AF541233

KUSHOK BAKULA RINPOCHE

The Architect of Modern Ladakh

Life and Times

KUSHOK BAKULA RINPOCHE

The Architect of Modern Ladakh

Life and Times

Sonam Wangchuk Shakspo

PENTAGON PRESS LLP

First published in 2025 by
PENTAGON PRESS LLP
206, Peacock Lane, Shahpur Jat
New Delhi-110049, India
Contact: 011-26490600

Typeset in Palatino, 10.5 Point
Printed at Aegean Offset Printers, Greater Noida

ISBN 978-81-987484-0-9

www.pentagonpress.in

Contents

Part II
Representing Ladakh in Jammu & Kashmir

Part VI
Fulfilling Destiny: Bakula Rinpoche – Russia and Mongolia

Epilogue

DR. KARAN SINGH

3, NYAYA MARG,
CHANAKYAPURI,
NEW DELHI-110021

FOREWORD

It is my pleasure and privilege to write this Foreword for the excellent work done by Sonam Wangchuk Shakspo on the life and times of Kushok Bakula Rinpoche. I first came into contact with Kushok sahib way back in 1952 when, at the age of 21, I was elected Sadar e Riyasat of Jammu and Kashmir. Kushok Sahib was revered as the Head Lama of Ladakh, and he was always the most prominent Ladakhi leader. A man of great wisdom and maturity, he worked closely with me to put Ladakh on the map of national consciousness. As can be seen from my correspondence with Pandit Jawaharlal Nehru (Jammu and Kashmir 1949-1964, Oxford University Press) I was, from the outset, deeply committed to the strategic and political importance of Ladakh whose symbol was Kushok Bakula Rinpoche and kept impressing this upon the Prime Minister in my letters and during our meetings.

In year 1952, I had the experience of flying along with Pandit Jawaharlal Nehru, Indira Gandhi, Sheikh Abdullah and senior army commanders to the newly constructed airfield at Chushul in eastern Ladakh, situated at an altitude of 14270 ft. above sea level, reportedly the highest airfield in the world. Kushok Sahib was also on the flight, which was truly an unforgettable experience. That was followed by my wife and I paying a visit to Ladakh in 1952. This was the first time that any member of Maharaja Gulab Singh's family had actually visited Ladakh despite a hundred years of Dogra Rule. The memory of the Dogra General Zorawar Singh was, of course, a powerful presence. The visit was a tremendous success. We landed at Leh to a rousing reception, the entire population of the town and surrounding village had turned out to greet us, led by the Head Lama Kushok Bakula Rinpoche. In the next three days Kushok Sahib took us around many of the important monasteries, including Hemis, Spituk (Pethub) and Shay and his own Samkar Gonpa. From that time onwards Kushok Sahib and I developed a close personal relationship which lasted until the end of his life.

During all the years that Kushok Sahib was involved in state and national politics, he paid special attention to the economic development of Ladakh. This period included several visits to Tibet where, on his return, he had in 1955 warned the Government of India of this severe danger facing Tibet due to the growing Chinese presence in the region. Kushok Sahib and I participated together in several international forums in the field of Interfaith, including a significant one in Windsor Castle, UK in 1995 hosted by HRH Prince Phillip.

Kushok Bakula was deeply involved in the 2500 Buddha Jayanti celebrations and was honoured in year 1988 by the Padma Bhushan Award. His appointment as Ambassador to Mongolia turned out to be much more than simply a diplomatic assignment. Mongolia was just recovering from brutal years of Communist Party dictatorship which ended only with the peaceful collapse of the Soviet Union, thanks to the wisdom and foresight of President Gorbachev of not using force at that critical juncture. During the Communist regime in Mongolia for many years' religion was cruelly suppressed, many of the Gonpas destroyed and the religious texts obliterated. At that time Kushok Bakula' appearance was a blessing for the deeply religious people of Mongolia, and during his stay there he virtually reintroduced Buddhism to Mongolia by restoring monasteries and restarting Buddhist prayers. During that time my wife and I made it a point to pay a visit to Mongolia. It was remarkable to learn that the people in Ulan Bator would often place their newly born children at the feet of Kushok Bakula, an honour surely never before extended to any Indian diplomat! Kushok Sahib had constructed a school for Buddhist teachings & training of young monks which he asked me to inaugurate.

To conclude, Kushok Bakula Rinpoche in his long and eventful life rendered valuable service to the nation in many capacities and was the architect of modern Ladakh. Personally, we had a very close relationship and would often discuss the regional problems of the state in depth. In his quiet unobtrusive manner, Kushok Sahib always presented an accurate picture of the problems of Ladakh. He was also, of course, a revered spiritual leader. Through this Foreword I pay my homage to his memory.

April 7, 2021 **Karan Singh**

Preface

It is almost impossible to do justice in a modest book like this or in any other written account, to the many facets and dimensions of Kushok Bakula Rinpoche's identity and legacy. Gyalsras (prince) Bakula or Rinpoche (as I always referred to him) was the harbinger of the poor and oppressed of Ladakh and beyond. A multi-faceted personality, he was a prince, grew up to be an astonishing scholar, virtuous philosopher, social reformer, a consummate statesman, an effective diplomat, and an extremely popular leader of the masses. He served the people of his native Ladakh and the Indian state for decades. More than this, he was a freedom fighter and above all, a remarkable Buddhist monk. The 13th Prime Minister of India, Dr. Manmohan Singh while dedicating the Leh airport after him, had aptly called him ***'The Architect of Modern Ladakh.'***

Rinpoche was an exceptional person right from his young days, a great lama of distinguished lineage with great personal capacities, virtues, and appeal. The Greek-British author and mountaineer Marco Alexander Pallis in his book "Peaks and Lamas", published in 1942; recalls his visit to Spituk (Pethub Monastery) in Leh. In Spituk, Marco Pallis found that the young head of the monastery, at that time was away from his seat and was pursuing his studies at the great monastery of Drepung in Lhasa. In the course of his visit, Mr. Pallis saw photographs of the young Bakula and was deeply impressed by his "nobility of countenance and the 'high character' revealed by the pictures." It was in his words, a face of 'rare distinction and beauty'; and 'a born prince'. He further wrote, "In this democratic age, not all of these perceptions will look entirely fitting, but we should nevertheless take note of this picture of Kushok Bakula as an exceptional person with great personal quality and appeal. He looked like a born prince who, if appearances did not belie him, would prove a worthy ruler of his community."

Chos or Dharma in Sanskrit, means duty. During the course of a long and highly eventful life, one might say that Bakula Rinpoche's personal Dharma was a weave of duty – on the one hand as public figure with responsibilities in a variety of official roles, and on the other as a Buddhist monk, dedicated to the teachings of the compassionate Buddha and the wellbeing of his fellow beings. He was a role model, steadfast in his adherence to the strict code of conduct that governs the life of a genuine Buddhist monk. Some might think that these two roles were incompatible or contradictory to each other. After all, Buddhist monks are enjoined to abandon worldly life and some would say that there is nothing more worldly than politics. Rinpoche himself acknowledged this and at first was very reluctant to take on the mantle thrust upon him by India's first Prime Minister Jawaharlal Nehru. But once he, on Pandit Nehru's insistence, accepted that mantle and made his peace with it as a way of pursuing the ethics of a Bodhisattva, his life came to exemplify how these two roles – as a monk and as a statesman – can not only be reconciled, but can and do actually complement each other. It was Rinpoche's moral integrity, his simplicity, and his humility as a monk that made him so effective in his public and political roles. It was his status as a public representative with the Indian state, with the ability to call upon India's senior leadership when needed, that furnished him with the wherewithal to pursue the benefit of beings to much greater effect. This would not have been possible if he had remained (as he himself might have preferred) within the confines of a monastery. Rinpoche was a role model, who laid down the benchmark for high moral standards in public life. His life is different from that of other religious figures in more than one way. While he was always sincere and faithful to his duties and responsibilities as a monk, he, at the same time, never shied away from being an activist who, in many ways, transformed the life of so many people, especially in Ladakh.

In the spirit of a genuine Buddhist monk, Bakula Rinpoche was never satisfied with mere sermonizing. He believed that in order to really benefit people one needed to do more than just make speeches and give sermons. Therefore, throughout his long life he remained deeply engrossed in the practical affairs of his communities, his country, and the wider world. In these qualities, Rinpoche was very much like Mahatma Gandhi and this was a comparison the 14th Dalai Lama himself would one day make, dubbing him "the Gandhi of Ladakh".

One of his favourite quotes, which he would often cite, was from Shantideva's Way of the Bodhisattva. It sums up his untiring dedication to the cause of serving others:

For as long as space endures and
For as long as living beings remain,
until then May I too abide to
dispel the misery of the world!

Bakula Rinpoche remained a father figure in Ladakh's political and religious life. In his long and distinguished career, he became a minister in the J&K Government, the first Member of Parliament from Ladakh and India's ambassador to Mongolia in a period spanning over fifty years. In 1977 Mr. Morarji Desai, the Prime Minister of the first non-Congress party government in India realizing that the Buddhist minority of India did not have a leader, appointed Bakula Rinpoche as a Member of the newly constituted National Commission for Minorities. Although a member of the Indian National Congress throughout his political career, he was above politics and respected by all as such. Bakula Rinpoche's stature emerged stronger after his retirement from active politics. The most remarkable feature of his life was that despite attaining high position and power, he continued to be a humble Buddhist monk.

His role in the campaign for Tibetan cause is well recorded. Bakula Rinpoche was also a Buddhist leader representing India on the world stage. He was the first senior Buddhist monk from outside Mongolia and Soviet Union who could preach Dharma there even at the peak of communist rule. Subsequently, after the collapse of communism, he was also responsible for a peaceful transformation and revival of Buddhism in the region. He was able to reach and preach in countries ruled by communists where no other monk could go. This was another distinct feature of his personality.

Bakula Rinpoche receiving the 'Padma Bhushan', one of India's highest civilian award from Mr. R. Venkataraman, President of India at the Rashtrapati Bhawan, New Delhi (1988)

Rinpoche receiving 'Polar Star' state award of Mongolia from Mr. N. Bagabandi, President of Mongolia. (2001)

In recognition of his tremendous contributions to India, to world peace, and to Buddhism, Rinpoche received many accolades and awards. In 1988 the President of India conferred upon him the Padma Bhushan, one of India's highest civilian award, in recognition of his services to the Indian nation. In 2001, he received the coveted Polar Star award from the President of Mongolia in recognition of his phenomenal services as a diplomat and for his role in the revival of Buddhism in Mongolia. The awards themselves mean little, but they illustrate the breadth and scope of Rinpoche's glorious legacy, a legacy which bestrides and lives on in the hearts of all those fortunate enough to have known him.

This book is based on the many conversations over decades I had with Rinpoche. In the following pages, I relate what knowledge I have gained of Rinpoche's life from working by his side for over twenty- five years till his last breath. In it, I have made an attempt to give some account of the high points of that long and eventful life using many resources, archival materials including Rinpoche's own recollections. Of course, there will be many omissions and I am sure, some errors, all of which are my own, and hopefully will not cause any offence. I am not a writer and my skill as a storyteller is limited, so I ask for the reader's forbearance.

It may also be pertinent to mention here that besides Bakula Rinpoche, Ladakh has had several other distinguished leaders who have contributed to the development of Ladakh since independence and their role cannot be underestimated. However, this book is about Bakula Rinpoche, his life and times in Ladakh and beyond.

I have set these details down at the request of Rinpoche's many disciples and devotees, who felt, quite rightly, that his momentous life needed to be set down on paper. The record of his life presented here is neither complete nor totally authoritative, but I hope, it will help to inform future generations – of Ladakhis and people around the world – about Rinpoche's life, by reminding them of the debt that all of us owe to Gyalsras Bakula Rinpoche.

Sonam Wangchuk Shakspo

J-177, Saket, New Delhi-110017.

Email: sonamwangchuk177@gmail.com

Acknowledgement

This book is a small tribute to the memory of Bakula Rinpoche, the legendary Buddhist monk, who not only provided spiritual guidance to the people of Ladakh and later in Mongolia and Russia but was also responsible for awakening them to an awareness of their civic and political rights and duties. It has been my great fortune to be near Rinpoche and observe his deep sense of compassion and dedication. Therefore, I owe my first gratitude to Bakula Rinpoche for his inspirational life and service to the people.

I am grateful to Dr. Karan Singh, former *Sadar-e-Riyasat*, Jammu & Kashmir State and a close associate of Bakula Rinpoche for writing the foreword.

I am thankful to Prof. Jamyang Gyaltsan, the editor of Bakula Rinpoche's autobiography in the Tibetan language which inspired me to write this book. In writing this book I have received support from several quarters. I wish to thank Mr. George Solomon Fitzherbert, Dr. Manjula Saxena and Mr. Nitin Vaidya for patiently and painstakingly reviewing my script and for their most valuable suggestions.

My Thanks also go to Mr. Nawang Tsering Shakspo and Mr. T. Namgyal Shakspo, Dr. Aashish Bhave, Mr. Anirban Ganguly, M/S Norbu Graphics, New Delhi, Mr. Morup Namgyal Shakspo, MD, Palkit Impex Pvt. Ltd., New Delhi, Mr. Pankaj Gujral, friends and well-wishers for their valuable support and suggestions. No less thanks are due to my wife Rinchen Wangmo for her invaluable moral support. This book would not have been possible without her. I also thank my sons – Rinchen Norbu Wangchuk and Rinchen Namgyal Wangchuk who evinced keen interest in the book and helped me in different ways.

Last but not the least, my most sincere thanks are also due to all my friends from Mongolia, Russia, Japan, China and other countries for their continued support and good wishes.

Sonam Wangchuk Shakspo

Author with Amb. Bakula Rinpoche in his chamber at the Embassy of India, Mongolia

My Association with Bakula Rinpoche

Like most children of my generation in Ladakh, I got my name from Gyalsras Bakula Rinpoche. As a child, my own first memory of Bakula Rinpoche was in the early 1960s, when Rinpoche was a minister in the Jammu and Kashmir Government. I remember accompanying my mother to listen to Rinpoche giving teaching and addressing public rallies in Leh. Rinpoche was held in very high esteem by the people of Ladakh. He was regarded as the ***'Head Lama of Ladakh'*** – a title bestowed upon him by the people for his outstanding role and contribution in promoting education, protecting monastic institutions and traditions of Ladakh. It was due to his wise counseling and political acumen that the people of Ladakh – Buddhists, Muslims and Christians stayed harmoniously united.

In Leh, Rinpoche would stay mostly at Samkar Gonpa (monastery) located in my village called Samkar, just outside Leh town. People from across Ladakh would flock to Samkar Gonpa to meet him and to seek his blessings. In his young age, Rinpoche was a striking personality. His royal lineage, his recognition as a Tulku or an incarnated lama and subsequent higher education in Lhasa had already made him a celebrity in Ladakh. His gentle yet forceful voice and his humility as a monk would leave a deep impact on the ordinary folks.

In 1964, when I was 8 years old, I was chosen as one of around one hundred boys and girls from Ladakh to study in New Delhi at the Ladakh Institute of Higher Studies (LIHS) which was established by the Government of India at Bakula Rinpoche's initiative and which was later renamed as Vishesh Kendriya Vidyalaya (VKV). After school, I joined St. Stephen's College, Delhi and in 1979 obtained my Bachelor of Arts (BA) degree.

Soon after, I joined the Minorities Commission as Rinpoche's Private Secretary and got an opportunity to travel to Russia and Mongolia. This trip to Russia and Mongolia was the first time I had ever travelled outside

India. Rinpoche was then the Vice-President of the Asian Buddhist Conference for Peace (ABCP) as detailed later in this book. In Moscow Rinpoche was admitted at the famous Bodkin Hospital for diplomats for a thorough check-up. Unexpectedly, Rinpoche's check-up and treatment there lasted over a month. This unscheduled stay in Moscow put me in an awkward situation. I had intended to apply for post-graduate study at University of Delhi but because of this delay, I missed the application deadline. Fortunately, destiny had designed a different course for me.

One day during our stay in Moscow, Mr. Inder Kumar Gujral, who was an old friend of Rinpoche and at that time was serving as India's ambassador in Moscow (he later became India's Prime Minister), invited Rinpoche for lunch. I accompanied Rinpoche to the embassy. I was very young at the time. During the course of our conversation, Amb. Gujral asked me about my studies and future plans. I told him about my predicament with the University of Delhi. Amb. Gujral listened patiently and asked me if I would be interested in pursuing my higher studies in Moscow instead? He said that he could arrange a scholarship for me. I was dumbfounded, but very happy. I sought Rinpoche's permission, and he agreed. Soon, I received a five-year scholarship from the Soviet authorities to study in the USSR. Initially I was sent to Tashkent, capital of Soviet Republic of Uzbekistan to do the preparatory course in Russian language, and then I was to study international relations at the Patrice Lumumba University in Moscow.

At this time Rinpoche asked me if I could study Mongolian language. This was an unexpected suggestion, and not something I had previously considered, since career prospects in India for someone who could speak Mongolian seemed very slim. So, I was hesitant, but I agreed and said I would find out about Mongolian language courses at the university. As it turned out, a Mongolian language course was not available, so I stuck to my original plan of study. In hindsight I have often wondered about this suggestion of Rinpoche's. He could never have known then that in ten years' time, he would be appointed India's ambassador to Mongolia and that I would go there with him as his assistant. But it suggests that he had some prescience about it. Later, working for Rinpoche over many years, I had many of these little incidents, which I would look back on and think, "how did Rinpoche know that?"

After a month's stay in Moscow, when Rinpoche returned to Delhi, I boarded a train to Tashkent, a journey which then took three days. In Tashkent I did an intensive course in Russian language at the University of Tashkent. It was an amazing and eye-opening experience, as I was among a batch of students that was truly international. There were fellow students from Latin America, the Middle East, Africa, and Asia as well as several Eastern Europeans, North Koreans, Pakistanis and Mongolians. My roommate was from Benin in West Africa. After one year of intense studies, I had gained basic knowledge of Russian and was ready to start my studies in Moscow.

But no sooner had I reached Moscow than I received a message from Bakula Rinpoche asking me to return to Delhi to work with him at the National Commission for Minorities. After all my hard work in Tashkent, and my excitement about the coming time in Moscow, this came as quite a blow to me. But of course, I accepted. After all, I owed my scholarship to Rinpoche in the first place. As a Ladakhi and a Buddhist, my loyalty to Rinpoche, of course, took precedence over my own personal wishes.

In 1985 when Rinpoche's term at the Minorities Commission ended, I found myself briefly out of work. Meanwhile, I had been offered a scholarship to study Japanese language in Tokyo, which I was eager to do. I departed for Tokyo, where I joined a private language college. It was a wonderful and unforgettable time. But barely six months into my stay there, I again received a message from Rinpoche asking me to return to New Delhi, as he had been re-appointed to the Minorities Commission. So, once again, I gave up my studies in Japan and returned to India to work by Rinpoche's side.

Same year I got married to Rinchen Wangmo, a niece of Bakula Rinpoche, whom I had known since my childhood. From that time onwards, I was pretty much at Bakula Rinpoche's side. The rest, as they say, is history.

PART I

THE EARLY YEARS (1917-50)

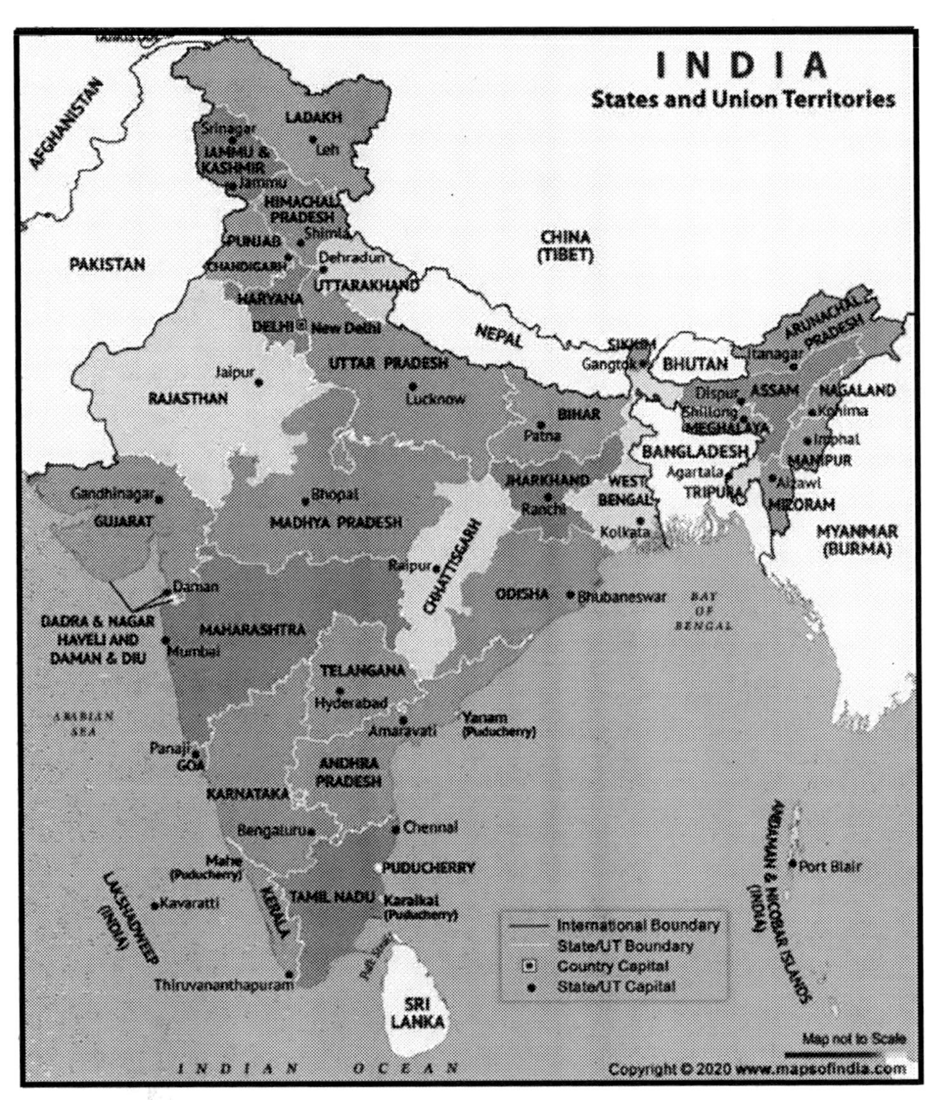

Political Map of India

One

Ladakh: A Brief Introduction

Situated in the northwest of India and bound by Tibet to the east, Lahaul and Spiti (in today's Himachal Pradesh) to the south, J&K to the west, and Xinjiang (the western-most province of today's China) to the north, Ladakh is known for the grandeur of its landscape and the vibrancy of its Buddhist culture. Greater Ladakh also includes the sparsely inhabited Northern Areas, Gilgit Baltistan, the Trans-Karakoram tract and the Aksai Chin. Situated on the trade route between the Punjab and Central Asia, Ladakh was, for centuries, traversed by caravans carrying textiles and spices from the south, and raw silk, carpets, and dry fruits from the north. Ladakh's rugged terrain and the absence of any paved highways forced merchants to entrust their goods to a relay-network of pony transporters which extended all the way to the Silk Route cities of Yarkand and Khotan. On this long route between the plains of India and the oases of Central Asia; Leh, the capital of Ladakh, was the half-way mark. Over the centuries, it developed into a bustling trading centre and its bazaars thronged with merchants from far-off places. However, in 1950, the People's Republic of China brought Tibet and Xinjiang under its control and with that, Ladakh's important position as a trade route and centuries-old trade link with the region ended abruptly.

Central Ladakh, with Leh at its heart, is the most populous part of the region, and is the political, social and cultural hub of Ladakh. Zanskar, a tangle of steep ridges and deep ravines to the south of the Indus valley, is an area of dramatic natural beauty which, even to this day, remains cut off from the rest of the world during the long winter months by heavy snow. Changthang to the east is famous for its wide-open expanses of wilderness which extend all the way across the Tibetan plateau. The sparsely populated Changthang region of Ladakh is celebrated for its unique species of sheep and large goats, which are the source of pashmina wool (Cashmere). The Nubra valley – north of the Indus valley is the gateway to the Siachen glacier and the Karakoram peaks. Its villages are relatively low-lying and are set among fertile farmlands. The upland plateau of Dras, known as the coldest place in India, and second only in the world to Siberia, is relatively green in the summer months, and apart from barley (the staple crop across the Tibetan plateau including Ladakh), also produces some wheat and buckwheat.

Since time immemorial, the high altitude and the harsh winter climate have been the natural protectors of Ladakh. Shielded by high mountain passes, it has escaped many major invasions, and this has fostered a sense of uninterrupted continuity in its way of life and its ancient cultural traditions. In its cultural and spiritual traditions, Ladakh has always been very close to Tibet, and all four of the major traditions of Vajrayana Buddhism: *Nyingmapa, Kagyupa, Sakyapa* and *Gelugpa* are preserved here. The *Gonpas*, or the Buddhist monasteries, are the repositories of Ladakh's art and culture. Perched on high cliffs, some look like they are literally hanging off the rocks. These vast, multi-storied, flat-roofed structures of stone and mud have survived for centuries and have always functioned as the nerve-centres of Ladakh's spiritual, educational, economic, cultural and artistic life.

Ladakh also has a sizable Muslim population, both Shia and Sunni, as well as a small Christian community. Relations between people of different faiths in Ladakh have tended to be very harmonious, with people sharing a common language as well as many bonds of tradition and culture. It is no exaggeration to say that Ladakh has long been a great example of peaceful religious coexistence. As a small Himalayan kingdom at the edge of the Tibetan cultural world, Ladakh was at its height in the early 17th century, when under the famous King Singye Namgyal (1616–42) its rule extended across Spiti and western Tibet right up to the *Mayumla* pass, beyond the sacred sites of Mount Kailash and Lake *Mansarovar.* Ladakh had been an independent kingdom from 10th century AD to the 19th century under Lhachen and Namgyal dynasties. In 1842, Wazir Zorawar Singh, a military commander of Maharaja Gulab Singh of Jammu and Kashmir conquered both Ladakh and Baltistan and brought the area under his control. In 1846, the British colonial government handed over Jammu and Kashmir to the Maharaja under the Treaty of Amritsar and subsequently became a part of the Republic of India following the Maharaja's decision to accede to India.

The Instrument of Accession is a legal document executed on October 26, 1947 by Maharaja Hari Singh, ruler of the princely state of Jammu and Kashmir. By executing this document under the provisions of the Indian

Independence Act 1947, Maharaja Hari Singh agreed to accede to the Dominion of India. Although the highland kingdom of Ladakh remained under Dogra rule for over one hundred years, throughout this time it retained considerable autonomy under its own royal family, and it continued to maintain its strong cultural, religious and linguistic ties with Tibet.

Today's Ladakh consists of two districts: Leh and Kargil, governed separately by the Ladakh Autonomous Hill Development Council (LAHDC) of Leh and Kargil respectively and was within the jurisdiction of the Indian State of Jammu & Kashmir (J&K). Together, the districts of Leh and Kargil have an average altitude of 3500 metres above sea level and constitute a total area of 59,146 sq. kilometers or 22,836 sq. miles. According to the 2011 census, the total population of Ladakh (including Leh, Kargil, and Zanskar) stood at 2,74,289. Known for its ancient Buddhist monasteries, distinct culture, high peaks, unique landscape and rivers, Ladakh is a popular tourist destination.

In the year 2019, Ladakh was made into a Union Territory. A bill was introduced in Parliament of India on August 5, 2019, calling for the bifurcation of the state of Jammu & Kashmir into two separate Union Territories of Jammu & Kashmir and Ladakh. The bill became a law on October 31, 2019. Thus, the long-standing demand of the people of Ladakh to free Ladakh from Kashmir, became a reality. In August 2024, Government of India granted approval for the formation of five new districts in Ladakh, increasing the Union Territory's total number of districts to seven. The *five new districts* are *Zanskar, Drass, Sham, Nubra, and Changthang.*

Prince of Mangtro (Matho) Palace, Ladakh after his recognition as 19th Arhat Bakula (1921)

Two

The Birth of a Prince

According to Bakula Rinpoche's autobiography in Tibetan Language "Rangnam Padma Karpe Thengwa", the fiefdom of Matho, a small area some twenty-two kilometers from Leh on the left bank of the Singye Khabap (Indus river), was bestowed upon Raja Tensrung Yurgyal in around the year 1837, during the lifetime of his father King Tsewang Rabstan. It was at around this time that the Stok and Matho palaces were founded, with the latter becoming the main seat of Raja Tensrung. Their family lineage was an illustrious one. It could be traced back to the early Ngari chieftain Skyide Nyima-Gon, considered to be the first king of Ladakh.

In the late 19th century, the Raja of Matho, Tashi Lhawang, had five princes, namely Nangwa Thayas, Thustob, Phuntsog Namgyal, Tsewang Namgyal, Chimet Dorje and two princesses – Lhadol and Dolma Skyidzom. Prince Thustob became a monk at the Drukpa Kagyu Hemis Monastery and rose to occupy the seat of *Lopon* (abbot). His younger brother Phuntsog Namgyal joined the Sakya Matho Monastery and was to become its abbot. Nangwa Thayas remained at the palace as the heir apparent in secular affairs. Princess Lhadol married a yogi (*Druba* in Ladakhi). Tsewang Namgyal joined another family as a *Makpa* (a husband who resides with his wife's family) when he married Tsewang Laskit of Nyemo Roopchan. This is a common practice in Ladakh when a household accepts a husband who comes to live with them and takes their family name. They had one son, named Jigmet Namgyal. Princess Dolma Skyidzom married King Tsetan Namgyal of Zangla. The youngest of the six siblings, Chimet Dorje Namgyal spent most of his adult life with his older brother Raja Nangwa Thayas at Matho Palace. He had a late marriage with Diskit Wangmo of the Ayu-Kalon family and their daughter was Princess Tsering Dolkar who married Sonam Gyaltsan Khangsar. Interestingly, Sonam Gyaltsan Khangsar was the son of Sheikh

Abdul Razak, who originally belonged to a rich Muslim family in Leh. Sheikh Abdul Razak converted to Buddhism and became a disciple of Lama Tagtsang Raspa (head of Hemis Monastery). He was given the Buddhist name Tondup Namgyal and his family was also re-named as the Khangsar family (which means "new household"). In view of the unique social circumstances leading to his conversion, Lama Tagtsang Raspa issued a decree through Hemis Monastery which vouchsafed special privileges for the Khangsar family that remains in force even today.

As for Raja Nangwa Thayas, he married Princess Eshey Wangmo of the Zangla royal household of Zanskar. Eshey Wangmo was herself the niece of the 18th Bakula Rinpoche Lobzang Eshey Stanba Gyaltsen. Together the royal couple had four children. The eldest was the Raja-to-be Tashi Phuntsog Namgyal. Of the two daughters Rigzin Wangmo married Sonam Tsepel of Spiti. Norzin Wangmo, married Sonam Tsepel, Shey-Lonpo. The fourth child, a son, was born at the Matho Palace on the auspicious *Saga-Dawa* or Vesak Purnima in the Earth-Horse year of the Tibetan calendar, which corresponds to May 19, 1917, in the western calendar. It was this child who would soon be recognized as the reincarnation of the 18th Arhat Bakula. Tragically, Eshey Wangmo passed away only seven days after the birth of her youngest son.

Three

The Successive Incarnations of Arhat Bakula

According to Buddhist chronicles, Arhat (*Nastan)* Bakula was one of the sixteen main disciples of the Gautama Buddha. The name Bakula is said to be derived from a particular type of grass which was dear to *Arhat Bakula*. It is said that Bakula used to be engrossed in prayers and meditation. He had renounced all worldly pleasures and attractions. In Buddhist murals, the Bakula Arhat is seen holding a brown mongoose in his hands who is pouring out gems. One day while Bakula was sitting on a hilltop, he saw Lord Buddha passing by. Seeing him, Bakula had a strong urge to meet him, but the way down was long. Had he tried walking down, the Buddha would have gone. Out of eagerness to meet him, Bakula skied downward from the hilltop. Buddha initiated him into his Sangha. All the monks of the Sangha were amazed at his uncanny talents. Just eight days after his initiation into the Sangha, Shakyamuni Buddha brought him into the fold of select disciples who were called *Arhats* or "one who is worthy" or a "perfected person".

When Lord Buddha's time of Mahaparinirvana was near, all the Arhats were around him. They pledged before the Shakyamuni Buddha that for the protection of Dharma, they will not leave the Samsara, until the time all sentient beings are freed from suffering. These Arhats were free from the cycle of Samsara and chose to sacrifice Nirvana for the benefit and gratification.

However, it was in the seventeenth incarnation that Bakula first reincarnated in Ladakh, as Kongchog Rangdrol Nyima of Lamayuru monastery, situated some 120 kms west of Leh. He eventually became the head of his monastery, at which point he was recognized as the incarnation of Bakula. Even today, his hermitage is considered one of the most sacred precincts of Lamayuru, regularly visited by pilgrims.

The eighteenth incarnation, Lobzang Eshey Stanba Gyaltsen, the uncle of Eshey Wangmo as mentioned earlier, was born in Zanskar (1860–1917), as a prince of the Zangla palace. At a young age, the 18th Bakula left Ladakh to pursue his higher studies in Tibet at Lhasa's famous Drepung monastery. There he received the degree of Geshe Lharampa, the highest qualification in Buddhist philosophy conferred by the Gelug school. After completing his studies, he returned to Ladakh and assumed control over the monastic affairs of the kingdom.

An interesting anecdote is told about the 18th Bakula. When Pratap Singh (1848–1925), the Maharaja of Kashmir, and his consort were without heir to the throne, they became morose. They tried every possible method to conceive a child, but to no avail. It is said that one of the Maharaja's ministers, who had recently returned from Ladakh, informed the king of Bakula Rinpoche's reputation for spiritual power, and suggested that the Maharaja invite him to the palace to conduct some special prayers. In his desperation, the Maharaja duly sent a royal invitation to Ladakh inviting Bakula Rinpoche. He accepted and set off with an entourage of senior monks. In addition to discussing affairs of state, the Maharaja spoke eloquently of the great sorrow afflicting the royal household. Bakula Rinpoche stayed at the Jammu Palace for a week conducting prayers. During the course of this stay, the royal couple became greatly devoted to Rinpoche. As a mark of their respect, it is said that the Maharaja would make a point of removing his crown before speaking with the lama and also discussed with him matters of administration.

When the time came for him to leave, the king asked Rinpoche what gifts or offerings would be suitable? Rinpoche replied that there was nothing he wanted for himself, but that if the Raja wanted to do some good deed, he should consider exempting all the monasteries of Ladakh from royal taxation. For at that time the monasteries of Ladakh were under a heavy tax burden which severely affected their proper functioning. The Maharaja was rather taken aback by this suggestion, but was impressed by 18th Bakula's forthrightness. He replied by seeking a clarification – surely the concession being requested was only for Bakula Rinpoche's own monastery, the Pethub Monastery? "No", Rinpoche replied firmly and requested that the privilege should be extended to every monastery in Ladakh. The Maharaja yielded to this request and ordered the full exemption of all monasteries in Ladakh from royal taxes. It was a tremendous gesture which gave the monasteries great respite and allowed them to continue into the modern age. This

18th Bakula Rinpoche Lobzang Stanba Gyaltsen giving a religious discourse to his disciples. (Early 20th century)

18th Bakula Rinpoche at the Royal Palace of Maharaja Pratap Singh in Jammu

exemption for monasteries in Ladakh remained in force even after India's independence and continues to this day, thanks to the efforts of the 19th Bakula Rinpoche as described in another chapter.

During his stay in the palace, Rinpoche and the Maharaja discussed various issues relating to Zanskar and Ladakh in general. The Maharaja also conferred upon Bakula Rinpoche a state medal and appointed him the official Tehsildar (revenue officer) of the Paldar Pangde region adjoining Zanskar. There are several photographs bearing testimony to the visit. Rinpoche is seen outside the Jammu Palace with a medal flanked by royal guards and decorated elephants. Rinpoche also became acquainted with the British Field-Marshal Lord Robert (1832–1914) who was transiting to Srinagar at the time. The 18th Bakula is also remembered for having built Samkar Gonpa (also known as Samkhar) near Leh in 1890. To this day Samkar is considered a particularly impressive example of Ladakh's traditional vernacular architecture. The Rinpoche eventually passed away at Stongde Gonpa in Zanskar.

It is said that before his demise, the 18th Bakula foretold the place of his next reincarnation. On his final visit to Matho Palace near Leh before he died, Rinpoche had gone to visit his niece Eshey Wangmo, wife of Raja Nangwa Thayas and gave her a *Oo-Lab* (placed over-head of a seat of a high lama), together with a *Gyab-yol* (an ornamental curtain) and a small silk carpet. As he gave these gifts to her, he said rather mysteriously that these items would be needed in the future. After the demise of 18th Bakula Rinpoche, the monks of Pethub Galden Targyesling Monastery began the search for his reincarnation. In keeping with tradition, a petition was sent to the 13th Dalai Lama, Thupten Gyatso in Lhasa, seeking his divination regarding the reincarnation. Another divination was also requested from the Matho oracle. It is said that during the Matho Nagrang festival that year, Nechung Chogyal (Tibet's state oracle) also made a brief appearance through one of the Matho mediums, and prophesied that the reincarnation would be born in the palace of a lineage-holder of Nyatri Tsenpo (the first king of Tibet). The Matho oracle also paid a visit to the queen Eshey Wangmo at Matho palace and presented her with a *Khadag* (a ceremonial offering-scarf) and a protection thread (Raksha Sutra). The oracle is reported to have said, "I expect that the sun of happiness will soon shine on this small land." It is also said that in an unusual display of respect for the queen, on the 8th day of the 2nd month of Tibetan lunar calendar, during the Matho festival, both the Matho oracles picked up the bigger piece of juniper wood from among the religious objects, smeared a bit of butter on it and sent it to the would-be mother of Bakula Rinpoche with a clear indication of things to come. On the same occasion the two Rong mediums also pointed out to the people a solitary bird, which was flying from the direction of Zanskar towards Matho Palace, shouting, "look!"

All these signs indicated that the youngest son of the recently deceased Queen Eshey Wangmo was the new incarnation. So, when the prince was just four years old, a team of monks from Pethub Monastery visited Matho Palace, bringing with them a variety of rosaries, cups and a few other items, among which one set had belonged to the previous Bakula. Various items were placed before the young prince to choose from. It is said that he correctly chose each of the items that had belonged to the previous incarnation. In addition, it is said that the young boy recognized the previous Bakula's cook and held his hand. The search team was convinced. So, they forwarded their observations to the Thirteenth Dalai Lama, Thupten Gyatso, for his appraisal. The Dalai Lama replied by giving his seal of approval and confirmation. At the same time, he conferred on the child a new name, Ngawang Lobsang Thubten Chognor. Henceforth this was to be the 19th Bakula Rinpoche's official name. But in Ladakh he was always known simply as "*Gyalsras Bakula*" or Prince Bakula.

In 1921, at the tender age of six, on an auspicious day, the young prince was escorted by a caravan of horses from Matho Palace to *Pethub Galden Targyesling Monastery* – popularly known as Spituk Monastery, located on a hillock near what is now Leh airport. From this day on, this monastery was to be the boy's home and chief residence for the rest of his life. In Pethub's grand assembly hall, the young prince was formally ushered onto his previous incarnation's throne for the first time.

Following his enthronement, Gyalsras Bakula (1917-2003) was placed under the care and tutelage of the accomplished master, the 3rd Rizong Sras Rinpoche Lobsang Tsultim Chosphel, who ordained him as a novice. Henceforth winters would be spent with him at Samstanling Monastery in Nubra memorizing scriptures and learning to read and write, and the summer months at Pethub for language and sutra studies under the Eshey Dawa of Stok. There were also several other celebrated teachers from his own monastery who guided the young *Rinpoche* during these formative years and introduced him to worldly etiquette. He lived an extraordinary life and became one of the most prominent Indian Buddhist monks of the twentieth century. He passed away in 2003 at the age of 86.

The 20th Bakula Rinpoche

After the demise of the 19th Bakula Rinpoche in year 2003, on February 26, 2008, H.H. the 14th Dalai Lama Tenzin Gyatso recognised a child born on January 23, 2006, as the 20th reincarnation of Bakula Rinpoche. The child's parents, Dorje Tsering and Sonam Dolkar reside in Kyagar Village, Nubra,

Ladakh. The 102nd Gaden Tripa, Rizong Sras Rinpoche, took on the role of root-guru for the young Rinpoche and many followers sincerely hope that the auspicious karmic relationship between Bakula Rinpoche and Rizong Sras Rinpoche will continue for the benefit of all mankind. On July 22, 2010, the Dalai Lama bestowed the name Tenzin Ngawang Jigmet Wangchuk upon the young Tulku at Samstanling Monastery in Nubra.

The much-anticipated enthronement ceremony for the 20th Bakula Rinpoche took place in the Grand Assembly Hall of Pethub Monastery in Leh on August 12, 2010. However, the event was subdued due to a devastating cloudburst that caused flooding and destruction in the Leh region. In December 2012, the young Rinpoche arrived at Drepung Losaling Monastery in Mundgod, Karnataka, to begin his studies. He is currently undergoing monastic studies there under the guidance of Loseling Khenpo Geshe Eshe Lhundup, Khensur Lobsang Samten and Geshe Thupstan Rabgyes.

On July 27, 2017, he made his maiden visit to Mongolia and assumed authority over Pethub Monastery there. The ceremony was graced by a galaxy of religious leaders, led by the 102nd Gaden Tripa, Rizong Sras Rinpoche. Now 18 years old, the 20th Bakula Rinpoche is diligently pursuing his studies at Drepung Losaling Monastery in South India.

The 20th Bakula Rinpoche Tenzin Ngawang Jigmet Wangchuk with H.H. the 14th Dalai Lama (2015)

Four

To Lhasa for Higher Studies

In 1926, barely ten years old, the young 19th Bakula Rinpoche left Ladakh to continue his higher Buddhist studies in Tibet. He set off for Lhasa accompanied by a small retinue which included the monk Lobzang Tsetan and other attendants from Pethub. Raja Nangwa Thayas, his father accompanied the caravan only as far as Nyemo village, about 35 kilometers from Leh. There, the Raja bade a tearful farewell to his youngest child. This was to be the last time that Prince Bakula would see his father, for by the time he returned from Lhasa fourteen years later (in 1940), the Raja had already passed away.

On the way to Srinagar, Rinpoche paid homage at several monasteries dotted along the route and also at the ancient nine-metre high (29.5 feet) Chamba (*Maitreya*) statue carved into the cliff-face at Mulbekh. It is pertinent to mention here that Ladakh in those days was completely cut off from the rest of the world. There was no road or any vehicular traffic. People had to walk for weeks under severe conditions to reach Srinagar, carrying with them food and fodder for the horses, mules and other animals. The route connectivity between Srinagar and Leh was a pony track-cum footpath. It would be a judicious assumption that foot-distance in 1948 may have been around 300 km.

The most dramatic part of the journey from Dras is the ascent up the *Zoji-la pass* (3528 metres, 11,575 Ft.), the pass in the great Himalayan range that serves as the gateway to Ladakh. The contrast in natural scenery when one crosses Zoji-la, which separates Ladakh from the rest of the world is breathtaking. On the other side is the Kashmir Valley, with its marvelous, lush greenery, the likes of which one cannot find anywhere in the wild and on this side lie the barren, rocky-mountains of Ladakh. Descending into the

Kashmir Valley and the verdant city of Srinagar surrounded by lakes, the young Bakula was delighted to see motor vehicles, bicycles, and horse carts for the first time in his life. From Srinagar the team then proceeded to Jammu by bus and from there by train to Rawalpindi (in what is now Pakistan). From Rawalpindi they took another train across northern India to Siliguri (in the north of West Bengal) and then proceeded up to Kalimpong and onward to Sikkim.

From Kalimpong the party entered Tibetan territory for the first time. After several day's travel, the caravan arrived at *Shigatse*, (officially known as *Xigaze*) Tibet's second city, and home to the celebrated monastery of Tashilhunpo, seat of the Panchen Lamas. After a few weeks' rest at Tashilhunpo, the party set out again for Lhasa. This part of the journey took several days, as they paid their respects at several important monasteries and pilgrimage sites along the way. Upon their arrival in the holy city of Lhasa, they proceeded directly to the great Drepung Monastery located just outside the city, where Bakula Rinpoche was warmly received by the monks of the Losaling Dratsang. He was housed in the residence of the previous Bakula in the Pethub Khangtsen which was also home to most of Drepung's numerous Ladakhi monks. For the next fourteen years, the Pethub Khangtsen was to be Rinpoche's home. He was enrolled in Losaling Dratsang and granted the status of a junior level *tulku* (reincarnate lama). Thus, his formal education began. Because of their proximity, Pethub Khangtsen enjoyed a particularly close relationship with its neighbour, the Nechung monastery, which was home to Tibet's famous state oracle. At that time, the Nechung Rinpoche Thupten Konchok was exactly the same age as Bakula (both were born in the Earth-Horse year) and the two soon became close friends. Many years later, when Nechung Rinpoche fled to India in the wake of the Chinese communist takeover of Tibet, the old friendship between the two was rekindled, and they remained in close contact thereafter.

After Bakula Rinpoche's admission to the monastic university of Drepung, a committee of senior scholars was set up to select a worthy teacher for the young Rinpoche. They shortlisted five prospective scholars all of whom were equally qualified in the relevant fields. But they could not reach a consensus on who should become his main teacher. Finally, at the request of Pethub Khangtsen, the manager of Nechung Monastery, who was named Ngawang Zangpo, forwarded the matter to the 13th Dalai Lama Thupten Gyatso himself, who after careful consideration appointed Geshe Lobsang Jungne of Gya-Khangtsen as Bakula's personal tutor.

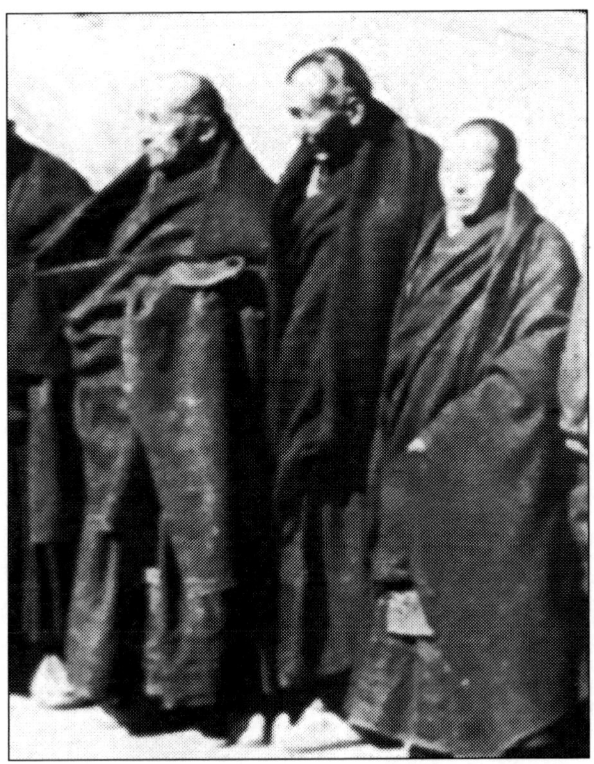

Geshe Lobsang Jungne (centre) Bakula Rinpoche's tutor in Lhasa

From that moment onwards, until the completion of his studies fourteen years later, Geshe Lobsang Jungne was his constant mentor, and a strong bond of affection was formed between them. Under his compassionate guidance Rinpoche studied all the core subjects, from elementary logic to the great treatises of Abhidharma (*Zod* in Tibetan, dealing with metaphysics, cosmology and phenomenology), Vinaya (*Dulwa* in Tibetan, monastic discipline and ethics), Paramita (*Pharchin*, the Mahayana "perfections" or virtues, including the virtue of wisdom found through the philosophy of emptiness), Pramana (*Tshad-ma namdrel*, valid cognition) and Madhyamika (*Uma*, the "middle way" philosophy developed influentially by Nagarjuna and other saints).

Geshe Lobsang Jungne was like a father to the young Rinpoche. Although on occasion he could be strict, he was always kind-hearted, and he led by example as a monk who himself was very disciplined in his daily habits. He was also a good storyteller, and he kept the young Rinpoche well-informed about the developments and debates going on in the field of religious education at that time in the different monastic institutions of Tibet.

Under the tutelage of Geshe Lobsang Jungne the young Bakula Tulku became one of the best students in Drepung.

In 1928, young Bakula took ordination as a *Rabjung* (ordained monk) from the 13th Dalai Lama. While studying the *Pramanavartika* (Commentary on Valid Cognition), he participated in the traditional winter debate sessions at Jangphu Monastery (known as *Jang Gunchoe*) for six consecutive years. Bakula Rinpoche worked hard to remove his intellectual ignorance both through dialectic study and through debate. He particularly excelled at philosophy, but he also developed a good command over the entire Tripitaka.

In 1940, during the *Monlam Chenmo* or great prayer festival in Lhasa, Bakula Rinpoche stood for his Geshe-degree final exams, which consisted of a series of public debates held over several days on a variety of subjects. As the culmination of many years' studies, this was a tremendously important and auspicious occasion at which all the senior monks of Drepung, Sera and Ganden Monasteries were in attendance. In the presence of many learned Geshes and highly respected scholars, young Bakula Rinpoche's knowledge of the scriptures, and his philosophical proficiency, were put to the test. Even Kyabje Ling Rinpoche, who had recently been appointed the 14th Dalai Lama's main tutor, was present at the debate held in the Jokhang's inner courtyard. Despite his nervousness, Rinpoche's years of diligent study shone through, and his performance was a resounding success.

During the return debate session, several of Tibet's most senior monastic figures – Reting Rinpoche's tutor, the one-time Ganden Throne Holder (*Ganden Tripa*) Amir Rinpoche, Sharpa Choeje, Tongdul Rinpoche and Jangtse Choeje Lhundup Tsondue sat on the panel. During this period, on the 16th day of the first Tibetan month (February 22, 1940), when the young 14th Dalai Lama Tenzin Gyatso was formally ushered onto the golden throne in Potala for the first time, Bakula Rinpoche was called upon to represent Drepung at a one-to-one debate in front of the regent Reting Dorje Chang in the Sishi Phuntsok Hall of the Potala Palace. His debating partner (or opponent) was Geshe Gedun Kelsang from Ganden Monastery. This was the culmination of Bakula Tulku's Geshe examination. Because of his clear grasp of the subject and his great skill in debate, he gained the first position in the order of merit and was thereby awarded the degree of "*Geshe Lharampa*" with distinction, the highest degree attainable in the Gelug tradition. Rinpoche recounts this with typical humility in his autobiography: "I completed my Geshe examination, and like a dog being called a lion, I was also praised with the title 'Geshe Lharmapa' of the First Order".

By the time of his graduation, Bakula Rinpoche had already become a popular student in the monastic communities of Drepung, Ganden and Sera.

He had been ordained as a Gelong (fully ordained monk) by Reting Dorje Chang who at that time was the Regent of Tibet during the minority of the 14th Dalai Lama. Rinpoche had been initiated into all branches of the Buddhist teachings, taking oral teachings from a great number of revered figures on the *sutras, agamas* and *tantras* and he had been empowered with the four *Abhisekhas*. He had also established a spiritual connection with the eminent scholar of the time Kyabje Phabongka Dorje Chang Chenmo, who was a master of Lamrim (especially Tsongkhapa's *Stages of the Path to Liberation*). Having completed all these studies, Bakula Rinpoche began to apply his learning to the practical tasks of living as a Bodhisattva – a being who strives to work for the benefit and liberation of all beings.

Five

Ladakh Beckons

Soon after his success in the Geshe examinations, Bakula Rinpoche received an urgent call from his monastery requesting him to return to Ladakh. At the time he had been planning to continue his studies by joining the Gyume Monastery in Lhasa. Had he done so, it could have paved the way for him to scale the monastic hierarchy and may eventually have led to him becoming Ganden Tripa, the most senior position in the entire Gelug tradition. But the call of duty from his homeland took precedence, and Rinpoche immediately sent a request to Reting Rinpoche, the Regent of Tibet seeking permission to return to Ladakh for three years. Permission was granted and at the same time Reting Rinpoche bestowed on Bakula Rinpoche the title *"Tsogchen Tulku"*.

He left Lhasa in the 3rd Tibetan month that year (1940), with the Tibetan Government providing escorts to accompany him all the way to the border. This time his route was not south via Sikkim, but west, directly to Ladakh across the open expanses of upper Tibet. On the way Rinpoche stopped again at Tashi Lhunpo in Shigatse (Xigaze), as he had done fourteen years ago and had sought an audience with the 10th Panchen Lama. The Tibetan Government also issued an order dated April 5, 1940, directing all Tibetan border posts and authorities to extend necessary assistance and security to Rinpoche and his entourage. **(Annexure 1)** During the long journey across western Tibet, Rinpoche also had the opportunity to make a pilgrimage to Mount Kailash, Lake Manasarovar and several of the retreat spots in that sacred area.

In September 1940, having crossed the barren highlands of the Changthang (northern plains) Rinpoche finally entered Ladakh. He was received at the border by a welcoming party of senior lamas, lay people and local government officials. On reaching Leh, after a ceremonial greeting, he was escorted back to Spituk (Pethub) Monastery where the monks of the four Dratsangs, namely Galden Targyesling (Pethub Gonpa), Chiskyob Ling (Samkar Gonpa), Gurfug Gonpa (Stok Gonpa) and Tashi Geyphel Ling (Sabu Gonpa) together with the local people, gave him an impressive and joyous welcome.

In Ladakh, Bakula Rinpoche was in great demand. He was invited to different monasteries and villages for teachings, various rituals and empowerments as well as sutra transmissions. He gave teachings on Refuge, on Karma (the law of causality), on the rarity of human birth, on the value of human life and on impermanence. He also advised people on religious practices and urged them to eschew bad habits like smoking and drinking alcohol, taking snuff and other intoxicants. He preached about long-standing social issues in Ladakhi society such as polyandry, excessive drinking (of a locally made alcoholic beverage called *Chhang*), rituals such as animal sacrifice and the hunting of wild animals. He implored people to respect the natural environment and to protect them for the posterity. He also criticized the caste system prevalent in Ladakh, whereby a section of the people was considered to be of less value than others. Rinpoche was determined to apply his spiritual education to practical goals and so he took it upon himself to address the challenges facing the society for the good of all.

Rinpoche was steadfast in his opposition to harmful practices and he made every attempt to educate people about them. He focused on the importance of adhering to meritorious conduct and eschewing sinful practices. He really took the words of Lama Je Tsongkhapa to heart that learning and teaching the tantras is insufficient for bringing about truly beneficial results. So, rather than conferring endless empowerments, Rinpoche instead insisted on the importance of proper conduct of the Three Refuges (the *Kanchog sum* – Buddha, Dharma and Sangha) and of the Law of Karma. And he always sought to teach by example – by living his own life in accordance with what he preached. As stated by Trijang Rinpoche, the junior tutor of the 14th Dalai Lama "He (19th Bakula Rinpoche) brought it (what he had learned in Tibet) back with him to his native land, just as a sailor returns with a great treasure of precious stones and anecdotes after a long journey."

Rinpoche also believed that before bestowing the deep and profound tantric teachings on others, he should first thoroughly understand and practice them himself. So, after his return to Ladakh, he practiced numerous sadhanas and cultivated the meditative absorption of Samadhi. Often, he would retreat to a meditation cell located in a cliff some distance behind his monastery. The simple two-room cell, deep in the rugged mountains behind Pethub monastery, provided him with the tranquil and pristine environment he needed for long solitary retreats. A small trickle of spring water, enough for only one or two persons, was the only source of water. Wild animals roamed about freely and the chirping of birds was the only sound to be heard. Sometimes Bakula Rinpoche would spend months there, meditating in this cell, diligently performing *Nyen-drub* (the recitation of a large number of mantra prayers) and *Sag-jang* (accumulating good karma and purifying bad karma). The little retreat-cell still exists today, but unfortunately its approach is restricted as it is now surrounded by military establishments.

Bakula Rinpoche's hermitage in the mountain behind Pethub monastery

In addition to continuing his profound study of the Five Great Treatises already mentioned, Rinpoche also took up the study of astrology under Padma Rinpoche of Dragthog Gonpa, known throughout Ladakh as a great expert. Likewise, Tsultrim Ngawang Chiprapa of Lukyil Gonpa, a recognized master in the field of Tibetan medicine, gave Rinpoche instruction on the medical treatise *known as the Gyud-shi* (*The Four Tantras*). From him Rinpoche learnt interpretations of the foundational texts as well as all the necessary transmissions, how to identify many medicinal plants and how to prepare pills from them. He also studied the complex and subtle Tibetan system of pulse analysis and other diagnostic methods, along with acupuncture and needle-treatment. For several years thereafter Rinpoche would use this learning to treat patients. But later, because of his many official responsibilities, his own personal devotion to the practices of *nyen-drub* and lack of time, he gave up his public medical practice.

Although Bakula Rinpoche's political achievements are unrivalled in the modern history of Ladakh, his own personal priorities were always clear, which were not political at all. Being a monk, he felt that his primary duty was to teach the profound insights of the compassionate Buddha to the common people. In this, his life mirrored the advice of Lama Je Tsongkhapa, as stated in the following stanza which sums up Bakula Rinpoche's core aspiration, his prayer, and his lifetime's work:

First, seek to listen to the teachings in full,
Then, take to heart as precepts all their doctrines,
And finally, practice day and night,
Dedicating all to the flourishing of the teachings.

Practice what you preach

As an illustration of his unwavering ethical integrity, Rinpoche took up his commitment to vegetarianism in 1945, long before vegetarianism came to be the norm in the monasteries. Bakula Rinpoche believed very strongly in practicing what he taught and also in setting an example for others. His conversion to a vegetarian diet followed an incident which pricked his conscience. This incident took place in Drok-yul in Ladakh, a place inhabited by a small community of Aryan Dard people in the Indus valley at the border with Pakistan, about 160 kilometers southwest of Leh and 62 kilometers north of Kargil. The Dards are thought by some to be the purest descendants of the ancient Indo-European Aryan race that settled in India. They are

Rinpoche among the Drokpas of Ladakh

handsome people with distinct physical features, their own language and their own social and cultural values, which are totally different from those in Ladakh. Drokpas or Brokpas are also known for their forthright and candid nature.

In 1945 Bakula Rinpoche was invited to give a religious sermon in one of the Drokpa villages. It was a festive occasion, and people had gathered in large numbers to receive the teachings. After the sermon, there was dance and music and it was during this that Rinpoche was offered lunch which chiefly consisted of mutton. Rinpoche had no appetite at that time and therefore ate very little. But villagers were unhappy at his modest help and insisted that he must eat more. At this point, one Drokpa said casual words to the effect that they had slaughtered a sheep especially for his meal! Rinpoche was shocked and dismayed at these words. It was a poignant and distressing moment as he realized that an animal had been killed especially for him. Recalling that moment Rinpoche told me that he could not say anything but silently prayed for the sheep. Immediately after that incident, Rinpoche made it known to everyone in Ladakh that henceforth he would be a vegetarian. That day onwards, he maintained a strict vegetarian diet. This asceticism of Rinpoche was noted by many throughout his life. Even before he gave up meat, he already strictly adhered to the *Vinaya* code whereby monks are allowed to take only one meal a day and eat nothing after lunch. Rinpoche was now a fully ordained monk. Following the Vinaya rules is a natural and integral part of the self-disciplined life that a monk is expected to lead and he was committed to this rule.

Six

Shridhar Kaul Dullu alias Masterji

This was a time of great change and uncertainty. In 1947 India achieved independence after centuries of British colonial rule. But the people of Ladakh, far removed from the main currents of Indian life, were still under the loose suzerainty of the Maharaja of Jammu & Kashmir. These developments spelt uncertainty rather than liberation because colonial rule in this region had been weak. Now Ladakh had to find a new place for itself in a world steaming with the currents of nationalism, modernism and development.

"During the 1940s Bakula Rinpoche developed a close relationship with a Kashmiri Pandit named Shridhar Kaul Dullu (1892–1967). Rinpoche affectionately called him "Masterji". Such was the lasting influence of Masterji on him that many years later, when Rinpoche penned his autobiography (published in 2001), he dedicated the work to him."[1]

Shridhar Kaul Dullu (1892–1967), a Kashmiri Pandit, was an inspector in the education department earlier. After having accepted the responsibility to lead the people of Ladakh in their political struggle, Rinpoche took his assignment as a politician very seriously. With no knowledge of any language other than Ladakhi and Tibetan, he had to, first of all, learn some Hindi or Hindustani. After his many years of traditional Buddhist education in Lhasa, Rinpoche was only dimly aware of the many changes taking place in the world (the Second World War had recently begun). Yet he could see that great changes were afoot and he recognized the urgent need for Ladakhis to start engaging with modern education and science.

Rinpoche with Pandit Shridhar Kaul (Dullu) alias Master ji

So, when he heard of the presence of a certain "*Masterji*" in the town, he met him, and soon they became close. They would have many long conversations about all kinds of things. They discussed not just current affairs and the Indian independence movement, but also the history of Buddhism, the extraordinary legacy of Kashmir in the development of both Buddhist and Saiva Tantrism in the centuries before the arrival of Islam in the area. As is known, many of the most revered saints of the Mahayana and Vajrayana Buddhist traditions such as Kumarajiva, Buddhajiva, Sribhadra and so many others, were originally from Kashmir. It was also from Kashmir, between the 7th and 11th centuries, that Ladakh and indeed Tibet at large received so many of their Buddhist teachings, transmissions and artistic styles that have been preserved with great care and devotion within Tibetan Buddhist culture to this day.

Pandit Dullu, although a born Hindu, subsequently became a devout

Buddhist. He had the concern of the people of Ladakh uppermost in his mind. Over the years, he became Rinpoche's guide and teacher. He was an extraordinary man in his own right, whose contribution to modern Ladakh should not be forgotten. Highly educated in the Kashmiri Pandit tradition, he was a great believer in modernity and was very progressive in his attitudes. As for his relationship with Rinpoche, he perhaps did more than anyone else to help him understand the political, educational and developmental challenges facing his homeland.

When Bakula Rinpoche returned to Ladakh from Lhasa in 1940, Masterji had only recently arrived on the scene. Until 1939, he had been involved in a pioneering education programme in the Kashmir Valley itself. That programme, which began in 1927 under the sponsorship of Maharaja Hari Singh, had focused particularly on giving modern educational opportunities to girls and was led by a number of forward-thinking Theosophists. This was in fashion among modernists of the time of whom Sridhar Kaul was one[2]. By the year 1932 there were as many as seventy schools being run by the Women's Welfare Trust in Kashmir alone. However, at every meeting of the trust, Pandit Shridhar Kaul always made known his passion for extending their work to Ladakh, which, he pointed out, had so far been completely neglected. One chance for doing the needful came in 1939, when the Maharaja appointed him education officer in Leh, a post that he discharged with tremendous energy and dedication until 1948.

From his association with Bakula Rinpoche, Masterji developed and nurtured a deep respect for Buddhism. From Masterji, Rinpoche learnt about the world, about the methods and content of modern education and about the situation in India and the world at large. He guided Rinpoche in learning the statecraft and became his close confidant and steered Rinpoche in his new role as a leader. Rinpoche sincerely respected Masterji as a teacher and regarded him as one of his main gurus. After Masterji's death in 1967 his son H.N. Kaul also worked with Rinpoche as his OSD and served with great dedication and brilliance. Mr. Kaul, who was my senior in the Minorities Commission, also ensured that his father's book on the history of Ladakh, *Ladakh Through the Ages,* made it to print.

NOTES

1. Bakula Thubbstan Chognor 2001. Rang rnam padma dkar po'i phreng ba.
2. Some of these details are gleaned from "Shridhar Joo Koul Dullu (1892–1967): A Pioneer Who Spread Light and Knowledge in Ladakh" by Autar Mota.

Seven

Pakistani Invasion and the Emergence of Bakula Rinpoche as a Leader

In 1947, when Rinpoche was some thirty years of age, India attained independence from British colonial rule amid partition and great suffering and upheaval. In the months that followed the former princely states, which until this time had exercised a significant degree of autonomy under the British, joined the Union of India one by one. However, the then ruler of Jammu and Kashmir, Maharaja Hari Singh, was undecided about what to do whether he should accede to the Indian Union, or in light of his kingdom's relative isolation from the Indian hinterland and its demographic and historical factors, should attempt to assert independence from both India and Pakistan, an option that he himself then favoured.

Returning to the life and legacy of the 19th Bakula Rinpoche, some further historical contextualization is required. The emergence of Bakula Rinpoche at this critical juncture was truly historic and a significant event in the annals of Ladakh. It was a time when great transformation was taking place with India becoming independent after centuries of colonial rule. Rinpoche played a decisive role in determining the future of his homeland at this crucial juncture, by ensuring that Ladakh remained an integral part of India. Firm in his convictions, he worked day and night, sparing no effort or material resources in his determination to improve the lives of the often-poverty-stricken people of Ladakh. Therefore, rise of Bakula Rinpoche was a leading light of considerable historical significance. But for the people of Ladakh who were still under the Dogra regime of Jammu and Kashmir, it was a difficult period. They had to find a place for themselves in the new political structure of the nation. Their voice would have been lost in the wilderness of its high and barren mountains, if the charismatic personality of Bakula

Rinpoche had not been entrusted with this new role as a political leader of Ladakh.

Seeing the imminent danger to Ladakh's security, Bakula Rinpoche gave a call to the People of Ladakh to raise their own defenses till the Indian Army could arrive, a step which saved Ladakh from falling into Pakistani hands. It was in this atmosphere of uncertainty, in October 1947, only months after the declaration of Indian independence, that some bands of tribal militia from the nascent Pakistan invaded Kashmir with the intention of "liberating" its Muslim population from Dogra rule and joining it with Pakistan. The invasion clearly exposed the extreme vulnerability of Hari Singh's kingdom to Pakistani domination, and it was this that spurred him to change track and sign the Instrument of Accession with India on October 26, 1947. The Maharaja handed power in the kingdom over to the National Conference, a secular socialist Kashmiri political party with links to the Indian National Congress, which had until recently been outlawed. The National Conference was headed by the charismatic leader Sheikh Mohammed Abdullah, popularly known as Sher-e-Kashmir, who was also a close associate of the Congress leader and the Prime Minister of India Pandit Jawaharlal Nehru.

It was in this way that the modern Indian state of J&K came into existence. However, Pakistan, which was created under the banner of Islam (in contrast to India which was avowedly a secular state), could never reconcile with this accession. Since Kashmir had a Muslim majority, there were many who believed that it should have been included in Pakistan, not in India, and as such, attempts to annex the region to Pakistan continued. However, the Maharaja's kingdom also included regions like Jammu and Ladakh. This contested status was, in some ways, a legacy of British imperial rule which preserved anachronistic political alignments through the system of proxy princely-states and which continues to haunt the region even today.

Maharaja Hari Singh's decision to join the Union of India enabled the Indian government to deploy forces into J&K, and also in Ladakh. But in every way, Ladakh remained distinct from the neighbouring regions. In Kashmir, the vast majority were Muslim, while in Jammu, the majority were Hindu. Ladakh, however, had always been a stronghold of Buddhism, despite a significant minority of Muslims. In contrast to the confusion and uncertainty which prevailed in Kashmir about the new political dispensation whether it would be better to join India, or Pakistan, or to attempt full independence; the people of Ladakh were unanimous and unequivocal in their support for joining the Union of India. However, this aspiration was under threat. In early 1948, Pakistani tribal raiders entered the Skardu region of Gilgit-Baltistan, in the north of Ladakh. They besieged and soon overran the district centre of Skardu itself. This incursion presented a real and imminent danger to the security of the whole of Ladakh. It was now only a matter of time before they would begin their advance on Leh.

Meanwhile the land route between Ladakh and the Kashmir valley was cut off due to snowfall, leaving the Himalayan kingdom isolated from the rest of India, with no chance of reinforcements to relieve the small Indian Army garrison at Leh. The only means left available for bringing in reinforcements and supplies was by airlift, but at that time there were no landing strips in Ladakh. The nearest serviceable strip was in Gilgit, but that had already fallen into Pakistani hands. And even if there had been suitable places to land, the treacherous air routes to Ladakh had not yet been charted and the high altitude and unpredictable mountain weather made the journey extremely hazardous for even the most modern aircraft of the period. Moreover, the region didn't have even the most basic ground infrastructure such as roads and bridges making any kind of military deployment very hard. But time was running out for the Ladakhis and any further delay could have made the situation irretrievable.

The Pakistani raiders, mostly Pathan tribesmen, were better-organized, better-equipped[1] and more in number than the meagre Indian garrison at Leh. During the winter, they continued to strengthen their positions, occupying the lower areas. In the spring of 1948, Bakula Rinpoche was scheduled to deliver some teachings at Lungnag, a very remote place in the interior of Zanskar, south of Leh, an area which until then had been untouched by the conflict. Despite the uncertainties of the time, he continued with his schedule as planned. But while he was there, the Pakistani raiders, in a surprise move, struck south and broke through to Padum, the main village of Zanskar, plundering Buddhist monasteries and villages along the way. The raiders were moving fast.

Describing the panic situation to me Rinpoche recalled that a young monk named Tashi Ngodup (also called Upasaka) who was known to Rinpoche came running to Lungnag to inform Rinpoche of the impending disaster. He was gasping for breath and could barely speak. Such was the fear consuming the fellow. For some time, he just kept mumbling "Paki" and no one could get any sense from him. Eventually he calmed down enough to narrate the horrifying acts of brutality being committed by the invaders. He described how Sonam Stanzin who was the Zildar, government appointed revenue officers, who was the village headman and a prominent local figure, had been brutally killed, his body strapped to a horse and sent back to his village as a message to the people to either surrender or face the consequences. The messenger also said that the raiders were aware of

Rinpoche's presence in the region and implored him to leave immediately. It was clear that Bakula Rinpoche must escape without delay.

Rinpoche left Lungnag the same day with a small party of attendants. They travelled day and night without halting, and after crossing Lingti and Changthang they reached Leh unharmed. Later it was learnt that the Pakistanis had detained some local people for their role in aiding Rinpoche's escape. Such was the fear of the Pakistani onslaught at that time that hundreds of families fled from Zanskar to the neighboring regions of Kullu and Manali, where they led a life of complete destitution. Back in Leh, Rinpoche learnt that Drass and Kargil had already fallen into enemy hands. He saw the panic among the people. He held meetings with local village headmen and appealed for calm and utmost caution.

Pandit Shridhar Kaul Dullu (Masterji) was in town, so Rinpoche asked him to go immediately to Srinagar and further to Delhi to inform the political leadership of the impending danger and urge them to send help immediately to save Ladakh from Pakistani occupation. Braving the difficult and long terrain, Masterji arrived in Delhi and conveyed his misgivings to the top civil and military leadership. Meanwhile the Indian army establishment was well aware of the developments and was doing everything possible to send additional help to Ladakh. They were clandestinely preparing part of the sandy expanse between Leh and Rinpoche's monastery called Spituk (Pethub) as a landing strip under a young Ladakhi engineer Sonam Norboo.

"However, the pressure on Leh, the capital of Ladakh, had yet to be fully relieved. The airstrip at this height of nearly 3256 metres (11,000 ft.) was able to handle Dakota operations but such flying imposed operational difficulties and unknown stresses on aircraft, including ice formation on wings. Major General K.S. Thimayya, the Divisional Commander had first thought of sending reinforcements by the Manali land route, but the situation was getting critical and on May 19, 1948, Army Headquarters were apprised of the imminent danger to Leh and requested arms and supplies to be urgently air dropped. The situation had become desperate owing to the disaster at Khaltse on May 22, 1948, and Major Prithi Chand in command reported that Leh could fall to the enemy unless reinforcements reached there within 24 hours. Large numbers of raiders were observed concentrated near Khaltse and could certainly brush aside the limited defense and capture Leh within 24 hours. Aware of enemy presence at Kargil, Major Prithi Chand dispatched Major Kushal Chand with few soldiers to defend the only bridge over Indus at Khaltse, the gateway to Leh. The enemy showed up on 22nd May and Maj. Kushal Chand, finding himself hopelessly outnumbered, set ablaze the centuries old wooden bridge and gained valuable time.

Meanwhile, Subedar Bhim Chand with 80 soldiers checkmated and inflicted heavy casualties on enemy intruders (estimated 900) in Shyok and Nubra valleys, in two nail biting actions. He was awarded the much-merited VrC and Bar while Col. Prithi Chand & Maj. Kushal Chand were decorated with the MVC. During the time Maj. Kushal Chand was engaged in dousing planks of the bridge with kerosene and setting it afire, Naik Bir Singh kept the enemy at bay, got fatally wounded and was awarded VrC (Posthumous). May be the moment of honour best belonged to Sepoy Togbe, the first Leh volunteer who showed boundless courage in the Shyok Valley encounters and was awarded the VrC."[2]

Such a desperate situation required a desperate remedy. There was no one in the Air Force who really knew whether Dakotas could fly at this altitude over the high Himalayas to land at the improvised strip near Spituk (Pethub) Monastery at Leh. The redoubtable Air Officer Commanding No. 1 (Ops) Group, Air Commodore Mehar Singh, DSO, then decided to pioneer the route himself, piloting a Dakota to Leh. General Thimmaya, the Divisional Commander decided to accompany him. The pioneering flight was dangerous and daunting but the distinguished pilot's skill and courage were rewarded by success and safe landing at Leh on May 24, 1948, a tremendous boost to the morale of troops and civilians. For most of the local people this was the first time they had ever set eyes on an aeroplane. Indeed, for many of them it was the first time they had seen a motor vehicle of any kind, since at that time there was not a single motor vehicle in the whole of Ladakh.

News of the landing of the first aircraft was received with great joy. May 24, 1948, was therefore a game changing day in the history of Ladakh. Locals, led by Kushok Bakula Rinpoche, gathered for the unprecedented spectacle as this "big metal bird" or a "flying horse" descended from the sky. Recalling that incident, Rinpoche told me that he invited General Thimayya to his monastery and had a long conversation with him. He expressed his gratitude to the Indian Army for saving Ladakh from falling into the hands of Pakistani forces.

Here it is pertinent to make a special mention of the legendary Col. Chewang Rinchen played a critical role in saving Ladakh from the enemies. His younger brother P. Namgyal was twice elected as Member of Parliament and went on to become a Union Minister. A small volunteer force was formed under his dynamic leadership which came to be known as the "Nubra Guards" which became the nucleus of the resistance against the invading Pakistanis. A prominent figure, his father Kunzang Dorjey was a loyal and a close associate of Bakula Rinpoche in Nubra valley. Col. Rinchen was just

17-year-old when first enrolled as a Jemadar in the Indian Army in 1948 and went on to rise to the rank of a Colonel by the time his long and glittering army career ended. He was twice awarded the Mahavir Chakra, first for having stopped the advance of Pakistani raiders in the Nubra Valley in June 1948 and the second for the bravery he displayed in the Turtuk sector in December 1971".[3] In the 1971 India-Pakistan war, Col. Rinchen and his comrades continued the unfinished task of 1948; and freed Turtuk from Pakistani occupation.

The first IAF Dakota plane piloted by Air Commodore Mehar Singh after it landed at Leh (1949)

Major General KS Thimayya DSO

Air Commodore Mehar Singh, MVC, DSO

Col. Prithi Chand, MVC

Maj. Kushal Chand, MVC

Major Hari Chand

Sub. Bhim Chand, Vir Chakra

Major Chewang Rinchen, MVC

"In Leh Major General Thimayya assessed the situation and returned to Srinagar with Air Commodore Mehar Singh. Reinforcements were then flown in the morning of May 31, 1948, six Dakotas of No. 12 Squadron being led by Air Commodore Mehar Singh himself. However, bad weather over the high mountains compelled the aircraft formation to turn back after flying halfway towards their destination. Troops of 2/4 Gorkha Rifles (GR) remained at Srinagar airfield and again boarded the aircraft before dawn on June 1, 1948. The perilous flight was uneventful and all six Dakotas landed at Leh, the troops were rushed to the 'front' near Spituk (Pethub) Gompa and quickly established the position. Leh was safe for the time being. By August 30, 1948, a total of 123 additional troops of 2/8 GR were flown to Leh, together with supplies of stores, equipment, ammunition, wireless sets, etc. With this induction, the defending forces at Leh had increased to nearly two battalions in operating strength."[4]

In the coming weeks more Indian Air Force (IAF) aeroplanes landed at the simple airstrip bringing military battle-hardened members of the Gorkha Rifles as reinforcements. A short while later a column of infantry troops and a large caravan of mules carrying supplies also arrived on foot from Manali. They had been trekking for weeks. These developments gave some succor to the people of Ladakh, but the situation on the ground remained fluid and uncertain. Even with the reinforcements, a few hundred Indian troops were still insufficient to repel the invaders. It was at this point that Bakula Rinpoche issued a call to the youth of Ladakh to join the Indian troops as volunteers. Meanwhile, Rinpoche was also able to prevail upon the emergency administration at Srinagar, Kashmir to take immediate steps for organizing local volunteers, irrespective of religious affiliation as National Guards. They had no military training, but hundreds came out enthusiastically to defend their land including Ghulam Qadir, now 95 years old from Partapur, Nubra who was one such volunteer. He still prides in flashing the identity-card signed by Bakula Rinpoche which is one of his prized possessions.[5] My father Tondup Namgyal Shakspo also joined the fight as a civil volunteer. The Indian army with the assistance of air strikes by the Indian Air Force and local volunteers were able to push back the Pakistani forces and destroy their positions and supply lines.

Hostilities came to an end when a ceasefire was eventually agreed between India and Pakistan on January 1, 1949. Major General KS Thimayya, GOC paid high tribute to "The LEHDETT, One Force too Many" and placed on record that "Their deeds and acts of gallantry against very superior forces in the Ladakh valley will go down in the annals of the Indian Army as one of the greatest feats." Let us stand up in salute to LEHDETT's spirit of devotion to duty and the unflagging vision of field commanders."[6] There were many casualties, and the medical facilities were minimal. When the situation became desperate, Bakula Rinpoche offered the army a portion of Pethub Monastery (which was close to the airstrip) to use as a make-shift medical centre for the injured soldiers and civilians.

The border, however, is still contested, with the areas of Skardu and Gilgit remaining in Pakistan to this day. In retrospect, the Pakistani invasion of Ladakh was a truly historic episode. It secured India's border with Pakistan and it saved Ladakh and its ancient Buddhist culture. Had things gone differently, Ladakh would have been a part of Pakistan and its Buddhist civilization would have been subsumed under a hostile ideology, suffering a fate similar to that of Tibet under Chinese occupation. Subsequently, Rinpoche sent a letter to Prime Minister Nehru through Major Hari Chand inviting him to visit Leh which was acknowledged by the Prime Minister Nehru **(Annexures 2, 3)**.

Recollecting the traumatic experience of that time Rinpoche told me that the ground strip where the Dakotas had landed belonged to his Spituk (Pethub) monastery. When the hostilities ended and the Pakistani forces were successfully repulsed, Indian Army felt the need of a permanent airport at Leh. The Army and Air Force authorities concluded that the ground prepared for the landing of Dakotas, which belonged to Pethub monastery, was best suited for the airport. An old revenue document testifies to this fact is attached. **(Annexure 4)** Rinpoche agreed to part with that piece of land. According to Lama Lobzang Lhundup, former abbot of Pethub Monastery there were some apprehensions among some of the senior monks, but Rinpoche overruled them and decided to give away the land for construction of the airport.

It is also relevant to mention here that like the 'Darbar Move' between Jammu and Srinagar when the entire bureaucratic set-up moves to Jammu from Srinagar and vice versa, Ladakh also followed a similar system. In the case of Ladakh Leh would function as the summer capital whereas Skardu become the winter capital of Ladakh. Many people from Ladakh who were government employees working in Skardu, got stuck there following the Pakistani incursions and they barely managed to escape from there. They brought with them the horror stories and the atrocities committed by the raiders.

Following this misadventure from Pakistan, government swung into action and Chushul airstrip in Changthang was completed by August 1952. Prime Minister Jawaharlal Nehru along with colleagues took the first flight into it and inaugurated it. On 23 July 1962, the first plane landed at *Daulat Beg Oldi* (DBO), the highest air strip in the world. Located at an altitude of

Rinpoche meeting General Cariappa in New Delhi (1949)

Rinpoche with his delegation at the residence of General Cariappa, New Delhi (1949)

over 16,000 feet, DBO lies a mere 8 km south and 9 km west of the Line of Actual Control (LAC), and is an airfield of strategic importance. Similarly, THOISE airfield in Nubra was also made operation in 1960. It lies in Shyok Valley. THOISE is not a real name but an acronym: Transit Halt of Indian Soldiers Enroute (to Siachen). It is about 160 km from Leh. Thoise is reached via the Khardungla pass, one of the world's highest roads used by motor vehicles.

Meanwhile, General K.M. Cariappa, Commander-in-Chief of the entire Indian Army who had learnt about Rinpoche's exceptional contribution during the conflict, invited Bakula Rinpoche to New Delhi to thank him personally for his contribution during the war. Rinpoche visited New Delhi and reciprocated the compliments by praising the sheer bravery of the general and the Indian Army and for saving the people of Ladakh and their homeland from aggressors. The meeting brought the two men close. The Army Chief was delighted by the success of the campaign and was genuinely moved by the leadership and patriotism shown by Rinpoche and the people of Ladakh. He also recognized the velour and commitment of the volunteer forces who had played such a vital role in the action.

NOTES

1. An entry on K.M. Cariappa on the website IndiaNetzone expresses the widely-held belief that these tribal invaders were aided by the nascent state of Pakistan: "As early as October 1947, Pakistan had started its hostile activities by providing covert logistic support to the tribals. Besides, its regular soldiers were given long leave to fight as 'deserters' and lead the tribals clandestinely. Since Pakistan had launched the offensive, it had all the tactical advantage in choosing the terrain for infiltration beforehand. Its lines of communication were shorter and more secure. On the other hand, India had numerous logistical problems. The mountainous region posed serious difficulties in transporting the medium guns of the artillery. Its wireless messages were often intercepted while the telephone lines were not reliable. The fighting units were strung over hundreds of kilometers far from each other and Delhi was far away from the scene of action."
2. Salute. Recalling an Audacious Mission: February-March 1948. Written by Lt. Gen. Baljit Singh, AVSM, VSM.
3. "An Ode to the Unsung Heroes of Ladakh" by Claude Arpi
4. The society for Aerospace Studies, Vol II, 2007, edited by Pushpindar Singh.
5. Remembering the 19th Bakula Rinpoche. A collection of memories from different parts of Ladakh. By Himalayan Cultural Heritage Foundation (2018
6. Salute. Recalling an audacious mission: February/March 1948. By Lt. Gen. Baljit Singh, AVSM, VSM.

Eight

Bakula Rinpoche and Prime Minister Nehru

For the Indian political elite, Pakistani incursion had brought into sharp focus the vital importance of Ladakh as a strategic border area. So, not long after his meeting with General Cariappa, Bakula Rinpoche, then a young man (age 32 years), received an invitation to visit New Delhi to meet the Prime Minister of India Pandit Jawaharlal Nehru. In the spring of 1949, accompanied by a delegation and Stanzin Wangbo Nangso as interpreter, Rinpoche set off on the long journey to New Delhi. They started out on horseback for several weeks to Srinagar, where they rested for a few days, then continued by road and rail to the Indian capital New Delhi. Rinpoche's meeting with Pandit Nehru was scheduled to take place at the sprawling Prime Ministerial residence *Teen-Murti Bhawan* on May 20, 1949. For Bakula Rinpoche there was a lot at stake in this meeting. Fate of Kashmir, and with it that of Ladakh, was still hanging in balance, with the UN calling for a plebiscite on its future. This was Rinpoche's first meeting with an Indian leader, let alone with the world-famous Pandit Nehru, the great hero of India's freedom struggle. Describing the moment Rinpoche told me that when he looked back on the event in later years, he remembered being rather tense and apprehensive before the meeting. But when he saw Pandit ji's simplicity and his warm and affectionate nature, he was greatly reassured and felt completely at ease speaking with him.

Rinpoche briefed Pandit Nehru about the aspirations of the people of Ladakh and also about the situation in general following the Pakistani attack. "The delegation urged the Prime Minister that the territorial integrity of the J&K State of which their country is a part, be maintained and that the State as a whole remain with India. The future security and prosperity of their region lie with India alone."[1] He urged the Prime Minister to ensure the security of Ladakh, and that it had no desire to join Pakistan. Bakula Rinpoche's words added weight to the petition that had already been submitted on May 4, 1949, to the Prime Minister on behalf of the Ladakhi Buddhist Association headed by Chewang Rigzin Kalon. This memorandum made a detailed case for Ladakh to remain a part of India. The people of Ladakh, it said, had cast their lot with India, and should not be bound by the outcome of any plebiscite held about the future of Muslim majority in Kashmir. Should such a plebiscite go in favour of joining Pakistan, argued the memorandum, Ladakh be allowed to join the Hindu-majority region of Jammu, or the East Punjab, and thereby remain within India. If such assurances were not given, warned the memorandum, Ladakh would have no choice but to reluctantly look at re-uniting with its closest neighbour Tibet, even though Tibet was at that time facing the imminent threat of Chinese invasion. The petition also underlined the strategic and commercial importance of Leh as a nerve centre of Central Asian trade and argued it was in India's strategic interests not to let it go.[2]

These points had to be spelt out explicitly to the Indian leadership, so as to clearly distinguish Ladakh in their minds from the neighbouring but very different region of Kashmir. Sheikh Abdullah, the charismatic leader of Kashmir at that time, had been a close associate of Pandit Nehru since the 1930s, and at that time was broadly speaking in favour of Kashmir's union with India. However, he was keen to assert Kashmir's special status and thus its autonomy within the union. His historical stand for autonomy was based on the Treaty of Amritsar (1846). This Treaty, executed by the British East India Company and Raja Gulab Singh after the First Anglo-Sikh War, established the princely state of Jammu & Kashmir under the suzerainty of the British Indian Empire. However, as Rinpoche pointed out, Ladakh's relationship with the Dogras was governed by a separate and earlier treaty resulting from the war of 1834 when Gulab Singh sent his General Zorawar Singh to take control of all the territory between Jammu and the Tibet boarder, leading to the conquest of Ladakh and Baltistan. Rinpoche argued, the arrangements which subjected the Ladakhis to the Dogras had ceased to be operative in the wake of the accession to India, so the constitutional link which tied Ladakh to the State of J&K should no longer be considered valid.

Rinpoche told me that he was struck by Pandit Nehru's personal faith in Buddhism and his genuine dedication to the cause of uplifting the plight of the poor and downtrodden in India. It was under Pandit Nehru's leadership that India adopted a secular, democratic and federal structure of government which as Bakula Rinpoche admitted, was the model best suited for catering to India's great diversity. Pandit ji had an optimistic nature and an unshakeable faith in the power of goodwill and honesty in matters of international diplomacy. He really exemplified the *Madhyamik Marg* or the Middle Path in his approach. This is quite obvious in his insistence on the *Panchsheel* or Five-Point agreement signed between India and China in 1954.

Narrating about this meeting to me, Mr. Wangbo Nangso, who was Rinpoche's interpreter, recalled that before meeting the Prime Minister Rinpoche had held an informal discussion with some of the senior Ladakhis present in Delhi so as to decide the issues that should be raised at the meeting. During that meeting Rinpoche had proposed that in order to make the Indian leader understand the situation first hand, Prime Minister Nehru should be invited to visit Ladakh. However, Tsewang Rigzin Kalon, a prominent Ladakhi aristocrat of the time who was also the President of the Ladakh Buddhist Association, advised Rinpoche against making such an invitation. He said it would not be practical since Leh at that time had no infrastructure or even basic modern amenities suitable for someone of the Prime Minister's stature. At the meeting, Rinpoche agreed with Tsewang Rigzin's point. However, when Rinpoche met Pandit Nehru in person, he felt so comfortable in his down-to-earth personality that he summoned the courage to invite Pandit ji to visit Ladakh. Meanwhile, Rinpoche had also sent a letter to Prime Minister Nehru to visit Ladakh. After the visit Rinpoche wrote another letter to Prime Minister Nehru. This letter was written in Tibetan which can be accessed at the National Archive of India, New Delhi.

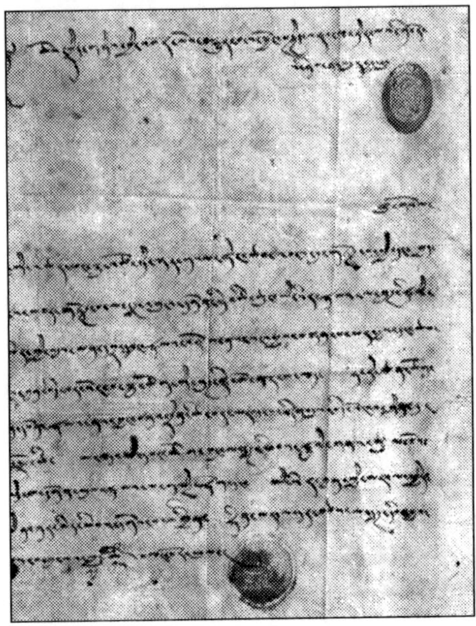

Letter from Bakula Rinpoche to Prime Minister Nehru

Bakula Rinpoche offering a silk ceremonial scarf to Jawahar Lal Nehru upon his arrival at Leh on July 4, 1949 (Times of India. July 12, 1949)

Rinpoche with Prime Minister Nehru, Prime Minister Sheikh Abdulla and others at Samkar Gonpa, Leh (1949)

Bakula Rinpoche addressing the VIP guests in Leh. Ms. Indira Gandhi, Sheikh Mohd. Abdullah, Pandit Jawaharlal Nehru, Prime Minister of India and other leaders are seated. Mr. Sonam Norboo is seen standing backside (July 5, 1949)

Pandit Jawaharlal Nehru, Prime Minister of India and Sheikh Mohd. Abdullah, Prime Minister of J&K in traditional Ladakhi dress (1949)
Photo courtesy: The Dispatch

Prime Minister Nehru presenting a portrait of Mahatma Gandhi (Leh. July 5, 1949)

In later years, for as long as Pandit Nehru was in office, Rinpoche always had easy access to the Prime Minister House the Teen Murti Bhawan, and this connection helped him significantly in the discharge of his duties as an elected representative of the people of Ladakh. Pandit Nehru would always receive him very warmly and make him feel completely at home. One of Prime Minister Nehru's personal staff who was later working in the Parliament House, once told me that Pandit Nehru had tremendous regard for Rinpoche and would personally receive him and see him off. The two men developed a close personal bond which continued till the last days of Pandit ji's life. While in Delhi, Rinpoche also called on his friend General K.M. Cariappa at his residence. Over tea, the General offered to arrange for Rinpoche a pilgrimage to many of the holiest Buddhist sites of northern India. General Cariappa provided Rinpoche and his entourage with a vehicle and all necessary logistical arrangements. He also offered to arrange everything for their return trip to Leh. So, having completed their pilgrimage to holy places, the party proceeded to Pathankot, then Jammu and onward to Srinagar. In Srinagar Rinpoche spent some days meeting senior Kashmiri figures, including the Kashmiri Prime Minister Sheikh Mohammed Abdullah, leader of the National Conference.

True to his word, Prime Minister Nehru visited Leh soon after Rinpoche's return. An Indian Air Force plane carrying Pandit Nehru and his team landed at Leh on July 4, 1949, on the same makeshift airstrip near Pethub Monastery which had first been prepared during the Pakistani incursion. On disembarking the aircraft, the senior dignitaries were greeted by a group of people led by Bakula Rinpoche. They were provided with horses for the ride up to the official residence, known as Wazir Bangla.[3] It was, one can only imagine, an interesting contrast for those VVIP visitors, transiting directly from an aeroplane to horseback in the rarefied high-altitude air of Ladakh, surrounded by dramatic scenery untouched by modernity.

At the Wazir Bangla, Rinpoche offered Pandit Nehru a ceremonial *Khadag* and gift and extended his warm welcome. In return Prime Minister Nehru presented him with a statue of Lord Buddha and an ivory casket with holy images. This was the first time that a top leader of India had ever visited Ladakh, and the local people, together with the local notables and officials, gave the visiting party a warm traditional welcome. The Prime Minister was accompanied by his daughter, Indira Gandhi. Sheikh Mohammed Abdullah was also in the party. There were also several journalists, including Delhi based photo-journalist P.N. Sharma and Sati Sahni, BBC India correspondent.

Primary goal of the Prime Minister's four-day visit was to enable him to make a first-hand assessment of the needs and challenges being faced by this unique region. During his stay he received a number of local delegations and listened patiently to their concerns, demands and aspirations. The visit was not without its cultural accompaniments. As it coincided with the annual grand festival of Hemis monastery, popularly known as the *Hemis Tsi-shu*. Rinpoche recalled that at the time he had a particularly well-behaved horse nicknamed 'Ziling', a Mongolian breed, sturdy and docile. So, he offered that Pandit Nehru could ride *Ziling* for the duration of his stay. Pandit ji graciously agreed and it was the astride Ziling that Pandit Nehru rode the forty-five kilometers to Hemis to attend the grand festival. Other horses were also provided for Sheikh Abdullah and the other dignitaries.

The rigors of everyday life in Ladakh at that time were a long way from the luxury of Teen Murti Bhawan but Pandit Nehru seemed to thoroughly enjoy the experience. Throughout his stay, the dependable Ziling was always close at hand. Along the way to Hemis, villagers and children came out and lined the road at various points to welcome these important guests. At Hemis Monastery Pandit ji was given a warm and traditional welcome. Stagtsang Raspa Rinpoche, the head of Hemis Monastery received the Indian Prime Minister. The elaborate Buddhist murals at Hemis left a lasting impression on the Prime Minister, as did the strength of Ladakh's living culture and traditions.

During the party's return journey from Hemis, a reception was held for them by locals on the banks of the azure-blue Indus river (known in Ladakhi as the *Singe Khabab* at Choglamsar. Large picnic tents were erected, and the reception was attended by many senior representatives of both Buddhist and Muslim communities of Ladakh. Perhaps to ascertain his assessment, it was at this meeting that Pandit Nehru asked the people as to who should lead the people as their representative? The assembled notables of the region, Buddhists and Muslims conveyed to Pandit Nehru and Sheikh Mohammed Abdullah their complete confidence in the leadership of the young Bakula Rinpoche and their unanimous desire that he should be their political representative.

Bakula Rinpoche recalled that after returning to Leh he was called to meet Pandit Nehru and Sheikh Abdullah at the Wazir Bangla. He was accompanied by Wangbo Nangso. Pandit Nehru patiently explained to Rinpoche the new democratic system of governance that was being established in India. Then, with an implicit recognition of Rinpoche's spiritual priorities and education, Pandit Nehru made him a fateful offer. The Prime Minister said that Rinpoche should consider combining his spiritual leadership with political leadership, for the sake of the welfare of his people. It was very important, he said, that the people of Ladakh were not left behind during this period of great change and social progress. And no one was better placed or better suited to discharge this duty of leadership, then Bakula Rinpoche himself.

Rinpoche was dumbfounded and rather confused by this surprise offer. Coming from none other than the Prime Minister of India himself, it could not be refused straight away. Yet, he didn't know what to do or say. Reflecting on this meeting in later years, Rinpoche recalled that it took considerable effort to gather his wits, but when he did, he politely refused the offer. He explained to Pandit Nehru that his vows as a Buddhist monk made it hard for him to take part in worldly affairs, and anyway, he said, he was completely ignorant about modern politics, knew little about India, and couldn't even speak a word of Hindi or English. Politics, he tried to convey, was really not his cup of tea.

But Pandit Nehru had already observed Bakula Rinpoche's astute leadership qualities, and the high esteem in which he was held by both the Buddhists and Muslims of Ladakh. He had already made up his mind about his suitability for the role and was not going to let Rinpoche off the hook so easily. Pandit Nehru reminded him, kindly but firmly of Buddha's teaching to work for the well-being of others. Well, he said, there could be no better opportunity than this, to help free the people of Ladakh from the shackles of poverty, ignorance and deprivation. He also promised that he would personally give Rinpoche his full support and eulogized about the rights of the people under the new democratic dispensation. Sheikh Abdullah who was present, also pledged his own cooperation in the discharge of Rinpoche's new role. Rinpoche was deeply apprehensive. He told Pandit Nehru that he had to think it over and that he would inform them of his decision before the Prime Minister returned to Delhi in a couple of days.

Describing the day, Rinpoche recounted that in the evening, Pandit Nehru's words were still echoing in his ears. Meanwhile news of the meeting and its import had quickly spread around the small town of Leh, and the people were discussing little else. A steady stream of local elders, including those from the Muslim community, came to Samkar Monastery to pledge their support for Rinpoche and tried to convince him to accept. In Ladakh, in those days, there were really very few people with the education, popular stature, and breadth of vision to take on such a role. But Rinpoche felt woefully ill-prepared, and the prospect of the volatile Indian political milieu was a very daunting one. However, he also realized that he could not just turn his back on the situation. His Bodhisattva vows impelled him to do whatever he could to help alleviate the sufferings of others, and as Pandit Nehru himself had pointed out, this was a tremendous opportunity to do that.

Finally, he decided he should submit to the demands of his people and accept Pandit Nehru's offer, despite his apprehension. He then withdrew for some solitary meditation to clear his mind and clarify his conviction. That way he managed to overcome his fears and developed a clear resolution and commitment for the way ahead. He would accept responsibility as political leader of Ladakh, but only on the condition that this would not interfere with his prior commitment to Buddhist ethics and the routines of monastic discipline. On that, he resolved, there would be no compromise. Thus, ever since that fateful decision, the whole of Bakula Rinpoche's long life would be characterized by the difficult task of balancing between political and spiritual commitments, and the need to reconcile all of his actions as a leader, with his primary moral commitment to benefitting the people. The next day Rinpoche once again met with Pandit Nehru and Sheikh Abdullah for lunch at Samkar monastery. Delighted by Rinpoche's acceptance, they reiterated their promises to give whatever personal assistance they could in the discharge of his duties. Mr. Sonam Norboo; who was then the Development Commissioner, Ladakh; were also present on that occasion.

Pandit Nehru's last engagement before leaving Ladakh, was a public address to the people of Leh and assured them of his continued support in the development of the region. He announced that a team of experts would be sent from Delhi to assess the requirements of the region and promised to help accelerate the region's development and integration with the rest of India. Pandit Nehru's short visit had an abiding impact on the people of Ladakh. It gave them a sense of security and belonging concerning the new democratic, secular and socialist India. In Pandit Nehru they saw a visionary, but also a man with a simple and a sincere heart, who genuinely cared for the welfare of the people. Soon afterwards, Sheikh Abdullah, who was by now the Prime Minister of J&K and leader of its ruling National Conference party, formally appointed Bakula Rinpoche as President of the National Conference in Ladakh. The National Conference was at this time completely dominant in the politics of Kashmir. With this, Rinpoche's long involvement in the often-tumultuous affairs of the State of J&K began.

Holy Buddha Relics Come to Ladakh

The repeated crop failure, excessive snowfall and attack by the Pakistani tribal raiders in 1948 had left a deep psychological scar and sense of fear among Ladakhis. So, during Pandit Nehru's four day visit Bakula Rinpoche took the opportunity to ask the Prime Minister Nehru whether the holy relics of the Lord Buddha and his two principal spiritual sons, *Sariputta* and *Mahamoggallana,* could be sent to Ladakh. This, he said, would have a very healing and beneficial effect on the people after the recent turbulence, and would also help to reinforce the people's sense of belonging to India. When Pandit Nehru returned to New Delhi, he did not forget this request, and following it up, he instructed the Ministry of Education to explore the possibility of sending the holy relics to Ladakh.

So, on the morning of May 24, 1950, a delegation accompanying the holy relics of the Lord Buddha and the two disciples, flew from Dum-Dum airport, Calcutta to Srinagar. The delegation included Venerable Dvariyavalisinghe, General Secretary of the Maha Bodhi Society of India; Bhikkhu Sangharakshita; Bhikkhu D. Sasanagiri Thero; Sheelbhadra; Bhikkhu U. Dhammaratana and Lama Angrup, a Buddhist scholar from Lahaul and Spiti. They were received at Srinagar airport by Bakula Rinpoche along with Bakshi Ghulam Mohammed, the then Deputy Prime Minister of J&K, and some other high dignitaries. The next day Bakula Rinpoche joined the delegation on its onward journey to Leh, again in special military aircraft.

At Leh, a grand ceremonial welcome awaited them. As the plane touched the tarmac there was jubilation marked by sound of music, fluttering religious banners and prayer flags. Long queues of people waited for hours to get a glimpse of the holy relics of Lord Buddha. For the next seventy-nine days, the relics were taken to all the major monasteries and villages of

Ladakh, so that people all over the region could receive their visual blessing. They were taken to the regions of Sham, to the upper and lower areas of Nubra, to Changthang, Zanskar and Kargil. The monetary and material offerings made by the people of Ladakh during this visit were passed on to the Mahabodhi Society.

Coming of the holy relics also helped Ladakhis forge their links with other Buddhist communities outside Ladakh and gave them the sense that they were now part of the mother India. This was important because geographically Ladakh was cut off from the rest of the world. The only outside place with which it had effective relations was Tibet, but those connections too were being slowly severed by the Chinese invasion of Tibet. In order to build on these new relations with Buddhist in other parts of India and outside, Bakula Rinpoche requested the *Maha Bodhi Society* of India to accept some Ladakhi students at the Mahabodhi Inter college at Sarnath, Varanasi. The request was accepted and the first batch of Ladakhi students was enrolled. Thereafter twenty more young novices from different monasteries such as *Hemis, Thiksey, Chemdey, Phyang, Likir and Pethub* were sent to study there under the supervision of Lama Lobzang and later Nyima Norbu. They were provided scholarships by the Ministry of Home Affairs, New Delhi. Subsequently, Rinpoche also sent a few young monks of his monastery to Sri Lanka to study Pali.

Bakula Rinpoche, Gergan Sonam and Stanzin Wangbo Nangso at Leh Airport as the Holy Relics taken to Delhi

(L to R) Togdan Rinpoche, Konchok Soṇam, Bakula Rinpoche, Thiksey Rinpoche and Stakna Rinpoche with other senior monks

Rinpoche with senior Ladakhi monks and members of the Mahabodhi Society of India with the Holy Buddha Relics (Leh, 1950)

NOTES

1. Ladakh Through the Ages by Shridhar Kaul and H.N. Kaul pg. 185
2. This memorandum was submitted to Prime Minister Nehru on May 4, 1949 by Mr. Chewang Rigzin Kalon, President of Ladakh Buddhist Association, as stated in conflicts in J&K impact on Polity, Society and Economics by V.R. Raghvan.
3. Today this site – in no small part due to the persistent efforts of Bakula Rinpoche – serves as the headquarters of the Ladakh Buddhist Association (LBA).

Nine

Rinpoche and the Baba, Lost and Found

The story of Bakula Rinpoche's elder brother, Raja Tashi Phuntsog Namgyal is very interesting. It is unbelievable but true and, therefore, it is worth a short digression from the main topic. It is also a story of human bond and relationship. I was the sole witness to this emotional meeting of two elderly brothers meeting after about 55 years of separation.

Raja Tashi Phuntsog Namgyal had married twice. His first wife was Tsering Lhazom of the Leh Kalon family. Tragically, very soon after the birth of their only son prince Thupstan Nyima (later recognized as the Rizong Sras Rinpoche) Tsering Lhazom passed away. Raja Tashi Phuntsog Namgyal was distraught, but after some time he remarried, this time to Rigzin Dolma of Solpon-Konchok.

Anyway, when Bakula Rinpoche returned to Ladakh in 1940, he was confronted with some very sad news. He already knew about the passing away of his father Raja Nangwa Thayas while he was in Tibet, but he had no idea about the mysterious disappearance of his elder brother Tashi Phuntsog Namgyal. It transpired that after the tragic death of his second wife, his brother lost all interest in worldly affairs. He had become reclusive, melancholic and deeply religious. One day, he left his home unannounced. Nobody knew where he had gone. It was a deep shock to the family. Divination indicated that he was still alive and that he had become a Hindu ascetic, steadfastly clinging to the banner of Dharma. The divination also suggested that he would only be found after about fifty to sixty years. Based on these divinations, Bakula Rinpoche was convinced that he was still alive. And over the years, he never gave up hope and continued the search for his missing brother. He visited many Buddhist as well as Hindu holy places and pilgrimage sites including the banks of Ganges at Varanasi and Haridwar, making enquiries and hoping to hear some word about his brother among the Hindu ascetics (*sadhus*) there. But it was all in vain. The family waited and waited, but there was no news. After some decades, the family gave up all hope of finding him alive.

But then, sometime in 1989, there was an interesting turn of events. Rinpoche received news of a person whose description sounded like it might be his lost brother. At that time, I was working as Rinpoche's secretary in the National Commission for Minorities, New Delhi. The report was about an elderly hermit living in a mountain-cave near Manali in Himachal Pradesh. The description was certainly intriguing for it was reported that the old *Sadhu Baba* could speak Ladakhi. Rinpoche was very eager to find out more to ascertain this person's real identity. So, he sent his *Chagzot* (Manager) Thupstan Targyes (*Gelong Shakspo)*, to Manali. Upon his return, the manager told Rinpoche that the *Baba* (as he was known locally) was living at Nehru Kund near Manali and that he did indeed appear to be his lost brother. Yet it was difficult to be conclusive since the old man would not disclose his identity to anyone and also because he behaved and talked in a very strange manner. The *Baba* apparently maintained no contacts with anyone and never revealed his identity to visitors. Occasionally, it was reported that he would admit that he was from Ladakh, but that was the only information anyone could glean.

However, it was clear that Baba could understand Ladakhi and most interestingly, he also appeared to know about some people and specific incidents in Ladakh's history that suggested he had to be Rinpoche's brother. But whenever he was asked directly about his identity, he would either laugh or reply with some misleading remarks. For example, Baba had once stated that he belonged to a particular family from Nubra in Ladakh. But when word was sent to this family, the reply came back saying that there was no-one missing from their family. So, this turned out to be another attempt by Baba to hide his identity. But as news of this mysterious figure spread in Ladakh, there was intense curiosity among the people and many people visited the place near Manali to see the hermit.

Raja Tashi Phunstog Namgyal's two children – Rizong Sras Rinpoche and Namgyal Wangmo – as well as his own sister Norzin Wangmo and other family members, went to see him. And they all returned convinced that the Baba was indeed Raja Tashi Phuntsog Namgyal. What in particular, made them believe was that as a young man Raja Tashi Phuntsog Namgyal had a distinct limp in his walk which this Baba also had. So, now, there were enough indications that the white bearded chain-smoking Baba in the foothills of Manali was indeed the long-lost brother of Bakula Rinpoche.

In mid-1990s Norzin Wangmo, his sister along with some family members had visited the Baba and identified him. At that time, Rinpoche was posted in Ulaanbaatar, Mongolia as Ambassador of India. Convinced that his brother had been found, Rinpoche decided to travel to India to meet him. I accompanied Rinpoche on this visit. From New Delhi we flew to Kullu and from there we drove, reaching the government guest house in Manali by evening. It was a cold autumn day in 1990. Rinpoche asked me to find directions to the exact location so that we could go there early the next morning. So, I made a reconnaissance visit and returned with the news that Baba was living in a cave at a place known as *Nehru Kund,* not far from the town.

The next day, early in the morning, we drove to Nehru Kund, about 20 kilometers outside Manali on the way to *Rohtang Pass*. Not far from there is the bridge over the Beas river. There was no village or settlement anywhere near the cave and he lived all alone. His room was actually a rock-cave with no window and only a dark metal sheet made from an asphalt container as a door. It was a damp, cold and foggy morning. As we reached the place, Rinpoche asked me to go first and inform the Baba about his visit, while he waited in the car.

So, I approached the cave and knocked on the metal sheet which served as a door. A voice came back asking in Hindi who was there. I removed the tin sheet and entered the room. Baba was sleeping on the ground and hadn't yet got up, and though I was speaking in Ladakhi, he was still talking to me in Hindi. I told him that Bakula Rinpoche had come to meet him and that he was waiting in the car outside. At first Baba did not believe me. Then he got up immediately and asked me to repeat my words. He seemed filled with an incredible innocent, childlike happiness. But before inviting Rinpoche into the room, he asked me to help clean up a bit. I looked around, bewildered – the room was so dusty and there was really nothing of any value in it. There was no bed, no table, no chair, and virtually no possessions. There were some bags hanging on the wall. That's all. It was cold so, I lit some firewood lying there to generate some heat. Baba asked me to prepare a clean seating area for Rinpoche while he pulled up a tin box and covered it with a piece of cloth as a makeshift table.

Baba was a heavy smoker and could not resist his morning cigarette. So, he started smoking which filled the room with even more smoke. As I came out of the cave, I saw Rinpoche was waiting anxiously. He told me he had heard the commotion and was concerned if everything was okay. I explained the inside situation and requested Rinpoche to wait a little while longer to give the dust and smoke from the cigarette some time to settle down. Having severed all worldly ties, Raja Tashi Phuntsog Namgyal had never disclosed his family and personal relationships for about 55 years. But when he saw Rinpoche, his younger brother entering the tiny shed, he could not control his emotions. He stood up from his bed, embraced Rinpoche tightly and said, "so happy to meet my brother". Later, according to the locals, who provided him with food and generally looked after him, told us this was the first time he had ever admitted to having any human relationship with anyone. I was the sole witness to this emotional reunion of two elderly brothers, one in his seventies and one in his eighties, who had not seen each other for about 55 years. Unimaginable but true. It was truly an emotional moment and not easy for me to watch. In their own ways and following different paths, they had chosen to renounce the world and family to follow the path of spirituality. Wiping his tears, Baba offered the Rinpoche a place to sit.

As they both settled down in this unexpected reunion, Baba's demeanour suddenly changed. As if re-asserting his stated position, he suddenly announced to Rinpoche that their meeting as brothers was just a one-off, and from now on when they meet, it is only as one sadhu or ascetic meets another. Then he seemed to go off into some kind of trance and started behaving strangely, while intermittently making pronouncements about impermanence. Then he picked up his simple flute and started playing it and singing a song. His talk was in an endless stream, smattered with quotes from Hindu and Buddhist scriptures, and invariably ending on the philosophical note of impermanence. He was somewhat eccentric in his behaviour. Sometimes he would suddenly burst out laughing for no apparent reason or pick up his flute mid-sentence and start playing it. His was the truly ascetic life, unhooked from worldly concerns. When Rinpoche inquired about his long absence, Baba told him that he had been in Burma and neighboring areas during World War-II, though we have never been able to verify this. After that, he said, he had been wandering from place to place until he settled in his current abode in the foothills of the Himalayas.

His knowledge of both Buddhist and Hindu philosophy was evident. Then he told Rinpoche that his most precious possession was a book rolled up in a cloth cover. Un-wrapping it and opening the book, he showed us a very old black and white photograph of the young Bakula Rinpoche which had been inserted between the pages. "You see, you are always with me", he said with a smile to Rinpoche. Whenever he addressed Rinpoche, he called him 'Raja Sahib'. Rinpoche would reply and say that he is only a Buddhist monk, so why do you call me Raja? Baba gave a philosophical

Bakula Rinpoche meeting his brother Raja Tashi Phuntsog Namgyal (Baba) at Nehru Kund near Manali (1990)

reply. A Raja, he said, is someone who lives in the hearts of people. He clearly knew about Rinpoche's hard work and achievements for the people of Ladakh and elsewhere. He also told Rinpoche that although they had not been in contact for many years, he had always followed Rinpoche's life and appreciated his noble deeds. Rinpoche then asked the Baba if he would like to return to Ladakh to visit his home and family. Like a sadhu, Baba's reply was that he would go if Laxman (the younger brother of Lord Rama) would go with him. To this Rinpoche nodded in agreement and promised to make the necessary arrangements. Then Baba started smoking again. Since the room had no window or ventilation it was quickly filled with smoke, and I could sense Rinpoche was finding it uncomfortable. I tried to tell Baba not to smoke but he could not stop himself. By this point I had become quite friendly with him. Pretending that I was a smoker too, I asked him for a cigarette. He gave me the packet and more importantly the match box. So, I took them and left the room. After some time, I returned, but only with the cigarettes, not the matches, to save Rinpoche from the discomfort!

The local people in the neighbouring villages respected Baba and they looked after him well. Generally, he seemed to be in good health and had a sound memory. Since that time, Rinpoche has met his brother several times. Baba also visited Ladakh and spent some time at the Matho palace near Leh, but he could not adapt easily to family life and soon returned to his hut in the mountains. On one occasion Rinpoche sent a warm Mongolian coat for his brother, which I delivered to him in Manali. I told Baba that it was a gift from Rinpoche. He accepted and asked me to thank him. Later on, I heard from others that he had never before accepted a gift and used it. When people tried to offer him things or money, he would take them, but as they left, he would immediately give it away to the local villagers. But this time he not only accepted the gift, but wore it all winter, which surprised many people.

During this period, Rizong Sras Rinpoche, his son, would regularly visit his father and look after all his needs. But sadly, in the autumn of 2003, while Bakula Rinpoche was recuperating from Pneumonia in Mongolia, the news came that his brother Raja Tashi Phuntsog Namgyal had passed away. For me it was a difficult situation to handle. Rinpoche's own health at that time was very poor. So, I was in a fix as to convey the sad news to Rinpoche or not. I immediately called Rizong Sras Rinpoche, his son, in India and asked for his advice. Rizong Rinpoche told me not to hold back but to tell him. On hearing the news, Bakula Rinpoche immediately sat down to offer prayers. He also gave instructions to the monks in his monastery to conduct special prayers for his brother. Raja Tashi Phuntsog Namgyal had died peacefully in the same hut near Manali at the ripe old age.

Ten

The 102nd Gaden Tripa Rizong Sras Rinpoche

Thupstan Nyima Tenzin Norbu, better known as Rizong Sras Rinpoche, was born in Matho Palace in 1927. His father Raja Tashi Phuntsog Namgyal was the elder brother of 19th Bakula Rinpoche. At a very young age he was recognized as the 4th incarnation of the Rizong Sras Rinpoche. As a result, he spent a lot of time in his early childhood being guided in basic monastic education by his uncle 19th Bakula Rinpoche, just as Bakula Rinpoche himself had been guided in his early youth by the previous incarnation of Rizong Sras Rinpoche. This Master-pupil relationship between Bakula Rinpoche and Rizong Sras Rinpoche continues even today. After the passing away of 19th Bakula Rinpoche, Rizong Sras Rinpoche took upon himself the responsibility of finding the 20th incarnation of Arhat Bakula and later his upbringing. In 2022, the 4th Rizong Sras Rinpoche also passed away and now when the 5th Rizong Sras Rinpoche is found, it is the turn of the 20th Bakula Rinpoche to take care of the 5th Sras Rinpoche.

Under Bakula Rinpoche's tutelage the young Rizong Rinpoche memorised Maitriya's *Abhisamaya-alankara* (Ornament for Clear Realization) and Chandrakirti's *Madhyamikavatara* (Introduction to the Middle Way). He also received detailed explanations of Lamrim (Tsongkhapa's Stages of the Path). Often, he would spend days with Bakula Rinpoche during the latter's meditation retreats. Even at a young age, Rizong Rinpoche showed unusual abilities, such as conducting an Amitabha retreat (on the Buddha of Longevity) and conferring its initiation. He also showed great aptitude in the study and contemplation of the Lamrim Chenmo) (The Great Treatise on the Stages of the Path to Enlightenment)

In 1945, following in the footsteps of his uncle Bakula Rinpoche, Rizong Rinpoche left for Tibet to pursue higher studies. From 1945 till 1959, he was enrolled at Drepung Losaling in Lhasa where he remained engaged in the thorough study of the Five Great Treaties and later received *Geshe Lharampa*, the highest degree in Buddhist philosophy. When Drepung was re-established in exile in Southern India, he served for one year as the Geskoe, or discipline master and followed by *Lama Umzey* (the lama who leads the prayer assemblies). Later he was appointed the Abbot of Gyume, a position he held for three years.

In 1984, Rizong Rinpoche was appointed Abbot of Drepung Losaling. During his tenure he both maintained and enhanced monastic discipline and raised the commitment of the monks to their studies. Not only was there a vast improvement in the level of study during his tenure, but he was also highly respected by the monks for his immense personal dedication and determination in reforming the monastic education at the monastery. With the aim of sustaining these improvements, he drafted "Guidelines and Regulations for Monastic Education" in which a variety of modern educational methods were to be integrated into the monastery's traditional systems of instruction. This was in accordance with the modernizing vision of the 14th Dalai Lama expressed support for these innovations and urged other monasteries to follow suit.

After completing his tenure as Abbot, Rinpoche then undertook a three-year retreat on Vajrabhairava at Samstanling Monastery in the Nubra Valley of Ladakh. In September 1995, the 14th Dalai Lama appointed Rizong Sras Rinpoche as the *"Jangtse Choeje"*. On October 26, 2009, Rizong Sras Rinpoche was summoned for Serjal (audience) with the Dalai Lama in Dharamshala and accorded the highest honour possible for any monk in the Gelug tradition. He was made the 102nd *Gaden Tripa*, the "Throne-holder of Ganden", which is the senior-most position in the Gelugpa school of Buddhism. There is a traditional Tibetan saying that "If he has the ability, then there is no stopping even for a beggar's son from becoming the Gaden Tripa as this position in the Gelug school is based entirely on merit, irrespective of birth or incarnation.

When the frailty of old age began to take its toll on Bakula Rinpoche, he had no hesitation in entrusting all his religious duties and responsibilities to Rizong Sras Rinpoche, his former student and esteemed nephew. Bakula Rinpoche was always seen as a great example of strict monastic discipline.

102nd Gaden Tripa Rizong Sras Rinpoche

Bakula Rinpoche with Rizong Sras Rinpoche at the Drepung Losaling Monastery, Mundgod, Karnataka

Rizong Sras Rinpoche's achievement was remarkable and unprecedented, for never in the history of Tibetan Buddhism had a lama from Ladakh been entrusted with the high position of Gaden Tripa. It was during the stewardship of Rizong Rinpoche as Gaden Tripa, that "*Gaden Trithok Khang*", office of the supreme head of Geluk tradition was re-established in India at Gaden Monastery in Mundgod, Karnataka. After serving for six years as Gaden Tripa, Rizong Sras Rinpoche retired from his position in October 2016. Rizong Sras Rinpoche remained active in service of the Dharma and travelled to many countries to teach the sublime message of the Awakened One. He passed away on the 8th December 2022, at the age of 96. The 14th Dalai Lama desired that the mortal remains of Rizong Sras Rinpoche be preserved in Rizong Monastery in Ladakh in the form of a "*Mardung*", a process when the body is preserved through an embalming process in the natural way.

PART II

Representing Ladakh in Jammu & Kashmir

1949–67

Eleven

Struggle to Save the Land of the Gonpas

Bakula Rinpoche was a reluctant politician. He had never imagined that he would spend most of his time in politics. But circumstances had conspired in such a way as to make his entry into the political arena unavoidable. He was also the kind of man who once having accepted the responsibility, would be unwavering in his resolve and dedication, discharging the duties that came with it. Rinpoche's political journey did not start out well. He naively believed that the new democratic government – both at the centre in New Delhi and at the provincial level – would usher in a new dawn for Ladakh. His optimism arose from the views of both Pandit Nehru and Sheikh Abdullah that showed in what esteem they both held the socialist ideal. He accepted their promises at face value and naively believed that all of the people's needs and valid aspirations would henceforth be addressed.

There was one incident which shook his conscience to the core. On July the 13th of 1950, the State Government of Jammu & Kashmir (J&K), under the socialist leadership of Sheikh Abdullah and his National Conference, passed a wide-ranging land reform act called the "Big Landed Estates Abolition Act". The aim of this legislation was to emancipate the common people by ending very obvious and deep-rooted feudal dominance of landlords (*zamindar*). Similar acts were being passed in other Indian states at this time, and they all had the full support of the central government. The plan was to completely overhaul the existing patterns of land ownership in favour of the ordinary and landless farmers. In J&K, the Act decreed that tenant farmers were eligible for 70% of the entire produce of any land they tilled. Moreover, and even more significantly, it now became illegal for single families or institutions to own more than a certain area. The Act ruled that any land in excess of 182 *Kanal*s (about 22 acres)[1] held by a single family or institution, would be confiscated by the government and redistributed to landless peasants. As a result, some 80,000 acres were confiscated in the state and turned over to some 2,47,000 tillers, without any compensation to the former owners.[2]

This redistribution was done in the name of social justice and more equitable distribution of wealth. In some areas of the state, it was certainly beneficial, as it put an end to the exploitation of landless peasants whose lives were often very hard. In the Kashmir Valley in particular, the measure was popular, but elsewhere in the state it did not find unanimous consent. For instance, in Jammu, since most of the landlords were Hindu and most of the tillers were Muslim, the reform took on a communal flavour and faced criticism on this very ground. Then, in Ladakh, though there were some aspects of exploitation in the land tenure system that needed to be addressed, the reform was not in harmony with mainstream sentiment, because it meant stripping the Buddhist monasteries of the economic basis of their very existence and it was mainly for this reason that the proposed reforms were seen by Ladakhis not as a form of liberation, but as an attack by outsiders on their religion.

It seems that it never occurred to the authors of the Act that the conditions in Ladakh were entirely different from those in Kashmir and Jammu. In Ladakh, due to the altitude, the dry climate and the sandy soil, the productivity of agricultural land was barely one-tenth of that in other regions, but this was not factored into the legislation. Moreover, Ladakh was sparsely populated, so the number of landless peasants was actually quite small. Nevertheless, a group of officials arrived in Ladakh from Srinagar bearing the government orders, and were determined to enforce the provisions of the Act, without exception. They conducted a survey and found that only twenty-one holdings in all – mainly monasteries – exceeded the limit on land ownership. The high-handed behaviour of these officials antagonized the Ladakhis as did their refusal to consider Ladakh's special circumstances.

For the majority of Ladakhis who were devout Buddhists, taking land from a monastery, without even seeking its permission or agreement, was deeply reprehensible. In fact, it was completely unthinkable. In those days, before the advent of modern schools or hospitals and such like, the monasteries were the heart of the communities. They weren't just place of prayer, they were also the centres of learning, where one would go seek education, or be treated by traditional doctors (*amchi*). They were also the centre of community ceremony, not to mention important family events, like births and deaths. Every major village had its own monastery, and they were the lifeline of the community in all kinds of ways, not just spiritual.

Also, the Buddhist monasteries were unlike the mosques or Hindu temples of Kashmir and Jammu. They were home to large permanent communities of resident monks and nuns. So, the agricultural land held by monasteries weren't just used for profiteering, they had to support large numbers of people – many more people than just one family. So, why should they be subject to the same land-holding rules as the estate of single landlord family? The monks relied on the land for survival. So, if their means of sustenance were taken away from them, the monks would have to leave their homes and the monastic communities would become smaller. Of course, this would inevitably mean the decline of Buddhism in Ladakh and this was just not acceptable to any Ladakhi. In fact, there were genuine fears among Buddhists at the time that such measures could sound the death knell for Buddhist culture in Ladakh.

On Bakula Rinpoche's call, the monasteries responded by sending petitions to the central and state governments but nothing came of their appeals as the state government was adamant. Unsurprisingly, to the Buddhists of Ladakh, this looked like a Kashmiri conspiracy to strike at the very root of their Buddhist culture, which had not only survived for so many centuries despite its proximity to the Muslim culture, but had even flourished. The heads of Ladakh's monasteries, therefore, resolved to protest against the implementation of the government orders. This might give them a stay of execution, but for how long, was a question no one could answer. Time was of the essence. So, it was decided that Bakula Rinpoche should lead a small delegation to take a petition to the leadership in Srinagar directly.

Accordingly, on September 10, 1950, Rinpoche left Leh accompanied by a team consisting of Gelong Rigdol Lharje, his manager, Gelong Padma Tsering, Manager of Hemis Monastery, Gelong Konchok Sonam of Phyang Monastery, and Sonam Wangyal who at that time was serving as Rinpoche's political assistant. When they arrived in Srinagar after journeying several weeks on foot, they went to meet Rinpoche's old friend and mentor *Masterji* – Sridhar Kaul Dullu who had, by this time, retired from government service and was living in Srinagar. Masterji helped them draft their petitions in English and also set up their meeting with the Prime Minister Sheikh Mohammed Abdullah. Sheikh Sahib was a self-important, charismatic and busy man, and arranging a meeting with him was not at all easy. In fact, it was several weeks before they were allowed to meet him. So, the Ladakhi delegation just had to wait. And when they did finally get an audience, Sheikh Abdullah was simply not interested in listening to their grievances. He even expressed irritation and annoyance at Rinpoche, accusing him of dressing the matter up and giving it a communal colour. "It was nothing of the sort", he said. "It was about progress, and about the emancipation of the poor." The delegation also met with other high-level government officials and tried to explain to them the ground reality of the situation in Ladakh as clearly as possible. But their petitions and entreaties were falling on deaf ears. The state government was simply not interested, and despite repeated efforts, their arguments were not bearing any fruit. The only assurance the government gave to the delegation was that the matter would be decided by the Constituent Assembly when it was formed.

The delegation discussed the situation amongst themselves and considered what options were available to them. In the end it was Master ji, who suggested that they should take their case to the central leadership in Delhi. If the authorities in Srinagar wouldn't listen to Rinpoche, maybe they would listen to Pandit Nehru himself. Taking his advice, the delegation planned for the onward journey to Delhi.

In Delhi once again, Bakula Rinpoche sought a meeting with Prime Minister Jawaharlal Nehru, and submitted a petition to him concerning the issues faced by the monasteries as a result of implementation of land reform. Prime Minister Nehru assured Rinpoche that he would do what he could, and also advised him to arrange a further meeting with Dr. Bhimrao Ambedkar, who at that time was the Union Law and Justice Minister. In his meeting with Pandit Jawaharlal Nehru, Bakula Rinpoche complained that the Sheikh administration in Kashmir continued to neglect Ladakh, as well as imposing a new ordinance prohibiting estates of more than 182 *kanals* of land, a huge blow to the monasteries. Subsequently, Prime Minister Nehru wrote a letter to Sheikh Abdullah on December 1, 1950:

> *"My Dear Sheikh Saheb,*
>
> *I have already [sic] written to you about Ladakh and the deputation of Lamas from there. I have a growing feeling that it is of considerable importance how Ladakh is treated. This is so not only because of Ladakh but because of the whole Kashmir problem, as well as because of developments in Tibet. All kinds of complications might arise, if we are not careful. I would therefore earnestly request you to take this matter in hand yourself and try to remove all legitimate grievances. It is clear that these people are feeling repressed and frustrated and have a sense of complete neglect by the Government. That is a bad feeling. If this has spread or might spread generally to the Lamas in Ladakh, it will influence large numbers of people there. As you will observe, we are facing a very grave international situation and are possibly on the verge of world war. The future is dark from the point of view of this unhappy world of ours. In this state of affairs, we have to carry all kinds of people with us to meet the dangers and perils that might arise."*[3]

Rinpoche with Chagzot Gelong Rigdol Lharje and Mr. Stanzin Wangbo Nangso

The delegation met Dr. Ambedkar, who gave them a patient hearing and assured that the matter would be resolved. While in the national capital, they also called on the President of India, Dr. Rajendra Prasad, the Home Minister, Sardar Patel as well as several other top officials. Finally, the Government of J&K officially agreed to modify the new law exempting monasteries of Ladakh. This was a major victory and the source of tremendous happiness for the small Ladakhi delegation. They returned at once to Kashmir, where they stayed for about ten days, and after receiving official sanction from the Jammu and Kashmir government to proceed, they returned to Ladakh and their respective monasteries to give them the good news.

Wazir Committee Report

Under pressure, the State Government decided to modify the Act to meet concerns expressed in various quarters. But before modifying the Act the State Government sought to convince itself of the reality of the situation. It set up an inquiry committee headed by then Chief Justice Janki Nath Wazir on February 2, 1952, to examine, among other issues, the working of land reforms. Besides other regions of the State, the Committee also visited Leh and found merit in the argument put forward by the Ladakhis seeking exemption from the Act. It submitted a detailed report to the Government of Jammu and Kashmir.

In its own words under the sub-heading "Gompas land – Exemption from Abolition Act", it said: "In Ladakh it was represented to the Committee by the tenants as well as the proprietors that the lands which are attached to the religious institutions of theirs called Gompas should be excluded from the operation of the Abolition Act. It was rather surprising that the tenants who were likely to gain by the operation of the Act on the lands attached to the Gompas, have unanimously decided that these lands should remain attached to the Gompas and be free from the operation of the Abolition Act. It was specially enquired from them why they were in favour of retention of the land with the Gompas. Their reply was that the lands which were attached to the Gompas were cultivated by the tenants and they had to pay only 1/4th of the produce to the Gompas. The Gompas share of produce was utilised for educational, religious and charitable purposes and for feeding the poor and the needy and, therefore, they would like that the Gompas should not be divested of these lands. It would hurt their religious feelings in case the Act was made operative on these Gompa lands. The Committee was told that on their representation the operation of the Act had been suspended for the time being by an executive order of the Government yet the demand of the public at large was that the exemption of the Gompas from the operation of the Act should be incorporated in the Act itself. This suggestion is commended to the Government for favourable consideration."[4]

By presenting a united front, the monasteries of Ladakh registered a significant victory. However, this was not to be the end of the matter. Various officials in the state government were unwilling to let Hemis Monastery, which was the largest monastery in all of Ladakh, get off so lightly. According to Konchok Namgyal, former President of Ladakh Gonpa Association, they were determined to see its large land holdings broken up. When the situation became untenable, on the request of Hemis monastery, Bakula Rinpoche again visited Srinagar to take up the matter with the authorities in Srinagar, and eventually the state government agreed that it too should be exempted. As a token of appreciation for his efforts on their behalf, Hemis Monastery gifted Bakula Rinpoche a piece of land in Leh town near Karzoo. Later, Bakula Rinpoche founded the All Ladakh Gonpa Association and transformed this land into its headquarters. The site later also became home to two other key institutions – the Central Institute of Buddhist Studies (CIBS) and the Lamdon Model Senior Secondary School before they were shifted to their present locations. This initiative laid the foundation for strengthening education and preserving Ladakh's spiritual heritage.

NOTES

1. In Kashmir, one *kanal* equals one eighth of an acre or around 4500 square feet.
2. These statistics are drawn from VR Raghavan (ed.) 2012 *Conflicts in J&K: Impact on Polity, Society and Economy*. Chennai: Centre for Security Analysis.
3. Lines of Control, From Empire to Nation-State by Kyle J. Gardner, Published online by Cambridge University Press.
4. Janki Nath Wazir Committee Report - an Enquiry Committee appointed by the Government of Jammu and Kashmir to examine the working of land reforms, price control etc. (2nd February 1953)

Twelve

Rinpoche Joins the J&K Constituent Assembly

With the signing of the Instrument of Accession on October 26, 1947 by Maharaja Hari Singh, Jammu and Kashmir formally became a part of the Union of India, albeit a loosely affiliated one. What all this meant was that the precise status of the state within the Union in the late 1940s and early 1950s was yet to be fully settled, and this was entirely because of the disputed status of the Kashmir Valley. It really had nothing to do with Ladakh, nor Jammu, which were only part of the same state as the Valley due to historical contingency and the settlements made under British colonial rule. At that time this was meant to be an interim settlement, but it was written into the Indian Constitution as the famous Article 370, and due to the conflict over Kashmir, it remained in place until August 5, 2019, when Parliament of India revoked the special status.

Meanwhile, with the future being uncertain, political power in the state got passed to the veteran leader, Sheikh Mohammed Abdullah and his avowedly socialist and secular National Conference party which had previously been outlawed under the Maharaja. In 1951, Dr. Karan Singh – who had succeeded Hari Singh in the largely ceremonial post of Sadar e Riyasat (similar to the post of Governor in other states of the Indian Union) – issued a proclamation directing the formation of a Constituent Assembly for the state of J&K, whose pressing duty was to be the drafting of a new constitution for the State. Sheikh Abdullah, for his part, was against joining with Pakistan, but nor was his support for joining India unequivocal. He, like Hari Singh, harboured ambitions for independence, and sought to use the state's strategically important location at the junction of India, Pakistan,

China and the Soviet Union in Central Asia. The unique location would enable him to leverage as much power as he could by playing countries against one another.

Returning to the early 1950s, the total number of representatives in the Constituent Assembly was fixed at one hundred. Forty-three of these would come from Kashmir, thirty from Jammu, twenty-five from the occupied territories (taken by Pakistan), and just two from the frontier constituencies of Ladakh, Kargil and Baltistan. This distribution of seats illustrates the extent to which the interests of Ladakh which comprised 2/3 of the state's territory, were to be swamped by those of its more populous neighbours. First meeting of the new assembly was held in Srinagar on October 31, 1951. Addressing the delegates, Sheikh Abdullah urged them to devote themselves diligently to the task of framing a constitution to safeguard the state's autonomy while also allowing for the conclusion of its formal accession to the Union. Bakula Rinpoche, as the National Conference's endorsed candidate, was the sole representative of Leh, Ladakh, while Syed Ibrahim Shah represented Kargil.

As he looked around him, Rinpoche could see the vast majority of delegates were Kashmiri. Naturally they would have the interests of the valley uppermost in their minds. Besides, he could not understand Kashmiri, Urdu, Hindi or English. This made Rinpoche apprehensive, as he realised how isolated his position was, and how difficult it would be to make the interests of Ladakh heard in such a setting. It was obvious that the Hindu delegates from Jammu had similar misgivings, as they too feared their region would be sidelined by the new political ascendancy. Fears of the Hindus in Jammu were well-known, and received a sympathetic hearing both from the Central government and in the Indian press at the time. As a result, in April 1952, Prime Minister Nehru sent Gopalaswami Ayangar, a former Prime Minister of J&K under the Maharaja, and now a member of the Rajya Sabha (the Upper House of the Indian Parliament), to Jammu to make a first-hand assessment of the situation. Delegations representing Hindus and Sikhs met with him and expressed their anxiety. Availing the opportunity on behalf of Ladakh, Bakula Rinpoche also presented Pandit Nehru's envoy with a memorandum. In this he urged the Government of India not to make the mistake of equating the entire state with just the Kashmir Valley, only because it was the most populous and most turbulent region politically. There were other complex and pressing issues facing other parts of the state, in particular the Buddhist-majority regions of Ladakh including Zanskar. Through various communications, Bakula Rinpoche impressed upon the Central government to pay attention to the particular geographical, environmental, religious, educational and cultural circumstances in those areas and that Ladakh needed to be dealt with according to their own requirements and not considered as mere extensions of Kashmir.

"As a way of ensuring against such mis-management, Bakula Rinpoche suggested that Ladakh should be granted a federal status within the state of J&K, similar to the status that J&K itself had within the Union of India. Further, he also suggested the creation of a Ministry of Ladakh Affairs within the state which would be headed by the elected Ladakhi member of the assembly along with a popularly-elected statutory advisory committee of ten members. No major decision passed by the Constituent Assembly in Srinagar – which affected the social, political, religious or economic life of Ladakh should be implemented without this committee's approval. At the very least, he urged, that Ladakh be given more adequate representation in the state legislative assembly and in the various departments of the civil service. He also suggested that Ladakh should establish its own panchayats (elected village governance bodies linked to government departments) as well as rural development agencies. Since this had been overlooked, he urged that development funds for the construction of roads and irrigation canals be also made available for Ladakh.[1]

HON'BLE MEMBERS OF J&K CONSTITUENT ASSEMBLY (1951)

Rinpoche seated second from the left side in front row

Bakula Rinpoche attending a session of J&K State Legislative Assembly, (1953)

In Feb. 1954, the Constituent Assembly ratified J&K's accession to India, by a unanimous vote. The new constitution drafted by the assembly then came into force three years later on Jan. 26, 1957, proclaiming categorically that the J&K is and shall be an integral part of the Union of India. The constitution also institutionalized what had been the temporary safeguards of regional autonomy stipulated in the famous Article 370 of the Indian Constitution. Meanwhile, Praja Parishad, a political party of Jammu, was spear-heading an agitation against conditional integration of J&K to India which found a lot of traction with the people of Jammu. Its main activity was to campaign for the close integration of Jammu & Kashmir with India and oppose the special status granted to the state under the Article 370 of the Indian Constitution.

Rinpoche also apprised Dr. Karan Singh, the Sadar e Riyasat and son of the Dogra ruler Hari Singh about the concerns of the people of Ladakh. He came to Leh for a three-day visit in 1952 along with his wife Maharani Yasho Rajya Lakshmi. This was the royal couple's first visit to Ladakh and they received a warm welcome from the people. Although Ladakh had been a part of the princely state of J&K for over a century, no member of the royal dynasty of Gulab Singh had ever actually visited Leh. This visit was particularly significant as it coincided with the historic opening of the Srinagar – Leh highway, which they inaugurated at Kargil. While in Ladakh the royal couple also visited Bakula Rinpoche's Samkar Gonpa. Dr. Karan

Rinpoche with a group of Ladakhi leaders meeting Sheikh Mohammed Abdullah in Srinagar (1951)

Bakula Rinpoche with Dr. Karan Singh, Sadar e Riyasat of Jammu and Kashmir and Maharani Yasho Rajya Lakshmi (Photo by P.N. Sharma)

Dr. Karan Singh, Sadar e Riyasat with Bakula Rinpoche, Tagtsang Raspa Rinpoche, Stakna Rinpoche, J. Dechen and Other Officials (Photo by P.N. Sharma)

Rinpoche and Dr. Karan Singh with a group of prominent Ladakhis (1952)

Dr. Karan Singh, Sadar e Riyasat and Maharani Yasho Rajya Lakhsmi with Bakula Rinpoche at Leh with school children

Singh was deeply affected by the visit and henceforth he was always very supportive of Ladakh, recognizing its vulnerability and the concerns of its people. Reminiscing about the visit, Dr. Karan Singh wrote in his autobiography: "Even more so than in Jammu, the Ladakhis were feeling uneasy and insecure under the Sheikh's administration. Forming as a distinct cultural entity, they felt that their position in the new dispensation with only two members in the State Assembly (on the basis of population) was extremely precarious and made them totally subordinate to the Kashmiris[2]".

NOTES

1. V.R. Raghavan, *Conflicts in J&K: Impact on Polity, Society and Economy.*
2. Dr Karan Singh: The Original Votary of Devolution of Powers between the Provinces of Jammu and Kashmir-(I), by The Northlines: Jagmohan Sharma.

Thirteen

A Legendary Maiden Speech

On April 12, 1952, Prime Minister Sheikh Abdullah presented his government's first annual budget proposal to the Constituent Assembly, which also functioned as the legislature. Expectations were high, and Rinpoche hoped that the new democratic government would begin the healing process by making positive efforts to iron out its biases and develop all three regions of the state on a fair and equitable basis. However, his hopes were rudely dashed. Ladakh was not only overlooked by the Sheikh's first budget; it was completely ignored. There was not a single mention of Ladakh in the Kashmiri leader's entire budget speech. There was not one specific proposal for Ladakh, nor did it even merit passing mention in the context of the wider state-wide initiatives. It was a shocking blow and a great disappointment for Rinpoche, confirming all his people's worst fears. It was up to Rinpoche alone, who had been elected to the Constituent Assembly, to do something about it.

The casualness, with which the new leadership was brushing aside even legitimate concerns of the Ladakhis; confirmed the suspicion in people's minds that despite all this new talk of progress and development, when it came to Ladakh, it was going to be business as usual. Government officers would continue to exploit the people, taking taxes and giving nothing in return. Ladakh would still be in a subservient relationship to colonial masters; now only the masters had changed. Naturally, there was considerable anger and bitterness among Ladakhis.

Following the budget speech, Rinpoche, in his indignation, was spurred into action. He immediately sought out his old friend and mentor, Masterji, who was now living in Srinagar. They discussed the situation at great length, going over all the possible avenues of redress available. Eventually, they agreed that since the only weapons they had were their voices, the best they could do was to make the strongest and most public gesture of protest possible. This was not only to let their dismay be known to Sheikh Abdullah and the National Conference, but also to the media, and in fact, to the entire world.

So, the next day, while the budget session of the assembly was still in progress, Rinpoche filed for permission from the Speaker of the House to address the chamber on the provisions of the proposed budget in his capacity as a member. He also requested that he be allowed to address the members in his own language, Ladakhi or Bodhi. After this, he said, an English translation of the speech, which he would provide, would be read out. These requests were accepted by the Speaker, and Rinpoche was scheduled to speak on May 12, 1952, in the assembly.

This maiden speech in the assembly had become the stuff of legend in Ladakhi lore. First of all, Rinpoche spoke in Ladakhi, which was itself a hugely symbolic gesture of caring for the common people. If someone else had done this, it might have seemed like they were trying to score a political point or trying to waste time, but coming from Rinpoche, there was nothing conceited or artificial about it. For him to speak in Ladakhi was not just natural but completely necessary, because Ladakhi and Tibetan (which are very closely related and share a single literary language) were the only languages he knew. Here, the symbolism was also tremendous. It was the first time that a Ladakhi had been heard on the floor of the assembly. Surely, in a democratic country, if representatives can speak in English or Hindi, they could also use their native tongue in their dealings with the government. If they don't, it's hard to see how our rich and eloquent languages will ever receive the long-overdue national-level recognition they deserve.

Since Rinpoche was, at that time, officially a member of the treasury bench, everyone in the assembly assumed that his speech would be in support of the government and its budget and that, coming from a gentle Buddhist monk, it would be little more than a ceremonial gesture of thanks and a message of tribute to Prime Minister Sheikh Abdullah. But nothing could have been farther from the truth. In fact, Rinpoche's speech was a passionate condemnation of the treatment of Ladakh as a conquered territory, in which he openly vented his anger, disappointment, and anguish at what he saw as a callous betrayal of Ladakh by the Kashmiri leadership and by Sheikh Abdullah in particular. Because no one in the assembly understood a word of what he was saying, every time he mentioned the name 'Jenab (Honourable Sir) Sher-e-Kashmir', members of the treasury bench on either side of him expressed their approval by thumping their desks. Rinpoche later recalled that he felt awkward, but he carried on nevertheless.

When he had finished his speech, the Speaker of the Assembly, as agreed upon earlier, directed the Secretary to read out the English translation that Rinpoche had provided. As the English version was being read out, it began to dawn on the delegates that the speech was, in fact, a damning condemnation of the government. A hushed silence fell over the chamber, which then quickly gave way to uproar as various members of the government, led by Sheikh Abdullah himself, began protesting indignantly, demanding that the reading of the English translation be stopped and that the English version of the speech be expunged from the Assembly record. **(Annexure 5)**

Mr. G.M. Sadiq, the Speaker of the Assembly, to his great credit, maintained his calm amid the pandemonium and displayed a fair-mindedness befitting his office. He refused to bow to the storm of outrage led by Sheikh Abdullah and the treasury benches and insisted that the English translation be read in its entirety, as had already been agreed. Sheikh Abdullah was spitting with rage, maintaining that the translation was not accurate and should be disqualified. However, the Speaker insisted that since the translation had been supplied to him by the "Head-Lama" himself, they had to presume it accurately expressed Rinpoche's opinions, which it did, though Masterji had added a certain colourfulness of expression to this English version.

Outside the assembly, copies of the speech were already being circulated to waiting journalists, as Rinpoche and Masterji had planned, and as a result, his speech received wide coverage in the national press over the following days. It even found its way into some foreign newspaper reports, much to the embarrassment of Sheikh Abdullah, who, at the time, was very keen to impress on the world and the United Nations that he was the contested state's sole mandated leader. Inside the House, the rumbling continued. Mr. D.P. Dhar, the Deputy Home Minister, raising a point of order, suggested that Rinpoche's speech should be expunged from the record because it had been made in the Ladakhi language, which was not recognised as an official language of the government. He also alleged that Rinpoche had been manipulated and misguided by irresponsible anti-government elements. This accusation, along with the insinuation that he was incapable of making his own decisions and having his own political views, was deeply insulting to Rinpoche. He felt very sad and angry that they seemed to be refusing to address the issues he had raised about education, rural development, and roads and communications, and he was shocked by the aggressive outbursts of Sheikh Sahib and the strangely dismissive attitude of Mr. Dhar.

Finally, after close consultation and discussion among the leaders, a solution acceptable to both sides was found. The Speaker announced a compromise whereby a probe would be immediately conducted to assess the authenticity of the English translation, and the speech would only be included in the proceedings of the Assembly if the translation was verified as being accurate. Mr. J. Dechen, a Christian from Ladakh who worked in Srinagar as a revenue officer, was given the task of comparing the two texts. The result was that there was no substantive discrepancy. As a result, Rinpoche's speech was accepted and recorded in the minutes of the Assembly, much to the discomfort and embarrassment of the government.

When the new session of the Constituent Assembly met three days later on May 15, 1952, the government ceded a few points made in Rinpoche's speech and promised to make amends. Though the government did not accept all of his criticisms, it did acknowledge that compared to the regions of J&K, Ladakh had been neglected in the provision of poverty-alleviation and other programmes. In recognition of this, some district-level posts were created for Ladakh, such as a Block Development Officer (BDO), an Assistant Registrar of Cooperatives, and an Assistant Information Officer. These were inadequate measures, but at least they were something.

In their book titled *Ladakh Through the Ages*, scholars Shridhar Kaul and HN Kaul, noted: "After the assembly session, Kushok Bakula saw the futility of his being in the legislative assembly until he was provided with an interpreter. He, accordingly, asked for one and as this request was turned down, he tendered his resignation as a member of the assembly at Jammu. It was due to persuasion of N. Gopalaswamy Ayyangar, the then Minister for States (Government of India), who came over to Jammu at the end of the session and persuaded Kushok Bakula to withdraw his resignation on the understanding that an interpreter would be provided to him. It was at this time that the Ladakhis' demand for constitutional safeguards was discussed by Mr. Ayyangar with the ministers of the Kashmir cabinet." [1]

Meanwhile, Sheikh Sahib was not amused. A few days later, he invited all the prominent Ladakhis in Srinagar, including Bakula Rinpoche, to his residence for tea. Here again, he publicly chastised Bakula Rinpoche and asserted that what *Kushok Sahib* stated in the Assembly did not reflect his own thinking but was the product of manipulation by others. He even accused Pandit Dullu by name. Bakula Rinpoche's political relationship with Sheikh Sahib thus began on a sour note from which, unfortunately, it never recovered.

Subsequently, in a statement in New Delhi on June 9, 1952, Kushok Bakula emphatically clarified that "the aspirations of the people of Ladakh were not a whit different from those of the people of J&K. That is why, the people of Ladakh desired to be masters in their own home under the protection of India. India first and India last is our slogan. We are resolved to stick to India at any cost unless, of course, India herself chooses otherwise," according to the book 'Ladakh Through the Ages'.[2]

In hindsight, it seems Sheikh Abdullah should have seen Rinpoche's discontentment with his administration coming from a mile away, especially when they failed to accord any importance to Ladakh in their first budget. The signs were always there. In the years following 1947, Rinpoche consistently articulated Ladakh's deep anxieties, particularly those of its Buddhist community, and their place in the larger framework of a Muslim-majority Jammu & Kashmir, according to scholars like Dr. Kyle Gardner, the author of *The Frontier Complex: Geopolitics and the Making of the India-China Border, 1846–1962.*

While presenting a paper at a conference organised by the Indian Council for Cultural Relations (ICCR), Government of India, in October 2016, Gardner noted that approximately 18 months before his historic speech on the Assembly floor, Rinpoche led a delegation before the Government of India in New Delhi, discussing Ladakh's grievances with Indian Prime Minister Jawaharlal Nehru.

After this meeting, Gardner remarked, Nehru sent a series of letters to Sheikh Abdullah urging "the need for imaginative [also "tolerant and tactful"[3]] handling of the Ladakh problem." Sheikh Abdullah responded that he would "give the matter his personal consideration."[4] While this meeting between Rinpoche and Nehru yielded some positive outcomes, correspondence from the Ministry of States noted "no lasting improvement" to the "Ladakh problem."

In the following year, Rinpoche wrote to Nehru:

> *For better or worse we have decided to stay in India and we remain with Kashmir, subject to certain safeguards which have been specified separately in the memorandum addressed to Sheikh Muhammad Abdullah – as long as Kashmir stays in India. This obviously means that in case the rumoured plebiscite is held for the whole state and not on a regional basis and the result is in favour of Pakistan, our connection with the State will terminate and we shall automatically merge without any intervening link with India. If, however, it becomes for any reason impossible for India to directly annexe [sic] our land, then, as the last course open to them, our people will seek political union with Tibet which in spite of our political connection with Jammu and Kashmir State for*

nearly the last 120 years has continued to be the great inspirer and controller of our spiritual life and which, whatever our political affiliations must be looked upon as our eternal and inalienable home. We fervently hope that India will not fail us at this critical juncture of our history.[5]

About 10 days earlier, on December 19, 1951, Rinpoche sent a nearly "identical letter" to Sheikh Abdullah. In both letters, according to Gardner's presentation at the ICCR conference, Rinpoche listed a series of demands from the people of Ladakh. These included:

1. The transfer of Zanskar, a part of Kargil Tehsil (district), along with the villages of Darchiks and Garkon, to Leh Tehsil (district).
2. Following this, the district should be divided into 15 constituencies, each with a population of approximately 5,000 people. "In short, he proposed a Provincial Constituent Assembly that would act much like the state government acted in relation to the national government," noted Gardner.
3. Reservation of seats for Ladakhi students in higher education, professional colleges and technical training, aiming to enhance the provision of essential local services through local personnel.
4. "The local legislature would be the only authority competent to make Laws for the province and to control its administration and naturally an Executive Council would be responsible to it. But no motion or Resolution affecting the religious or social system of any community inhabiting the province would be brought before the Legislature unless so desired by the community concerned," stated Rinpoche.
5. "A governor deputed by the Centre would represent the Central Government and be the connecting link between the province and the centre. He would exercise the same functions as the constitutional head of the State would do in the State," stated Rinpoche.

Furthermore, Rinpoche proposed an alternative arrangement to the initial one offered in his letter, in which Ladakh would be a federating unit of Kashmir. However, towards the end of the letter, Rinpoche made a staggering suggestion related to the "recent developments in Tibet."

Rinpoche stated: "In particular, it would be impossible for the people of Ladakh to be content with their lot if it happens in any way to be less enviable than that of their brethren across the border. The situation is pregnant with portentous possibilities and must be tackled with vision and foresight if Ladakh is to continue to be a part of the state."

"Lastly it must be clearly stated that Kashmir's accession to India is an essential condition for Ladakh remaining a part of the State. This means that in case the rumoured plebiscite is held on an all-state basis and the result is in favour of Pakistan, the connection of Ladakh with the State will cease automatically and it will directly form a part of India and in case India is, for any reason, unable to take over our land, we shall naturally be restored to our home, Tibet, which, even after our political connection with Kashmir, has never, for a moment, ceased to be our spiritual guide, master and director," he added.

Showing real political acumen, Rinpoche garnered the Union government's attention by "using a veiled threat to join Tibet" as leverage, noted Gardner. Unfortunately, progress was slow, and over time, Rinpoche's correspondence began to articulate a growing exasperation with the situation. Towards the end of March 1952, another secret memo noted that "the Government of India received telegraphic representations purporting to come from Kushak [Kushok] Bakula (Rinpoche), bitterly complaining about the corrupt and communal attitude of the Kashmir officials stationed in the district."[6]

These reports of disaffection in Ladakh made their way to the national press. Moreover, the Jammu & Kashmir government "seemed to realise that the situation called for remedial action and requested the advice of the Minister of States."[7]

When Rinpoche got up and delivered his historic speech on April 12, 1952, Sheikh Abdullah and his advisors should have been under no illusion about its contents. As stated earlier in the chapter, following all the hullabaloo in the Assembly over the translation of Rinpoche's speech, Shri Gopalswamy Ayyangar, the Union Minister for States, visited Jammu in April 1952 to discuss "the problem of Ladakh" with Sheikh Abdullah and other members of the state government. According to archival records:

> *He [Ayyangar] also gave an interview to Kushak Bakula who acquainted him with the grievances of the Buddhist [sic] population. The Jammu & Kashmir Ministers said that the publicity which had been given to the agitation of the Ladakhis had caused them much embarrassment and that they would have no objection to the area being taken over by India. Such a solution was, however, considered to be inadvisable [by the government of India] and it was thought that the best course would be to appoint an officer deputed by the Government of India to be Administrator of the whole area; a system of local Advisory Councils such as was provided in the Constitution for the Assam Tribal Areas could also be set up.* [8]

Despite the Government of India's position, Rinpoche continued to articulate the political concerns of Ladakh's Buddhists, particularly the demand for "internal autonomy."

According to Gardner's presentation, on July 23, 1952, Rinpoche sent a "most confidential note" on "Kashmir Government's Sinister Designs on Ladakh" to Dr. Kailash Nath Katju, States Minister, Government of India. In this note, he discussed various issues, including the presence of a "pro-Pakistan" clique comprising some influential members of the Muslim and Christian communities. He also highlighted the Kashmir government's attempts to "create disruption among the Buddhists" and, in particular, to form a party that would create a sentiment that the Buddhists have no confidence in Rinpoche.

In the note, he also alleged that Sheikh Abdullah had organised a secret meeting in Srinagar "to see if they could arrange the public expression of lack of confidence in me by some men of Ladakh" and detailed how attempts were about to be made "to convert the Buddhist majority into a minority." Furthermore, he raised the spectre of joining Tibet, despite the growing presence and threat of China's communist government in the region.

In a later section of this note titled, "Our Future," Rinpoche expressed his most vehement language yet:

> *It is clear as crystal from all this that unless India intervenes immediately, Ladakh will be lost to it one way or the other. Let India grasp this fact clearly: the existence of the Buddhist community in Ladakh is the only factor which guarantees to it the possession of this important frontier. We shall prefer to be wiped out of existence, but we shall not permit ourselves to be hurled into the blazing hell of Pakistan. To prize our Buddhist culture above our very lives therefore, the thought of the advent of Communism into our land is a dreadful nightmare for us but if India casts us to the wolves we shall, as we have repeatedly declared, prefer being restored to our home Tibet even under Communist regime to being tied to the chariot-wheels of Pakistan. Our culture [and] ideals can live and thrive only under the direct sunshine of India's protection and not under its shadowy long-distance guardianship exercised through the non-conducting medium of a virtually independent Islamic Kashmir.*
>
> *In the note, Rinpoche further stated: "Our demand for internal autonomy is being thrown overboard. Shri Gopalaswamy Ayyanger [sic] had reassured me during my recent interview with him at Jammu, that India would depute an administrator to the District. But the Prime Minister of Kashmir has informed me that he has not agreed to this proposal and*

> *that India has not agreed to the direct merger of the District with itself. This is most unfortunate for us and gravely harmful to the interests of India itself. The need of the hour is the appointment of an Administrator by India. ...To save the Frontier, India must save the Buddhists of Ladakh and to save the Buddhists of Ladakh it must take [sic] over administrative control of the District without the loss of a moment."*

However, despite the tensions created by Rinpoche's strong public advocacy, it was having immediate results. At a joint press conference in July 1952, Pandit Nehru and Sheikh Abdullah announced that the new dispensation in the state would provide for regional autonomy. This was considered a considerable victory for the cause of Ladakh. Seeking to assuage any lingering sense of hostility that his budget speech may have aroused, Bakula Rinpoche held a press conference on January 15, 1953, in order to clarify his position. He stated:

> *"I am no enemy of Kashmir. In fact, Ladakh wants to have the closest ties with Kashmir. But if freedom is good for Kashmir, it is good for Ladakh also. We want to have an effective voice in the administration of our area and we want a relentless, remorseless and ruthless war to be carried out against poverty, ignorance and disease in Ladakh. That is the long and short of the matter. I do not want to pull any wool over the eyes of the state authorities and let there be no misunderstanding in any quarter about our aims and objectives".*[9]

Meanwhile, the relationship between the two leaders in whose hands the fate of Ladakh lay – Abdullah and Nehru – had become strained and soon reached breaking point. On August 8, 1953, Sheikh Abdullah was dismissed from the post of Prime Minister by the Sadar e Riyasat, Dr. Karan Singh. Soon afterwards, he was arrested and accused of conspiracy against the state and conspiring to create an independent Kashmir in the infamous "Kashmir conspiracy case." Sheikh Abdullah would spend the next eleven years of his life in jail.

After the J&K constitution came into force, general elections were immediately held in J&K, in which Bakula Rinpoche was re-elected unopposed as a member of the legislative assembly (MLA). It was a seat he occupied without interruption from 1951 until 1967, during which time he also held various ministerial positions in the Council of Ministers of the J&K State.

NOTES

1. Shridhar Kaul and H.N. Kaul, *Ladakh Through the Ages: Towards a New Identity* (New Delhi: South Asia Books; 2nd Edition, May 1993), p. 202.
2. Ibid., p. 198.
3. Ganesan, DSI, "Political Developments in Ladakh, 30 April 1952
4. Ganesan to N. Gopalaswami Ayyangar, 1 April 1952.
5. NAI, Ministry of State (Kashmir), Secret, 19(16)-K52. "Buddhists in Ladakh; Representations from head Lama of Ladakh; General position re: Ladakh."
6. Ganesan, Deputy Secretary to Govt. of India, Ministry of States, "Political Developments in Ladakh, 30 April 1952.
7. Ibid.
8. Ibid.
9. Shridhar Kaul and H.N. Kaul, *Ladakh Through the Ages: Towards a New Identity* (New Delhi: South Asia Books; 2nd Edition, May 1993), 192.

Fourteen

The Post-Abdullah Years

After the dismissal of Sheikh Abdullah, the post of prime minister was taken by Bakshi Ghulam Mohammed. Bakshi was a member of the National Conference from its founding and rose to be the second in command to Sheikh Abdullah. He served as the Deputy Prime Minister of the State of Jammu and Kashmir between years 1947 and 1953, but disagreed with Abdullah's advocacy of independence for the state in 1953. Bakshi was the longest serving Prime Minister of Jammu and Kashmir, whose rule saw the formulation of the constitution of Jammu and Kashmir and a normalisation of relations of Jammu and Kashmir with the central government. Soon after, he made a public assurance that development in the state would be shared in equal measure by all the three regions, and that the Valley would not be given special priority. This again was welcome news. Soon afterwards Rinpoche along with several Ladakhi leaders personally met Prime Minister Bakshi Ghulam Mohammed and submitted a memorandum to him which contained several concrete suggestions for how to improve the educational, economic and social conditions of Ladakh. The new government took heed of these suggestions and initiated some restructuring of its Ladakh policy. Technical experts were sent to Leh and Kargil to assess the challenges and survey the potential for small-scale industrialization, road construction, and the development of telecommunication facilities.

In an address to the assembly on October 5, 1953, Bakula Rinpoche again reiterated his demand that along with Hindi and Urdu, there must be provision for teaching Bodhi in all government schools in Ladakh, and that textbooks must be developed for this purpose without delay. He also insisted that the medium of instruction in primary schools should be Bodhi, not Urdu. He repeated his demands for the digging of irrigation canals, the construction of roads and the development of healthcare facilities. He also expressed his hope that the people of Ladakh would get their share in the benefits of poverty-alleviation and educational initiatives that were being launched in Kashmir. In order to ensure that Ladakh was not overlooked again and to accelerate the pace of development and bring coordination among various government departments, Rinpoche reiterated the demand for creation of a separate Ladakh Affairs Ministry at the cabinet level to deal exclusively with matters related to Ladakh. He had also put this demand earlier to the central leadership and to Pandit Nehru himself who would always empathise with him and gave a patient hearing. Rinpoche believed that under the wise and positive leadership of Bakshi Ghulam Mohammed, Ladakh would emerge from the despotic tyranny and exploitation of the previous government.

Bakshi Ghulam Mohammed promised a fair deal for the people of Ladakh. A welcome intervention was the appointment of an IAS (Indian Administrative Service) officer directly responsible for the Ladakh region. In contrast to Sheikh Abdullah's authoritarian style of leadership, his tenure was marked by a softer approach, which helped ease tension in the Ladakhi region, especially when he agreed to Bakula Rinpoche's suggestion about the creation of a separate cabinet level ministry of Ladakh Affairs. This was a major step forward.

In November 1953, Bakula Rinpoche was inducted into the state's Council of Ministers as a Deputy Minister charged with running the newly created ministry of Ladakh Affairs. It was for the first time that anyone from Ladakh had been appointed to such a significant rank. The news was widely welcomed by the people of Ladakh. After his assumption of office on November 9, 1953, as a Deputy Minister Kushok Bakula Rinpoche told a press conference that: "Monks, as a rule, have no time for politics. I broke this century old tradition only because I had the interests of Ladakh at heart."

However, the high hopes his appointment had created were unfortunately short-lived. In an unprecedented and authoritarian manner, the government attached two unusual conditions to Rinpoche's official appointment as a Deputy Minister. (i) That his headquarters would be at Leh and not at the state capital of Jammu or Srinagar and (ii) that the Deputy Commissioner (DC) of Ladakh would function as his ex-officio Secretary. These conditions were unconstitutional and were a clear attempt to control and sideline Rinpoche, whose popular mandate in Ladakh was something the political elites in both Srinagar and Jammu envied and feared. Rinpoche felt that these conditions would make his position ineffective. If he was confined to Leh, he would not be able to hold the state government to account during its deliberations and decision making.

Bakula Rinpoche in conversation with Prime Minister Nehru at Srinagar (1954)

Dr. Karan Singh, Sadar e Riyasat administering oath of office to Rinpoche (1953)

Rinpoche with Bakshi Ghulam Mohammed, Prime Minister of Jammu & Kashmir (1953)

Dr. Karan Singh Sadar e Riyasat with the newly appointed council of ministers headed by G.M. Sadiq, Chief Minister

Moreover, by imposing a bureaucrat of their own choice on him, the state authorities were ensuring that his hands would be tied in all practical matters. It was even hinted to him indirectly that he should not interfere with the administrative work of the Deputy Commissioner. Since Rinpoche's functions as Deputy Minister had not yet been properly defined, Rinpoche used this as his point of leverage. He sought clarification from Prime Minister Bakshi about his role and warned him that to confer an office without any real power would not only be dishonest, but would also be a backward step. At the same time, he wrote a detailed letter to Prime Minister Nehru about the developments and sought his intervention to defuse the situation. Rinpoche could see that to be a nominal head of government ministry, but without any real agency, would lead to many false expectations among the people and that this would create many problems later on. He told Prime Minister Bakshi Ghulam Mohammed quite frankly that he had never sought political office in the first place and that he was only there in order to serve the people and if conditions were not created that enabled him to render real and meaningful service to the people, then he would simply resign.

Prime Minister Bakshi understood the implications of this threat and immediately cleared the ambiguity so that Rinpoche would henceforth enjoy full powers as Deputy Minister in charge of Ladakh Affairs. In the next state budget, Prime Minister Bakshi ensured that adequate allocations were made to Ladakh for medical aid, education, irrigation, and general relief and grants for community projects. These were positive steps, but still, they did not commensurate with the enormous challenges facing the Ladakh region.

Fifteen

Freedom from Exploitation and Tyranny, Working for the Transformation of Ladakh

Though Bakula Rinpoche had opposed the National Conference's land reform policies as unsuitable for Ladakh's particular circumstances, he did see the pressing need for greater social justice in the region. He recognized that in modern developmental terms, the situation in Ladakh was woeful. A significant proportion of the local population, both Buddhist and Muslim were illiterate and lived in abject poverty. Healthcare was non-existent and infant & maternal mortality rates were unacceptably high. The general standard of education was very low, with all but the senior monks being essentially illiterate. Levels of numeracy were hardly any better, and modern science had barely been heard of, let alone taught. Tackling these issues, dealing with the Kashmiri leadership, preserving the value of Ladakh's traditional culture and the conservative and religious sentiments of the people was never going to be easy. It was evident to Rinpoche that the road ahead was going to be a difficult one, full of obstacles, particularly for a political novice.

On the ground, the reality was different from the promises made. It was a rude awakening for Rinpoche to find that the very state which was expected to and, therefore, was assigned with the task of safeguarding Ladakh's legitimate rights to autonomy and freedom, and advancing its access to modern public services such as transport, health and education, had itself struck hard at their very foundation. It soon became abundantly clear that Ladakh was very low on the list of priorities for the new leadership too. In fact, so low as to be almost completely invisible. No attention was given to Ladakh's special circumstances and needs, nor to the will of the people in the enactment of certain "modernizing" reforms. Instead Ladakh was treated as a mere appendage of Kashmir, treated as if whatever is right for Kashmir must also be right for Ladakh. In the face of this situation, Rinpoche fundamentally only had two choices. He could either submissively accept Ladakh's fate as an insignificant backwater and acquiesce quietly to the priorities and agendas of his superiors within the National Conference (as Sheikh Abdullah seemed to think he would), or he could stand up for Ladakh and fight for its right to better treatment. Rinpoche was a gentleman and a monk. Perhaps it was because of this that Sheikh Abdullah and others thought he would be easy to placate. But Rinpoche was also a very clear-sighted person, a man of tremendous conviction and grounded in personal moral integrity. Besides, he was not someone who could be easily dominated, for he was impervious to flattery and did not care at all for status and privilege. Nor would he submit to any intimidation or threats. In this respect Rinpoche was very much like Gandhiji, and this was a comparison the 14th Dalai Lama himself would one day make, dubbing Rinpoche as "the Gandhi of Ladakh". Given these personal qualities, it was only a matter of time before his confrontation with the authorities would begin.

Rinpoche decided that what was required first of all, was clear information about the living conditions of the people. He convened several meetings of village elders at which he consulted respected figures in the community, listening to their views and offering his own perspectives. He also visited every village in the land, so as to consult the common people directly and inform them of the new horizons and prospects in being part of the new India. These meetings were never just about political and administrative issues. There was always a wider spiritual and moral dimension to them. In pursuing the dream of a more prosperous future, he would say, there are always two points which must never be forgotten. First, when planning changes and development initiatives start, we must always consider the long-term need of the people and secondly, we must never be blinded by narrow self-interests, bias towards our own family or our own region or community.

Secondly, it is fair to say that common people in Ladakh were simple folk, devoid of cunningness and dishonesty. This was true irrespective of religion. But due to lack of education, they tended to be overly submissive and meek. They were not used to demanding their rights, or expecting anything more than what they were accustomed to. In some cases, this made them vulnerable to naked exploitation by unscrupulous officials, as well as landlords who also operated as lenders. This was not acceptable to Rinpoche. But no matter how downtrodden the people were, no matter how hard their living conditions, there was really no culture of protest. People would accept their situation and carry on. Bakula Rinpoche saw that this had to change. People needed to be made more aware of their basic rights to a life of dignity. He realized that in order to improve people's lives but without creating harmful social unrest, there had to be first of all modern education for the children, an increase in awareness, and above all, people had to unite in a shared vision for the future.

So. Rinpoche and his associates travelled from village to village, speaking to communities about these new things called "rights", which are due to all citizens in a free democratic country. Young children with drums were sent out into the fields and villages to spread the message of change, urging people to unite and mobilize. There was resistance to sending children to school. People preferred to have their children at home so that they could assist with family chores and work in the fields. Rinpoche used all his powers of persuasion to convince them that education would help them in the long run. This was something he always cared about very much and therefore left no stone unturned in his attempts to provide access to education for every child in Ladakh. At a time when roads or modern communication facilities of any kind did not exist, Rinpoche travelled on horseback and on foot to educate the people about their democratic rights and responsibilities. Often his tours would last for weeks and at each and every village he would speak to a gathering of the people and motivate them, emphasizing the value of education, and encouraging them to send their children to school wherever possible.

During our conversation, Rinpoche recalled that in those days, except for a handful of rich families, the ordinary people of Ladakh were by-and-large subsistence farmers who had very little, if any, disposable income. People were starving and everything they had was home-made. People's clothes were generally old and tattered and their home-made shoes, were often even worse. People picked up blankets or items of clothing or shoes from the army camps. Hides were used during winter and in some extreme cases; poor people without blankets of their own would sleep huddled up inside hay-stacks known as *Foograg*s in Ladakhi, in order to survive the bitterly cold winter nights. The situation had considerably worsened in the years 1948–49, when Ladakh experienced not only the destructive tribal incursions, but also a particularly heavy snowfall which devastated crops in some areas and brought many families to the point of starvation.

Rinpoche with an old Ladakhi couple

Rinpoche addressing a group of villagers in Sham area

Rinpoche addressing a group of villagers in Leh area

A group of Ladakhis, young and old

Empowering the youth with modern education (Leh, 1949)

Bakula Rinpoche with his entourage on a visit. Gelong Thupstan Targyes, his manager is to his left

But all of this optimistic activity couldn't hide the fact that old habits die hard. Far from being treated as equals, poor people continued to be worked to the bone. It soon became clear that officials charged with the administration of Ladakh under the new regime were no better than the old ones. There were even instances of peasants being thrashed and the small properties inherited from their ancestors, being snatched from them due to some trivial issue of paperwork, or merely on the whim of these petty tyrants. Heavy taxes continued to be collected in both cash and kind simply to sustain the salaries and rations of these government servants. Such was the terror that officials evoked in those days that even a peon working in a government office had considerable clout and had to be treated with respect. In the past, when government officials of various ranks went on tour, villagers cowered in front of them. They always had to have horses ready for their use, as well as yaks, *Dzo* (a hybrid between a yak and cow), mules and donkeys – whatever they needed to carry their baggage. And wherever they went, they had to be fed and housed – often they demanded meat – all at the expense of the villagers. The ruthless collection of *Jensi* (revenue tax) further added to their woes. And if the tax couldn't be paid on time, or a horse was not good enough or not to their taste, or the pack of animals were delayed, officials would think little of having villagers thrashed in public as a display of power and to teach the wider population a lesson. It is fair to say that the poor in those days were only a bit better than slaves.

Rinpoche would also often recollect about the hardship he encountered during those tours. With neither roads nor vehicles, there was no choice but to ride a horse or walk. So, people would only travel if there was a genuine and pressing need. In those days even travelling to Diskit, the district headquarters of the Nubra area (120 kilometers from Leh), was a majorly hard task. It would take about three to four days from Leh and involved crossing the 5359 metre (17582 Ft.) high Khardong Pass, which even in summer months was used to be covered with snow. Although Ladakhis are accustomed to high altitude, this was a tough climb even for them. People would generally spend a night on either side of the pass at *North Pulu* and *South Pulu*, since the final ascent in the thin mountain air was grueling. Snowstorms were common at the higher altitudes, and sometimes thick freezing clouds would reduce visibility to zero.

On reaching the crest of the pass, people would call out prayers to the Buddhas and the spirits of the mountains, making offerings, and tying many coloured prayer flags before beginning the descent down the other side. Such journeys had to be well-prepared, as there was often nowhere to obtain food and other essentials for long stretches along the way. They also had to ensure that one had enough fodder for the horses, yaks, mules and donkeys, and that the animals were fit and up to the job. *Tsampa*, roasted barley flour,

Bakula Rinpoche riding his horse "Ziling" on a visit to a far-flung area

Rinpoche crosses a twigs/rope bridge near Phugtal Monastery in Zanskar

which is the staple food of Ladakh and the wider Tibetan cultural region, was the main food consumed during such journeys, mixed by hand into a dough with butter and tea. Only a few essential utensils would be brought, such as a long cylindrical butter-tea churn known as a *Gurgur* or a *Solgur*.

Kargil was more backward as compared to Leh. Once, during an official visit to the Kargil region, many people came to Rinpoche who was then a minister, to apprise him of the difficulties they were facing. Due to debt burdens compounded by a recent crop failure, there were acute food shortages in the area, and some families were on the brink of starvation. Recounting the incident Rinpoche told me that when he heard of their plight he was appalled. He immediately called for a meeting with local officials and directed them to distribute all the provisions currently held in the government granary at Baru to the needy people. The officials complied, and the food store was emptied and distributed free of charge. Sometime later, this would land Rinpoche in some serious trouble with the state government. Since Rinpoche was not the Minister for Food and Supply, he, therefore, did not technically have the authority to distribute government food stores free of cost. Rinpoche was only saved from the trouble when Bakshi Ghulam Mohammed – who by that time had succeeded Sheikh Abdullah as Prime Minister intervened personally in the matter and gave his executive approval for what Rinpoche had done. He did however caution Rinpoche against taking any such rash steps in the future.

Recollecting that time, Haji Abdul Hamid Tanveer, a prominent Shia spiritual leader from Kargil writes that in those days, Kargil only had a Middle school and students from Drass and Shakar Chiktan would be put up in a dilapidated house that was used as a hostel. Bakula Rinpoche used to visit Kargil and surrounding villages regularly and would strive hard for the proper development of the area. He upgraded the Middle school in both Leh and Kargil as High schools. Another veteran Agha Sayeed Jamaluddin Mossavi, a prominent Shia cleric from Manji, Kargil also echoed similar sentiments. He noted that Bakula Rinpoche would never discriminate on the basis of class, region or religion. He along with Agha Ibrahim Shah fought against *Bab and Jinsi* (taxes). 'Bakula Rinpoche had put Ladakh on the political landscape of J&K State,' he said.[1]

Bakula Rinpoche also faced resistance from vested interests and government officials but he was determined and ensured that the Government of Jammu and Kashmir took Ladakh seriously. There is another incident which demonstrates his compassionate nature and commitment to public service. In the 1970's the Government of Jammu and Kashmir sanctioned a power station for supplying electricity to Leh Town and the surrounding areas. Unfortunately, district authorities could not find a suitable plot of land in Leh Town for the power station. When the issue was brought to the notice of Bakula Rinpoche immediately agreed to give a prime piece of land which belonged to his monastery and located near the present-day head office of J&K Bank in Leh town for the purpose. Such was his dedication to public cause and the emancipation of the poor. Rinpoche was truly a leader of the masses, an ideologue and symbol of honesty and integrity who championed the interest of the poor and oppressed communities of Ladakh.

Exploitation and Tyranny of the Landlords

One of the most revolutionary steps undertaken by Bakula Rinpoche was to free the farmers and the poor from the clutches of Landlords. It wasn't just at the hands of government officials that the people suffered. Greedy landlords were sometimes as oppressive as the bureaucrats. The way debts were managed by the rich and landlords in those days was particularly exploitative. At the time there was a prevalent practice known as "recovery of five for a loan of four". This meant that if a rich farmer had loaned a poor peasant four *khal* of grain (usually barley) for planting in the spring, he would have the right to be repaid five *khal* in the autumn. But in effect the recovery was very complex and at a very high rate. Because of this practice, poor farmers were constantly debt-ridden and often they were malnourished as well. And as if being indebted wasn't bad enough, they also had to show their gratitude for the loans by providing free labour to their creditors during the spring ploughing and planting season and the autumn harvest season. If, due to poor weather or some other misfortune, a poor farmer was unable to pay back the "five for four", then his debts were carried over to the following year, creating a permanent burden of debt from which it was impossible to escape. Sometimes the modest land-holdings of such peasants would even be confiscated to cover their unpaid debts, leaving families landless and destitute. Theirs' was a life of bare survival summed up in three words: *tattu* (donkey), *sattu* (barley flour) and *pattu* (handmade woolens). But even in the face of such hardship, it was very difficult to convince them that the future could be different.

Seeing the desperate situation, the poor people were in, Rinpoche called for freedom from the clutches of heavy debts. He visited major villages and called upon the people to raise their voices against such injustices in a democratic society. He called upon the J&K Government to stop this practice immediately and free people once and for all from the burden of debts.

The campaign had the desired effect and, in the end, the government came up with the "Distress Debtors Relief Act 1949" which freed the farmers from all the accumulated debts. The poor farmers welcomed the move whole heartedly. Throughout this struggle the poor farmers stood rock solid with Rinpoche. In the end, even the rich and influential bodies did not oppose its implementation and there was only a meek opposition from some quarters. A debt cancellation board was set up to oversee the settlement of debt cases, and to write off all historic debts which were deemed unjust. Mr. Sonam Wangyal, a close confidant of Rinpoche, was appointed as a senior member of the Board. This was a revolutionary step and came as a great relief to the poor people of Ladakh who would otherwise have continued to toil under the intolerable burden of historic debts from which there was no chance of escape. For them it was a triumphant occasion and would not believe that such a thing could ever happen.

In Leh, Rinpoche gave a call to the people to assemble where he enlightened them about their democratic rights in the new environment and freedom from subjugation and tyranny of the landlord. Mr. Tsering Samphel, now 80 years old, who was a close associate of Rinpoche who was part of this campaign and a witness to this celebration, told me that heeding to Rinpoche's call, the people managed to collect all the account books (ledger or Bahi Khata) from the landlords and made a bon-fire in the middle of Leh bazar. He described the incident as the real sign of freedom and emancipation of the common people from bonded-labour. This was the first major achievement for the people of Ladakh under the new democratic regime which greatly infused their faith in the system and they were now more determined to continue their struggle and to rid Ladakh from exploitation and discrimination.

NOTES

1. Remembering HE the 19th Bakula Rinpoche. A collection of memories from different parts of Ladakh (201 Himalayan Cultural Heritage Foundation (2018).

Sixteen

Rinpoche's Contemporaries and his Loyal Brigade

As described earlier, Pandit Shridhar Kaul Dullu (Masterji) was the sole guide and teacher for Bakula Rinpoche during his early years in politics. He would help and guide Rinpoche in every possible way. But without the public rallying behind him, Rinpoche could not have done much. Fortunately, there was a small band of dedicated people who stood shoulder to shoulder with Bakula Rinpoche during these important years. They would also mobilise people and go from village to village to educate the masses and prepare them for the long struggle. Without them Ladakh would not have seen political transformation and success. They were spread all across the region and were prepared to make all sacrifices for the development of Ladakh.

Foremost among them was Sonam Wangyal who was at that time Rinpoche's political assistant. He was from a very poor family, but he was articulate, hardworking and a prolific speaker. He was also a shrewd politician who in the course of time became a Member of the Legislative Assembly (MLA) and later, a minister in the J&K government. Another towering personality of the time was Tsewang Rigzin Kalon, who with his aristocratic background yielded considerable influence on the people. Elizer Joldan, a dedicated school teacher, also played an important role in the development of Ladakh's education policy. Other important foot soldiers of Bakula Rinpoche included Tsering Stobdan Lhajingpa from Nye village, Norburam from Stok, Tashi Dorje Stachakpa from Sakti, Tsewang Targyes from Hundar and Kunzang Dorjey from Sumur in Nubra and Meme Zanskarpa from Bazgo. Each one of these leaders represented different regions of Ladakh and commanded deep respect from their local community. The presence of these dedicated and active leaders ensured that there was always good communication and participation of the public at demonstrations (an important part of Indian democratic politics), even at short notice.

Many Muslims also joined and followed Bakula Rinpoche in his struggle against injustice and for the development of the region. Munshi Abdul Sattar, a freedom fighter was a well-educated leader who was appointed Secretary of National Conference Party in Ladakh. He was among those who had pleaded with Pandit Nehru back in year 1949 to make Bakula Rinpoche the sole leader of the people of Ladakh. Sheikh Jamaluddin of Leh who was a government teacher by profession and the Imam of the Leh Jama Masjid was another important leader. Ghulam Rasool (Baba Kulu) of Thiksey Betong was among the closest associates of Bakula Rinpoche who remained steadfast in his loyalty towards Rinpoche. A good orator, he was very popular among the masses, both Buddhists and Muslims.

It is a great testimony to the loyalty that Bakula Rinpoche inspired in those who knew him, that all of these men despite the considerable pressure they faced from various quarters, stood firmly by Bakula Rinpoche throughout. Abdul Haq, Mohd. Hussain Abidi, Haji Hussain Mohammed, Ghulam Sultan Shangku, Haji Ghulam Mohammed Barchapa, Sheikh Javed of Thiksey to name a few, remained throughout alongside Bakula Rinpoche. Some of them even faced social boycott from their own community for supporting Bakula Rinpoche.

Numerous women also took an active part in the mass mobilization initiated and led by Rinpoche. Although illiterate, these women leaders were vociferous and fought shoulder to shoulder with their menfolk. Prominent among them were Dolma Kharpon, Stanzin Zangmo Tsangspa Yogma, Eshey Tsomo Gangba, Chorol Raku, Palkit Lamagon, Ashey Malo, Phuntsog Palmo Matho Lasopa, Spaldon Shuma, Tondup Thagang and Yangchan Chocho Tsangspa, just to name a few. There were many others who joined the struggle and made sacrifices. They went from village to village and guided the people. Demonstrations were held frequently at Leh so that the opposition of the Ladakhis to the government's attitude could not be ignored.

There were many from Kargil too. Prominent among them included Aga Sayeed Mehdi Heniskot, Agha Ibrahim Shah, Agha Sayeed Ibrahim, Kacho Mohammed Ali Khan of Pashkyum, Agha Zakir of Suru, Aga Mohammed Shah of Kartrse, Munshi Habibullah, Haji Rangeen Ali, Agha Raza from Suru to name a few. In Zanskar, Raja Sonam Tondup Namgyal, Nawang Phuntsog, Sonam Namgyal Pikongma, Nawang Chotak were some

Sadar e Riyasat Dr. Karan Singh with Bakula Rinpoche and Mr. Sonam Wangyal

(L to R) Sonam Wangyal, Chorol Raku, Dolma Kharpon, Dr. Karan Singh, Bakula Rinpoche, Palkit Lamagoon, Tondup Thagang, Ghulam Rasool Betong, Tashi Rigzin Langto, Sonam Stobdan Nye Lazhingpa, Tsewang Targyes Bazgo Zanskarpa, Munshi Abdul Sattar, Tashi Wangyal Sakti Stakchagpa, Norburam Stok and Tsetan Nakpo

Maharani Yasho Rajya Lakshmi, wife of Dr. Karan Singh with some Ladakhi Muslim women in Leh (1960s)
Photo by P.N. Sharma

of the senior local leaders who led the public mobilisation. Zanskar also had a team of leaders who were vociferous and dedicated to their cause and would remain in constant touch with Rinpoche. Notable among them were Nawang Tashi, Tsewang Chotar, Gyaltsan Tsazar, Sonam Wangchuk Lonpo, Gyalsras Nima Norbu, Lama Ngawang Tsering and others.

But in Leh, there were some mischief-makers too. Some government officials tried to paint him and his colleagues as trouble-makers and enemies of the new government. Besides that, there was a section of Ladakh's aristocracy which did not take kindly to Rinpoche's modernizing revolution, as it threatened to undermine whatever feudal powers they still retained. But among the general populace, the mood was buoyant and Bakula Rinpoche's movement continued to gain momentum among the poor which gave Rinpoche the desired courage and made his task easier.

Seventeen

Pilgrimage to Mount Kailash and Lake Mansarovar

For centuries Tibet has been a source of spiritual inspiration for millions of Buddhists, Hindus, Jains and *Bonpos*. Its sacred mountains and lakes, and historic monastic centres were the places of pilgrimage for people across the Buddhist world. In particular, Gang Rinpoche or Mount Kailash is considered by the faithful to be the king of all mountains, which in Buddhist scriptures is referred to as the centre of the world. Mount Kailash is by far the holiest mountain in Tibet, stretches to 6,714 metres in height. Every year tens of thousands of people make a pilgrimage to the mountain, circumambulating this towering and dazzling peak. In 1954, the year of the Wood-Horse in the lunar calendar was considered particularly auspicious for making pilgrimage to the holy mountain. Such occasions only fall every sixty years. Bakula Rinpoche too, then a minister in the J&K Government, decided to make the pilgrimage to the holy mount Kailash, known as Gang Tise in Tibetan.

He set off from Leh on July 20, 1954, and the team consisted of four monks and others. Passing through *Gya-Miru* and crossing *Taglang-la,* before reaching Tashigang, which lies in Tibetan territory. The monks of Tashigang Monastery and the local people accorded Rinpoche a warm welcome.

Reminiscing on this memorable visit, Bakula Rinpoche recalled that in accordance with official protocol as a government minister of the state of J&K, he was received in Tashigang by a group of Tibetan and Chinese officials. This was the period known as "uneasy co-existence" between the old Tibetan government and the new Chinese communist forces which had begun to enter Tibet in the early 1950s but had not yet taken over full control. By 1954, Rinpoche recalls that the strong presence of the Chinese military was already visible. After that, the team reached *Gar-Gunsa* (winter camp) and Gar-Yarsa (summer camp). From Gar-Yarsa they reached a township called Mon-tser (also known as *Menser*). Historically, the local people paid revenue tax to both the Tibetan authorities and the King of Ladakh, then a protectorate of the Maharaja of J&K whose royal title included *"Shriman Indar Mahindar Rajrajeshwar Maharajadhiraj Shri Jammu Kashmir Naresh Tatha Tibet Deshadhipati"*. Local people, Rinpoche recalled, pleaded with him to help them incorporate their land into India.

For the benefit of the readers, I am giving below the story as described to me by Rinpoche himself. Rinpoche next visited a temple at the holy site of *Tirtapuri* also known as *Pretapuri*. This site is believed by the faithful to be the Palace of Dorje Pagmo (*Vajravarahi*) and Demchog (*Chakrasamvara*). There is a traditional saying that without visiting Tritapuri, no merit can be earned by making pilgrimage to Gang Rinpoche (Mount Kailash) and Lake Mapham (*Manasarovar*). The main sacred image in this temple is a statue of Guru Padmasambhava. Traditionally, the caretaker of this temple was sent from Hemis Monastery in Ladakh. From here, the team proceeded towards Mount Kailash. Lake Mapham (Manasarovar) is likewise considered sacred in all four religions. For Buddhists, Mount Kailash is the sacred abode or mandala of the assembly of the sixty-two deities centred around the tantric deity Khorlo Demchok (*Chakrasamvara*). It is also considered the abode of Yenlagjung (*Angaja*), one of the sixteen 'Arhats' or original disciples of the Buddha Shakyamuni, surrounded by an entourage of one thousand five hundred further disciples. It is a uniquely sacred site.

For the Brahmanical Hindus, Mount Kailash is the abode of Lord Shiva, his consort Parvati, their son Ganesh and his courtiers. Near the mountain is a rock known in Tibetan as *Teu Poezin Drag* (Monkey-holding-a-joss-stick Rock) which resembles the Hindu deity Hanuman making an offering. The *Dolmey Trukyi Zingbu* is recognized as the pool where Parvati took her bath. And the rock *Drag Rinchenpung* is believed to depict Shiva's son Ganesh receiving religious teachings. Jains or *Gyalwapas* believe that Mount Kailash is the place where Rishabanath (*Rishabhdevji*), the first of their twenty-four Tirthankaras, sat in penance for many years, until he achieved a physical state devoid of all obscurations. After that, he remained there in deep contemplation to attain the power to abstain from the ten non-virtuous actions and thus attain freedom from the very cycle of existence. For the Bonpos, this mountain, known as *Lachen Gangkar Tise*, is the sacred mountain the centre of their ancient civilisation of *Zhangzhung*. It is believed, that Shenrab Miwo, the founder of their faith, visited it and gave his teachings here. As a result, there are many Bonpo temples and hermitages in the area, where many sages are believed to have attained realization.

There are many sacred temples and cave-hermitages in the area surrounding the circumambulation route, some of which have historic ties with Ladakh. At the back-side of the mountain, along the pilgrim route, is a pass called Dolma-la at a height of 5,723 metres (18776 ft) above sea-level. This is a uniquely sacred place considered to be the abode of the twenty-one Dolma (Tara) deities. It is at an extremely high altitude that takes your breath away, quite literally. Climbing down from that pass, one reaches a lake called *Kapala*. Further down again is an excellent footprint of the Buddha set on a boulder. It took Rinpoche and his party four days to make the full circumambulation. This was because they moved only by day, and each evening Rinpoche would enter a hermitage cave and perform offerings to *Machig Labdon* (a great Tibetan yogini) until late in the night. Once after circumambulating the sacred mountain and reaching the large prayer flag in front of the peak, Rinpoche felt unwell there and had to rest for seven more days.

Before proceeding to the holy Lake Mansarovar, Rinpoche performed a "mirror divination" which showed a huge boulder blocking the way. Accordingly, he decided to only have a visual blessing at the Lake, and offered a fervent prayer and could not make a circumambulation of the holy lake. The monastery there has many unique and sacred objects that, over the centuries, are believed to have self-arisen from the lake. Nestling at the foot of Mount Kailash, the Mansarovar Lake, known in Tibetan as *Mapham-Yutso,* is one of the world's loftiest freshwater lakes. The lake is a very popular allusion in Buddhist literature and is associated with many teachings and stories. Buddha, it is reported, stayed and meditated near this lake on several occasions. To the west of it is Lake *Rakshastal;* to the north is Mount Kailash. Outwards from the lake, rolling brown and orange hills stand against a backdrop of distant snow-covered peaks, punctuated with occasional settlements. On its northern side it is protected by an expanse of impenetrable desert, Lake Mansarovar has always been an intimidating area to travelers. With no trees to break the winds, the landscape is dramatically open and harsh. Buddhists also associate the lake with the legendary lake Anavatapta (Sanskrit; Pali *Anotatta*) where Queen Maya is believed to have conceived Lord Buddha. The lake has a few monasteries on its shores, the most notable of which is the ancient Chiu Monastery built on a steep hill, looking as if it has been carved right out of the rock. The lake is also considered the main source of four major rivers which flow from it in four directions. These are:

Maja Khabab – from the mouth of the peacock **(Ganga)**

Tachog Khabab – from the mouth of the horse **(Brahmaputra)**

Langchen Khabab – from the mouth of the elephant **(Satluj)**

Sengge Khabab – from the mouth of the lion **(Indus)**

Not far from Mansarovar Lake is another lake called *Langkar Lake*. Its shape resembles a complete human skin spread out, as a reminder of mortality. Hindus call this lake *Rakas or Rakshas Tal*. While returning home after his pilgrimage, Rinpoche and his team continued to Rutog, which was a richly verdant and extremely beautiful area. In former times merchants from Ladakh trading with eastern Tibet used to live and trade here. The two soldiers sent by the Chinese government to be Rinpoche's escorts came up to this point and returned back from there. Bakula Rinpoche and his team then continued to Gar-Yarsa (summer camp) where a trade representative of the Indian Government received them.

Mon-ser or Mensar was known in those days as a bandit-infested area, and this was a matter of some concern for them. But to their pleasant surprise, many people came to receive Rinpoche and his team, all of whom were well-dressed and bearing *khadag* (white ceremonial scarves) in their hands to welcome him. Some of them approached Rinpoche to request teachings, which he gave, following which several among them surrendered their weapons in front of Rinpoche and vowed not to resort to criminal activities in the future. Rinpoche was very pleased. This incident was narrated to me by Sonam Gyaltsan Khangsar who accompanied Rinpoche on this trip as his liaison officer. As they continued their journey through Chushul, Serchu, Changla and Sakti, a large number of people gave them traditional welcomes and some also accompanied them onward to Pethub Monastery, Leh.

Eighteen

On an Indian Government Mission to Tibet

India decided to celebrate the 2500th Buddha Jayanti on a grand scale. The Organizing Committee was headed by Dr. S. Radhakrishnan, Vice-President of India. Bakula Rinpoche was appointed a member of the organizing committee. It held its first meeting on May 20, 1955 which among others, decided to send Bakula Rinpoche as a special emissary of the Government of India to Tibet to coordinate with the Tibet government in Lhasa which at that time still had its own government despite the recent onslaught by the Chinese communist army. Rinpoche gladly accepted the call as he was eager to visit Lhasa again, which he had last seen in 1940. His stay in Tibet was scheduled to last five months. Sadly, this was to be Rinpoche's last visit to Tibet as an independent nation.

Bakula Rinpoche, who was then Deputy Minister for Ladakh Affairs in the Jammu & Kashmir Government also understood the political ramifications of his visit. Rinpoche recalled that Mr. T.N. Kaul, one of India's foremost diplomats, had confided to him that a senior Chinese diplomat had met him and asserted that Rinpoche's visit would be treated as 'a private pilgrimage' and hence Rinpoche is not required to carry a passport or a visa. The reason behind such a move, according to Rinpoche, was that China was not keen to acknowledge India's sovereignty over Jammu and Kashmir and Ladakh in particular. Mr. Kaul clearly saw the implications of the Chinese diplomat's contention. But after a discussion during which he insisted that the trip was officially sponsored by the Indian Government, the Chinese diplomat reluctantly agreed to put a visa stamp on Bakula Rinpoche's diplomatic passport. It later transpired that the Chinese

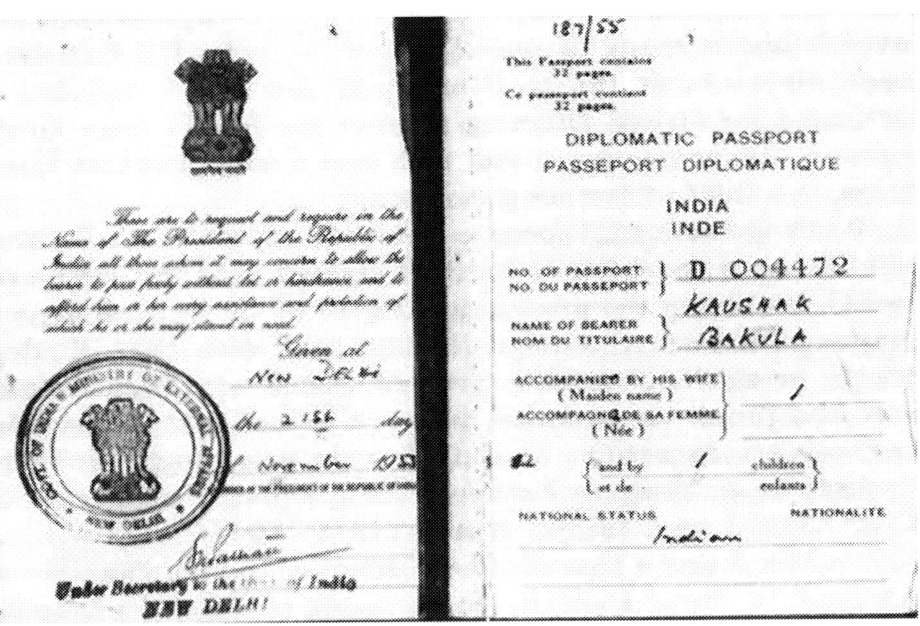

187/55

This Passport contains 32 pages.

Ce passeport contient 32 pages.

DIPLOMATIC PASSPORT
PASSEPORT DIPLOMATIQUE

INDIA
INDE

These are to request and require in the Name of The President of the Republic of India all those whom it may concern to allow the bearer to pass freely without let or hindrance and to afford him or her every assistance and protection of which he or she may stand in need.

Given at New Delhi the 21st day of November 1955

Under Secretary to the Govt. of India
NEW DELHI

NO. OF PASSPORT / NO. DU PASSEPORT: D 004472

NAME OF BEARER / NOM DU TITULAIRE: KAUSHAK BAKULA

ACCOMPANIED BY HIS WIFE (Maiden name) / ACCOMPAGNÉ DE SA FEMME (Née): /

and by / et de: / children / enfants

NATIONAL STATUS / NATIONALITÉ: Indian

4

Countries for which this Passport is valid
Pays pour lesquels ce Passeport est valable

China

The validity of this passport expires
Ce passeport expire le:

20th November, 1956

Issued at / délivré à: New Delhi

date / date: 21st November 1955

5

HOME ADDRESS

Indian Home (i.e. full address or village or town and district):

Ministry of Ladakh Affairs, J&K State

Father's name and address (i.e. full name and address or village or town and district):

Shri Nawang Thayas

OBSERVATIONS

Copy of Diplomatic Passport issued to Bakula Rinpoche for visiting Lhasa, Tibet in 1955-56

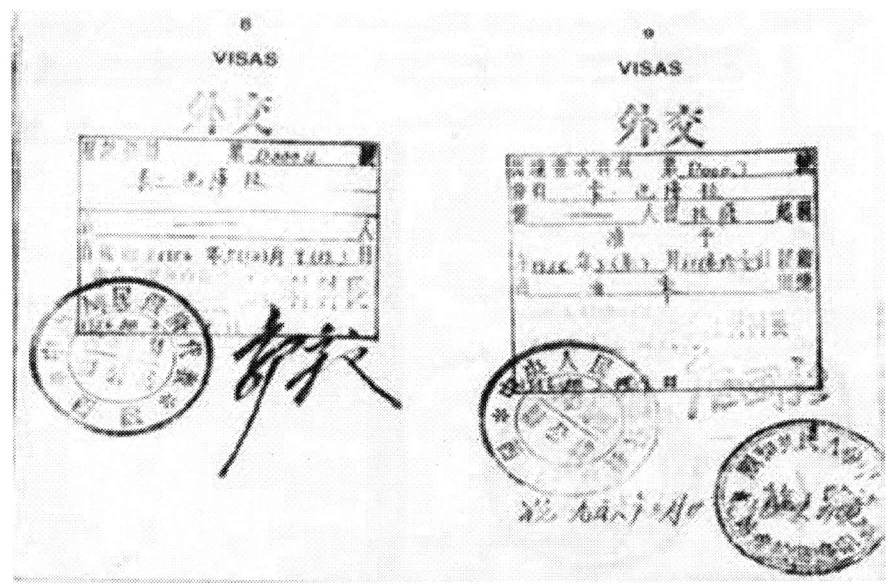

Visa issued by Chinese Embassy, New Delhi, India

Government had already circulated a new map in which the whole of Aksai Chin area was shown as a part of Tibet. Rinpoche travelled to Tibet on a Diplomatic Passport with a Visa stamped by the Chinese Embassy in New Delhi, dated December 18, 1955.

Accompanied by a small group of officials and attendants, Rinpoche departed Leh for New Delhi in November 1955. On November 18, 1955, he called on Dr. S. Radhakrishnan, Vice-President of India, in New Delhi who was also the Chairman of the Organizing Committee. He also met with Prime Minister Pandit Jawaharlal Nehru, and discussed arrangements for the upcoming 2500th Buddha Jayanti celebrations and its diplomatic significance for India-Tibet-China relations. Leaving Delhi, he proceeded to Sarnath and Bodh Gaya, where the Buddha Jayanti celebrations would be held. He then continued from there to Kalimpong where he stayed for a week. In Kalimpong he met among others, Gyalo Dhondup, the elder brother of the Dalai Lama, the Tibetologist Dr. Yuri (George) Roerich of Russia and Shakabpa, an esteemed Tibetan scholar, statesman and former Finance Minister of Tibet. All these briefed him on the sensitive situation prevailing in Tibet at the time. From Kalimpong he went to Gangtok where Apa Pant, the Political Officer of the Government of India, received him very warmly at his residence. Journey from Gangtok to the Tibetan border at Nathu-la was undertaken in five stages. Nathu-la, the pass that demarcates the border

Bakula Rinpoche meeting with the Panchen Lama at Tashi Lhunpo Monastery, Tibet (1955)

between Sikkim and Tibet, lies at an altitude of about 4310 metres (14140 Ft).

Fortunately, despite the oncoming winter, there was no snow on the passes at the time so the route was easily negotiable. At Sarchu Thang, in Tibetan territory, one Phuntsog Wangchuk, deputed by the Tibetan authorities in Lhasa, received Rinpoche. The next day, they reached Yutung where Rinpoche stayed for the night at Ṭungkar monastery. Other members of his delegation stayed at the residence of Major Chibbar, the Indian Trade Agent posted there. Their next stop was Phari where one Mr. Ko, a senior officer of the Chinese Foreign Bureau, along with an interpreter and five guards, received the delegation. Near Phari, they visited two small temples and then left for Gyangtse, a major trading centre in south-central Tibet.

On December 14, 1955, Rinpoche left Gyangtse for Shigatse (Xigaze), home to Tashi Lhunpo monastery. The delegation stayed in Shigatse for two weeks, during which time Rinpoche had three audiences with the 10th Panchen Lama Choekyi Gyaltsen at his residence. Panchen Lama also hosted Rinpoche and his team for lunch and discussed the upcoming visit to India. The Panchen Lama was eagerly looking forward to it. On every occasion that they met the Panchen Lama, they found that Mr. Ko of the Chinese

Foreign Bureau was present. It seemed he was the security official charged with attending to Panchen Lama.

During this sojourn Rinpoche had the opportunity to visit Tashi Lhunpo Monastery several times. He also met the Ladakhi monks who were studying there. There were considerable numbers of Ladakhis at the monastery at that time, perhaps as many as three hundred. Nirmal Sinha and Sonam Stobdan, who were the officials accompanying Rinpoche, also called on two of the Panchen Lama's non-ecclesiastical government ministers.

Journey from Shigatse to Lhasa took only one and half days by motor vehicle on the newly-constructed road, as against the ten days it had taken previously when Rinpoche had lived at Drepung Monastery in the 1930s. The Tsangpo (Brahmaputra) had to be crossed by means of a big ferry at a point called *Staktukha*. Rinpoche reached Lhasa on December 29, 1955. On arrival he stayed for a couple of days at the residence of Mr. P.N. Menon, who was at that time India's Consul General at Lhasa. With him Rinpoche discussed the currently precarious situation in Tibet. The Tibetan government was still in place and still operating, but was being increasingly sidelined by the new Chinese military authorities. A soft-spoken diplomat, Mr. Menon was India's last Consul General in Lhasa. He made the team feel at home and provided all necessary assistance and hospitality. The Indian Consulate in Lhasa was located in the centre of the town and was known as Deki Ling.

In Lhasa Rinpoche and his team were allowed to go wherever they liked. After the brief sojourn at *Deki Ling*, Rinpoche and his team were put up in a house provided by the Tibetan government. However, Rinpoche did not stay there and instead moved back to his old quarters in the Pethub Khangtsen of Drepung Losaling Monastery where he had formerly spent many years pursuing higher education. The large community of monks at Drepung gave him a warm ceremonial welcome. In particular, Rinpoche was keen to visit Drepung Monastery to meet his former tutor Geshe Ngawang Jungne, who was at that time holding the seat of *Khen Tripa* (Chief Abbot), of Drepung monastery. This visit had brought back many happy memories, Rinpoche recalled.

At the time of his arrival in Lhasa, the 14th Dalai Lama, who at that time was twenty years old, was in retreat, so Rinpoche could not meet him immediately. A fifteen-day program was chalked out for Rinpoche by the authorities, in which he would visit some famous monasteries and hermitages in the surrounding area, such as *Trak Yerpa and Drikung Thil*. Access to these places in those days was only by mule or horseback. By now it was mid-winter and it was very cold. At that time Rizong Sras Rinpoche, his nephew (and later the 102nd Gaden Tripa), was still studying at Drepung Losaling. Rinpoche returned to Lhasa on January 25, 1956, to participate in Rizong Rinpoche's '*Damja*' an important vow-taking religious ceremony. The same day he also had a meeting with General Chiang, who was the highest-ranking Chinese Army Officer in Lhasa at that time.

Next day, 26th January1956 was India's Republic Day. Celebrations were being held at the Consul General of India at Deki Ling. The honour of unfurling the Indian national flag was given to Bakula Rinpoche, and he also addressed the august gathering. Also present there were Palden Thondup Namgyal, the young Chogyal of Sikkim, along with several senior Tibetan and Chinese officials. Many Indian nationals, who were mostly traders, living in Lhasa at the time, also attended the celebrations.

On January 30, 1956, Rinpoche had an audience with the 14th Dalai Lama at the Potala Palace. During this meeting, gifts were exchanged and Rinpoche informed the Dalai Lama about the purpose of his mission in Tibet and conveyed to him the greetings of the President and Prime Minister of India. He told him that the top brass of the Government of India was very much looking forward to his first visit to India. He also informed the Dalai Lama that all necessary arrangements were in place and that no efforts would be spared to make the visit a fruitful one. The Dalai Lama expressed joy and eagerness to visit India, especially to make a pilgrimage to the holy sites. Rinpoche was greatly pleased by this rare opportunity to meet with the Dalai Lama. From January 31 to February 2, 1956, Rinpoche also attended the Dalai Lama's teachings delivered at the Potala Palace. It was during this teaching at Potala that Bakula Rinpoche met 42nd Sakya Trizin, the 41st head of the Sakya Order for the first time.

On February 7, 1956, Rinpoche and his party began their pilgrimage to the Ganden and Samye Monasteries. This time, it took them fourteen days to complete the round trip. Ganden, which is some forty-five kilometers from Lhasa, was a vast monastery, which had been established in the early 15th century by *Je Tsongkhapa*. The Samye monastery, which lies a few days trek away from Ganden, is much older. It is the first Buddhist monastery ever established in Tibet in the 8th century, and according to tradition, the great mystic saint Guru Padmasambhava actually helped with its construction.

Tibetan New Year or Losar fell when the team was at Samye. For Rinpoche this was very special. After a short period of rest, Rinpoche was again keen to return to Lhasa, so as not to miss the annual *Lhasa Monlam* or prayer festival. The congregation was to commence on the 2nd day of the Tibetan first month (February 16, 1956). The Tibetan Government provided a guest house just below the Potala to serve as Rinpoche's residence. As a result, he was able to attend the entire congregation.

On February 28, 1956, Rinpoche attended the first meeting of the Tibetan Government sponsored Council of Tibet's Tulkus (high-ranking incarnate lamas) which was held at Lhasa. Rinpoche was invited to address the gathering, which he did. In a hard-hitting speech in the presence of high-ranking Chinese officials, he expressed his dismay at the growing interference of the Chinese military authorities in the internal affairs of the monasteries. In 1956, Tibet was still theoretically an independent nation. Only the control of its foreign affairs and defence had been signed away to China in the controversial Seventeen Point Agreement signed in 1951. In matters of internal governance and especially in the realm of religious affairs, the Tibetan Government was still meant to be in charge. Rinpoche could also clearly foresee the anxiety and fear among the population at the daily interference in their way of life and freedom by the overbearing Chinese military authorities.

In Lhasa, the top Chinese Communist Party leader also hosted a luncheon in honour of Rinpoche, to which many senior Tibetan aristocrats and senior Chinese officials were invited. Rinpoche remembers making a brief speech and thanked his host for bestowing this honour. But he also cautioned them against the indiscriminate and wanton destruction of Tibet's sacred monuments under the garb of development and called upon the Chinese Communist authorities to exercise restraint. Rinpoche emphasized to the gathering that Tibet is a unique repository of Buddhist culture and thus a treasure for the Buddhist world. Therefore, no damage should be done to its cultural heritage. He also urged them to respect the religious sentiments of the people of Tibet. China was, by this time, already the de-facto power in Lhasa and they appeared to be consolidating their position in other parts of Tibet too. This speech was remembered with pride by many of Rinpoche's Tibetan acquaintances who later took asylum in India. They admired Rinpoche for his outspoken courage in articulating what many of them felt.

Rinpoche also recalled one incident which, he felt, was an indication of how intimidated the Tibetans felt by the Chinese during this time. By this time Rinpoche was strictly vegetarian, which was rare in Tibet in those days. At the lunch, a friend of Rinpoche advised him not to mention anything about his food preferences, as that might be considered impolite and could offend his hosts. Such was the fear among the Tibetan officials. But when the Chinese hosts asked Rinpoche about his food preference, he stated it quite clearly and they served him a good vegetarian meal.

During his five-month stay in Tibet, Bakula Rinpoche took the opportunity to meet various old friends and acquaintances, and in this way, he got to know how people felt about the new situation they found themselves in vis-a-vis the Chinese. Almost everyone, it seemed, was deeply anxious about the intentions of the communist military forces now garrisoned in their homeland. According to information provided to Rinpoche, there were about 12,000 Chinese all over Tibet, many of them soldiers and the rest engaged in the construction of roads. A few schools for Tibetans where the Chinese language was taught had been opened at Lhasa and Shigatse. One hospital equipped with an X-ray machine had been opened at Lhasa. Although in this period the Chinese communists had declared to the Tibetans that their policy would be not to interfere with religious affairs, this assurance became increasingly hollow as they increased their grip on every other aspect of life in the country.

In early March 1956 Rinpoche had a final audience with the Dalai Lama at Potala Palace during which he formally took his leave. A few days later, at the close of the prayer congregation, Rinpoche bade farewell to the great city of Lhasa on March 11, 1956. The Chinese authorities placed at his disposal a jeep and another vehicle with one Chinese officer and five guards charged with accompanying the delegation to the last place within their jurisdiction at the Indian border. After two days the team arrived at Shigatse where they spent another week at Tashi Lhunpo where Rinpoche met with the Panchen Lama and finalized arrangements for his India visit. He left Shigatse on March 19, 1956, reaching Gyangtse and onward to *Yutung* in two days. Travelling down from Yutung, the team arrived at Gangtok and then to Delhi, and from there back to Jammu, where he submitted a report on his mission to the government of J&K.

In New Delhi, Rinpoche met Prime Minister Pandit Nehru at Teen Murti Bhawan and gave him a detailed account of his visit and apprised him of the situation in Tibet and the likely fall-out of Chinese incursions in future. Rinpoche told the Prime Minister about his meeting with the Dalai Lama, Panchen Lama and other dignitaries and explained to Pandit Nehru that the situation in Tibet was extremely fluid and dangerous, and that the Tibetan population was tense. He was unambiguous in his assessment that the Chinese had made major inroads into all Tibetan areas and that unless something was done to help them, complete Chinese takeover of Tibet was imminent. He also urged the Prime Minister to discuss the situation with the Dalai Lama during his visit to India and work out a clear strategy. According to Rinpoche, he strongly pleaded with the Prime Minister to consider giving political asylum to both the supreme religious leaders of Tibet, the Dalai Lama and Panchen Lama, if any such request was made by them during their coming visit. To prove his point, Rinpoche told Prime

Minister Nehru that having seen the imminent threat of Chinese communist occupation of Tibet, he had taken the precaution, when leaving Lhasa, of bringing with him all the precious holy objects held at his residence in Drepung Monastery in Lhasa to Ladakh.

In order to convince the Indian government of the impending danger from China, Rinpoche tried all means available to him and placed the ground situation before them. Meanwhile, the situation deteriorated and anxiety grew all around in the Indian establishment. Time was running out and the measures taken were too little too late. Sino-Indian relations were made even worse when, in 1959, India received nearly 100,000 Tibetans. Then, a series of incidents between India and Chinese soldiers and officials in the northeastern and northwestern Himalayan began to push Indian public opinion against China. In 1962, Pandit Nehru and his Chinese counterpart Mr. Zhou Enlai held meetings in an attempt to de-escalate tensions, but those ended when China and India failed to agree on the major crisis that defined the boundary in the western sector. War broke out in 1962 in which India suffered a humiliating defeat and ceded a major chunk of its territory to China. In short, Rinpoche made all out efforts but failed to convince the Indian government. He was deeply disappointed on this account. In his seminal book 'India after Gandhi', the noted Indian historian Ramachandra Guha also refers to how Rinpoche had warned the Government of India in year 1955, of the severe danger facing Tibet and its potential fallout on India of growing Chinese presence in the region.

Nineteen

India Hosts the 2500th Buddha Jayanti

When India attained independence on August 15, 1947, after nearly two centuries of British colonial rule, questions arose as to what should be adopted as the national symbols of free India. Free India chose Babasaheb Dr. Bhimrao Ambedkar, an Indian jurist, economist, social reformer and political leader who later embraced Buddhism, as head of the committee drafting the Constitution of India. It adopted an inclusive constitution and declared India a sovereign and democratic republic and assures its citizens justice, equality and liberty which are principles embodied in Buddhist philosophy. The Constituent Assembly of India ultimately turned to the Buddhist heritage to furnish it with suitable symbols. Buddhism in some ways represented New India's aspirations and ethos as well as its great historical legacy for world culture.

The Ashoka Chakra in the Indian Tricolor is symbolic of the law of Dharma and denotes motion. Thus, the *Dharma-chakra* came to be at the centre of India's national flag, while the four-headed lion represents capital of the Buddhist Emperor Ashoka, and the fearless proclamation of *Dharma* to the four quarters of the world, was adopted as the National Emblem of India. This was also adopted as the official seal of the Republic.

It was on the Day of Vesak two and a half millennia ago, in the year 623 B.C., that the Buddha was born. It was also on the Day of Vesak that the Lord Buddha attained enlightenment and Mahaparinirvana. In keeping with this newly invigorated resonance of Buddhism for the new Republic of India, it was decided that there should be an elaborate celebration of the 2500th anniversary of Lord Buddha's birth, as the Buddha Jayanti or Vesak in 1956. Pandit Nehru himself took a personal interest in the arrangements for this international event which would also serve as a platform for India to project itself as a leading power in the new post-colonial Asia. The organizing committee was headed by Dr. S. Radhakrishnan, Vice-President of India. Bakula Rinpoche was appointed a member of the organizing committee.

The Buddha Jayanti celebrations commenced on May 23, 1956, and lasted for a full year, with important Buddhist figures coming from all over the world to participate in this auspicious event. Prime Minister Jawaharlal Nehru had planned the celebrations on a grand scale. Buddhist leaders and eminent scholars from many countries of the world were invited. The guest included the 14th Dalai Lama and 10th Panchen Lama and their tutors, 16th Gyalwa Karmapa, 41st Sakya Trizin, Chogyal of Sikkim, leaders from various South Asia and Southeast Asian countries including Mr. U. Nu, first Prime Minister of Burma, Eshi Dorzhi Sharapov, Pandito Khambolama of Soviet Union, T. Gombodoo and Prof. Sh. Luvsanvandan from Mongolia were also among those who participated.

On May 24, 1956, Dr. Rajendra Prasad, the first President of India, announced that the ridge area of Delhi, a large park and a green-belt area in the capital was henceforth to be known as the "Buddha Jayanti Park". He also announced the formation of a Department of Buddhist Studies at the University of Delhi and seven other universities. (Currently, 22 universities in India have department of Buddhist studies). Facilities for Buddhist pilgrims to visit the Buddhist holy places like Sarnath, Bodh Gaya, Kushinagar etc. were all completed in time for the celebration.

In May 1956, the 14th Dalai Lama, who, at that time, was only 21-years-old, arrived in New Delhi with a large entourage of Tibetan dignitaries. He was extended a ceremonial welcome as a Head of State and presented with a guard of honour on arrival at Palam Airport. Among those present at the airport to receive him were Dr. S. Radhakrishnan, Vice-President of India, Prime Minister Nehru, Bakula Rinpoche and other dignitaries. In New Delhi, the Dalai Lama stayed at Hyderabad House, whereas the Panchen Lama stayed at Kota House. In terms of state protocol, Bakula Rinpoche who was then a minister in the J&K Government, was assigned the task of accompanying the Dalai Lama and the Panchen Lama and functioned like their official chaperone. He travelled with them to different Indian cities. The Tibetan dignitaries stayed in India for quite a long time, visiting many holy sites as well as several industrial centres and historical monuments. The mother of both the Holinesses, along with their principal tutors Ling Rinpoche, Trijang Rinpoche and Nyulchu Rinpoche, tutor of the Panchen Lama was also part of the delegation. Once, during a ceremony in Sarnath, the Panchen Lama wore Bakula Rinpoche's *Chogos* (robes) and for this reason Bakula Rinpoche forever thereafter treasured those robes. To be with these exalted figures – the most important religious figures in the entire Tibetan Buddhist cultural world, of which Ladakh was a part – was rare and a tremendous privilege. Rinpoche also hosted a reception in honour of the two Holinesses at Kashmir House, New Delhi. Present on the occasion were eminent scholars and Buddhist spiritual leaders from many countries. Arrangements were also made for their pilgrimage to all the Buddhist holy places in India.

In Ladakh too, the Buddha Jayanti was celebrated with great religious fervor. Buddha Purnima, the thrice-blessed day of Lord Buddha's birth, enlightenment and *mahaparinirvana*, was celebrated at Leh in May 1956, on a grand scale. Celebrations lasted for three days, and were attended by the speaker of the J&K legislative assembly and government ministers along with many other dignitaries. Special funds were provided by the state government for the purpose. That year on October 14, 1956, Dr. B.R. Ambedkar, the chairman of the committee which drafted the Indian Constitution and the champion and leader of India's disenfranchised Dalits, led an estimated half a million followers who for generations had been humiliated because of the Hindu caste system, to embrace Buddhism. This mass conversion brought an unprecedented transformation in Indian society.

Vesak, the Day of the Full Moon in the month of May, is the most sacred day to millions of Buddhists around the world. The UN General Assembly, by its resolution of 1999, recognized internationally the Day of Vesak to acknowledge the contribution that Buddhism, one of the oldest religions in the world, has made for over two and a half millennia and continues to make to the spirituality of humanity.

Prime Minister Nehru, The Dalai Lama and Dr. S Radhakrishnan, Vice-President of India. Bakula Rinpoche and Burmese leader Mr. U. Nu are also seen in the picture (1956)

The Dalai Lama, inspecting a guard of honour on arrival at Palam airport, New Delhi (1956)

Pandit Jawaharlal Nehru, Prime Minister and The Dalai Lama exchanging greetings at Delhi airport. Dr. S. Radhakrishnan, Vice-President of India, Bakula Rinpoche and Apa Pant are also seen in the picture (1956)

The Dalai Lama at a reception hosted by Bakula Rinpoche, Minister, Government of Jammu and Kashmir at J&K House, New Delhi, Tashi Rabgyes, Private Secretary to Bakula Rinpoche is seated on extreme right (1956)

Panchen Lama appreciating Kashmiri products at the J&K Emporium in New Delhi (1956)

The Dalai Lama, Panchen Lama, Bakula Rinpoche and monks offering prayer at the Mulagandhakuti Vihara, Sarnath (1956)

(L to R) Bakula Rinpoche, Kachen Nyulchu Rinpoche Lobsang Choepel, senior tutor of H.H. the 10th Panchen Lama and Kyabje Ling Rinpoche, senior tutor of H.H. the 14th Dalai Lama (New Delhi, 1956)

Twenty

Measures to Protect and Strengthen Ladakh's Buddhist Heritage

Besides psychological and many structural reforms e.g. freeing the people of Ladakh from bondage and heavy debt of landlords, abject poverty, promoting school education for children, infrastructure and later formation of a separate ministry of Ladakh Affairs in the Government of Jammu and Kashmir, were some of the landmark achievements of Bakula Rinpoche's early years of public life. Over the years, Rinpoche remained focused and was successful in establishing several institutions which helped accelerate the pace of development in Ladakh.

All Ladakh Gonpa Association (ALGA)

Due to its close cultural and religious affinities with Tibet, Ladakh is sometimes described as "Little Tibet". After the Chinese occupation of Tibet in the 1950's and the gradual undermining of Tibetan culture under the Chinese communist occupation, the importance of Ladakh as a place where Tibetan Buddhist culture could continue to thrive in conditions of freedom, was greatly heightened. Moreover, the Chinese occupation, and particularly the aftermath of the 1959 Tibetan uprising and the flight of the Dalai Lama, led to the border between India and Tibet being sealed shut, with all trade ties and contacts between the two sides abruptly severed. This was a major setback for Ladakh, since historically the holy sites of Tibet were major places of pilgrimage for Ladakhis, and there were also many cultural, religious and trade ties which were now suddenly disrupted. With Tibetan culture now under grave threat of extinction in its homeland, it became a matter of tremendous importance that Ladakh take steps to preserve and strengthen its Tibetan Buddhist heritage. This could only be done by making the latter fit enough to meet the challenges of modernity that lay ahead. Efforts were, therefore, made to reform Ladakh's religious bodies, and new accountable democratic institutions were put in place to govern the region's religious and cultural institutions.

Over the years, two organizations, namely the Ladakh Buddhist Association (LBA) and Ladakh Gonpa Association (LGA) were established. While the former represented the Buddhist population of Ladakh, the latter became the central body of Ladakh's monasteries representing all major traditions. In this highly significant task, which included forming the LGA too, Bakula Rinpoche's role and contribution have already been described in an earlier chapter. The LBA, established in 1949 was in fact formed from the pre-existing Young Men's Buddhist Association which had been established in 1934. Raja Jigmet Dadul Namgyal of Stok, served as its first president. The organization was committed to the preservation and propagation of Buddha's teachings and the Buddhist heritage of the region. It also supported work in the socio-economic, cultural and linguistic fields.

The "Big Landed Estates Abolition Act" episode impressed on Rinpoche the importance of all different Buddhist schools of Ladakh coming together if they were to be effective in defending their shared interests. Like his predecessor, the 18th Bakula Rinpoche Lobzang Eshey Stanba Gyaltsan, who had pleaded with Maharaja Pratap Singh and got all the monasteries of Ladakh exempted from royal taxation, the 19th Bakula Rinpoche too was completely dedicated to preserve and protect Ladakh's unity and preserve its unique identity.

With the aim of forging unity amongst all the different Buddhist communities and sects represented in Ladakh, Rinpoche spearheaded the establishment of a central body to represent their shared interests. In turn, Rinpoche offered the piece of land he received from Hemis Monastery, as a gift, to the new organization, to build its headquarters. This became known as the All-Ladakh Gonpa Association (LGA). For forty-two years, Bakula Rinpoche remained its founder-president.

All Ladakh Gonpa Association (ALGA) is the central organisation of the Buddhist Monasteries and it aims to preserve and strengthen monastic institutions. It is worth mentioning that two of the most important educational institutions in Ladakh, namely the Central Institute of Buddhist Studies (CIBS) and the Lamdon Senior Secondary School first operated from here and only later moved to their present locations.

Over the years, LGA together with the LBA also played an active role in voicing the legitimate socio – political demands of the people. It also organise the annual "Ladakh Monlam Chenmo" congregation attended by monks from all the four major monastic traditions and also carry out other religious activities. A new complex "Dharma Centre" was built by the Association at Choglamsar near Leh. On August 3, 2025 His Holiness the 14th Dalai Lama consecrated the "Dharma Centre". Under bright morning sun, people from all walks of life lined up to greet him. At the Dharma Centre His Holiness was received by Ven. Tsering Wangdu, President of All Ladakh Gonpa Association.

Building of Jokhang or Chokhang Temple

The establishment of Ladakh Gonpa Association which brought all the monasteries of various Buddhist traditions in Ladakh under one umbrella organization, was a major accomplishment. Another major achievement for Rinpoche was the construction of the *Jokhang* or Chokhang temple at Leh. Around the city of Leh, and in all the major villages of Ladakh, there are ancient monasteries. However, each monastery is affiliated to one or another particular sect or tradition, and as a result there was no ecumenical space in which the followers of all the traditional schools could get together. This impeded the ability of Ladakhi Buddhists to unite and coordinate their activities. To remedy this situation Bakula Rinpoche embarked upon a plan to build a Jokhang Temple at Leh, mirroring the famous Jokhang Temple in Lhasa which is a major site of pilgrimage for all the followers of Tibetan Buddhism. The breakthrough in this plan came when Bakula Rinpoche, by now a minister in the J&K government, was successful in obtaining clearance from Prime Minister Bakshi Ghulam Muhammad led government for allotment of Wazir Bangla – the former residence of the colonial representatives in the heart of Leh town – as the site on which the new Jokhang Temple could be built.

A campaign was started to raise funds for building the temple in which all the Rinpoches of Ladakh and prominent citizens took part. Donation in the form of cash and material was collected from across Ladakh. On the auspicious Saga Dawa of the Earth Dog year of the sixteenth rabjung of the Tibetan calendar (1958), the 19th Bakula Rinpoche Lobzang Thupstan Chognor laid the foundation stone for the Jokhang Temple amidst great fanfare. An architectural plan was prepared and executed by local artisan and craftsmen. The Jokhang was built with active support from people across Ladakh. The main image installed inside the temple was the gold-gilded statue of Jowo Rinpoche (Buddha Shakyamuni) similar to one in Jokhang Temple in Lhasa and 10th Panchen Lama Chokyi Gyaltsen facilitated the transportation of the statue from Tibet to Ladakh.

In 1959 the 6th Ling Rinpoche, the senior tutor of the 14th Dalai Lama visited Ladakh and consecrated the Jowo statue and the Jokhang temple.

A plaque at the gate of Jokhang Vihara, Leh. "Gyalsras Bakula Rinpoche, the spiritual and political leader of Ladakh, laid the foundation-stone of Jokhang Vihara on the auspicious Vesak Day in 1958"

Jokhang (Chokhang) Leh, Ladakh. (1959)

The 14th Dalai Lama Tenzin Gyatso paid his first ever visit to Ladakh in August 1966, and he too blessed the temple. Likewise, supreme heads of all other Tibetan Buddhist Traditions as well as many other revered Lamas and saints from home and abroad have visited Jokhang in Leh and augmented its sanctity.

In 1968, soon after Bakula Rinpoche's first election to the Lok Sabha, he invited His Royal Highness *12th Chogyal* of Sikkim Palden Thondup Namgyal (which at that time was an independent kingdom) to visit Ladakh. Rinpoche had first met him in Lhasa, Tibet in year 1955 and knew him well. He was also a member of the Board of management of the Namgyal Institute of Tibetology in Sikkim founded by Chogyal Palden Thondup Namgyal. The Chogyal of Sikkim together with his wife Gyalmo Hope Cooke visited Ladakh in October 1968. They were in India on a state visit. Sikkim, like Ladakh, was a Himalayan Kingdom following the traditions of Tibetan Buddhism and thus the two regions have many cultural and linguistic affinities. Thousands of curious people turned out at the Jokhang to welcome and greet the royal couple on their first visit to Ladakh.

In modern days, Ladakh Buddhist Association (LBA) has also become a unifying front of the Buddhists of Ladakh, aiming to look after their political interests, bringing social reforms in Ladakhi society and to preserve their art, culture, language and traditions. For the people of Ladakh the compassionate Buddha resides in this Jokhang. Venerable Rinpoches and scholars, irrespective of sectarian consideration deliver teachings to the public. Various religious events such as Vesak celebration and other such events are also held at Jokhang Leh. On the advice of Bakula Rinpoche, the great scholar Kachen Eshey Tondup, a scholar of unrivalled knowledge began the practice of giving religious discourses to lay people inside the temple. He taught *Lamrim* (the graduation path to enlightenment) as well as history, grammar, and poetry. This tradition of public teachings by learned monks and scholars continues to this day and has helped greatly in giving the common people a thorough understanding of the Buddhist path. The people of Ladakh shall remain ever-grateful to Bakula Rinpoche for his far-sightedness in helping establish this holy place.

However, in recent times, the old building had developed structural issues and suffered from inadequate space and infrastructure. Consequently, after much deliberation, it was decided that the old temple would be demolished and a new one constructed on the same site. Work began in 2025 and at the request of Mr. Chering Dorjey, President of the Ladakh Buddhist Association, His Holiness the 14th Dalai Lama, Tenzin Gyatso, laid the foundation stone for the new temple on 3rd August 2025. It was a grand ceremony attended by a large gathering of devotees.

In recognition of the pivotal role played by the 19th Bakula Rinpoche in the construction of the old Chokhang, the Ladakh Buddhist Association requested the 20th Bakula Rinpoche Tenzin Ngawang Jigmet Wangchuk to participate in this important event. Accordingly, Rinpoche arrived from Drepung Monastery in Mundgod, Karnataka and attended the ceremony in Leh. The new temple is expected to be completed by 2027.

Model picture of new Jokhang (2025)

HH The 14th Dalai Lama laying the foundation stone on August 3, 2025.

Establishment of Central Institute of Buddhist Studies (CIBS)

Also severely disrupted by the developments in Tibet were the educational opportunities of Ladakh's monastic populations. Chinese Communist occupation and the destruction of Tibet's religious culture and communities had brought an abrupt halt. It was thus imperative that an alternative source of traditional Buddhist education be made available immediately, so that these precious traditions would not be lost and forgotten.

On the initiative of Bakula Rinpoche, a meeting was convened in Leh in year 1959, with representatives from all the major monasteries in Ladakh following different traditions. In it Bakula Rinpoche put forward an idea to establish a School of Buddhist Philosophy (as it was then known) at Leh. Each of the ten major monasteries representing all the four major Buddhist traditions would contribute and send certain number of monks each year to be enrolled there. All the monasteries agreed to provide supporting materials to ensure the school's smooth functioning. Aim of the institute was to facilitate education for monks in the Five Great Treatises of Buddhist philosophy, as well as Buddhist art and useful modern subjects such as Hindi and English.

On the auspicious day of October 23, 1959, the school was inaugurated by the 6th Ling Rinpoche, the senior tutor of the 14th Dalai Lama. Initially the School had only five monk students, but gradually the numbers increased. In those very early days, the school operated from the headquarter of the All-Ladakh Gonpa Association at Karzoo, Leh, set-up on the land offered to Bakula Rinpoche as a gift from Hemis Monastery. Geshe Eshey Thub was appointed the school's first principal with Geshe Eshey Thabkas and Yuru Khanpo Konchok Stanzin as senior teachers. Shiv Kumar Sharma was the Hindi teacher. Lobzang Samstan, now in his 80s, who was among the first batch of monk-students, told me that the facilities at the school in those early days were basic and that sometimes students would not even get enough to eat. However, as time passed, things gradually improved. He remembered the frequent visits of Bakula Rinpoche to the school to enquire about the welfare of monks and staff working there. For about two years the school remained at Karzoo and then it shifted to Pethub or commonly called Spituk. Later, as the number of monk students increased, its management became more difficult due to the growing costs. So, in 1962, Bakula Rinpoche took up the matter with Prime Minister Jawaharlal Nehru and requested that the school be funded by the central government's Ministry of Education. To his great joy and satisfaction, Pandit Nehru accepted he request. The name of the school was changed from the School of Buddhist Philosophy to the Central Institute of Buddhist Studies (CIBS) as it is now known. It functions under the direct administrative control of the Ministry of Culture, Government of India and receives generous grants from the central government.

A new campus was set up at Choglamsar which was inaugurated by the 19th Bakula Rinpoche. Over a period of time, the level of academic activity at the Institute was gradually raised to include post-graduate level courses. The Institute forged an affiliation with the Sampurnanand Sanskrit University in Varanasi. Today its courses are available not just to monks, but also to nuns and lay students. In 2016 it was granted the status of 'Deemed to be University' by the University Grants Commission (UGC). Branch schools of the institute have been opened in all the major monasteries of Ladakh where preparatory philosophy courses are offered to young monks.

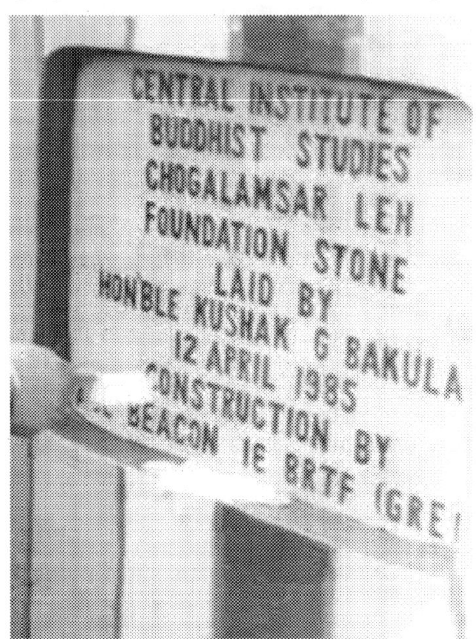

Foundation stone of CIBS, Leh laid by Bakula Rinpoche (1985)

Bakula Rinpoche inaugurating the new campus of Central Institute of Buddhist Studies (CIBS), Choglamsar, Leh

The institute also has a full-fledged branch school in Zanskar and in other places. Many of its alumni now occupy senior public positions and serve the community. From its humble beginnings, the Institute is now firmly a part of Ladakh's educational landscape and Ladakh owes deep sense of gratitude to Bakula Rinpoche and Prime Minister Jawaharlal Nehru.

Ladakh Bauddh Vihara, Delhi

In those days only very few Ladakhis had the resources to venture out of their homeland. And those who did, whether on pilgrimage, or in trade, or seeking medical treatment and so on, would at some point find themselves in the national capital, Delhi. But for most ordinary Ladakhis, visiting Delhi in those days was a terrible and traumatic experience. Ladakhis could be seen wandering lost in the streets and sleeping at the railway stations for want of accommodation. Most Ladakhis were both poor and illiterate, so there was no way they could afford to stay in hotels. And at that time there was only one Buddhist temple in New Delhi, known as Buddhist Vihara, Birla Mandir, but it was very small and could only accommodate few visitors at a time. Conditions were especially difficult during the hot summer months. So, there was an urgent need for a proper shelter for the people, and this really occupied Rinpoche's mind. Rinpoche, therefore, decided to raise the matter with Prime Minister Jawaharlal Nehru and submit a petition in this regard. Pandit Nehru was most gracious in his response and promised to look into the request. Shortly thereafter, he directed the Central Public Works Department (CPWD) to identify a suitable place which soon came up with a plot of land on the banks of the Yamuna river, where a temple and rest house for Ladakhi pilgrims could be built.

Officials, however, clarified to Rinpoche that the cost of construction would not be borne by the government and only the land had been granted free of cost. So, it was left to Rinpoche to raise the required funds for the construction of the temple and the two-storey guesthouse blocks on either side. Given the hopeless financial situation in Ladakh at that time, raising sufficient funds from there was going to be impossible. Rinpoche recalled meeting Pandit ji yet again and asking him for monetary assistance in building the Vihara. According to Rinpoche, Pandit ji could be sometime become very short-tempered, especially when faced with demands that he felt were unjustified. But despite his irritation, Pandit ji was a very kind-hearted and compassionate man. After his initial outburst, he told Rinpoche that he would look into his request and see what could be done. Later the prime minister instructed the CPWD to construct two blocks of the guest house. This was a great relief, but there were still no funds available for building the temple, even though the CPWD had already commenced construction of its two blocks. Rinpoche urgently needed to generate funds to build the temple, so he elicited donations from Ladakh and also sought financial assistance from the state government of J&K. This was all done in a tremendous rush.

Thus, on Rinpoche's request on February 23, 1963, a magnificent temple in Buddhist architectural style, with double-storied guesthouse blocks on either side was inaugurated by Prime Minister Jawaharlal Nehru at Bela Road in the area of Old Delhi. The Central Public Works Department (CPWD) which operates under the Central Government, handed over its management to 'Ladakh Baudh Vihara Society', a registered society. A governing body was set up to regulate its activities and safeguard its interests and Lama Lobzang was appointed as its Honorary Secretary. The Vihara looked magnificent against the backdrop of the river Yamuna. Rinpoche commissioned a statue of Lord Buddha and his two disciples from Nepal as well as twelve large *thangka*s depicting his life-story, to be displayed inside. A library equipped with some rare manuscripts, books, *thangka* paintings and holy art objects were also assembled. Rinpoche had grand plans for the future of this Vihara. He hoped it would develop into a Buddhist cultural centre of international repute in the national capital.

On November 27, 1968, the 14th Dalai Lama paid his first visit to the Vihara. A large crowd of devotees, including many from Ladakh gathered on that occasion. His Holiness emphasized the urgent need to collect the original works of Buddhist philosophy and other philosophical writings, so that the Vihara could become a place for genuine research and the translation of the Buddhist scriptures into various Indian languages. The vihara also hosted Sakya Trizin Rinpoche, the head of Sakya tradition. He stayed at the vihara for several weeks giving teachings to a large gathering. Over the years, many other distinguished spiritual masters, including the 16th Gyalwa Karmapa, Dudjom Rinpoche, Ling Rinpoche and Trijang Rinpoche, two tutors of the Dalai Lama and many other highly-realized Buddhist masters from Sri Lanka, Thailand and Burma and elsewhere have visited the temple. Top national leaders such as Prime Minister of India Jawahar Lal Nehru, President Giani Zail Singh, Prime Minister Lal Bahadur Shastri, Prime Minister Indira Gandhi, Deputy Prime Minister G.L. Nanda, Dr. Karan Singh and others also visited the vihara and paid their respects.

However, the Vihara which Rinpoche had established with great expectations, suffered complete neglect in the subsequent years. Its Governing Body which had representatives from various ministries and Delhi Administration on it, was defunct for many years. Conditions at the vihara were difficult. Most of the guest rooms which had been intended for travelers and pilgrims from Ladakh, were rented out on a permanent basis, mainly to the families of Tibetan traders creating considerable resentment among Ladakhis.

Prime Minister Nehru inaugurating Ladakh Bauddha Vihara, Delhi.
Bakula Rinpoche sitting in the middle (1963)

Rinpoche speaking at the inauguration of Ladakh Bauddh Vihara, Delhi (1963)

Prime Minister Nehru planting a Bodhi Tree sapling at Ladakh Bauddh Vihara, Delhi. Also seen in the picture are Bakula Rinpoche, Rizong Sras Rinpoche, Gulzari Lal Nanda, Anand Bhante and Lama Lobzang (1963)

Bakula Rinpoche with Prime Minister Mr. Lal Bahadur Shastri at Ladakh Bauddh Vihara, Delhi. Also seen are: Mrs. Brookner, a well-known painter of Hungarian origin, Mrs. Savita Ambedkar, wife of Babasaheb Dr. Bhim Rao Ambedkar, Mr. G.L. Nanda, Home Minister and Bhikshu Ananda (1965)

In 1982, I was entrusted with the responsibility of its management. As a first step in the effort to revamp the functioning of the institution, it was decided to reconstitute the governing body of the Vihara. Urgent requests were sent to various ministries of the Central Government, the Government of Delhi and Delhi Development Authority (DDA), and other prominent public bodies to nominate representatives to join the governing body. With the governing body in place, a formal meeting was held under the chairmanship of Bakula Rinpoche, president of the Vihara. It took some important decisions. Notices were issued to all permanent occupants to vacate the rooms. This was a difficult task but we eventually succeeded, thanks largely to the active support of Mr. P.P. Srivastava, the then commissioner of Municipal Corporation of Delhi (MCD) and a member of the governing body. Facilities at the vihara were restored to serve the community for which it was intended. A new tariff system was also introduced which helped generate the funds to run the vihara effectively. Secondly, although the Vihara temple had been built only 26 years ago, the building was in precarious condition. Its roof made of wood and tiles were unsuited for Delhi's weather condition. It had developed severe cracks all over causing leakages during the rainy season. The matter was discussed in the Governing Body and a new structural plan was prepared and work began but before it could be completed, I had to leave for Mongolia.

Meanwhile, encroachments and unauthorized structures came all around the vihara complex. A flyover on the Bela road (Ringroad) was built which further added to its woes. As a result, the Vihara which occupied an important place in the capital's social and cultural map, lost its sheen. However, all is not lost, and with the determined efforts of people across Ladakh, what remains of this once-prestigious Vihara can still be salvaged.

School in Delhi for Children from Ladakh and Border Areas

The Chinese aggression of 1962 brought Ladakh into international spotlight for the first time, and it was only after this, that the Government of India finally began to recognize the strategic importance of this area. However, despite this newfound attention being lavished on the region by the central government, in Ladakh people remained poor, and it was very hard for Ladakhis to find good education since the schools in Ladakh lacked both infrastructure and suitably-qualified teachers. Coming from a Ladakhi background it was very hard for youngsters to gain admission into national-level colleges and institutes, when they had to compete with students from other more developed regions.

With this situation in mind, Bakula Rinpoche spearheaded an initiative to establish a co-educational boarding school for children from Ladakh and other border regions in New Delhi. By locating the school in the national capital, he felt that the school would give the youths a broader perspective on their opportunities, and would also help integrate them with the rest of the country. In order to get the project off the ground, Rinpoche once again took the route which had repeatedly proved itself to be the most effective means of getting things done. He brought the proposal directly to Prime Minister Pandit Jawaharlal Nehru. Pandit Nehru always had an open-door policy towards Rinpoche, and he always gave his ideas and perspectives a sympathetic hearing. On this occasion too, Pandit ji was forthcoming with his support and practical assistance. He asked Rinpoche to meet Dr. K.L. Shrimali, who was the Union Education Minister and the entire process was completed soon. And so, it was in 1964 that the Ladakh Institute for Higher Studies (LIHS) was established in Delhi under the supervision of the Ministry of Education.

A team of officials along with Lama Lobzang, who was then the Hony. Secretary of LBV, Delhi went to Ladakh to select the first cohort of students (boys and girls). Other students were also enrolled from almost all Himalayan border areas of North East India. All students were on full bursaries, so there were no expenses, to be borne by the parents. They were taken care of by the Government of India, and in addition each student was paid a stipend. The author was one among these fortunate students and remember Rinpoche would always encourage us to study hard so that the students could return home and work for the future of their regions. Boys and girls from the entire Himalayan belt – from Ladakh, Himachal Pradesh, Arunachal Pradesh, Nagaland, Mizoram, Manipur, UP Hills, and Sikkim – were admitted to this institute. Later, in tune with the changing demands, its curriculum was changed and it was affiliated with the Central Board of Secondary Education (CBSE), New Delhi. This made it possible for the students to study science and other modern subjects. At the same time LIHS was renamed as *Vishesh Kendriya Vidyalaya* (VKV) and henceforth functioned under the jurisdiction of the Central Schools Organization.

In 2002 however, the school was threatened with closure by the government. It was around that time Rinpoche (who by this time had retired as ambassador) raised the matter with Mr. Murli Manohar Joshi, Minister for the Human Resources of India. During the latter's official visit to Ulaanbaatar he had come to meet Rinpoche at his monastery. In the course of their conversation Rinpoche explained in detail about the background of the VKV in Delhi and requested that the minister should intervene to save the school from closure. Mr. Joshi promised to look into this matter on his return to New Delhi. His office order dated July 29, 2002, (**Annexure 6**) instructed the Kendriya Vidyalaya Sanghathan (KVS) to maintain the status quo until a final decision was taken in this regard. Again, it is matter of regret that despite Rinpoche's best efforts and the minister's personal intervention, KVS decided to discontinue this facility, thus depriving children from Ladakh and other border areas of great educational opportunities. Efforts to re-start this premier institution are still on but without much success.

Land for Lamdon Model School

In subsequent years Ladakh produced many young talents who made great contributions in the spread of education. In year 1970, a group of young men came together and established Lamdon Social Welfare Society in Leh. Lamdon Senior Secondary School was founded under the auspices of this society. This school, like the CIBS, began with a small number of students at Karzoo, the headquarters of Ladakh Gonpa Association. For all his work in strengthening traditional institutions and its Buddhist heritage, Rinpoche was also a keen advocate of modern education and therefore supported their initiative wholeheartedly. He firmly believed that Ladakh needed its youth to be well educated so as to be able to face the challenges that lay ahead.

In 1973, when the management of the school decided to build a school campus with all facilities including sports and hostel. They needed land for the purpose and approached Rinpoche for help. Rinpoche acceding to their request, made available to them a large chunk of land which belonged to his Samkar Monastery. This was to be Ladakh's first ever private school. It pioneered modern education in the Ladakh region and today Lamdon is the biggest and considered to be one of the best schools in Ladakh with a well-equipped campus. At present the school has over three thousand students, as well as branches in every region in Ladakh. Nobel laureate the Dalai Lama has visited the school several times and has supported its activities. Over seven hundred students are currently being provided free education under various sponsorship schemes. The school has hostel facilities for both boys and girls.

The Dalai Lama's Maiden visit to Ladakh

Despite his preoccupations, Rinpoche always had time for what he regarded as his much more important duties, both personally, as a monk, and publicly, as a public figure for his people. For centuries Ladakhis had looked to Tibet for spiritual guidance and leadership. Tibet had held aloft the flag of Buddhism, spreading their beneficence throughout the world. After his arrival in India in 1959, the 14th Dalai Lama then just 24 years old, was hosted by the Government of India in Mussoorie, a hill-station just north of

Dehradun, and later he was relocated in Dharamshala in Himachal Pradesh, where he has since resided.

The people of Ladakh were extremely keen to invite The Dalai Lama for what would be his maiden visit to the Ladakh region. His Holiness had been living in India for 7 years and that they were extremely keen to receive his blessing. Therefore, on behalf of the people of Ladakh Rinpoche decided to seek an audience with the Dalai Lama and placed his request before him. His Holiness gave his consent to visit Ladakh.

Ladakh was at that time a restricted area and all visitors required prior permission from the central government. Therefore, in the summer of year 1966, Rinpoche who was then a minister in the Jammu and Kashmir government, met Prime Minister Lal Bahadur Shastri and sought his assistance. Prime Minister Shastri assured Rinpoche his support and soon all the necessary clearances from the central government were obtained. However, in view of its special status of J&K, it also needed the consent of the State Government. This permission was mandatory and it was not forthcoming despite best efforts of Bakula Rinpoche. Chief Minister Ghulam Mohammed Sadiq had some security apprehensions and he also felt that the visit would antagonise the Chinese. This was totally uncalled for and Rinpoche was deeply saddened by his approach. The situation came to a boiling point and during a cabinet meeting, Rinpoche strongly protested and accused the Government of being insensitive to the religious sentiments of the people. When his efforts failed, he made his feelings known by walking out of the meeting. People of Ladakh were also deeply hurt with the attitude of the State Government and there were protests against the State government across the region. Eventually their persistent efforts paid off and the state government gave its approval. It was in this way that the 14th Dalai Lama blessed Ladakh with his presence for the first time from August 25-30, 1966, where he received a rapturous welcome from the local people.

Kalachakra Teaching at Leh

It is believed that Lord Buddha graced the king of a mythical land called Shambhala with these sacred transmissions and that this king and his successors preserved them there for many centuries. Later, the teachings were re-introduced to the human realm especially, in India. The Kalachakra initiations have since been passed on to an unbroken succession of great masters, including highly-revered figures like Atisa Dipankara Jnana Sri and Lama Tsongkhapa, leading directly to the present 14th Dalai Lama.

It has been 10 years since His Holiness had visited Ladakh for the first time. Bakula Rinpoche, along with the Ladakh Buddhist Association and

The Dalai Lama in Leh. Bakula Rinpoche is seen walking ahead of the motorcade (1966)

Gathering at the Kalachakra Teaching at Choglamsar, Leh

Ladakh Gonpa Association were of the opinion that it was the appropriate time for them to request the Dalai Lama to deliver the Kalachakra initiation in Leh. Accompanied by Sonam Gyaltsan, President and Tsering Samphel, General Secretary, Ladakh Buddhist Association called on The Dalai Lama in Dharamshala. His Holiness was gracious enough and agreed to deliver Kalachakra in Leh. Thus, another milestone was crossed in September 1976, when The Dalai Lama paid a holy visit and delivered the rare and auspicious Kalachakra (Wheel of Time) initiation at Choglamsar in Leh. The teachings of the Kalachakra Tantra are said to have come from the historical Buddha Shakyamuni himself.

The Dalai Lama traveled by road from Dharamshala and the State Government headed by Chief Minister Sheikh Abdullah extended all courtesies and facilities accorded to a state guest. He also hosted a reception in honour of His Holiness in Srinagar. Tibetan Muslims in large numbers had gathered in Srinagar and had the opportunity to pay their respects. Some could not control their emotions and were seen crying. From Srinagar His Holiness's journey to Leh resumed. He stopped at Drass and Kargil where the local people accorded him a very warm reception.

The Dalai Lama delivered the Kalachakra teachings at *Zhive-Tsal* near Leh in September 1976, which was attended by over 50,000 – an unprecedented gathering in Ladakh's history. People from across Ladakh, from the neighboring areas of Himachal Pradesh and rest of India attended the teachings. Since Ladakh had only recently been opened to foreigners and a number of international visitors also attended the teaching. District administration headed by Mr. M. Rehman, IAS sought the assistance of the defence forces and the IAF helicopters showered flower petals at the teaching site. It was a very pleasing moment.

According to Sonam Gyaltsan it was during the teaching that General Morlin who was the then General Officer Commanding (GOC) in Ladakh arrived at the teaching site. He sought to meet the Dalai Lama urgently and later he was seen whispering something to the Dalai Lama. It was revealed that the General had informed the Dalai Lama about the death of Chairman Mao Zedung, the founder of the People's Republic of China who died on September 9, 1976. Later the Dalai Lama said that although he committed cruelty and injustice against his people but personally, he does not carry hatred against him. Instead, he impressed upon all to develop compassion.

It rained persistently throughout the teachings, but the masses of gathered devotees were undeterred and remained steadfast until the end. The Dalai Lama spoke publicly about how moved he was by the audience's fortitude and unwavering devotion. On behalf of the people of Ladakh

Bakula Rinpoche made sacred mandala offering to the Dalai Lama for his long-life. Since his exile in India, the 14th Dalai Lama has given the precious Kalachakra initiations 34 times, the last one having been delivered at Bodh Gaya in year 2016 touching hundreds of thousands of eager participants from across India, and the world. In July 1988, His Holiness delivered his 12th Kalachakra teachings in Zanskar and gave a second time in Leh in July 2014, which was attended by over 1,50,000 people.

The LBA and the LGA, supported generously by the people of Ladakh, constructed a magnificent *Photang* (palace or residence) for the Dalai Lama at Choglamsar, near Leh which was appropriately named *Zhive-Tsal* or Peace Garden. It is a source of joy and deep satisfaction for Ladakhis that he continues to visit Ladakh during the summer months, and travels to various parts of our region. The 14th Dalai Lama has always emphasised on the need for interfaith dialogue and communal harmony in the world. In Ladakh Buddhists and Muslims have been living in peace and harmony for centuries and the Dalai Lama applauded this on many occasions. During his visit to Leh in 1994, His Holiness inaugurated the newly built Imam Bara in Leh town. This was a unique occasion. According to Ashraf Ali Barcha, President, Anjuman Imamia, Leh, this gesture was appreciated worldwide and sent a strong message for religious harmony and peaceful coexistence. The Dalai Lama would also occasionally visit the *Idgah* for lunch hosted by the Anjuman Moinul Islam, Leh.

Tackling Caste Discrimination in Ladakh

Sometime in mid-1980s, during a visit of the 14th Dalai Lama to Leh, a group of people considered as 'low caste' in Ladakh approached him and complained to him about the discrimination they faced in Ladakhi society. Blacksmith and musicians, they said, were maltreated and discriminated against in all spheres of life. Marriage was impossible outside their social group and they were routinely discriminated against and treated shabbily. People would not even share food or utensils with them at social gatherings and they were always seated separately. Children from such groups, they said, were also barred from becoming monks in the monasteries, despite their sincere devotion to Buddhism. Such caste discrimination in the old society in Ladakh was prevalent in both Buddhist and Muslim communities.

Bakula Rinpoche was present on that occasion. He told the Dalai Lama that this regrettable aspect of the traditional social system was indeed still prevalent in Ladakhi society despite efforts by religious leaders to eradicate them. Rinpoche also informed the Dalai Lama that there were many other evil customs still practiced in Ladakh such as hunting wild animals, polyandry, excessive drinking of *chang* and other forms of alcohol, animal

The 14th Dalai Lama with Gergan Konchog Sonam, Bakula Rinpoche and Thiksey Rinpoche (1966)

The Dalai Lama with, Bakula Rinpoche and Mr. Sonam Targyes, liaison officer. Paljor la, His Holiness's assistant is also in the picture

sacrifice and so on. Since his return to Ladakh in 1940 from Lhasa, Rinpoche himself had been making sincere efforts to end such practices, but unfortunately as old habits die hard, his work was far from complete.

The Dalai Lama was perturbed to hear this. He called it unethical, against the Buddhist teachings and explained to the people there the irrationality of such behavior, which undermines the wellbeing of others and therefore own self too. He said he was particularly shocked by such behaviour amongst people who are followers of Lord Buddha. He told the gathering that such treatment of others based only on one's birth was unacceptable. One of the petitioners said that he was a musician by trade and that musicians are considered low caste in Ladakh. The Dalai Lama was upset and wanted to do something. Then to the surprise of everyone present, and in his own characteristic way, he said that he would like to visit his home. This was unthinkable. People could not believe their ears and shifted uncomfortably in their places, not knowing how they should respond. The Dalai Lama decided to go to this musician's home that very day itself. And so, he did, accompanied by Bakula Rinpoche. The two high lamas went to that house where they accepted tea and food with the musician and his family.

The Dalai Lama, in the presence of a large gathering of local media who had come along, played the musician's drums with his own holy hands. He wanted to demonstrate through his actions that there was nothing 'unclean'

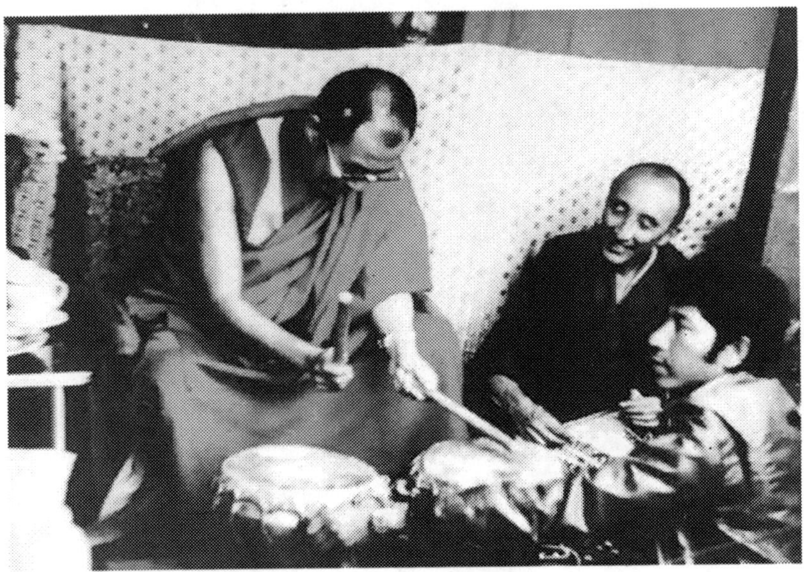

H.H. The Dalai Lama plays a musical instrument in Leh. Bakula Rinpoche is seated on his left (Photo by Vijay Kranti)

about such people, and convince the audience gathered there to do away with such irrational and negative notions. The Dalai Lama also paid tribute to the traditionally castigated professions of musicians and blacksmiths, accepted food and tea served by them and asked people to abandon such unnecessary prejudices against their own fellow people. Since that time there has been a considerable shift in social attitudes in Ladakh, although some remnants of the old thinking still remain. I was very fortunate to have witnessed this episode as a young boy which changed the face of Ladakh in so many ways.

Pethub Monastery: A Major Renovation

The Pethub monastery, which is perched on a hillock overlooking the Indus river, near Leh, has a long and illustrious history. It was founded in the 11th century. The Buddhist saint and translator Lotsawa Rinchen Zangpo (958–1055), is believed to have visited the site, and it is said that he predicted that a monastery called Pethub Gonpa (meaning an exemplary monastery) would come up at this site and would help in propagating the Lord Buddha's sublime teachings in the region. Amidst all of his other official duties Bakula Rinpoche

Bakula Rinpoche with his Manager (Chagzot) Gelong Thupstan Targyes

never forgot his personal duties as the head lama of his own home monastery – *Pethub Galden Targyesling* or Pethub Monastery and its subsidiaries. He always kept a watchful eye on it and ensured that it did not suffer any undue neglect. During this phase his manager for over fifty years, Gelong Thupstan Targyes *(Gelong Shakspo)* who was Rinpoche's *Chagzot* (manager) for over fifty years, (from 1962 till 2014) shouldered all the responsibilities.

In 1990, Bakula Rinpoche commissioned a new twenty-one feet gold-gilded bronze statue of the Buddha from the finest craftsmen in Nepal, which was installed in Pethub's main assembly hall. It contained priceless holy relics and these included a statue of the Buddha which had belonged to the 13th Dalai Lama, as well as holy hair relics of the two main tutors of the 14th Dalai Lama given to Rinpoche by HH the 14th Dalai Lama himself. These and other revered objects were sealed within the statue in accordance with tradition. According to Rinpoche, he had various motivations for commissioning this statue. First and foremost, he believed that it would help prevent war and natural calamities and would bring good fortune to all sentient beings in general and the people of Ladakh in particular. Secondly, it would help ensure that Ladakh received timely rainfall and snowfall, so that its people could be contented and prosperous; and thirdly it would help ensure that the monasteries of Ladakh and the Buddha Dharma more generally thrive, bringing peace and harmony to the world.

In the 1980s, unfortunately, some cracks appeared in some of its mud and stone structure, the causes of which could not be established with certainty. It is possible that it had something to do with the monastery's close proximity to the new airport. Heavy explosives had been used at the nearby hillock to level the ground so as to extend the runway for use by fighter jets and heavy military aircraft and many believed this to be the cause. Such activities, so close to this ancient monastery, shook its foundations, both physically and metaphorically. However, government agencies brought in to inspect the damage, would not accept liability. The experts instead suggested that the damage was more likely to have been caused by rainfall, which had been scarce in former times, but had increased noticeably in recent years due to climate change. These changing weather patterns had resulted in the shifting of the foundation rocks on which the monastery stands. It gradually became clear that these cracks were widening and that something had to be done to address the problem. Soon portion of it became literally unsafe for the monks to live in any longer and they started shifting to alternative accommodations. The monastery's annual festival – the *Pethub Gustor* – attended by thousands of people when traditionally the monks would perform a masked dance in the monastery's main courtyard, had to be shifted to a new location below the monastery since the main building was now considered unsafe. Experts were consulted and they informed Rinpoche that it was a serious problem and to restore and rebuild the necessary parts of this large and historic structure would be expensive. At that time, it was estimated that some two crores (Twenty million) Indian rupees were required. Even for a person of Rinpoche's standing and wide connections, to raise such a sum would be an uphill task.

Given their potential responsibility for the damage, Rinpoche first approached the Ministry of Defence for funding, but was rebuffed. Other government departments were also unresponsive. So, eventually, Rinpoche approached the Planning Commission of India (now called *Niti Ayog*) for a financial grant on the grounds that this was not only a historic monastery but also a very important place for the local community. At that time Mr. K.C. Pant whose father Mr. G.B. Pant, former Home Minister of India in Pandit Nehru's cabinet, was the Vice-Chairman of the Commission. Fortunately, Mr. Pant was magnanimous in his response and released the required funds in their entirety so that the work could start immediately. The rebuilding and restoration work were supervised by engineers of the National Hydroelectric Power Corporation (NHPC), and this difficult work was completed in a record six-month period.

After this, the annual *Gustor Festival* – held on the eve of the Ladakhi New Year on the 27–29th of the 11th month of lunar calendar – could resume once again in its old location. The new building below the monastery that

Pethub Galden Targaisling Monastery, Leh, Ladakh

had been constructed to hold the Gustor when the old assembly hall was faltering, was now converted into a temple dedicated to the Sixteen Arhats. Rinpoche had brought exclusive ceramic statues of the Sixteen Arhats from Beijing, China which were installed there. A school for young monks was also started there. This temple was formally inaugurated in July 2001 by the 17th Gyalwa Karmapa Ugyen Trinley Dorje, during his first ever visit to Ladakh.

Similarly, in the past, monks from Pethub, like Bakula Rinpoche himself, undertook their monastic studies at Drepung Monastery in Lhasa, which had its own Khangtsen (hostel). This housed monks from all over Ladakh who traveled to Lhasa to gain Buddhist education. After the 1959 influx of Tibetan refugees to India, many major Tibetan monasteries were re-established in exile. In particular, Drepung Loseling Monastery was relocated to Mundgod in Karnataka, South India and Rinpoche decided to re-open Pethub Khangtsen, a hostel facility for monks from Ladakh at Mundgod. Over the years many monks from Ladakh and other remote Himalayan regions have been able to successfully pursue their studies and return to their respective monasteries to serve the communities, thus reinvigorating Himalayan Buddhist tradition in many ways. Rinpoche also sent young monks from his monasteries in Ladakh to other monastic institutions such as Sera, Gyume, Namgyal and other Monasteries.

Twenty-one

Working with Successive Kashmiri Regimes

In Jammu and Kashmir despite some positive developments on the political front, things were not moving as smoothly as Rinpoche had hoped. His extensive visits to different parts of Ladakh and his interaction with the local people brought home to him the reality that the future of Ladakh, under the current dispensation, was neither safe nor secure. So, while the rest of India seemed to be advancing along the path of democracy and freedom, the people of Ladakh still faced deeply-entrenched and institutionalized discrimination and marginalization.

In October 1963, under the Kamaraj plan, Bakshi Ghulam Mohammed, despite not belonging to the Congress Party, was persuaded by Prime Minister Nehru to resign and thus eleven years of Bakshi's tenure came to an end. The former speaker Shams-ud-Din Kath, a Bakshi loyalist took over as Prime Minister and, in this way, Bakshi was able to retain indirect power even after relinquishing his office. Rinpoche this time was inducted as a minister of cabinet rank in the new government. But this lasted only a few months and the government had to resign following rumours of the mysterious disappearance of the holy relic of the Prophet Mohammed – a hair from his beard known as the *moo-e-muqadas* – from the Hazratbal mosque in Srinagar. Trouble immediately flared in Srinagar, and on December 27, 1963 tens of thousands of angry protestors took to the streets, catching the government unaware while it was operating from its winter capital in Jammu.

Narrating the incident Rinpoche told me that it was explosive situation and poised to run out of control. No minister was prepared to go to Srinagar fearing strong public protest and anger. In this hour of crises Rinpoche's response as a minister was very clear and decisive. By now he was a prominent face of the valley. In an effort to defuse the tension and to reassure the people of the Valley, Rinpoche offered the Chief Minister to visit Srinagar to meet the agitators as a representative of the government. The visit was approved and he proceeded to Srinagar. On his way to Srinagar, Rinpoche was stopped several times by demonstrators, but ultimately, he was able to make his way through. In Srinagar, he held several rounds of talks with the leaders of the agitation, and on behalf of the state government assured the people that every possible effort would be made to find the missing holy relic.

More discussions followed and with the intervention of Lal Bahadur Shastri who visited Hazratbal Dargah in Srinagar in 1964, the holy relics were soon found and after being publicly verified by Mirak Shah Sahib as genuine, the relics were re-enshrined in their rightful place. This restored peace to the Valley.[1]

In February 1964, Shams-ud-Din was replaced as the Prime Minister by Mr. G.M. Sadiq, who on January 26, 1965, announced the formation of Indian National Congress Party in J&K. The Congress Party and National Conference were now working together to run the government. It was during the Sadiq regime that the designation of Prime Minister (known as the Wazir-e-Azam) was changed to that of Chief Minister, and the designation Sadar e Riyasat to Governor. On July 26, 1964, Bakula Rinpoche was inducted into the Council of Ministers as a Minister of State for Ladakh Affairs, Health and Local Self-Government. But subsequently in a cabinet reshuffle, he was denied the Ladakh Affairs portfolio. Later, Mr. Sadiq tried to make amends by creating a Ladakh Development Board headed by Rinpoche with Agha Ibrahim Shah, the member of legislative council (MLC) from Kargil, as its vice chairman. However, the Board only had an advisory role and its task was to advise the government on policies for good governance and the speedy development of Ladakh. It lacked any real authority or funds. As a result, it proved rather ineffective, and in time came to be seen as another unwelcome interference by the Kashmiri leadership.

The half-hearted efforts on the part of the government, to bring infrastructural development to the region were hardly commensurate with the growing needs and aspirations of the people of Ladakh. So, to put it mildly, Rinpoche's relations with the state government throughout this period continued to be strained. The animosity of the Kashmiri leadership towards Bakula Rinpoche came out in the open again in 1967, when Rinpoche's state assembly seat became vacant on his assumption of the newly-created seat for Ladakh in the Lok Sabha (the lower house of the national parliament). Bakula Rinpoche had nominated his former assistant Sonam Wangyal to contest the old seat in his place, but Rinpoche's opponents in Srinagar were intent on using the election to sow division among the Ladakhis. A splinter group calling itself Congress-B sprang up in Leh and announced that they were contesting the seat. It was obvious that this splinter group was receiving lavish patronage from the Kashmiri establishment. Although, in the end Sonam Wangyal managed to win the election nevertheless, defeating Kushok Thiksey Khanpo Rinpoche, the episode was interpreted by many as yet another failed attempt by Srinagar to undermine Rinpoche's authority in Ladakh.

The neglect and discrimination experienced by Ladakh at the hands of the state government of J&K since independence meant that the people of Ladakh were still, by and large, without any of the benefits of modern development, whether in the fields of healthcare, education, or economic opportunity. The vast majority of the region was without electric power and there was no industry worth the name. In addition, people had to endure the long and harsh six-month winters without adequate supplies of essentials coming in from outside, as the Srinagar-Leh was closed throughout this period. The only sources of economic opportunity available to the people were the Indian defence establishments which not only recruited young Ladakhis into army and paramilitary forces but also generated small sources of income for the people in the surrounding areas, since the military bases became markets for their surplus goods such as vegetables and fruits.

NOTES

1. *Hanging by The Relic* by R.S. Gull.

Twenty-two

Sino-India War and the Formation of Ladakh Scouts

Although, on the political stage, there was a lot of bonhomie between India and China in the 1950s, a deep undercurrent was brewing within the Chinese communist regime. The Chinese had already firmly established their foothold in Tibet, with the last presence of Tibetan self-government coming to an end in year 1959, when the Dalai Lama fled to India along with around 1,00,000 refugees. The situation on the border was changing rapidly. Earlier, despite Rinpoche's expressing his apprehensions in the strongest terms, India was caught unaware when the Chinese first invaded Tibet. Now India faced another problem, this time on its own border.

Coming back to the border situation, the inevitable happened in October 1962, when China's Red Army launched a sudden and a massive attack on Indian Posts in NEFA and in Ladakh. The People's Liberation Army (PLA) moved deep into Indian territory, occupying thousands of square kilometers. This aggression and the humiliating defeat, exposed India's weakness and vulnerability. Prime Minister Nehru perhaps realized his own serious errors of judgment in assessing the situation in Tibet and in the Chinese attitudes towards India. He may also have remembered the cautionary alarm bells that Bakula Rinpoche had sounded after his return from Lhasa in year 1956, and also during their subsequent meetings.

Although the Indian army was lacking neither in valour nor morale, it was poorly trained, ill-equipped and lacked infrastructure and good supply-lines. It was easily overwhelmed by the Chinese PLA, which was a battle-hardened fighting force. Compounding the hardship of the Indian soldiers was the high altitude and harsh wintery conditions in the Himalaya which the Indian soldiers found very hard to endure. Many young Ladakhis who had volunteered to serve the nation in this hour of distress, also bore the brunt of the Chinese assault. For ordinary Ladakhis, this period was the most traumatic and anxious time of our history. People knew about the destruction going on in Tibet since the 1959 uprising, and the subsequent Chinese atrocities there. The mere thought of a similar situation in Ladakh filled the people with terror.

After a month of violent aggression, the Chinese thankfully called a ceasefire on November 20, 1962. Many soldiers had suffered serious injuries and were left with physical handicaps. There were heart-rending scenes and the helplessness of our soldiers was palpable. The Indo-China war has gone down in history to be one of India's most disastrous defeats. The battle of Rezang La was the only bright spot for India in the 1962 war with the communist China and for his unfaltering courage, leadership and exemplary devotion to duty, Major Shaitan Singh was awarded Param Vir Chakra, the highest wartime gallantry award.

Rinpoche also recounted this deeply distressing time of desperation. To oversee the situation and to assess the needs of the soldiers there, Rinpoche paid several visits to Chushul, the most active front of the Chinese assault. The people of Ladakh, though poor and ill-equipped had come out collectively in support of the Indian soldiers, and many joined the Indian Army. Women prepared food and volunteered by carrying loads and in road-building and so on.

Major Shaitan Singh, PVC

Bakula Rinpoche greeting Prime Minister Nehru

An enthusiastic crowd welcomes Prime Minister Nehru in Leh (1963)
(Photo by P.N. Sharma)

Bakula Rinpoche, Pandit Jawaharlal Nehru, Prime Minister of India with other dignitaries and officers of the Indian Army at Chushul, Ladakh (1963)

Rinpoche addressing the people in Leh Town. Prime Minister Nehru standing next to him (1963)

On a lighter note, Rinpoche had an interesting memory from this period. Once, he was flying from Srinagar to Chushul in an Indian Air Force Dakota plane. With him was his assistant at the time, a Kashmiri gentleman named D.N. Moza. Rinpoche was seated in the cockpit while Moza was seated in the back of the plane which had no window. Unfortunately, due to bad weather conditions in the Chushul area the plane could not land and had to return to Srinagar. Mr. Moza who had never visited Ladakh before, was, therefore, unaware of the topography. After some time, the plane landed at Srinagar. Mr. Moza, not knowing any better, said to Rinpoche: "How nice Chushul is just like Srinagar". Rinpoche was amused, and they had a hearty laugh.

Prime Minister Nehru, accompanied by Mr. Y.B. Chavan visited Leh in the summer of 1963. Bakula Rinpoche received the dignitaries at Leh airport and later accompanied them to the sensitive border regions. Later, at a public meeting at Leh's Lal Chowk, Pandit Nehru assured the people of the government's full support for the region's security and development. Rinpoche also addressed the gathering and put-forward several crucial demands including sending of a fact-finding team to assess the development needs of the region and special administrators for Ladakh appointed by the central government. I was only around eight years old at that time, and was among the fortunate group of school children who received sweets from Pandit Nehru after the meeting.

In March 1968, Bakula Rinpoche, who was then a Member of Parliament, warned the Indian government about the vulnerability of Ladakh. In a statement in the Lok Sabha on March 29, 1968, he said: "Pakistan, in collaboration with China, wants to endanger our independence. During the Indo-Pak war of 1965, the Indian army had twice cleared the hills (Kargil area) from Pakistani forces, but later, following the Tashkent Agreement, our army had to leave those strategic hills. I am not criticizing the Tashkent Agreement, but I would like to warn the Government of the serious consequences of our decision to leave those hills. Pakistan can destroy our airport in minutes. Why does the government leave these places of strategic importance to the defense of our country, unattended?"

Formation of Ladakh Scouts Regiment

In 1948, following an attack from the Pakistani Tribals, the Nubra Guards had been raised from local Ladakhi warriors to petrol India's mountainous border in the Ladakh region. In 1952, the Nubra Guards were merged with the Jammu & Kashmir Militia. In 1963, following the Sino-Indian War, Ladakh Scouts was formed by spinning off the 7th and 14th Battalions of the J&K Militia and it became an infantry regiment of the Indian Army. Primary role of this new unit was to do reconnaissance and respond along the high-altitude border regions. Sheer grit and courage and heroisms exhibited by the Ladakh Scouts have become the subject matter of legend. Valiant young men of the Ladakh Scouts also fought against the Chinese aggression in 1962 and all the subsequent wars with Pakistan. They are a highly decorated regiment of the Indian Army. Raja Kunzang Namgyal, the erstwhile ruler of Ladakh was commissioned into the Indian Army and joined the Ladakh Scouts. Col. Chewing Rinchen, a native of Nubra who led the 'Nubra Guards' and was twice decorated with the Maha Vir Chakra for heroism, was among this fine band of soldiers. Subedar Tsering Motup, who won the Ashok Chakra and Subedar Sonam Stobdan, MVC are among the many highly-decorated soldiers of this regiment.

After the border conflict with Pakistan in 1971, there was a long period of relative peace between the two hostile neighbors. Pakistani forces had made various attempts to infiltrate the Ladakh region in the past, and there was a lingering apprehension that such a scenario could emerge again. In 1997, Pakistan commenced deliberate shelling of the Kargil sector, targeting the Srinagar-Leh road. Rinpoche was in Mongolia when he learnt about the indiscriminate and unprovoked shelling of civilian areas in Kargil town by the Pakistan Army, and he was very distressed. There had been casualties, a great loss of property and feelings of panic and insecurity were spreading among the people. Rinpoche immediately wrote to the Mr. Inder Kumar Gujral, Prime Minister of India on October 3, 1997, requesting to send immediate relief and assistance to the people of Kargil, and to assure them that they would be compensated for the loss of lives and property. The Prime Minister replied and also informed Rinpoche that one crore rupee (ten million) were released from the prime minister's relief fund, which was earmarked for immediate assistance to the families of those killed or injured, and for the reconstruction of damaged houses. (**Annexure 7**).

In 1999, Pakistan once again targeted Kargil, Ladakh. This was both a shock and a big embarrassment for the BJP-led National Democratic Alliance (NDA) government of Prime Minister Vajpayee, since the attack came soon after the Prime Minister's much-publicized 'Bus-diplomacy'. This time their target was the National Highway (NH-1) which links Srinagar with Leh and passes through Kargil. They had clandestinely occupied some strategic and vintage hills which remained unnoticed by the Indian security establishment. Had the Pakistani forces been successful in strengthening their position, the Srinagar-Leh Highway would have faced a barrage of Pakistani artillery and could easily have been blocked. This would have cut the supply-lines of all Indian border posts, including the Siachen Glacier which the Pakistanis, seemingly planned to annex. However, when the

Rinpoche with the officers and jawans at Ladakh Scouts Regimental Centre (LSRC), Phyang, Leh

Col. Chewang Rinchen, MVC-Bar, SM

Naib Subedar Chhering Mutup, AC

Col. Sonam Wangchuk, MVC

Brig. Rinchen Dorje, VSM

Indian army realised what was afoot, its response, code-named Operation Vijay, was decisive. There was a massive mobilization of troops, including the Ladakh Scouts, and air power was also pressed into service. In the last week of July 1999, the Indian Army launched its final assault and defeated the enemy. They were able to regain control of all the territory south and east of the Line of Control (LoC). Fighting ceased on July 26, 1999, and that day has ever since been designated Kargil Vijay Diwas (Kargil Victory Day) in India. Several Ladakhi soldiers were decorated with gallantry awards for their role in this conflict. For his exceptional bravery and gallantry during 1999 Kargil War, a young Ladakhi officer, Major Sonam Wangchuk was awarded the Maha Vir Chakra. Local civilians also volunteered to help in the war effort.

In a letter to General V.P. Malik, Chief of Army Staff on July 20, 1999, Rinpoche highlighted the courage and valour of Ladakh Scouts seen during the conflict and their indispensable role in securing victory for India. In his reply, General Malik praised the saga of bravery and comradery of Ladakh Scout jawans and recommended that the Ladakh Scouts be upgraded to a regular regiment of the Indian Army. (**Annexure 8**)

Pride of its homeland, the Ladakh Scouts was made an Indian Army Regiment in year 2000. In year 2013, they celebrated their golden jubilee, fifty glorious years in service of the nation. On August 21, 2017, Mr. Ram Nath Kovind, President of India, visited Leh and presented the President's Colours to Ladakh Scouts Regimental Centre. The President complimented the Ladakh Scouts personnel for their outstanding performance in all spheres and their exceptional valour and sacrifice while upholding the sovereignty of the nation. Col. Rinchen Dorje, VSM, a son of the soil, was until recently the Commandant of the Ladakh Scouts Regimental Centre. He has since become a Brigadier in the Indian Army, the first Ladakhi to achieve this feat.

Twenty-three

Call for Ladakh to be Made a Union Territory

To return to the political milieu of the late 1950s and early 1960s, it was becoming increasingly clear to Bakula Rinpoche that the Kashmiri leadership were doing everything they could – to obstruct his efforts to advance Ladakhi interests, especially on the developmental and political fronts. They put endless bureaucratic hurdles in his way, and by fomenting communal, factional and sectarian divisions in Ladakh itself, they tried to undermine his authority. In light of this, Rinpoche gradually came to the conclusion that he should call for Ladakh to be brought under direct central government rule as a Union Territory, along the lines of the North Eastern Frontier Area (NEFA), present day state of Arunachal Pradesh. This, however, was not a new idea. In fact, it had been floated intermittently ever since Indian independence.

Initially Bakula Rinpoche had been cautious about raising a demand for UT status formally. He knew that this was likely to antagonize the political leadership in Srinagar, and he did not want to alienate any potential allies without first exhausting all other options. However, by the mid-1960s, his views had changed. Faced with repeated frustrations and disappointments, Rinpoche came to believe that breaking away from J&K was the only way to achieve meaningful progress in his homeland. He therefore reiterated his demand for UT status for Ladakh which alone can ensure self-governance for the people of Ladakh.

In September 1964, Rinpoche met Lal Bahadur Shastri, who had succeeded Pandit Jawaharlal Nehru as Prime Minister of India, in New Delhi. He discussed the situation in Ladakh and warned him that frustration and

Public demonstration in Leh. Ladakh demanding Union Territory status (1970)

Rinpoche addressing the people. Also seen in picture Nawang Rigzin Jora, Thiksey Rinpoche and Thupstan Chhewang.

discontent were running high in Ladakh, and that public agitation could ignite at any time. He, therefore, urged the central government to take a greater interest in the affairs of the region. In his letter to the Prime Minister Shastri, he once again raised the issue of bringing Ladakh directly under the supervision of the central government administration. "The Buddhists of Ladakh, who can have a future only in association with India, have all along urged the Government of India to take this border district into its direct control. The late lamented Pandit Nehru assured us off and on that this would be done in the course of time and in the meantime responsible administrative officers for the district would be deputed from the Centre. This was undoubtedly a step in the right direction provided these officers were carefully selected which, I am sorry, does not seem to have been done in the case of the present Deputy Commissioner. Since the portfolio of Ladakh's ministry was taken away from me, things have been going from bad to worse. No work worth the name has since been taken up and different communities are at loggerheads and even the Buddhist community is sought to be split up into hostile factions.

I entered upon a political career and took up ministerial office not to satisfy any personal ambition but to serve my people and to strengthen the ties which bind our people with India. By giving me a portfolio other than that of Ladakh Affairs, I am effectively debarred from accomplishing either of these purposes. I am therefore seriously thinking of resigning as a minister and devoting myself as a private person to the sacred task of restoring peace and amity between the different communities, uniting them closer and closer to India, our cultural mother and the guarantor of our progress, prosperity and political rights."[1]

At a press conference in New Delhi on August 15, 1967, the twentieth anniversary of Indian independence, Bakula Rinpoche once again publicly raised the demand for UT status. He said: "If I am asking for the Central Administration for Ladakh, it is for the betterment of all Ladakhis. I am doing so to strengthen the country's defense, while those who ignore Ladakh are doing a great harm to the security of the nation."

Unfortunately, due to various compulsions, no government in New Delhi ever considered this long-standing demand of the people to declare Ladakh as a Union Territory seriously. But in Ladakh, this demand would flare up again whenever there was a confrontation or disagreement with the State Government of Jammu and Kashmir. The struggle of the people of Ladakh for Union Territory status, therefore, continued unabated.

NOTES

1. Ladakh through the Ages by Shridhar Kaul and H.N. Kaul. p. 191.

PART III

A Decade in the Parliament

(Lok Sabha 1967–77)

Twenty-four

In Parliament, Learning the Ropes in the National Capital

The Jammu and Kashmir state government were indifferent to the plight of Ladakh. The region had only two representatives in the state assembly and could easily be ignored. Moreover, Ladakh had no voice whatsoever in the national parliament in Delhi. Ladakh was then a part of Gandarbal Constituency in the Kashmir valley and no MP had ever visited Ladakh. As a result, under the leadership of Bakula Rinpoche, demands for the creation of a separate parliamentary constituency for Ladakh in the Lok Sabha (the Lower House of the Indian Parliament) grew louder and louder. Numerous petitions were filed arguing that Ladakh's strategic importance, its distinct environmental, linguistic, cultural and ethnic character, justified a separate parliamentary seat. It was also argued that although Ladakh had a relatively small population, the region boasted two thirds of the State's total territory and was considered to be the largest district in the whole of India. Another crucial factor was that Ladakh used to remain cut off from the rest of the country for many months every year when the high-altitude Zojila pass which connected Leh to Srinagar was closed due to heavy snowfall. Rinpoche also argued that a separate parliamentary seat for Ladakh would help strengthen national integration and border security in this most sensitively strategic area, which had already been attacked by both China and Pakistan since Indian independence.

In the year 1967, a Delimitation Commission appointed by the central government acceded to these demands and recommended the creation of a separate seat for Ladakh in the Lok Sabha, with the constituency covering both Leh and Kargil. At this time, Rinpoche was already serving as a minister in the J&K government, so when the new Lok Sabha seat was created, the party leadership of the Indian National Congress, decided to field Bakula Rinpoche as their candidate.

In a country as diverse as India, the Congress Party served as a unifying force which represented the ideals of the constitution and the aspirations of the freedom movement from which it had been born. Rinpoche was a member of this organisation and remained with it throughout his political career. He represented Ladakh for two consecutive terms during the fourth and the fifth Lok Sabha. While in year 1967, his election had been unopposed, in year 1971, there was a rival candidate, namely Sonam Wangdus, a local Buddhist youth who enjoyed support and patronage from the J&K National Conference Party. The Kashmiri leadership was continuing with their divide-and-rule policy. Their strategy was two-fold. On the one hand, they sought to galvanise all the Muslim votes in the region, and, on the other, they sought to divide the Buddhist votes. Sonam Wangdus, though himself a Buddhist, was projected by the National Conference as a savior of Muslims. But the people of Ladakh were unconvinced, and Rinpoche won the election again by a comfortable margin.

Members of Fifth Lok Sabha (1972).
Rinpoche standing in the middle of the 4th row

Rinpoche's jump from the state-level political milieu of J&K, to India's national parliament was a big change, and a major step forward for the cause of Ladakh. Although his new role was less hectic on a day-to-day basis, his responsibility was now even greater. The people of Ladakh were putting all their hope in him to strike a better deal for the region and ensure better livelihoods and prospects for the people. He was initially put up at New Delhi's Kota House before moving to 26, Janpath, in the heart of Lutyens' Delhi, which henceforth would be his official residence for the next ten years. The proximity of this sprawling parliamentary complex to the corridors of power of the Indian nation, gave Rinpoche the opportunity to serve the people more effectively.

According to Rinpoche, the most striking aspect of this new position was his newfound ability to express himself freely. As a minister in J&K Rinpoche was bound by many protocols, restrictions and rules, whereas Members of Parliament are much freer and have direct access to the power centre. They can and do wield considerable power in their constituency. MPs hold the central government accountable by raising important questions with the union ministers on the floor of the parliament and they also play a crucial role in nation-building activities by participating in important debates. Becoming an MP also made Rinpoche eligible for a diplomatic passport, and it was with this that his role as a Buddhist leader across the world, especially in the regions of the Soviet Union, Mongolia, and East Asia began. Since this aspect of Rinpoche's career was a very important part of his legacy, it is a subject to which I will return to in detail, in Part-VI.

In Parliament, Rinpoche enjoyed visiting the Central Hall. It is formally used only for the address by the President to the joint sitting of both Houses. For the rest of the period, it is an exclusive coffee and talk shop for MPs, former MPs and Senior Journalists. Unlike today, the security situation in parliament in those days was relaxed, and as Rinpoche recalled, he could take guests for lunch inside Parliament House at the Railways canteen or the Coffee house. It was also here that Rinpoche developed his taste for coffee. Rinpoche also visited different parts of India and was charmed by India's diversity and the vibrancy of its cultural traditions.

As an MP, Rinpoche regularly raised issues in parliament concerning Ladakh. He was persistent and insistent in his demands for a better deal for the region which, he argued, had faced continued neglect at the hands of the state government of J&K. On March 29, 1968, while participating in a debate in the Lok Sabha on Jammu and Kashmir, Rinpoche called for the abrogation of Article 370 and the State's full integration with the Republic of India. He argued that the legitimate demands of its people, particularly those relating to Union Territory status, the recognition of Ladakh under the constitutional 'scheduled tribes', matters relating to regional autonomy, divisional status, as well as issues of the equitable allocation and distribution of funds, were being repeatedly and systematically ignored.

Interestingly, while the government of J&K received its plan funds from the central government on the basis of land area, the state government allocated funds to Ladakh on the basis of population. Such was the blatant neglect and discrimination meted out to Ladakh. This situation was forcing the peace-loving people of Ladakh onto the streets in protest. In this way, he continued to actively participate in various debates and speak on issues related to Ladakh. I place below, copies of some select speeches delivered by Rinpoche in the Lok Sabha drawing the attention of the Government towards issues related to Ladakh. (**Annexures 9, 10**)

In parliament, Rinpoche joined many other MPs raising their voices against the appeasement policy of successive central government administrations with regard to the state of J&K. The fact that the central government appeared to condone corruption and turn a blind eye to the serious electoral frauds being committed in the state only added fuel to the fire. Corrupt politicians in J&K were never held accountable for their misdemeanors.

A notable aspect of Rinpoche's multi-faceted personality was that during his long and distinguished political career, he maintained a close and cordial relationship with leaders of all the major political parties. His standing as a statesman transcended party lines. In year 1969, Rinpoche invited a team of MPs representing different political parties to Leh to assess the situation. Among them present was Mr. Atal Bihari Vajpayee, who later became Prime Minister of India and Mr. L.K. Advani, leader of BJP. Addressing a gathering in Jokhang Vihara in Leh, the headquarters of Ladakh Buddhist Association, Mr. Vajpayee supported the LBA agitation for UT status and called for accelerating the pace of development in Ladakh.

Frustrated by the fact that his calls for UT status had so far been ignored, Rinpoche sought recognition for Ladakh by advocating the renaming of the State of J&K. During a Lok Sabha debate on July 27, 1973, for example, Bakula Rinpoche publicly called for renaming the State as Jammu, Kashmir and Ladakh. After all, Ladakh constituted two thirds of the land area of the entire state. In response to Rinpoche's persistent demands in parliament, the central government finally agreed to send a team of MPs to make an on-the-spot assessment of the situation in Ladakh. This happened in 1976. In the same year, the Government of India also set up a commission headed by Justice P.B. Gajendragadkar, ex-Chief Justice of India, to look into regional imbalances in the state and to recommend measures for equitable development of its three regions in the future. In Leh, Bakula Rinpoche was made the chairman of the pleading committee set up to put the case before the Gajendragadkar commission, with Sheikh Jamaluddin acting as secretary and Sonam Wangyal, Ghulam Mohammed Barchapa, Sonam Dorje, Tsering Samphel, Nuruddin Zargar, Tashi Targais, Sajad Hussain, Sonam Phuntsog and Eshey Lhundup as its members.

A comprehensive and detailed four-part memorandum was prepared and submitted to the commission. Although the Gajendragadkar Commission accepted many of these points and also recommended change in the name of the State to "Jammu, Kashmir and Ladakh", at the end nothing very substantive emerged from this commission, since Kashmiri politicians were once again successful in maneuvering in such a way as to ensure that its recommendations were put into cold storage. In a press statement made in New Delhi on September 13, 1973, Bakula Rinpoche opposed Sheikh Abdullah's demand for restoration of pre-1953 position in the State of Jammu and Kashmir. Instead, he reiterated the demand of the Ladakhis for Central administration or (UT status) for their homeland. Going a step further, he suggested abrogation of Article 370 of the Constitution which provided a special status on the State of Jammu and Kashmir. He also suggested setting up a Development Council for Ladakh which should be headed by an administrator, which should enjoy legislative and administrative powers. In 1974, following the Indira-Sheikh Accord, Sheikh Abdullah was reinstated as the Chief Minister of J&K. After his release, Sheikh Abdullah once again became involved in the politics of the region. He perhaps realized that pursuing confrontational politics was futile and instead decided it was time to settle issues by a process of reconciliation and dialogue. He also visited Leh and Kargil, and in a public meeting announced that he would grant the long-awaited regional autonomy to the different regions of the state to ensure equal development for the three regions (i.e. Jammu, Kashmir and Ladakh). However, after assuming power, Sheikh Sahib conveniently forgot his promises once again.

While recounting a meeting, Rinpoche, then a sitting MP, told me that Sheikh Abdullah tried to rekindle their old relationship, and hinted that Rinpoche could be accommodated as a cabinet minister if he agreed to join the National Conference Party. Rinpoche told me that he politely declined the offer. This refusal served to further deepen the historic rift between Sheikh Sahib and Rinpoche and paved the way for frequent confrontations

Bakula Rinpoche with Sheikh Mohammed Abdullah at Samkar Gonpa, Leh (1975)

between the two in the coming years. Bakula Rinpoche represented Ladakh in Parliament for two terms from 1967-77. During these ten years he regularly raised issues of public concern and was able to achieve considerable success.

Opening of Ladakh for Tourism

Desperate to improve people's economic livelihoods, Bakula Rinpoche pleaded in Parliament for Ladakh to be opened up for tourism, especially for foreign tourists. Ladakh is an area of outstanding natural beauty and majestic views, and its cultural heritage, as a part of the Buddhist world, is rich and deep. The people are also known for their warmth and hospitality. Potential for tourism was obvious, and the people were very keen to access this extra source of potential income. But their aspirations were thwarted by the security concerns of the government which meant that the region remained closed to visitors. Eventually their efforts, along with Bakula Rinpoche's personal interventions on the matter with Prime Minister Indira Gandhi bore fruit. In year 1974, the border district of Ladakh was opened to tourists for the first time. Today, Ladakh has become a favorite destination for tourists and this generates much-needed employment and income for many families.

Bakula Rinpoche also played a crucial role in improving connectivity to Ladakh, particularly in advocating for commercial air services to the region. Before the introduction of commercial flights, the Indian Air Force operated military aircraft to transport people, especially during winters, when Ladakh remained cut off due to heavy snowfall. However, with the opening of Ladakh to tourism, there was a growing need for regular civilian air services.

As a Member of Parliament and later as a Member of the Minorities Commission, Rinpoche persistently raised this issue, drawing the government's attention to the importance of air connectivity for the people of Ladakh. His efforts bore fruit when, in 1978, the first commercial flight landed at Leh airport, marking a major milestone in the region's development. This initiative not only benefited the local population by ensuring year-round connectivity but also contributed significantly to the growth of tourism and economic development in Ladakh.

The high barren mountains, the pristine environment of crystal-clear lakes, turquoise-blue rivers, rare species of wildlife combined with age-old monasteries and villages, colourful local tribes and Buddhist culture made Ladakh a very attractive and even inspiring, place to visit. The tourism industry is now a major socio-economic sector. When Ladakh first opened for tourism in year 1974, as per the government records, there were 527 tourists – 500 foreign visitors and 27 domestic visitors. Now, almost 50 years later, the number of tourists has grown to 4.5 lakh (4,50,000) in eight months from January 1 to August 31, 2022.[1] Tourism generates revenue, provides both skilled and un-skilled employment opportunities in the hotel, guest-house and restaurant businesses, and creates demand for the agricultural sectors, and opportunities in transport, portering etc. Ladakh is now well-known as a popular destination for trekkers, mountaineers, bikers, rafting and all kinds of adventure sports enthusiasts. Besides ancient monasteries and Buddhist culture, it has the largest brackish lake in Asia, the longest glacier outside the polar region, and the world's highest space observatory. All of these world records add to its allure.

However, though tourism helped generate a lot of income, it also had its negative side. In an interview with the author, Rinpoche was deeply concerned with the negative impact of tourism on the youth of Ladakh. He pleaded with the people to protect their agricultural land as well as their rich cultural heritage. He emphasised on the need for environment and nature conservation and to stop unrestricted exploitation of natural resources. In nutshell his advice to the people was to ensure that tourism becomes a long term and a sustainable source of income for the people and not a cause of Ladakh's undoing.

Opening of All India Radio (AIR) in Leh and Kargil

Another issue of major concern was the total lack of information and communication network in the region. In early days, other than village-level loudspeakers provided by the ministry of Information and Broadcasting through its unit called Field Publicity Office which would broadcast news and some other programmes in Hindi and Urdu, there were no other means available for dissemination of information and communication facilities. Radio station was a far-cry in Ladakh. On the other hand, being in close proximity, both China and Pakistan would take advantage of this situation and broadcast propaganda material. Rinpoche was deeply concerned with this situation and therefore asked Government of India to set-up radio units in Leh and Kargil so that news and programmes could be produced in Ladakhi language. On several occasions he raised the matter in parliament that while Radio China and Pakistan continue with their propaganda, people living on the Indian side of the border as well as people elsewhere in Ladakh region, have no source of information and entertainment in their language.

On 4th May 1970, replying to Bakula Rinpoche in Parliament, Mr. I.K. Gujral, Minister for Information and Broadcasting stated in Parliament: "Work in connection with the setting up of a radio station at Leh is already in progress and when the station starts functioning, the programmes for listeners in Ladakh and its neighbourhood will be increased considerably".

(Annexure 11) Soon, a Ladakhi unit was set-up in AIR, New Delhi where a programme of one hour and twenty-five minutes duration consisting of news commentaries, talk, music, documentaries and newsreels were made. The program was sent by air to Srinagar on a daily basis and broadcast from there. Sonam Spalgyes worked as first producer of the program and Ms. Samten Dolma who was working in the Kashmir Service of AIR assisted him. This was a good beginning and helpful. Soon thereafter, a Ladakhi unit was opened in Radio Kashmir in Srinagar but Rinpoche was not satisfied.

At the end, Rinpoche's persistent efforts in the parliament paid off and the Government opened the Radio Kashmir (AIR) station in Leh. It was inaugurated by Sonam Wangyal, Minister of State for Planning and Co-operatives, Jammu and Kashmir on June 25, 1971. K.P. Shungloo was appointed as the first Station Director. This was a major achievement and establishment of AIR Leh benefitted the people of Ladakh tremendously, especially in learning modern agriculture farming and in the preservation of Ladakhi language, art and culture.

Promotion of Sowa Rigpa or Traditional Medicine

Tibetan medicine (Sowa Rigpa) or Amchi system of medicine has been a part of Buddhist science since time immemorial. It originated in Tibet and is also practiced in the Himalayan regions of India. Sowa Rigpa has similarities with Ayurveda. With the spread of Buddhism, it also became widely popular in many other countries such as Mongolia, Bhutan, Nepal, Russia etc. In Ladakh, Sowa Rigpa has long served as the only formal medical system. Modern medical science was non-existent in Ladakh in pre-independence time and people were dependent only on the Amchi system of medicine.

According to Amchi Rigzin Wangtak, who was the President of Ladakh Amchi Sabha from 2003-2006, it was in year 1970, that Bakula Rinpoche took the initiative in providing a formal structure to this ancient system of medicine in Ladakh. Along with some prominent local Amchis, Bakula Rinpoche set-out to establish a society in Leh which was called *'Ladakh Amchi Sabha'*. Bakula Rinpoche was its Founding-President and Amchi Tsewang Namgyal was chosen as Secretary. In 1972 'Ladakh Amchi Sabha' was registered as a Society which incidentally became the first registered society in Ladakh.

In year 1976, Dr. Karan Singh, Union Health Minister for Health and an old friend of Bakula Rinpoche, visited Ladakh. During the visit Rinpoche also discussed with Dr. Karan Singh the need for strengthening Amchi system of medicine and extending government patronage to it. This meeting resulted in the Ministry of Health sanctioning a monthly remuneration to all the registered Amchis of Ladakh. A post of Amchi Research Officer was also created and Gyurmed Namgyal was appointed as Research Officer at Leh. Ladakh Amchi Sabha also received a piece of land to establish a Centre. On 10th September 2009, Government of India approved the Indian Medicine Central Council (Amendment) Bill, 2009, which gave official recognition to 'Sowa Rigpa' making India the fourth country after China, Bhutan and Mongolia to do so.

In November 2019, Government of India approved the establishment of the 'National Institute of Sowa-Rigpa' (NISR) in Leh, Ladakh as an autonomous organization under the Ministry of Ayush, Government of India. The Institute is expected to provide opportunities for students of Sowa-Rigpa not only from India but also from other countries. NISR, Leh is currently headed by Dr. Padma Gurmet. The Government's objective is to establish NISR as an apex institute for Sowa Rigpa with aim of bringing a valid and useful synergy between traditional wisdom of Sowa Rigpa and modern science and also to promote inter disciplinary research and education of Sowa Rigpa. It must, however, be said that the establishment of NISR at Leh, is the culmination of the efforts made by the Ladakh Amchi Sabha in 1972 to promote Sowa Rigpa. Amchi system of medicine or Sowa Rigpa also became widely popular throughout India thanks mainly due to the work done by Men-tsee-khang or the Tibetan Medical and Astro Science Institute, Dharamshala.

Meeting Foreign Dignitaries

A major development stemming from Rinpoche's period in parliament was his exposure to various foreign dignitaries in the Indian capital. It was during his tenure as an MP that he first met the Buddhist leaders of Japan, Mongolia, USSR and other South Asian countries. The connections which were forged during this period, paved the way for the historic cooperation of later years. In 1973, Prime Minister Indira Gandhi invited Rinpoche to an official banquet being hosted in honour of Mongolia's Communist leader, Prime Minister Yumjaagiin Tsedenbal who was on a state visit to India.

This was also the period of the Vietnam War and Rinpoche expressed his deep concern for the suffering of the people of Vietnam. This was an issue Rinpoche often raised at that time. He made several interventions in parliament pleading for an early end to the war. And after the war he himself visited Vietnam, Laos and Cambodia as a guest of the communist regimes that had taken control in those countries.

NOTES

1. Source: *Official website of LAHDC*, Leh.

Twenty-five

A Voice for the Voiceless. Raising the Tibet Issue

Having himself lived for so many years in Tibet, and being intimately familiar with the tragic plight of the Tibetan people and their culture and sacred religious traditions, Bakula Rinpoche related to their hardships very personally and made every possible effort to help the community in exile whenever he could. From the very beginning Rinpoche was closely associated with the resettlement of Tibetan refugees in India. He travelled to Dharamshala for regular consultations with the 14th Dalai Lama and his administration.

The issue of Tibet – the exile of some 100,000 Tibetan refugees in India and the destruction and suppression of so much of its traditional culture – was something that pained Bakula Rinpoche deeply. In the Lok Sabha (Parliament) and outside, Rinpoche was open and outspoken advocate for the Tibetan cause and some Tibetan leaders even described him as the unofficial spokesman of the Tibetans. Rinpoche opposed the Indian government's Tibet policy of recognizing Chinese rule in Tibet. He often reiterated that to condone communist China's occupation and annexation of Tibet, was a serious mistake from the perspective of India's national interests. This had actually removed a crucial buffer zone between the two Asian giants. He also condemned China's rampant exploitation of Tibet's natural resources, which was seriously disturbing the fragile ecological balance in the entire region.

In 1954, Prime Minister Nehru had signed the *Panchsheel Agreement* with the Chinese Premier Chou Enlai to promote friendship and peace between the two Asian giants. However, as became clear in later developments, the agreement had not been made in good faith, since Communist China was harboring other designs. By 1959, the Chinese takeover of Tibet was all but complete, forcing the Dalai Lama to seek asylum in India. And with that, all semblance of Tibet's independence was lost.

As mentioned in an earlier chapter, after his official visit to Tibet in year 1955, Rinpoche had an hour-long discussion with Prime Minister Nehru in New Delhi, at which he had used all his diplomatic skills and powers of persuasion to convince Pandit Nehru of the imminent danger facing Tibet and thus, also India. He told Pandit Nehru in explicit terms that the situation in Tibet was going from bad to worse, and that as a result of Chinese intrusion, Tibetans were now feeling intensely vulnerable and insecure. Rinpoche pleaded with Pandit Nehru to intervene on Tibet's behalf and gave a detailed account of what was happening there and the growing Chinese dominance. But those were the days of *Hindi-Chini Bhai-Bhai* (India-China brotherhood) and as a result, Pandit Nehru failed to take Rinpoche's apprehensions seriously, and even advised him against such negative talk. He expressed his optimism about the future of Tibet and the future of Indo-Chinese relations. On this matter, history proved Pandit Nehru wrong. What happened in Tibet is well-documented. According to Rinpoche, Pandit Nehru must have felt a sense of guilt and remorse when he saw how things had turned out, since he had failed to act promptly and decisively when there was still some chance of making a difference. However, Rinpoche confided to me that there was no 'I told you so' kind of communication with Pandit Nehru or anything along that line.

With the full-scale Chinese occupation of Tibet, these discussions came to an abrupt end. After the Chinese occupation of Tibet in 1959, many Tibetans were re-settled in exile. On March 31, 1959, Rinpoche met with Tsewang Rabten Lukhangwa, the last Prime Minister of independent Tibet in New Delhi. They held a detailed discussion about the situation in Tibet and the condition of Tibetan refugees in India. Rinpoche often recalled this poignant moment with a deep sense of sadness. In their meeting, Lukhangwa impressed upon Rinpoche to do everything possible in the resettlement of Tibetan refugees in India, especially in Ladakh. He also called upon Rinpoche to work for saving Tibetan culture and heritage in India. Within Tibet, it was suffering a real beating under the Red Chinese forces and getting worse by the day, he said. He realised that Bakula Rinpoche, who was then a minister in the Government of Jammu and Kashmir, had considerable influence in the Government of India dispensation and enjoyed close proximity with Jawaharlal Nehru, Prime Minister of India. Rinpoche promised Lukhangwa to do everything humanly possible for saving the rich Tibetan culture and also in the resettlement of Tibetan refugees.

Rinpoche recalled that he was well acquainted with Dr. K.L. Shrimali who was Education Minister in the Union Council of Ministers in the (1955-60) and later the Vice-Chancellor of Banaras Hindu University and who had been introduced to him by Pandit Nehru himself. Later. Rinpoche would approach him regularly and resulted in the establishment of Central Institute of Higher Tibetan Studies (CIHTS), Sarnath, Namgyal Institute of Tibetology, Gangtok, Sikkim, Tibet House, New Delhi and several other institutions.

Shortly after his exile from Tibet, the 14th Dalai Lama established the Central Tibetan Administration (CTA), based on democratic principles which is also referred to as the Tibetan Government-in-Exile, based in Dharamshala, Himachal Pradesh. It has an elected legislature and an executive branch known as the Kashag or cabinet. In addition to political advocacy, the CTA administers a network of schools, social services and other cultural activities for the Tibetan exile communities in India. The 1960s and 1970s were very difficult times for the Tibetan refugees. There was very little money, and facilities were very basic. Many had left everything behind in Tibet, escaping to India with nothing but the clothes on their backs. Moreover, the Tibetans were not used to the climate of India and were particularly susceptible to various illnesses and diseases which are not found in Tibet. Employment for the refugees was scarce and in the early days many had no choice but to work as manual labourers building roads and so on. Many Tibetan perished in these early years. But gradually with assistance from the Government of India and various international aid organizations and donors, and thanks to their own entrepreneurial efforts, they were slowly able to build up their communities and even in recent decades, to prosper. Subsequently, many of the Tibetan monasteries in exile in India have now grown into large monastic universities, like they had been in Tibet, many of them housing several thousand monks.

People in India were by and large, very sympathetic to the plight of the Tibetans, and accepted their arrival without any rancour. The Government of India was also very generous in its assistance to the Tibetans, especially at the pitiable economic and social conditions in which many of its own citizens live. Responsibility for overseeing all this initial resettlement work was delegated to the Indian Government's Department of Rehabilitation, which fell under the Ministry of Home Affairs. Resettlement camps were set up at various states, but the largest were in the southern Indian state of Karnataka, where all rudimentary services were provided for the refugees, including schools for children, cultivable land, and essential though modest financial support. Sera, Drepung, Ganden Monasteries and their affiliates were all re-established in Karnataka.

Group photo of heads of different Buddhist traditions at Swarg Ashram, Dharamshala, Rinpoche seated on the extreme right (9th November, 1963)

Rinpoche with last Prime Minister of independent Tibet Mr. Tsewang Rabden Lukhangwa at Maha Bodhi Temple in New Delhi (31st March 1959)

Bakula Rinpoche with Gelek Rinpoche and Samdhong Rinpoche

On Rinpoche's personal initiative and support, several camps were also set-up in different parts of Ladakh and are still there today. For proper resettlement of Tibetan refugees in Ladakh and for better coordination, the Government of Jammu and Kashmir appointed a special officer designated as Assistant Commissioner (TR). Other steps were also taken to ensure survival of Tibetan Buddhist culture and its monastic tradition. Appreciating his valuable contributions towards the Tibetan cause, His Holiness the Dalai wrote "The assistance rendered to Tibetans by him during the difficult times is to be remembered with gratitude."

However, one positive development in this otherwise long drawn saga, was the spirited efforts made by the then Prime Minister of India Lal Bahadur Shastri. But unfortunately, destiny had other plans. As described in the book '*His Holiness The Dalai Lama, An illustrated biography*' by Mr. Tenzin Gyeche Tethong "In 1965, when His Holiness was visiting refugee settlements in South India,.war broke out between India and Pakistan. He was asked to not travel until the situation settled. While he waited, he received a message from W.D. Shakabpa, his representative in New Delhi, said that the Indian government was prepared to recognize the Tibetan government in exile and that he would receive a definite answer once the Prime Minister returned from Tashkent. Unfortunately, Prime Minister Shastri died suddenly (and according to some reports, mysteriously) in Tashkent on January 11, 1966. Once again, the matter of Tibet and its independence became a casualty."[1]

On February 15, 1968, referring to the Chinese occupation of Tibet, Rinpoche stated in the parliament that: "India's relations with China cannot improve until the issue of Tibet is settled. India has committed a blunder in its policy by allowing China a free hand in Tibet and for which we had to pay a very heavy price. Regrettably, India did little to help the Tibetans. India did not even try to raise the issue in the United Nations. An ancient Buddhist heritage was burnt and world-famous Buddhist monasteries were demolished by the communists in order to annihilate Buddhist culture. These have been mentioned in the report of the International Jurist's Commission."

According to Rinpoche, after taking refuge in India and in the early 1960s, H.H. The Dalai Lama had on several occasions pleaded with Prime Minister Nehru to raise the issue of Tibet in the United Nations. However, despite the staunch advocacy of Bakula Rinpoche and others in this regard, no successive government in Delhi has ever seriously considered changing its policy on Tibet. Rinpoche has always emphasized that India should take a firm stand and not succumb to Chinese diktat. In parliament he pleaded that relations between sovereign nations should be based on reciprocity which he felt was not the case in our relation with China. This kind of undue consideration and gesture only exposes India's meek disposition towards China. It is difficult to understand why our mandarins in New Delhi take such a submissive line.

With the initiative and efforts of Rinpoche, in both houses of Parliament (the Lok Sabha and Rajya Sabha), an all-party Indian Parliamentary Group for Tibet was formed. He worked closely with the Bureau of H.H. the Dalai Lama in New Delhi, Central Tibetan Administration in Dharamshala, Prof. Samdhong Rinpoche, Lodi Gyari and other Tibetan leaders, so that their positions could be faithfully represented in Parliament. This group did what it could to help the cause of Tibet.

Ironically, Buddhism in India got a new lease of life and later became popular all over the world, thanks largely to the presence of The Dalai Lama in India and through the monastic institutions which were established in different parts of the country. Monk scholars from these monasteries have made great strides in the spread of Buddhism or the Nalanda tradition in different parts of the world. These institutions helped Tibetan culture flourish outside Tibet, but inside Tibet it was another story.

In February 1979, on the eve of his China visit, Rinpoche wrote a letter to Mr. Atal Bihari Vajpayee, Union Minister for External Affairs conveying the sentiments of millions of people that India should not entertain any suggestion from the Chinese government for the return of the Dalai Lama to Tibet or China without his consent. In his reply dated February 27, 1979,

Mr. Vajpayee wrote: "During my conversation with the Chinese leaders when the question of the Dalai Lama and Tibetans was referred to, I informed them that we had made it clear that it was in deference to the Dalai Lama's spiritual position and in recognition to the needs of the Tibetan refugees, who voluntarily came to India, that asylum and resettlement facilities were extended by India. If the Dalai Lama and the Tibetans consider that the conditions are suitable for their return to the places of their origin, we, from our side, would not stand in their way to do so." (**Annexure 12**)

On one occasion Chotak Gyatso, a young Tibetan monk broke in and created a ruckus in the Lok Sabha, the Lower House of Indian Parliament while it was in session. He had been allowed into the Lok Sabha's visitor's gallery with a pass issued on the personal recommendation of Bakula Rinpoche, Member of Parliament. Thus, he was able to sneak in some pamphlets which he threw in the House and started shouting slogans demanding freedom for Tibet. This was considered a serious breach of security. Though his action helped secure some media attention, this also caused Rinpoche some trouble which fortunately did not take a very serious turn. The matter was resolved and no action taken.

Rinpoche's advocacy on behalf of Tibetans continued throughout his long career. When, much later, he was based in Mongolia as India's ambassador there, and started to gain a following in China, he actually visited Tibet (in 1992) and held in-depth discussions with Tibetan communist party officials there, as described in a later chapter. Bakula Rinpoche was unique in his ability to talk to all sides, winning the trust and respect not only of the Tibetan exiles in India, but also, despite his strong criticisms, of the China-backed authorities in Tibet. His sincerity and humility, combined with his complete integrity when it came to matters of principle, won him respect wherever he went.

NOTES

1. His Holiness the Dalai Lama, An illustrated biography. By: Tenzin Gyeche Tethong (Roli books)

Twenty-six

The Saga of the Leh-Manali Road

An important issue which was very close to Rinpoche's heart was the need to improve Ladakh's road infrastructure and communication links with the rest of India. He felt it was very important for Ladakh to have more than just the single road connection via Srinagar. The Kashmir Valley was a volatile region and therefore, another road link to the south, connecting with Himachal Pradesh; it was felt, to be very beneficial because that would make Ladakh less dependent on its relationship with Kashmir. The failed intrusion by Pakistani forces in 1948, who managed to infiltrate right inside Ladakh and repeated Chinese incursions, also called for an alternative road at an early date. An alternative, in the form of a Leh-Manali highway via Serchu, which crosses four passes including Rohtang la (pass), should have made perfect option for the Indian government. From time to time, Rinpoche also pleaded with the leadership in Delhi about the need for an alternate road connectivity with Leh via Padum in Zanskar and onward to Manali which would not only reduce the distance dramatically but would also be safe from enemy attack. But the government had its own priorities and there was no progress on this road.

Matters however were not to be so straight-forward, as Rinpoche discovered during his decades long campaign for the road's construction. In a speech made in Parliament on March 29, 1968, Rinpoche drew the attention of Lok Sabha towards the critical need to complete the Leh-Manali road. "It is essential to construct Leh-Manali road. Late Pandit Jawaharlal Nehru visited Ladakh in year 1949, and I had put forward this request to him at that time. Thereafter when Dr. Karan Singh visited Leh as the 'Sadar e Riyasat', I had again laid stress on the construction of Leh-Manali road but unfortunately at that time it was not considered necessary. Today, I want to reiterate this demand in the House and to say that the construction of Leh-Manali road is absolutely necessary both in terms of providing an alternate road link to Ladakh and to take into account defence needs for the country. Traders who come to Ladakh from Delhi and Amritsar have to take a longer route via Kashmir. If Leh – Manali road is constructed, the distance will become shorter and it will also benefit the traders."

In response to his demand Rinpoche, then an MP, received a letter dated April 17, 1968, from Sardar Swaran Singh, Minister of Defence, which indicated that the Government of India was seriously pursuing the matter, and that work was being done to build the road (**Annexure 13**). The letter said: "During your discussion on the Demand for Grants of the Ministry of Defence for the year 1968–69, you had suggested that the construction of Leh-Manali road should be expedited. Leh-Manali road is being constructed as a project of Border Roads Development Board. The funds required for this and other roads included in the programme of the Board are provided out of the Transport Ministry's budget. I did not have sufficient time to deal with all important points raised by the Honourable Member in course of my reply on the floor of the House. I, therefore, thought I should let you know the position in regard to this road, which is within my area of responsibility as Deputy Chairman Border Roads Development Board.

Work on the Leh-Manali road had been started in 1964. In order to achieve maximum speed, its construction was taken up from both ends. About 65% of the formation cutting work has been completed. Our engineers expect that a fair-weather road should be available for use by vehicles by the end of the next year. Considering the limited construction season and formidable problems of logistics, the tempo of work has been satisfactory. A close watch is, however, being kept on the progress of work because, like you, we are conscious of the importance of this road both from Defence and development angles."

It was a good statement from the Defence Minister and there was a good intent on the part of the Government of India. However, nine years later the road was still incomplete. Then in year 1977, the Congress Party lost power and a coalition government led by Morarji Desai of the Janata Party as Prime Minister was formed at the Centre for the first time. With this change of government, the priorities of the central government also changed, and even its lackluster efforts came into jeopardy. Progress on the road almost came to a halt. Naturally this was a matter of considerable concern, so Rinpoche raised the issue with Prime Minister Desai himself. In a letter dated February 26, 1979, Rinpoche who was, by now, a member of the National Commission for Minorities, called for the PM's personal intervention to ensure the completion of the project (**Annexure 14**). In the letter he reiterated the importance of Leh-Manali road from the defence point of view and that the commissioning of the road will considerably cut down expenses on transportation.

Rinpoche received a reply dated March 7/8, 1979, from Mr. Morarji Desai, Prime Minister of India which, to put it mildly, came as a great shock. What amazed Rinpoche most was the callousness and shortsightedness of the governments and security establishments towards critical issues of national defence and our preparedness. Despite the severe losses and humiliation of the defeat in 1962 at the hands of Chinese forces, and Pakistan's continued infiltrations into Kashmir, no urgency was shown at all. The Prime Minister's letter read "At one time the Army authorities had projected this need but now in view of the development in the situation and other facilities that are available, they are not interested in this road. The possibility of civilian traffic on this road is also very thin, particularly since there are many physical difficulties to be experienced on the Rohtang, Baralacha, Lechalang and Taklang-la, which are 12,000 to 17,500 feet high. While it is true that this provides a shorter route to Leh than via Srinagar, even the tourist traffic is more likely to be combined with a visit to the Kashmir valley rather than with a visit to Manali, particularly in view of the difficult road journey.... Taking all these factors into consideration I do not think it would be possible for the Government to improve this road so that it can be used by civilian traffic, nor would it be easy to use this road as an alternative to the Srinagar-Leh road when that road is blocked for the simple reason that at all times even this road is likely to present numerous difficulties." (**Annexure 15**)

This letter gives enough indication of the prevailing mindset among the defense establishment in New Delhi at that time about security considerations, which left Rinpoche utterly baffled. When Morarji Desai had to resign as Prime Minister in July 1979, due to factionalism within the ruling alliance, Chaudhary Charan Singh took over as prime minister. Bakula Rinpoche took this opportunity to take the issue up once again. But the response this time was even more enraging. In his letter of reply dated October 11, 1979, the new prime minister simply referred back to the letter of his predecessor and said there was no change in the government's position. (**Annexure 16**)

The NH-1 passing through Kargil was always vulnerable to Pakistani artillery attack since it passed close to the Line of Control (LoC). This became painfully evident again during the Kargil War in 1999, when the Pakistani army took control of the high points overlooking the highway and started shelling the area. It is only after years of delay and hesitation, did the government finally took measures to complete the road. This was in large part due to the continued pressure from the army and various parliamentarians cutting across party lines. However, the road is still only open for traffic in summer months. During Prime Minister Atal Bihari Vajpayee's tenure, the construction of tunnels at Rohtang Pass and Baralacha pass was approved. This would make the road an all-weather highway connecting Ladakh with the rest of India. A 9.2 km tunnel named as "Atal Tunnel" was inaugurated on October 3, 2020, by Mr. Narendra Modi, Prime Minister of India. However, the condition of this road even today requires drastic improvement and tunnels at various passes, though it is used by many foreign and domestic tourists during the summer.

Nyemo-Padum-Darcha Road

On May 7, 1979, Rinpoche accompanied by a delegation from Zanskar met with Mr. Morarji Desai, Prime Minister of India and reiterated the demand for an alternate road to connect Nyemo (Leh) with Darcha in Himachal Pradesh. It was pointed out that the Srinagar-Leh Road is unsafe and vulnerable to enemy attack whereas Nimmu (Nyemo) – Padum – Darcha would be not only shorter in distance (298 kilometers) and has only to cross Shinkun la, it is also secured from China and Pakistan. Nyemo is near Leh whereas Padum is the capital of Zanskar and Darcha in Lahaul and Spiti in Himachal Pradesh. Poor connectivity is one of the main reasons for the area's poverty.

Even until recently, Padum, the administrative headquarter of Zanskar, had only police wireless which was the only source through which local people would communicate outside the region. For other civic amenities, they had to make the arduous journey across several high passes to Kargil city, some 250 kilometers away.

From earlier times, people of Zanskar used the Chadar trek over the frozen Zanskar river to reach Leh. It was traditionally the only means of travel in the area during the harsh winter months. The 18th Bakula Rinpoche (1860-1917) who was born in Zangla Palace in Zanskar would undertake the difficult journey to Leh on the 'Chadar Trek' during winter. Midway he would stop in a cave. The 19th Bakula Rinpoche had also travelled on this route and used to halt at the same spot. This cave now known as 'Bakula Cave' on the Zanskar river has since become a holy spot for the local people.

Since becoming a Union Territory, there has been notable progress in power, telecommunication and road infrastructure facilities in Ladakh. In addition to the existing Kargil-Padum Highway which has been the lifeline of Zanskar during the summer months, Nyemo-Padum-Darcha Road through the 5,091 metre (16,702 Ft) Shinkula Pass in Ladakh has been made operational in April 2024 and covers 298 kilometers. It will not only provide an alternate connectivity but will also reduce the distance between Leh and Padum considerably. Whereas the distance from Padum to Leh via Kargil is 480 Kilometers, this alternate route will reduce the distance between Nyemo (Leh) to Padum to only about 200 kilometers and takes only about 5 hours.

Twenty-seven

Scheduled Tribe Status for Ladakh

In India, Scheduled Castes (SCs) and Scheduled Tribes (STs) are those demographic groups which were identified by the Constitution of India as having been historically oppressed, disadvantaged and disenfranchised, and which therefore required positive discrimination and government assistance to alleviate their situation and bring greater equality to Indian society. The constitution provided a three-pronged strategy to improve the situation of SCs and STs: (i) Protective arrangements would provide punitive measures against discrimination and atrocities against SCs and STs; (ii) Affirmative action in the allotment of government jobs for SCs and STs and (iii) A reservation system to ensure access for SCs and STs to prestigious higher education establishments as well as earmarked educational and developmental resources for SC and ST communities.

The neighboring tribal districts of Himachal Pradesh, as well as in the Himalayan regions of North-Eastern India, local people enjoyed the protections and benefits earmarked for them. When people in Ladakh became aware of benefits of ST status, they came to see it as their legitimate right and the demand for it grew louder each passing year. Many saw it as a prerequisite for progress within India, and the lack of it as the main reason why Ladakh had suffered such neglect.

Baseless rumours were being spread in some quarters of Ladakh that Bakula Rinpoche had refused Scheduled Tribe status when it was offered by Prime Minister Nehru. Rinpoche emphatically denied having received any such offer from any quarter and there was no official document to prove such peroneus claims. Moreover, back in the late 1950s, the status of J&K was still very uncertain. ST status for Ladakh was nowhere in the conversation. Besides, provisions of the Indian Constitution did not automatically apply to the State of J&K and under article 370 of the Constitution, J&K enjoyed a special autonomous status. Any application for scheduled tribe status for Ladakhis needed approval by the Government of J&K which was never going to happen under a National Conference regime.

While raising the matter in the Lok Sabha on March 29, 1968, Rinpoche reminded the House that whenever he demanded the inclusion of the people of Ladakh on the Backward class and Scheduled Tribe list, it was rejected by the Government of India. Congress Party was established in J&K on January 26, 1965, and soon after on February 19, 1966, a delegation of the Ladakh Congress Committee headed by Bakula Rinpoche submitted to Prime Minister Indira Gandhi demanding ST status for the people of Ladakh. Although the final decision rested with the central government, it alone could not grant the demand without also receiving the consent of the state government. Inevitably, this created a long delay which further heightened the sense of frustration, especially among the educated youth of Ladakh for whom there were few higher education or job opportunities. Persistent denial of this legitimate demand over decades drove the people onto the streets as happened during the mass agitations of the early 1980s.

The Mass Agitation

The source of this unrest was clearly the ongoing social, economic and political neglect suffered by the region at the hands of the J&K authorities. In the early 1980s, in the wake of atrocity and injustice in Zanskar and then the police brutality in Leh, the political situation in Ladakh became more tense than it had ever been. This re-ignited the demand for 'Free Ladakh from Kashmir' and for granting of the Scheduled Tribes status. Rinpoche took the lead and worked actively to find peaceful resolutions to these growing fissures which were becoming increasingly difficult to contain. To express their anguish at the police high handedness, the people observed Leh bandh on December 8, 1980, the Ladakhi New-Year.

A united alliance comprising of political parties and communities was formed under Rinpoche's leadership. On his part, Rinpoche urged that if this campaign was to be successful, then the people, Buddhist and Muslims, needed to unite or else it would continue to be ignored. So, in order to pursue the demand vigorously, the Ladakh Action Committee (LAC) was formed in Leh with the following key members:

Chairman:	Kushok Bakula Rinpoche.
Vice Chairman:	Togdan Rinpoche.
	Akhon Mohammed Raza.

General Secretary:	Mr. Tsering Samphel.
Secretary:	Mr. P.T. Wangyal.
Accountant:	Mr. Sonam Gyaltsan Khangsar.
Cashier:	Sheikh Mohammed Yusuf.
Members:	Mr. P. Namgyal, M.P.
	Mr. Sonam Gyaltsan, MLA.
	Mr. Sonam Wangyal.
	Mr. Tashi Targias.
	Mr. Tashi Tondup.
	Mr. Norbu Gialchan.
Spokesmen:	Mr. Akbar Ladakhi, T. Samphel
Advisory Committee:	Kushok Stakna Rinpoche.
	Mr. Rigzin Namgial Kalon.
	Mr. Tashi Tondup.
	Mr. Norbu Gialchan.
	Haji Ali Raza.
Senior Advisors:	Mr. P. Namgyal, MP.
	Mr. Skalzang Angdoo, MLA.

There were major disturbances in Leh in year 1980, and the situation was becoming tense. Police action in the face of public protests had hardened people's stance, and there were those calling for stronger confrontational tactics to press home the demands of the Ladakhis. Rinpoche, however, intervened and in order to diffuse this tense atmosphere, and in an attempt to convert the level of public discontent into concrete gains, the Ladakh Action Committee (LAC) formally launched its call for peaceful agitation on January 5, 1981.

This immediately captured the attention of the authorities in Srinagar, and after sustained dialogue with the Leh district administration, Sheikh Mohammed Abdullah (who was now again in the driving seat as Chief Minister) sent a negotiating team (a cabinet sub-committee headed by the J&K finance minister Devidas Thakur) to Leh. This sub-committee's visit took place from January 12–15, 1981. The LAC, led by Bakula Rinpoche, submitted a draft proposal to them, which among other things included demands for:

- Greater regional autonomy and renaming of Jammu and Kashmir State as Jammu, Kashmir and Ladakh
- Scheduled Tribe status for the people of Ladakh
- Divisional status for Ladakh as J&K state has only two divisions
- Fairer allocation of central government plan funds to Ladakh
- Promotion of tourism

- Commissioning of hydroelectric projects in the region
- Improvements to its communication and road infrastructure
- Higher reservation quotas for Ladakhi students in professional and technical institutions in Jammu and Srinagar
- Promotion and use of Bhoti (Ladakhi) language in government offices and institutions
- Better marketing facilities for locally-produced food and vegetable products
- An industrial development plan for Ladakh
- Improved transport facilities
- Implementation of much-needed irrigation projects

The cabinet sub-committee assured the people that the state government would carefully and sympathetically consider these demands. In particular, with regard to the demand for ST status, it promised that the state government would express its support for the measure and make necessary recommendations to the central government. Regarding the allocation of funds, it accepted the suggestion that a concrete formula should be evolved on the basis of scientific data concerning the extent of the problem facing Ladakh in comparison with the rest of the state.

On the question of regional autonomy, the sub-committee promised that a decision would be taken in due course, but it also asserted that the region's specific needs were already being catered to by the separate Ladakh Affairs Ministry. This last statement angered the agitators, because apart from the very brief period in which Bakula Rinpoche had been in charge of the Ladakh Affairs Ministry at its inception, the Ministry had ever since been headed by non-Ladakhis, who showed little interest or sympathy with the region's needs. The Ministry was thus regarded as an ineffective smokescreen which did not guarantee any real level of local autonomy. "This assurance and other decisions are contained in the record note of the discussions signed by the Deputy Commissioner, Leh on January 18, 1981, on the authority of the Chairman, Cabinet Sub-Committee."[1]

Based on the assurances given by the Cabinet Sub-committee, and taking them in good faith, the LAC agreed to suspend the agitation. Unfortunately, however, the state government once again did not honour its commitments and instead played the usual game of delaying tactics and divisive confrontational politics. As a result, the LAC was soon forced to resume its agitation. In a press release on May 14, 1981, Bakula Rinpoche, as chairman of the LAC, declared that unless the government implemented the assurances given by the cabinet sub-committee, the people of Ladakh would resume

Rinpoche addressing a public meeting at Leh Chowk. Also present are: Mr. P. Namgyal, Union Minister of State for Surface Transport, Mr. Rigzin Namgyal Kalon, Stakna Rinpoche and other leaders

Mr. Tsering Samphel, Secretary, Ladakh Action Committee speaking at a public rally

their agitation across the district on an intensified scale, responsibility for which would rest squarely upon the shoulders of the authorities in Srinagar. (**Annexure 17**)

It was highly regrettable that the state government had backtracked on the commitments given to the LAC only a year earlier. Regular *dharna*s (sit-ins) and public meetings were held in Leh and all over Ladakh. Once again, the police resorted to high-handedness and the peaceful demonstrators were baton-charged. Government started using brutal force to curb the growing unrest and many arrests were made. A delegation of the Ladakh Action Committee led by Bakula Rinpoche and Mr. P. Namgyal, MP Lok Sabha, called on Prime Minister Indira Gandhi in New Delhi to apprise her of the situation in Leh. She assured them that an official group of observers would shortly visit Leh to look into the grievances being expressed. This team arrived and was led by Mr. P. Venkatasubbiah, the Union Minister of State for Home Affairs.

Meanwhile, the Jammu and Kashmir Government continued with its delaying tactics. The State Government transferred Mr. S.S. Blowria, IAS and in his place appointed Mr. C. Phunsog, IAS, a Ladakhi officer as Deputy Commissioner of Leh. Public resentment and anger remained high on account of official apathy and police high-handedness. There was a protest march in Leh and the police resorted to tear gas shelling and an indiscriminate *lathi*-charge to break up a demonstration. This exacerbated the situation and in the ensuing clashes between protestors and police, there was indiscriminate firing by the police, and two innocent people were killed. In Ladakh, live ammunition on the people were used by the police for the first time in living memory. Lobzang Tsondus, a senior monk at Likir Monastery and Tashi Wangchuk, a youth from Saspol bore the brunt and were killed in police firing. Scores of others were also wounded. January 24, 1982, is considered a black-day in the otherwise peaceful history of Ladakh. This outrage added fuel to the fire and the agitation intensified in the coming days and weeks. The author was present in Leh at that time and witnessed this outrageous incident.

The situation became very tense in Leh and the villages around it. In protest, large numbers of people had gathered in the Jokhang temple in Leh town, the headquarter of Ladakh Buddhist Association, but the police forcibly entered the temple and chased them out with batons and teargas was used. This was unwarranted and also deeply offensive. Entire area was put under a continuous curfew for four days and later handed over to the army. Innocent people were beaten, houses were ransacked and many were kept unlawfully in police custody for several days without any charge. All of this was unprecedented in Ladakh's history. The situation was further compounded with the severe winter conditions. Leh had never known such hardship and sorrow. The district administration's response was to impose a strict curfew and the army was called in to stage a flag-march through the town. Such was the high-handedness of the police that even Mr. P. Namgyal, MP, was twice manhandled by police for violation of the curfew. Such incidents were illustrative of the unwarranted behaviour of the police and their callous disregard for rights and liberties of the local citizens.

The cremation of those killed by the police was planned for January 28, 1982. However, the district administration refused to hand over the bodies of those killed in police firing, as they feared the funeral would excite further public protest. It was then that Bakula Rinpoche and other leaders intervened. They entered into negotiations with the authorities and insisted on the return of the bodies, so that they could be given a proper cremation. Bakula Rinpoche and other senior members of civil society gave assurances that the cremation would be conducted peacefully and with proper decorum. So, there should be no police personnel present during the funeral procession. Finally, the district administration agreed. Bodies were handed over and the curfew was suspended for one day.

A record number of people, from all of Ladakh's religious communities, came out to mourn and witness the last rites of those killed in the police firing. As had been promised, the funeral procession passed off without any untoward incident. Nevertheless, the administration re-imposed curfew again afterwards, and then invoked Section 144 to prohibit gatherings of more than four people. Volunteers of the LAC, however, defied this prohibition and courted arrest by continuing to congregate daily.

These incidents proved that justice for people was a distant dream, and that the government would go to any lengths, including the use of lethal force against its own people. People's anger was directed towards the state government and they continued to come out in large numbers to protest the police brutality. Government officials decided to abstain from work in support of the public demand. People also demanded a judicial probe into the killings on January 24, 1982, but the state government gave no response. No expressions of sympathy for the bereaved families were forthcoming, nor any form of compensation. Instead, Dr. Farooq Abdullah, the son of Sheikh Mohammed Abdullah, who had now taken over as the Chief Minister of J&K, issued a bland and predictable public statement which was misleading and full of distortions, camouflaging and belittling the recent police misdemeanours. That the chief minister considered the shooting and killing of two people by the police as a 'trifling incident', further angered

Rinpoche leading the funeral procession of those killed in police firing

Rinpoche with Mrs. Indira Gandhi, Prime Minister of India at Leh, Ladakh To move at appropriate place

the people of Ladakh. However, the sustained popular pressure on the administration was by now having some effect. And after some hectic negotiations, Chief Minister Farooq Abdullah made an announcement in Leh on October 14, 1982, conceding Scheduled Tribe status for Ladakh. He assured the people that he would write to the Government of India recommending that ST status be granted without delay.

However, once again his assurance proved to be misleading, and nothing concrete emerged over the coming days. On October 21, 1982, Bakula Rinpoche and Mr. P. Namgyal, MP again called on Mrs. Indira Gandhi herself, briefed her on the situation in Ladakh and asked her to visit Ladakh to see the situation for herself. They were forceful in reiterating their demand for ST status, and for greater regional autonomy. On February 3, 1983, they held a joint press conference in New Delhi in which they highlighted the growing anger and frustration among Ladakhis. (**Annexure 18**)

Prime Minister Indira Gandhi visited Leh and Kargil on April 14, 1983. In Leh she intervened to publicly break the hunger strike of Sonam Wangyal, Nasir Ali and Tsering Stobdan by offering them juice, promising that the request for ST would be considered favourably in Delhi. This visit from the most powerful figure in the entire country heightened expectations, but people's optimism soon evaporated when again no specific announcement was issued by the central government with regard to the core demand of ST status.

Meanwhile, there was another change of guard in the J&K government. In July 1984, Ghulam Mohammed Shah, the estranged son-in-law of Sheikh Abdullah, became new chief minister after toppling his brother-in-law Dr. Farooq Abdullah by defecting from the National Conference along with twelve other senior party MLAs. Having elicited the tacit support of the Congress Party who held twenty-six assembly seats, Mr. Shah was, in this way, able to bring the government of his brother-in-law down. He then launched his own party, called the Awami National Conference. The new government began serious negotiation with the LAC leading to considerable success.

Chief Minister G.M. Shah, along with Devidas Thakur, Minister of Finance also visited Leh and met with Bakula Rinpoche. They were once again assured that ST status would be granted for Ladakhis, and that he would formally submit the state government's support to the central government. A delegation of the LAC headed by Bakula Rinpoche met with the new Chief Minister at his office in Srinagar on August 28–29, 1984, which also included P.Namgyal, M.P. and Sonam Gyaltsan, MLA, Sonam Wangyal and other leaders of the LAC. Fortunately, G.M. Shah kept his promise, and soon thereafter the required formal recommendation was sent to the

Rinpoche speaking at a public meeting with Prime Minister Mrs. Indira Gandhi at the dais, Leh

Mr. G.M. Shah, Chief Minister of Jammu and Kashmir with Rinpoche at his monastery in Samkar, Leh

Rinpoche addressing the people at the historic Polo Ground, Leh following the acceptance of Schedule Tribe demand by the State Government. Also seen on stage are P. Namgyal, Minister of State for Surface Transport, Govt. of India, D.D. Thakur, Minister of Finance, Govt. of J&K, G.M. Shah, Chief Minister of Jammu and Kashmir and Akhon Mohammed Raza

(L to R) Mr. Ghulam Nabi Azad, Bakula Rinpoche, Rajiv Gandhi, Akbar Ladakhi and P. Namgyal in Ladakh

Government of India. This was done despite some opposition within his own government. The people of Ladakh have not forgotten this and Shah is still considered in Ladakh as a true benefactor of the region. With this, the LAC had passed their most difficult hurdle, but years went by and the final formal declaration of ST status was still pending. On March 12, 1986, the State was thrown into jeopardy again when the J&K government was dismissed by the then Governor Jagmohan, following communal riots in south Kashmir.

It was a very frustrating time for Ladakhis, as it seemed like the process had stalled again. Bakula Rinpoche, who was serving as a member of the National Commission for Minorities met Prime Minister Rajiv Gandhi and conveyed the sense of frustration, despair and desperation felt by Ladakhis about the government's apparent indecision on this case. In an ardent letter dated September 22, 1989, to Prime Minister Rajiv Gandhi, Bakula Rinpoche requested Prime Minister's personal intervention to ensure the matter be settled without further delay. Making an oblique threat to resign from the National Commission for Minorities should his request be denied, Rinpoche wrote: "It is regrettable that the feeble voice of Ladakh is unable to make any impact on the Government whose compulsions in the Valley seem to out-weigh the vital interests of the strategically important Ladakh region. I am afraid, making the Ladakhis a scapegoat may not be in the overall national interests in the long run. As my efforts in safeguarding the interests of the microscopic Buddhist minority in the State of J&K are not bearing the desired fruit, it is becoming extremely difficult for me to justify my association with the National Commission for Minorities and safeguard my cherished credibility." (**Annexure 19**).

This letter had the desired effect. Finally, on October 7, 1989, within days of this letter, the presidential notification with regard to ST status for Ladakh was formally issued. The news was received with immense jubilation throughout Ladakh. It was a historic moment and a major achievement for which the people of Ladakh made tremendous sacrifices and showed complete unity. Fulfillment of this long-standing demand would help the Ladakhi youth achieve their dreams and accelerate the pace of development there. In a letter dated October 8, 1989, to Prime Minister Rajiv Gandhi, Rinpoche thanked him invoking the memory of his grandfather Pandit Nehru: "It was Pandit ji's wish to see Ladakh flourish in its pristine glory and take rapid strides towards development. You seem to be instrumental in transforming that wish into a reality. Ladakhis are immensely grateful to you."

NOTES

1. *Ladakh Through the Ages* by Shridhar Kaul and H.N. Kaul, p. 273.

PART IV

ON THE NATIONAL COMMISSION FOR MINORITIES (1978–89)

Twenty-eight

A Stint in the National Commission for Minorities, No Chance of Retirement

The purpose of Rinpoche's political career was always to serve the people and never an end in itself. He had accepted a public role on the solemn urging of Pandit Jawaharlal Nehru who had made him agree to it by invoking the Buddhist principle of working for the wellbeing of others. However, a lot had changed in Ladakh during the decades since the late 1940s. Now there were many talented and educated individuals among the Ladakhi youth who were not only qualified and talented but also eager to take up political responsibility. So, Rinpoche felt that he could now safely retire from active politics and leave it in the capable hands of the new generation. Besides, he felt it was hard for him to keep up with the rough and excessively demanding political life. Further, this decision was also influenced by the imposition of emergency under Mrs. Gandhi when democratic institutions were severely curbed and people's right and political dissent not tolerated. Rinpoche was disappointed with this decision and felt that this was a very sad period of otherwise a very vibrant democracy in India. In year 1977, therefore, at the end of his second term as an MP in the Lok Sabha, he announced that he would retire from active politics and not contest the year 1977 parliamentary election for the 6th Lok Sabha. In his Ladakh constituency, he gave his blessing to the Congress Party candidate, Rani Parvati Devi alias Diskit Wangmo, who became the first woman Member of Parliament from Ladakh. She defeated Ali Kargili, an independent candidate.

The election brought a new coalition government to power at the centre under the leadership of Prime Minister Morarji Desai and dominated by

Jayaprakash Narayan's Janata Party. With this a new era of coalition politics had begun in India. The new Government had decided to set-up a commission to monitor and safeguard the practical application of those portions of the Indian constitution which safeguarded religious freedom as well as all the laws that had been passed by the national parliament and state legislatures since independence concerning the political, social and economic rights of India's minorities. The Minorities Commission was also charged with investigating specific complaints regarding the deprivation of such rights, taking up such cases with the appropriate authorities. Five religious minorities, namely Muslim, Christian, Sikh, Buddhist and Zoroastrian (Parsi) were initially recognized by the Union Government, to which the Jains were added somewhat later. Rinpoche was appointed as a member of this commission representing the Buddhist community. He had no inkling that this was in the offing, so it came as a complete surprise. It later transpired that Mr. Morarji Desai himself had decided on Bakula Rinpoche as the best person for the job. Given Rinpoche's long association with the Congress Party, it is also a testimony to Rinpoche's integrity as a leader who was sought out for such a high position even by the Congress Party's bitterest opponents. The fact that Rinpoche in this new position was once again to be based in New Delhi where he commanded respect from a broad spectrum of people within the ruling political class, gave the Ladakhi people a much-needed sense of security. It also established Bakula Rinpoche's standing as a statesman whose stature transcended political divisions and was recognised as such in the power corridors of New Delhi.

When the Government of India set up the National Commission for Minorities in New Delhi in February 1978, its first chairman M.R. Masani, sought the cooperation of the Chief Ministers of the State Governments including the J&K Chef Minister for the discharge of its function. However, in the State of J&K, Rinpoche's old political adversaries in the National Conference, including Sheikh Mohammed Abdullah himself, who had returned to power as Chief Minister, unfortunately continued the old policy of obstructing Rinpoche wherever they could. This became clear soon after his appointment as member of the Minorities Commission, when Rinpoche decided to undertake an official visit to Ladakh, then a part of Jammu & Kashmir. In keeping with official protocol, the Commission filed a request with the J&K government asking that all due courtesies and cooperation to the Member be extended during the official visit. But, in a blatant U-turn on their earlier stand for the creation of the Commission, the state government denied consent for Rinpoche's visit, and even tried to assert J&K's immunity from the commission's jurisdiction under Article 370 of the constitution. Clearly the Kashmiri change of heart with regard to the Minorities Commission was due to Rinpoche's induction into it.

It was only after Mr. Dhanik Lal Mandal, Union Minister of State for Home Affairs, made a statement in the Lok Sabha concerning complaints he had received with regard to the minorities in J&K that this issue of the remit of the new commission for minorities on the Jammu and Kashmir State was further discussed in the J&K State Assembly. The matter was discussed in the Assembly on March 10, 1979, during the zero hour. Mr. A.G. Lone of People's Party criticised the Central Government for lending credence to such "baseless reports". Mirza Afzal Beg also wanted the Centre not to encroach upon the State's rights and the Chief Minister who intervened the debate announced in the Assembly that the government was examining whether the Minorities Commission's jurisdiction extended over the State. In a humiliating display of shortsighted partisanship, assembly members allied with the Chief Minister and denounced the new commission as yet another attempt by the central government to interfere with the internal politics of J&K, which they said, was contrary to Article 370.

On March 12, 1979, the Assembly adopted a resolution to set-up a committee headed by Mr. Devidas Thakur, Finance Minister, to examine whether the Minorities Commission's jurisdiction extended over the State and also to study who constituted a minority in the State. Sheikh Abdullah surprisingly informed the Assembly "that there had been no advance consultations between the State and the Centre" in the matter. He added, "one person from the State had also been nominated on the Commission. Probably this member had referred the complaints in question to the Commission," It was obviously a reference to Kushok Bakula Rinpoche. The Sheikh's assurance to Mr. Masani earlier when the commission was formed, is proof enough to establish that there was an advance consultation which Sheikh Abdullah denied on the floor of the House. This denial and the furore which was unleashed in the Assembly prompted a press statement by Rinpoche on March 16, 1979, clarifying that as a member of the Minorities Commission there was nothing to stop him from placing the grievances of Ladakh's minorities before the Commission. As a leader of Ladakh, he further pointed out, he owed a special duty to the minorities in the region and could not, as such, afford to be a passive spectator to their sufferings. He gave expression to his regards for the Kashmir Chief Minister who, he regretted, continued "having grouse against me unabatedly since 1949." He asked if the Chief Minister believed that the grievances of the Ladakhi Buddhists were baseless then why did he fight shy of the Commission's proposed official visit to the State? Answering the question himself, Rinpoche observed that there could be no reason other than the fear that his presence might have exposed facts. He felt pained at the Chief Minister's failure to realise that over the years, the people of Ladakh had emerged as an awakened community pulsating with new life and aspirations.

In a rejoinder to Bakula Rinpoche's statement, J&K Government's Works and Power Minister, Mr. Sonam Norboo, on March 19, 1979, denied the alleged unfair treatment to the Buddhist minority in Ladakh region and said that such a charge against the State Government was an "exercise in futility and a bid at mud-slinging". Mr. Norboo had successfully contested the year 1977 State Assembly election from Ladakh as a Congress Party candidate but later had joined the National Conference and got a berth in the State Cabinet.

This was yet another failed attempt by the Kashmiri leadership to undermine Bakula Rinpoche's influence in the region. However, it is worth observing that although Rinpoche had some political differences with Mr. Norboo, as reflected in several such incidents, they always maintained cordial and cooperative personal relations. An engineer by profession, he played a leading role in the construction of Leh airfield, Srinagar-Leh road and also made many long-lasting contributions to the development of Ladakh. For his distinguished services, he was awarded the 'Padma Shree' in year 1961.

Eventually, the Commission sought the intervention of Prime Minister Morarji Desai himself to help resolve the issue of whether it did or did not cover the state of J&K. Initially the state authorities tried to maintain their contention, but later they succumbed to the pressure from the central government and cleared the way for Bakula Rinpoche's official visit. As per protocol, Rinpoche was given the due courtesies afforded to a central minister by the State Government. He visited Srinagar where he held official discussions with the State officials. Later, on his arrival at Leh, Rinpoche was given a grand reception with thousands of people lining the road from the airport to Leh. During his visit to Ladakh, Rinpoche once again went out of his way to look into issues pertaining to all of Ladakh's communities, not just Buddhist but all sections of its population.

For a long time, the issue of Scheduled Caste reservation for Dalits who had converted to other religions has been a burning issue. Rinpoche met with senior Dalit leaders including Dadasaheb Narayan Kumbhare, Member of Parliament, Vamanrao Godbole, Rajabhau Khobragade, MP, Dadasaheb Gaikwad, MP, Sadhanand Fulzele, BP Maurya, Dadasaheb Rupawate, R.S. Gavai, and others to discuss strategy to tackle this issue and other issues concerning Dalits. Mrs. Savitha Ambedkar, wife of Babasaheb Dr. Bhimrao Ambedkar would often visit Rinpoche at his residence in New Delhi and discuss issues of concern with Rinpoche. He strongly advocated for the Scheduled Caste reservation rights for Dalits converted to Buddhism. Later, in year 1990 after an amendment to the constitution, the Dalit Buddhists were included in the list as Scheduled Castes.

Rinpoche with Mr. Sonam Norboo (Padma Shree), Cabinet Minister, Government of Jammu and Kashmir in New Delhi

With Prime Minister Mrs. Indira Gandhi accompanying a group of Buddhist leaders, members of parliament and prominent monks from various parts of India (New Delhi, 1974)

In his stint as a member of the Minorities Commission for 10 years from 1978-89, Rinpoche visited different States to understand the plight of the Dalit community and submitted various reports to the Government of India. Also, during these years, Rinpoche took up scores of issues facing Buddhist communities in different parts of India in the Himalayan region of Ladakh, Himachal Pradesh, Sikkim, Arunachal Pradesh, some of which are detailed later in this section. He also took up the rehabilitation of Chakma Buddhist refugees from Bangladesh. These were the continuation of issues with which Rinpoche had long been involved in India. Rinpoche made sincere efforts in the amelioration of the problems facing the Buddhists of India but perhaps the most important development during his decade on the Minorities Commission was the growth of Rinpoche's stature on the world stage as a Buddhist leader.

The Mahabodhi Temple in Bodh Gaya

For a long time, the Buddhists from home and abroad, have been campaigning to regain control of the Mahabodhi Temple. This campaign was partially successful when in 1949, in the wake of Indian independence, control of the site was passed on from the Hindu Mahant to the state government of Bihar. Under the terms of the Bodh Gaya Temple Act of 1949, the state government is responsible for the protection, management, and monitoring of the temple and its properties. The Act also made provisions for a temple management committee and an advisory board to oversee its day-to-day maintenance. As a member of parliament and later as Member, National Commission for Minorities Bakula Rinpoche served on this committee for many years.

This holy complex is visited every year by millions of pilgrims from all over the world. In a letter to Prime Minister Rajiv Gandhi dated August 20, 1987, Rinpoche drew his attention to the poor state of affairs at the holy site and suggested some measures to help improve it. In the letter, Rinpoche mentioned that the masterplan for Bodh Gaya, which had been approved by Prime Minister Nehru, was yet to be implemented and its vision remained only on paper. Rinpoche pointed out that while other minority communities were given full control over the management of their religious shrines, Buddhists had been denied this right. He therefore demanded some corrective measures. In year 2002, Mahabodhi Temple was declared as a UNESCO World Heritage site.

Rinpoche maintained pressure on this issue for many years and brought it to the attention of successive governments. A letter addressed to Bakula Rinpoche from Prime Minister P.V. Narasimha Rao dated June 16, 1992, bears witness to this. In this letter the Prime Minister gave further assurances

Rinpoche paying tribute to Dr. Bhim Rao Ambedkar at Deekshabhoomi, Nagpur

Bakula Rinpoche speaking at the Deekshabhoomi, Nagpur

and stated that the cabinet committee on political affairs (CCPA) would soon take up the issue and resolve it favourably. Unfortunately, since Buddhists in India are still a very small minority group, nothing substantive emerged and political forces in Bihar were still against handing over its entire management to Buddhists.

Preserving the Holy Buddha Relics

The holy Buddha relics are in display at the National Museum, New Delhi. As for the origin of the holy relics, these were objects which had been discovered by archeologists in Piprahwa, a spot about twenty-two kilometers from Siddhartha Nagar in Uttar Pradesh, which has been identified with the ancient site of Kapilvastu. It is the place where Lord Buddha spent the early years of his life. In those times, Kapilvastu was the capital of the Shakya dynasty whose ruler, King Suddhodana, was Lord Buddha's father. During the time of Lord Buddha, in the 6th century BCE, the Shakya domain was one of sixteen independent principalities of northern India. The ruins of the royal palace are spread over a large area which are today covered by several villages, mainly Piprahwa and Ganvaria. A large stupa was also there and was said to house the bone relics of Lord Buddha. This was attested to, in an ancient Brahmi inscription found at the site. Once excavated, text was found in the stupa mentioning in it 'Devaputra' (ref. to Lord Buddha). Two other mounds were also excavated at a short distance (1.5 km) away from the village. These are considered to be the ruins of King Suddhodhana's palace.

However, despite these discoveries, nothing substantial was done to develop these sites and the holy relics themselves remained in an enclosure in the National Museum in New Delhi. In September 1993, the Holy Buddha Relics were brought to Mongolia where it received a tumultuous welcome. It was for the first time that the holy relics had been sent outside India. Fortunately, this visit to Mongolia paved the way for other Buddhist countries to follow suit and subsequently the holy relics were sent for public exposition in several Buddhist countries.

Bakula Rinpoche believed it was high time the central government recognized the significance and sensitivity of the Holy Relics for Buddhists and took steps to rectify the situation. In a letter dated December 2, 2002, addressed to Mr. Jagmohan, the Union Minister for Culture, he wrote that instead of displaying and treating the holy relics of Lord Buddha as museum pieces at the National Museum, New Delhi, this priceless national treasure, which could attract millions of people from across the world, should be housed in a special complex in a suitable place of pilgrimage such as Bodh Gaya, Sarnath or Kushinagar. Alternately, Rinpoche suggested in his letter that a separate enclosure for displaying holy relics should be constructed within the compound of National Museum, New Delhi. Mr. Jagmohan assured of a serious consideration of the proposal. **(Annexure 20)** Subsequently, in a letter, the minister stated that after due consideration, and in consultation with the relevant state governments, the Ministry of Culture had decided to relocate the holy relics to Piprahwa in Uttar Pradesh (in the district of Siddhartha Nagar) where the relics had originally been discovered. However, Rinpoche did not agree as according to him Piprahwa, which was not on most pilgrims' route, the relics would be unsafe there and as such this was not a satisfactory resolution. He instead suggested that they should be retained by the National Museum, New Delhi but housed in a separate section within its compound. The matter did not move further and the holy relics of Lord Buddha continue to remain in the National Museum.

Promoting Language and Culture

For many years a major demand of the many Himalayan natives in India had been to bring the Tibetan language, also known as Bhoti or Bod-yig language, under the purview of the 8th Schedule of the Indian Constitution which pertains to the safeguarding and promotion of India's native languages. Dialects of Tibetan are spoken by a variety of Himalayan peoples spread across several states of India: Arunachal Pradesh (which includes the Monpa regions); Himachal Pradesh (Kinnaur, Lahaul and Spiti); Ladakh (Leh and Kargil); Sikkim; parts of Uttarakhand and the northernmost areas of West Bengal. Numerous appeals had been made to the central government in the past to this effect, but still it was not recognized as an official Indian language at the national level. In the 1950s, on the request of Bakula Rinpoche who was serving as a minister, the J&K government had implemented a decision to include Bodhi in the school curriculum in Ladakh up to the 8th standard. Rinpoche himself made his speeches in the assembly in Ladakhi in the state assembly.

On January 11, 1974, a conference was organized at Bodhgaya which was attended among others by profound Buddhist scholar Lama Tenzin Gyaltsan also known as Khunu Rinpoche. The conference agreed to set up an organization called the Frontier States Buddhist Society or "Seemant Pradeshiya Bauddha Maha Sabha". Khunu Rinpoche was elected its President and Bakula Rinpoche the Vice-President. The meeting emphasized the need to promote and protect the local languages in the Himalayan region of India. This meeting was the first such effort and proved to be a major step in the promotion and protection of the language. Rinpoche visited Kinnaur, Lahaul and Spiti regions of Himachal Pradesh, present State of Uttarakhand, Arunachal Pradesh, Sikkim, Darjeeling etc. and in an effort to

(L-R) Mr. P. Namgyal, Member of Parliament, Tsona Rinpoche (Arunachal Pradesh), Prime Minister Rajiv Gandhi, Bakula Rinpoche and Lama Chosphel Zotpa

strengthen Buddhist culture in the Himalayan region. Many students from the region were also enrolled at the Ladakh Institute of Higher Studies which was established in New Delhi and which later came to be known as Vishesh Kendriya Vidyalaya (VKV).

In February 1989, Rinpoche together with Mr. P. Namgyal, MP, Tsona Rinpoche, Lama Chosphel Zotpa from Zanskar, Ladakh and other leaders met with Prime Minister Rajiv Gandhi to further press the demand for inclusion of Bhoti or Tibetan language in the Eighth Schedule of the Indian Constitution.

Over the years some progress has been made in this regard, but the language is still not recognized officially at the national level. In June 2018, a new body called the "Indian Himalayan Council of Nạlanda Buddhist Tradition" (IHCNBT) headed by Maling Gombu, was formed with its headquarters in New Delhi. The author is associated with it as a Member-Secretary. In April 2022, IHCNBT signed an MOU with the National Institute of Open Schooling (NIOS), Government of India which provided for inclusion of Bhoti language and Boudh-Darshan in its syllabus for school curriculum. This was a major progress and considered a steppingstone for inclusion of Bhoti language in the 8th schedule of the Constitution of India. It got a further momentum when in December 2024, the Ministry of Home

Affairs, in principle, agreed to recognize Bhoti and Urdu as official languages of the Union Territory of Ladakh.

Financial Assistance to Buddhist Monasteries/Institutions

After visiting different Himalayan regions of the country Rinpoche also felt an urgent need for the maintenance and security of Buddhist antiques and manuscripts which would help the people preserve them for posterity. Unfortunately, many precious items had already been lost or smuggled out of the country over the decades, and much of what remained was in poor condition. Centuries old wall paintings, as well as many ancient religious structures in Ladakh and elsewhere, were in a dilapidated condition. Moreover, the numerous rare manuscripts housed in our monasteries had yet to be catalogued. These matters were taken up for discussion by the commission, and with cooperation from the relevant government agencies, various concrete steps were taken. Major renovations were undertaken at Leh Palace and other important historical sites by the Archeological Survey of India.

One satisfying outcome of Rinpoche's efforts was the establishment of a fund under the auspices of the central government's Ministry of Culture to provide for financial assistance to the monasteries and other Buddhist institutions across India for their repair and maintenance. In 1985, the Ministry of Culture, Government of India, launched a pilot project to help Buddhist monasteries. Under the scheme, the beneficiary Buddhist monasteries/institutions received financial assistance to the tune of Rupees 30-50 lakhs annually. This scheme continues to be in operation to this date and has benefited Buddhist monasteries/ institutions across India. Scholarships were also provided for Buddhist monks under this scheme to pursue their studies. This has greatly helped many Buddhist monasteries/ Institutions across India, especially those in remote mountainous areas of Ladakh, Arunachal Pradesh, Sikkim, and Himachal Pradesh.

Twenty-nine

Zanskar's Woes

It is said that the name Zanskar comes from the natural occurrence of copper in this region, since the Tibetan word for copper is "zang". Zanskar is an arid high-altitude region of dramatic ravines covering some 7,000 square kms with elevations ranging between 3,500 and 7,000 metres (11482-22965 Ft) above sea level. The inhabited regions of Zanskar basically consist of the country lying along the two main tributaries of the Zanskar river and around their confluence. The first of these tributaries, the Doda, has its source near the Pensi-la pass (4,400 m, 14435 Ft), from where it runs south-east along the main valley towards Padum (the administrative centre of Zanskar). The other river is formed from two smaller tributaries: the Kargyag with its source near the Shingo-la (5,091 m, 16702 Ft); and the Tsarap, with its source near the Baralacha-la. They converge below the village of Purne to form the Lungnak (also known locally as the Lingti or the Tsarap). This then flows north-west along a narrow gorge until it enters the central valley of Zanskar where it unites with the Doda to form the Zanskar river. This then flows north-east until it joins the Indus at Nyemo near Leh.

Zanskar is also known for Sani Monastery and Kanika Stupa. This Stupa dates back to the time of the famous Kushan Emperor, Kanishka (127CE). Kanika is a commonly used form of emperor Kaniska's name. He is famous in Buddhist literature as a promoter of Buddhism. The fourth Buddhist Council was held in nearby Kashmir in 72 AD under the patronage of Kushan King Kanishka. Sani seems to be the only monastery in the region which has a history going back as ancient as the Kushan period.

Tied with ancient monasteries, of which the Sani, Dzongkhul, Bardan, Rangdum, Karsha, Stongde and Phugtal are the most prominent, the story of Zanskar was unfortunately one of total neglect. Being a quite sparsely populated region, Zanskar is cut off from the outside world for most of the year by snow on its high passes. Then, there has always been very little political will to cater to the needs of these isolated communities. But people in these remote villages fondly remember visits of Bakula Rinpoche as back as in the 1940s who used to undertake extremely difficult journeys when there was no road or any transport other than horses, mules and yaks were available. During winter heavy snowdrifts sometimes reach rooftops of the local houses and movement becomes extremely arduous. The region had no electricity, and tele-communication facilities or other basic services like food (public distribution system), medical facility, veterinary etc. were woefully insufficient.

Bakula Rinpoche had a fascination with the region and visited every nook and corner of Zanskar. While in Zanskar he would also visit the ruins of Zangla Palace where his predecessor, the 18th Bakula was born. In one of the rooms in this mud-brick building that offers fascinating views of the Zanskar river and its entire valley far below, Hungarian scholar Alexander (Sándor) Csoma de Kõrös[1] had compiled the first Western dictionary of the Tibetan language in 1823.

At that time of the Pakistani invasion in 1948, Ladakh had no political representation at the state level, so people were without any means of appealing their cases. According to Bakula Rinpoche, after the Pakistani raiders were repulsed, the Central Government had, in fact, sanctioned some money for relief for Zanskar but unfortunately not a rupee of this found its way to the region.

In 1979, the composite district of Ladakh was divided into two districts. A separate district had been created for Kargil, and despite the protests of people from Buddhist-majority Zanskar it had been included as a tehsil or sub-district of Muslim-majority Kargil. Zanskar's link with Kargil is only the highway linking the two. Both are culturally, ethnically and geographically far apart from each other. This was a major sore point and was considered one of the main reasons Zanskar had continued to be marginalized and overlooked by the Jammu and Kashmir government in the area of economic development, education, and infrastructure and remained the most backward area of the entire state. The erstwhile Jammu and Kashmir Assembly had an MLA representing Zanskar Constituency. But regrettably, the J&K State Government had manipulated the area of the constituency in such a way that it always elected a Muslim candidate and not once a Buddhist candidate got elected.

In year 1979, a delegation from Zanskar visited New Delhi to apprise the government of the issues they were facing. They met Bakula Rinpoche who was then a member of the National Commission on Minorities and pressed for among others, the following main demands:

(i) A separate district for Zanskar should be created to safeguard the interests of this marginalized community,

(ii) To accelerate and early completion of Nyemo-Padum road, also known as Chadar Road,

(iii) Opening of an Amchi Research Centre, and

(iv) Opening of a branch of Central Institute of Buddhist Studies (CIBS) Leh.

It was shortly after this, in September 1980, that the discontent in Zanskar boiled over into public protest. The trouble started when the people of Karsha village demanded the retention of a diesel generator-set which had been brought to the village for the visit of the 14th Dalai Lama to Zanskar. The district authorities now wanted to shift the generator to Kargil. For the Buddhist locals this was yet another example of the callous disregard with which the district authorities in Kargil treated the Buddhists of Zanskar. Locals came out onto the streets in vocal protests, which the police dealt with very badly. The protests ended in the police opening fire, and the protestors being brutally lathi-charged. News of this spread like wildfire and the wails of the people of Zanskar found powerful support in Leh where people of all political shades came out in support.

A peaceful procession was held in Leh on November 30, 1980, to protest against the police atrocities in Zanskar. Invariably any such occasion is also an opportunity for the people to vent their anger against the State Government of J&K. In the ensuing stand-off with the police, many high-ranking monks and laymen were lathi-charged and subjected to tear-gas. The people were outraged, and in the ensuing mayhem, two government buildings were regrettably set on fire by agitators. On December 8, 1980, a bandh (general strike) was observed in Leh, and that year people did not observe the festivities of 'Losar', the Ladakhi New Year as a gesture of solidarity with the people of Zanskar and those who had suffered at the hands of police brutality.

Rinpoche visited Zanskar and Kargil in years 1983 and 1986 (August 21-30, 1986) and toured the region to take stock of the situation and meet the local people. After returning to New Delhi on November 20, 1986, he met with the Prime Minister Rajiv Gandhi reiterated the demand for a separate district for Zanskar and also submitted a detailed report which highlighted the following points brought to his notice in Zanskar and Kargil:

1. The Government of J&K may be requested to take early and effective steps to prevent Gujjar shepherds from Jammu to graze their livestock on Rangdum pastures.
2. The Government of India, Department of Culture, be requested to consider the demand of the people of Zanskar for setting up an 'Amchi' Research Centre, and the State Government may be requested to consider favourably the demand of the Amchis of Zanskar for a uniform rate of honorarium in the two districts.
3. The Government of India, Department of Culture, may be requested to consider the demand of the people of Zanskar to set up an institute or a branch of the Central Institute of Buddhist Studies (CIBS) Leh at Tungri near Padam (where the Dalai Lama delivered the Kalachakra sermon a few years back)
4. The State Government may be requested to favourably consider the demand of Buddhists of Leh and Zanskar regarding introduction of Bodhi as the medium of instruction in the primary stage.
5. The State Government may be requested to set up the already approved Block Development Office at Karsha to consider construction of a canal from Phey-Rantakasha-Padam and the early posting of a doctor to Karsha
6. Construction of an all-weather road connecting Zanskar to Leh via Neemu-Padam-Manali.
7. The Ministry of Communications was apprised of the difficulties faced by the people of Zanskar in the absence of postal and telephone facilities and requested to take steps as indicated in the Report.
8. In Kargil, people demanded that the Government of India should appoint one 'Amir Haj' for Kargil for the next Haj season.
9. The State Government may be requested to expedite completion of Stakna and Suru Hydel Projects and to undertake construction of Parkachik Hydel Project in Kargil.
10. The State Government may be requested to take necessary steps regarding promotion of tourism in the Zanskar area.
11. The State Government may also be requested to consider the request of the people of Zanskar for posting of local Police Officers in the area.

If the problems of governmental neglect and indifference were bad in Leh under successive J&K regimes, they were even worse in the neighboring area of Zanskar and Kargil. In particular, local people complained about the terror posed by the Kashmiri shepherds. Rinpoche was deeply concerned about the regular infringements onto the Rangdum pasture lands by bullying and gun-toting Gujjar Bakarwal shepherds from Kashmir. They came with their livestock to this verdant area to graze their cattle, denying access to the pastures to the local inhabitants. This had been a cause of severe tension for the local people for several years and required urgent government action. Repeated representations by the people of Rangdum to the district authorities in Kargil had been ignored, and due to this tacit support from both the authorities and police, the Gujjars began intruding further into Zanskar. Matters reached a gruesome and shocking climax on July 12, 2000, when three Buddhist monks of Rangdum Monastery were gunned down by Gujjar assailants. This was the first instance of such an atrocity in Ladakh. It shook the Buddhists of Ladakh to their core and raised unprecedented levels of indignation and communal tension. It is deeply regrettable and indeed shameful that no concerted action was taken by the State Government of J&K to identify the culprits of this heinous crime and bring them to justice.

In 1995, the Ladakh Autonomous Hill Development Council (LAHDC) Leh came into existence after prolonged agitation by the people of Leh. For the people of Zanskar this presented another opportunity to address their long-held grievances. When the Government of India approved LAHDC status for Leh, they also offered a similar reform package to Kargil district so that the people of the area could reap benefits of this new arrangement. However, leaders in Kargil declined the offer, much to the disappointment and outrage of Zanskar.

Only later did the Kargil leaders change their stance, and in 2003, after a gap of eight years, the Ladakh Autonomous Hill Development Council (LAHDC) Kargil was also constituted. But even with the new dispensation, Zanskar was again electorally marginalized, and the discrimination against them continued. As a result, a public boycott of the LAHDC Kargil elections was declared in Zanskar.

It was the summer of 2003, that Mufti Mohammed Sayeed accompanied by Nawang Rigzin Jora, Minister for Science and Information Technology, visited Samkar Gonpa where Rinpoche was convalescing from a bout of pneumonia. Even in his fragile physical condition, Rinpoche seized this opportunity to put the grievances of the people of Zanskar before the Chief Minister and urged him to ensure that they received due representation and consideration in the newly-formed LAHDC, Kargil. He also expressed his own view, shared by the majority of Zanskar, that Zanskar deserves to be a separate district and this alone could ensure the region overcoming its difficulties.

Rinpoche addressing the people of Zanskar at Padum, Zanskar

Rinpoche on his way to Zanskar in an Army Nissan vehicle (1986)

Chief Minister Mufti Mohammed Sayeed was moved by Rinpoche's passion and conviction on this issue, and recognized the great compassionate mind that Rinpoche was. He assured Rinpoche that the demand to increase the electoral representation of Zanskar on the council would be positively considered by the state government, and pleaded with Rinpoche not to bother himself with such issues and instead take care of his health. He also requested Rinpoche to advise the people of Zanskar against boycotting the upcoming council elections as that would only exacerbate the situation. Numerous negotiations were then held between the representatives of Zanskar and the state government which eventually resulted in Zanskar receiving three seats out of a total of twenty-six. The final settlement of three seats was still woefully inadequate. But they were given assurances that the number of seats allocated to Zanskar would be increased further in subsequent years, and that Zanskar would also get one post of Executive Councilor and of the nominated seat in the LAHDC, Kargil Act.

NOTES

1. Bernard Le Calloc'h, "Alexander Csoma De Koros, the Heroic Philologist, Founder of Tibetan Studies in Europe", *The Tibet Journal*, Vol. 10, No. 3 (1985), pp. 30–41.

Thirty

Border Trade and the Opening of Kailash Route from Ladakh

Once a flourishing centre of Silk Route trade, Ladakh's economy virtually took a nosedive following the annexation of Sinkyang (Xinjiang) and Tibet by Communist China. People were deeply concerned over the deteriorating situation on the border and the stoppage of border trade with Tibet. Rinpoche understood its grave implications on Ladakh's economy and therefore, took up the matter with the Government of India at the highest level.

"With Partition and the Chinese invasion of Tibet, Ladakhis suddenly found their identities retracted through three political categories: Pakistan, India and China. This political – and spatial – tension combined with longer and less noticeable trends lasted for decades before independence. Its effect was a paradoxical one: Ladakh was simultaneously made more consequential to the political considerations of India and its neighbors, just as it found itself economically isolated.

Matters did not improve after independence. Bakula Rinpoche bemoaned the impact of the end of the central Asian trade on Ladakh: "Due to the discontinuance of and stoppage of caravan from Sinkyang (Xinjiang), he wrote, "widespread unemployment had taken place, at the same time the prices of articles of daily consumption had gone very high." Since a "large number of people from Ladakh had trade connections with Tibet," Bakula Rinpoche continued, "now, due to the communist Chinese incursion in Tibet, it will be stopped also. In view of the rapid deterioration in economic condition of Ladakh, if no steps are taken to give productive work, a critical situation might develop."[1]

Restoring Ladakh's traditional border trade with Tibet and allowing

Indian pilgrims visiting Mount Kailash and Lake Mansarovar to cross into Tibet from Ladakh, had been a long-standing demand of the Ladakhis and Tibetans alike. Locals provided shelter for the travelers, load bearing animals and fodder supplies for animals thus playing a pivotal role. For centuries, trade routes between Tibet, Central Asia and India had been the lifeblood of Ladakh's economy and had nourished and sustained Ladakh's vibrant culture. In fact, much of the finest wool (known as pashmina or Cashmere) used in Kashmir's world-famous woolen scarves was traditionally procured as a raw material from Tibet and Ladakh, where there existed an age-old and well-established barter trade system. The closure of the border in the wake of the Chinese annexation of Tibet was, therefore, a severe blow not only to the economy of Ladakh, but also to Kashmir's woolen industry in general. Reopening this trade route would revitalize Ladakh's economy and breathe new life into the abandoned communities on both sides of the border. On various occasions therefore, Bakula Rinpoche requested the Government of India to consider reopening the border for purposes of pilgrimage and trade as soon as possible. Rinpoche made similar representations during his meetings with local officials in Lhasa during his visit there in 1992, as detailed in a later chapter.

Ladakhi Traders with their products on the Silk-Route (Photo by AADAR)

As a result of these representations sustained over many years, in the early summer of 1994, Rinpoche received a letter dated May 18, 1994, from the Ministry of External Affairs in response to his letter on this subject to Prime Minister P.V. Narasimha Rao **(Annexure 24)**. The letter stated that a proposal concerning this matter had been sent to the relevant Chinese government departments and that their reply was now awaited. Furthermore, as per directive from the central government, the Secretary of the Department of Ladakh Affairs (J&K Government) had made extensive local enquiries on the matter, including interviews with veterans who had traveled this route to Lhasa **(Annexure 26)**. This report concluded that if the trade route to Tibet was re-opened through Demchok, the population on both sides of the border would benefit and historical links would be restored, which would be in the interests of border security and peace between these two large Asian nations. In the past wool, silk, velvet, salt and meat used to be imported from the Tibetan side, while locally produced barley, wheat, butter, fruits, carpets, animal skins and textiles would be exported from the Ladakh side.

In the above-mentioned letter, the State Government of J&K also asserted that it was possible to cover the 633-kilometer route from Leh to Tarchen-Parakha (the base camp for Kailash-Mansarovar) in two days. The road does not need to traverse any major passes, is free from the risk of avalanches and with some maintenance, could be used year-round. It was also noted that Leh airport provides good connectivity via regular commercial flights to several Indian cities. Also, the hospitals in Leh were well-equipped to deal with problems such as altitude sickness that might be encountered by first-time visitors. The army even had the facility of a pressurized chamber which could replicate sea-level atmospheric pressures, thus avoiding the necessity, in extreme cases, of patients being flown out to lower elevations.

Unfortunately, these overtures from the Indian government were met on the Chinese side by a stony silence. The Chinese approach to the complex boundary question between the two countries, continued to be governed by a hardliner and uncompromising approach. As a result, no progress was made. But one glimmer of hope was that the Chinese government did finally agree to a very limited opening of the Nathu-la border crossing in Sikkim for the Kailash-Mansarovar yatra. This was in addition to the travel facility available through the Lipulekh pass in Uttarakhand since 1981.

NOTES

1. NAI, Ministry of States, 1951, I-K/51. From Bakula, Head Lama of Ladakh, and Sonam Wangyal, Representative of zamindars of Ladakh, to the Secretary of State Affairs.

Thirty-one

Formation of the Ladakh Autonomous Hill Development Council (LAHDC)

In July 1989, Leh witnessed another sudden bout of public disturbance following a clash between rival groups of youths from the two communities which unfortunately took a serious turn. At the time Bakula Rinpoche was away in Moscow and I was with him. It was only when we returned to New Delhi that Rinpoche learnt about the traumatic events in Ladakh, which had rocked the otherwise peaceful region. More significant than the fights themselves was the psychological impact, they could leave – a trail of bitterness and communal divide that could seriously undermine Ladakh's long tradition of communal harmony. Rinpoche had no doubt that the incident had been instigated by provocateurs – political forces in Kashmir who stood to gain from communal disharmony. They have been trying to undermine Ladakh's inter-religious co-operation for decades, and this was its latest manifestation.

It all began after an altercation between two groups of youths. On July 7, 1989, Nawang Rigzin Jora, Joint Secretary of Leh District Congress Committee who later resigned and became General Secretary of the Ladakh Buddhist Association (LBA), was beaten by some local Muslim youth for his vociferous nature and scathing criticism of the administration. When a police complaint was filed, the police duly arrested the individuals involved and detained them. Yet, very soon they were inexplicably released from custody, apparently under instructions from the higher government authorities in Srinagar. This enflamed public opinion, and Buddhists began to protest. The news of the incident spread quickly throughout the region and people came out in large numbers in Leh to protest against the bias of the local police and the district administration then headed by Varghese Samuel, IAS. The Buddhist and Muslim were becoming polarized, and this deeply saddened Rinpoche, who knew that the two communities had lived peacefully together for centuries in Ladakh. But it was clear that the situation was not going to be alleviated unless the legitimate grievances of the Buddhist community were addressed. The age-old communal harmony of the Ladakh region was being sorely tested, and communal tensions were running high.

The LBA, now headed by Thupstan Chhewang demanded the appointment of a commission of inquiry to investigate the matter. On July 10, 1989, the demand was formally submitted to the Divisional Commissioner and the Deputy Inspector General of Police (DIG) while on an official visit to Leh, along with a clear warning that if such a commission was not appointed without delay, the LBA would be forced to launch an all-out agitation. Unfortunately, the demand fell on deaf ears. The Jammu and Kashmir state government's refusal to take the grievances of Ladakhis seriously opened old wounds and the anger in Ladakh about the dismissive attitude of the J&K authorities reached new heights. Since no visible action was being taken by the government, the LBA true to its word, announced the commencement of an indefinite agitation against the state government to vent their grievances. Had the state government acted on their demand, the course of events would have been very different. An investigation into the beating of Rigzin Jora would have exposed those divisive forces who were fomenting trouble in Leh, and disciplinary action against them could have diffused the problem. But this was not to be. Instead, the J&K state government chose to do nothing, and took no steps to restore confidence among the Buddhists. The state government itself was, therefore, largely to be blamed for the deteriorating communal situation ignited by this incident.

People of Ladakh came out on the streets in full force under the banner of the LBA, unequivocally demanding Union Territory status for Ladakh and to 'Free Ladakh from Kashmir'. Tensions were high and the situation was deteriorating rapidly. On August 24, 1989, Bakula Rinpoche rushed to Leh where he held urgent discussions with senior district officials, as well as with the LBA, the Ladakh Muslims Association and other senior leaders. Along with Mr. P. Namgyal MP and other senior figures from both the communities, Bakula Rinpoche publicly appealed for calm and urged people to maintain communal harmony and to resolve their differences peacefully through dialogue. Appeals were also made to the state and the central governments for immediate intervention so as to diffuse the situation and restore order to the district. This initiative of the local elders, both Buddhist and Muslim, gave some solace and things showed signs of settling down.

But unfortunately, the draconian policing approach adopted by the authorities in the ensuing days quickly reversed the situation.

Earlier, during the height of the disturbances, Section 144 had been invoked, which prohibits gatherings of more than four people at a time, and this regulation had remained in force in Leh much to aggravating resentment of the Buddhist youth. Protestors had taken to making their opposition to this oppressive rule known by staging regular symbolic public protests outside the Jokhang temple in small groups of four. Meanwhile, local Muslims also joined the agitation. These were entirely peaceful expressions of dissent, and they did not threaten public order at all. However, there were elements in the Kashmir government which saw benefits in communal disharmony in Ladakh which were conducive to the political agenda they nurtured. So, rather than taking the public into confidence and diffuse the situation as a cue for loosening the policing in the capital, the response of the J&K government was to add fuel to the fire with a completely unnecessary and ill-advised escalation. This came when the state government abruptly withdrew the local police force and the Central Reserve Police Force (CRPF) which until then had been containing the situation in Leh, with the notorious Kashmir Armed Police (KAP). The KAP is made up mostly of personnel from the Kashmir Valley, and this further exacerbated the sense of outrage amongst the Buddhist youth, who were by now acutely conscious of their subordinate status within the Muslim-majority state.

The apprehensions felt by the people of Ladakh about the arrival of the KAP were not unfounded, and it was not long before the situation escalated with tragic consequences. It was obvious that the J&K state government had decided to crush the agitation by force. They were not interested in addressing the people's legitimate grievances and instead were determined to come down heavily on any expressions of dissent. Matters came to a head on August 27, 1989 when a small group of protestors came out of the Jokhang temple in Leh and staged a symbolic protest in defiance of Section 144. It had become a regular occurrence in those days. This time, however, the police response was totally out of proportion. It was clear that the district authorities had been preparing for a confrontation with the protestors and had decided to use this as a pretext to teach them a lesson.

In a clearly pre-planned operation, the police cleared the area outside the Jokhang and deployed a large number of armed KAP personnel around the temple complex. All exit points were covered, and when the small group of protestors emerged and made for the main road, police forces charged them with batons, leaving several protestors injured. This unprovoked atrocity enflamed the situation, and in retaliation people started shouting slogans and pelting stones at the police station. In the scuffle that followed, police resorted to the brazen use of live ammunition and opened fire indiscriminately on the crowd, without even the customary warning shots. Three people, namely Tsewang Dorje, Nawang Rinchen and Tsering Stobdan were killed and many others were injured. The police then forcibly entered the precincts of Jokhang, desecrating its holy spaces, and many arrests were made inside the temple. Soon afterwards, Leh town and the neighboring areas were handed over to the army. Martial law was not officially declared, but it was martial law in all but name, with armed military personnel patrolling Leh and the surrounding villages in combat uniform, and curfew imposed. The situation was further aggravated when the government shut down power and telephone lines. Leh had been turned into a virtual military garrison. To this day, this episode is remembered as a dark day and a very sad chapter in the otherwise tranquil history of Ladakh.

Mr. Nawang Rinchen

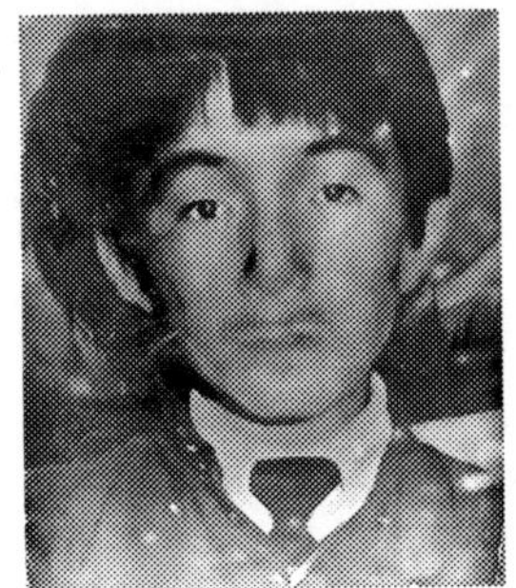

Mr. Tsering Stobdan

Mr. Tsewang Dorje

In the ensuing days of lock-down in Leh, the police arrested the top leadership of LBA including Thupstan Chhewang and took them to Srinagar. A number of Muslim youth leaders were also arrested. People vehemently protested these arrests.

Public discontent was reaching an all-time high. On September 2, 1989, state government employees in Leh went on an indefinite strike in support of the LBA agitation. As a result, the district administration came to a grinding halt. The people of Ladakh had been pushed to the wall, and were resolved to bring their agitation to its logical conclusion.

Rinpoche, along with other senior leaders, while trying to placate the public, appealed to the State and the Central Governments for their immediate intervention in defusing the tension. After sustained discussions and joint appeals by community leaders from both sides, some semblance of peace gradually returned to Leh, allowing Bakula Rinpoche to return to New Delhi. There he met with Prime Minister Rajiv Gandhi on September

22, 1989, and apprised him of the situation. Rinpoche gave the Prime Minister a detailed account of the tragic events which had gripped Leh, and the trail of bitterness they had left behind. Rinpoche also submitted a detailed report **(Annexure 21)** in which he suggested the following measures to restore normalcy:

- To discuss the core demand for Union Territory status for Ladakh, a Union Minister should be sent to Leh to hold tripartite talks between the Central Government, State Government and the Ladakh Buddhist Association;
- Essential supplies should be immediately dispatched to Ladakh before the closure of the road for winter;
- Immediate steps should be taken to end the strike of government employee so that the local administration could resume its duties;
- Scheduled Tribe status should be declared for all the people of Ladakh (Buddhist and Muslim) without any further delay, as it had already been recommended by the State Government and the Registrar General of India.

A sustained and peaceful agitation by the people of Ladakh finally bore fruits and as a result, in October 1989, the President of India formally promulgated the Constitution (J&K) Scheduled Tribes Order 1989 which declared eight tribes of Ladakh as Scheduled Tribes. Further, the Government of India in trying to end the agitation for Union Territory status for Ladakh, commenced tripartite talks in Leh on October 29, 1989, in the presence of Sardar Buta Singh, Union Home Minister, which culminated in the signing of an agreement assuring Ladakhis that an Autonomous District Council would be set up on the lines of the Darjeeling Gorkha Hill Council. The agreement was signed by P.P. Srivastava, Additional Secretary in the Ministry of Home Affairs on behalf of the central government, Ashok Jaitley, Additional Chief Secretary represented the J&K government, and Thupstan Chhewang, President of the LBA. **(Annexure 22).** The agreement was signed in the presence of the Union Home Minister Buta Singh, two ministers of the J&K government, namely Mangat Ram Sharma and Mohammed Shafi, as well as Bakula Rinpoche, P. Namgyal, and other authorities. The author was also present assisting Bakula Rinpoche in the meeting.

Although the LBA made a major climb-down on its demand of Union Territory (UT), this agreement, in which they settled for Hill Council status, meant a significant victory for Ladakh. With the signing of this agreement, peace and some semblance of normalcy returned to Ladakh. At last, the people of Ladakh were happy that they would have some measure of genuine democratic representation and local autonomy. The details however still needed to be hammered out, and negotiations with the central and state governments on the modalities of the Autonomous Hill Council began in earnest. Bakula Rinpoche was, however, not able to take part in these negotiations as he had to leave India soon afterwards to take up his new assignment as the Indian Ambassador to Mongolia.

Unfortunately, the negotiations did not proceed as smoothly as he might have hoped. The concerned parties found it hard to reach a final settlement, and new obstacles kept getting in the way. As a result, peaceful agitation in Leh resumed. Many youth activists and striking government employees were arrested and police atrocities also continued. Public anger against the State government remained high. On March 5, 1990, Ambassador Bakula Rinpoche wrote a letter from Mongolia to the then Prime Minister V.P. Singh, who headed the Janata Party Government, requested his personal intervention in unlocking the stalemate that was threatening the fragile situation in Ladakh **(Annexure 23)**. Unfortunately, the central government was at that time in a precarious position due to political instability which saw several successive governments at the centre fall in quick succession. Because of this gridlock at the national level, the final implementation of Hill Council status for Ladakh was again delayed.

On November 30, 1992, Bakula Rinpoche wrote another letter to Prime Minister P.V. Narasimha Rao cautioning that the delay was threatening to re-ignite the agitation and requested his personal attention. In response Rinpoche received a letter dated December 29, 1992, from the Prime Minister of India. In it the Prime Minister reiterated that "Efforts are continuing for developing a framework for appropriate institutional safeguards, which could meet the aspirations of the people and the development needs of the region." **(Annexure 24).**

Finally, in October 1993, the Government of India formally accepted the proposal for the formation of the LAHDC through an official notification. It was a major step forward. But the celebrations turned out to be premature yet again as there were still some obstacles to be cleared in the process. A series of discussions followed involving agitation leaders which helped remove the impasse. At last, the Government of India LAHDC Act, 1995 was passed by the Parliament of India heralding the de-centralization of planning process with the involvement of people at the grass-roots level. LAHDC, Leh was constituted in accordance with the Ladakh Autonomous Hill Development Council Act, 1995. The council came into being with the holding of elections on August 28,1995.

The Council came into being with the holding of elections to the 26-

member Ladakh Autonomous Hill Development Council, Leh (LAHDC) on August 28, 1995. Indian National Congress party secured an overwhelming victory in the election. Thupstan Chhewang was elected as the first Chairman and Chief Executive Councilor (CEC) along with Nawang Rigzin Jora, Sonam Dawa, Akbar Ladakhi and Tondup Sonam as Executive Councilors (ECs). A victory rally was organized at the Polo Ground in Leh, following the formation of LAHDC, Leh. Addressing the large gathering Bakula Rinpoche declared that the ultimate solution to Ladakh's grievances was Union Territory status for the region and that the LAHDC, Leh is only a stepping-stone in that direction.

The formation of LAHDC was a significant development with far reaching consequences for Ladakh which also heralded democratic decentralisation of the planning process with the involvement of people at the grassroots level. The same status was also granted to Kargil district where the people of Kargil had made no such demand. Initially they refused but later there was a rethink and finally LAHDC, Kargil was constituted in 2003. A new Council Secretariat comprising an assembly hall and a mini-secretariat, was built for the LAHDC, Leh. Its foundation stone was laid by Bakula Rinpoche on 27th September 2001.

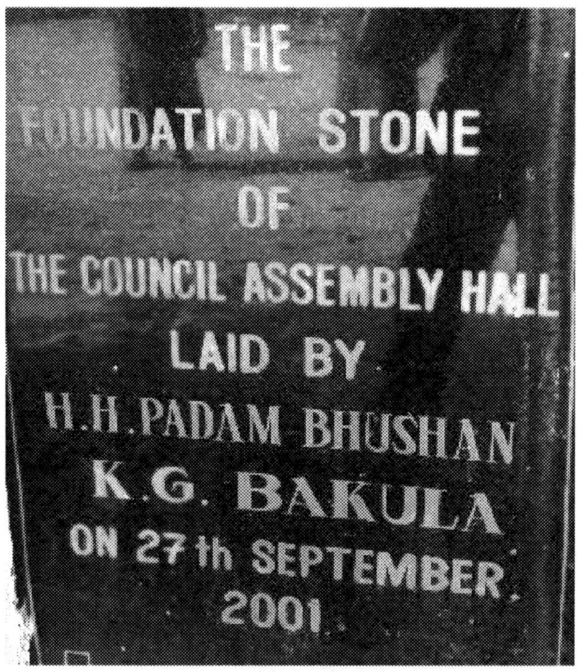

Foundation stone plaque of the LAHDC Assembly Hall, Leh

The successful outcome of the agitation was the hallmark of a new generation of educated leaders who refused to bow to pressure and brought their campaign to its logical end. In this, they were supported throughout by the ordinary people of Ladakh. It is also pertinent to mention here that the agitation succeeded yet again because the people of Ladakh were united in their resolve. Rinpoche always cautioned the people against forces trying to divide them. He had appealed to the people of Ladakh and their political leadership to stay united in their resolve for greater development of the region and for the protection of their unique cultural identity. It was hoped that the people of Ladakh stay united and focused in their resolve to defend their unique cultural identity. Failure in this resolve, Rinpoche feared, will do great harm to Ladakh and will only strengthen the hands of those who always sought division among the Ladakhis.

Thirty-two

Union Territory Status for Ladakh: A Mission Accomplished

As described in an earlier chapter, people of Ladakh under the leadership of Bakula Rinpoche have been persistently pursuing their demand for Union Territory status since 1949. This became a reality on 5th August 2019, when in a move in Parliament which surprised everyone, Amit Shah, Union Home Minister announced that the State of Jammu and Kashmir would be bifurcated into two Union territories – Jammu & Kashmir and Ladakh. It was introduced in the Rajya Sabha on 5th August 2019, and was passed on the same day. It was then passed by the Lok Sabha on 6th August 2019, and it received the President's assent on 9th August 2019.

Mr. Amit Shah, Home Minister, presenting the Jammu and Kashmir Reorganisation Act, 2019 (Image Credit: LSTV)

The Home Minister also announced that Article 370 and Article 35A of the constitution, that grants special status to the state of J&K, has been repealed. He said that while J&K will have a legislature, Ladakh will be a UT without it. However, it was made clear that the Ladakh Autonomous Hill Development Council (LAHDC) of Leh and Kargil will continue to function with the existing powers which would ensure democratic participation of the people in the running of a Union Territory. Thus, Ladakh, bound with the state of Jammu and Kashmir since 1842, was finally free from Kashmir. It became a Union Territory, a separate political entity administered directly by the Central Government in New Delhi.

Participating in the debate on the Jammu and Kashmir Reorganization Bill in Parliament, Jamyang Tsering Namgyal, Member of Parliament from Ladakh recalled the long and sustained struggle and sacrifices of the people of Ladakh and the exceptional leadership role played by Bakula Rinpoche for UT status for Ladakh. There was jubilation and instantaneous celebration across Ladakh. People of Ladakh expressed their gratitude to the Central Government. Homage was paid to all those who laid down their lives. Rich tributes were also paid to religious leaders and other leaders of the struggle.

The Bill passed by both the houses of Parliament came into effect on 31st October 2019. On this day Mr. R.K. Mathur took over as the first Lt. Governor of the Union Territory of Ladakh. However, while people in Leh district celebrated this feat, a section of people in Kargil District was upset and outraged. This, however, is not a new phenomenon as, on earlier occasions too, political leadership in Kargil behaved the same way.

However, despite these positive developments, dissatisfaction and disillusionment continues among the people. People had aspired for genuine autonomy and UT status with legislative powers throughout their long struggle, both in terms of administrative and financial matters which is lacking under the new set-up. UT without a legislature is like "old wine in new bottles", only the masters have changed. Earlier it was Kashmiri politicians and now it is bureaucrats controlled by Delhi. Therefore, the need of the hour is to restore democracy in Ladakh, empower the people with genuine legislative power and dispel all the misgivings.

It is to be noted that the people of Ladakh demanded UT status to safeguard their unique cultural identity and its fragile environment. It is also a fact that 97% of Ladakh comprises tribal population. Therefore, the people of Ladakh came out demanding the 6th Schedule of the Indian constitution, which provides for the administration of the tribal areas to safeguard the rights of the tribal population. Political and religious bodies

Bracing extreme temperature, a large crowd gathered in support of 6th Schedule. Leh, February 4, 2024

of Leh and Kargil came together in support of their four-point demand which included the following:

(i) Statehood/UT with legislature,

(ii) constitutional safeguards under the Sixth schedule of the Constitution of India,

(iii) creation of two Lok Sabha parliamentary seats for Ladakh, and

(iv) formation of Public Service Commission.

These long-standing grievances, coupled with the prolonged delay in talks between the two sides and the government's indifference to the four-point demand—particularly the demand for inclusion under the 6th Schedule—deeply upset the people. The 6th Schedule provides measures of autonomy and self-governance to the Scheduled Tribes in the hill region of Northeast India. Incidentally, 97% of Ladakh's total population are Scheduled Tribes. The provisions of the 6th Schedule are provided under Article 244(2) and 275 (1) of the Indian Constitution and one of the most important features of the 6th Schedule is the empowerment of District Councils to make laws on certain specified matters like land, forests, canal water, shifting cultivation, village administration, inheritance of property, marriage and divorce, social customs and so on. However, all laws made under this provision shall have no effect until assented by the Governor of the State.

Unfortunately, the local administration's continued disregard for the agitation caused the situation to steadily deteriorate. Growing frustration also drove many unemployed youths to join the movement, expressing their anger against the authorities. On September 10, 2025, environmentalist and Magsaysay Award winner Mr. Sonam Wangchuk, along with many others, began a hunger strike in Leh in support of the four-point demands. The situation worsened when two elderly participants in the hunger strike collapsed and had to be hospitalised. September 24, 2025, turned into another dark day in Ladakh's history. Violence erupted in the town, prompting the security forces to open fire on demonstrators without issuing the customary warning shots. Around 80-90 people were injured, many sustaining bullet wounds. Four young men — Tsewang Tharchin, Rinchen Dadul, Jigmet Dorjay, and Stanzin Namgyal — lost their lives in police firing. Among those killed in the police firing was a retired soldier of the Ladakh Scouts Regiment, a veteran of the Kargil War. Another youth, Stanzin Dorjey, later took his own life in solidarity with the movement.

Following the violence, the district administration imposed a strict curfew in Leh and suspended mobile internet services. Section 163 of the Bharatiya Nyaya Sanhita (the new version of Section 144, prohibiting the assembly of five or more persons) was enforced for several weeks. Numerous arrests were made, and police cases were filed against many protestors. The administration accused Mr. Sonam Wangchuk of inciting violence and arson, leading to his arrest under the National Security Act (NSA) and

subsequent transfer to the Central Jail, Jodhpur, Rajasthan. Meanwhile, Leh Apex Body (APEX) and Kargil Democratic Alliance (KDA) strongly protested the brutal and excessive force used by the administration to control the mob and also refuted allegations of the involvement of foreign hand and anti-national forces behind the agitation. It also demanded immediate and unconditional release of all those under detention and demanded an impartial judicial inquiry, headed by a retired judge of the Supreme Court of India, to investigate the incident. In protest, both APEX and KDA suspended their talks with the Ministry of Home Affairs until these demands were met.

On October 18, 2025, the Home Ministry, through an official notification, announced the formation of a Judicial Commission headed by Justice Dr. B. S. Chauhan, former Judge of the Supreme Court of India. The Commission is tasked with examining the circumstances leading to the violence, the police action, and the resultant loss of lives. This step is expected to help break the deadlock and pave the way for the resumption of talks. While the long struggle and campaign of the people of Ladakh to free Ladakh from Kashmir saw a happy ending with Ladakh becoming a Union Territory in 2019, people of Ladakh continue to crave for their democratic rights, legislative powers and constitutional safeguards under the 6th Schedule of the Indian constitution to protect their identity and preserve their cherished cultural heritage and environment. Their struggle continues and the people are hopeful that the Government of India will enter into a serious negotiation with leaders of Leh APEX and KDA and find a solution.

PART V

A BUDDHIST LEADER AT WORLD STAGE

Ladakh Shanti Stupa

Thirty-three

Ladakh Shanti Stupa

Bakula Rinpoche had a long association with the Buddhists in Japan. In 1971, he had visited Japan for the first time to attend the annual ceremony marking the US atomic bombing of Hiroshima and Nagasaki in year 1945 and to participate in a conference against nuclear weapons. He saw heart-wrenching scenes of the cities being wiped out and the subsequent hunger and disease that ravaged the survivors. That bombing had brought into sharp focus the devastating effects of nuclear weapons and the horrors they can unleash on humanity. This visit had a lasting impact on Rinpoche and spurred him to participate actively in peace movements.

During his stay in Japan, he met with many Japanese Buddhist priests as well as scholars of Buddhism and developed close friendships with many of them. In particular, Rinpoche remained in close contact with Nichidatsu Fujii Guruji who had visited India as early as year 1933, where he met Mahatma Gandhi and joined Gandhi's non-violent struggle for India's independence. It was from that time that Gandhiji incorporated the Lotus Sutra *(Na mu myo ho ren ge kyo)* into his roster of daily prayers. It was Gandhiji who gave Fujii the title "Guruji", as he is now known world-wide. The miniature of "Three wise-monkeys" was gifted to Gandhi ji by Fujii Guruji. Throughout his life, Fujii Guruji practiced a path of peace based on Buddhist ideals. The order he founded, called Nipponzan Myohoji, has built more than one hundred Shanti Stupas or Peace Pagodas in different parts of world, including Rajgir, Vaishali, Darjeeling, Dhauligiri (Orissa), Wardha and Ladakh in India, and also in the USA, the UK, Australia, Japan, Sri Lanka and other countries. Ever since their meeting in 1971, Rinpoche worked closely with Fujii Guruji. Rinpoche was a frequent participant at the annual peace rally in Japan and at other gatherings to protest against nuclear

Nichidatsu Fujii Guruji

weapons. Rinpoche also attended the funeral of Fujii Guruji, when he passed away at the age of 100 in Japan on January 9, 1985.

Bakula Rinpoche was very keen that one Shanti Stupa (Peace Pagoda) would also be built in Ladakh, particularly in light of the fact that Ladakh was a sensitive and highly militarised border area surrounded by two hostile neighbours. He told Fujii Guruji that being located geographically near the junction of several major powers (Pakistan, India and China), it would be highly symbolic, inspirational and a source of hope for a peaceful world. Accordingly, Rinpoche requested Fujii Guruji to build one such Stupa in Leh as a symbol of peace. He offered to provide all necessary logistical support and secure all the necessary government permissions and so on.

Fujii Guruji gladly accepted the request, and work began immediately. On behalf of his organization *'Nipponzan Myohoji'*, Fujii Guruji appointed Bhikshu G. Nakamura to supervise the construction work. The author was deputed by Bakula Rinpoche to accompany Nakamura to help him with all logistical issues in Leh. After careful consideration and visiting several possible sites, Changspa Hill, from which one gets a panoramic view over the Leh valley, was chosen for the project.

Rinpoche after laying the foundation stone for Ladakh Shanti Stupa (1983)

Rinpoche addressing the gathering after laying the foundation stone of Ladakh Shanti Stupa. Author is seen translating Rinpoche's speech

Volunteers at work at the construction of Ladakh Shanti Stupa

The foundation stone for the Ladakh Shanti Stupa was laid by Bakula Rinpoche on April 4, 1983, at a ceremony attended by a large gathering of local people, government functionaries including Mr. C. Phunsog, IAS, DC, Leh and senior lamas. The ceremony was also attended by monks of Nipponzan Myohoji as well as numerous other Japanese donors and guests.

To accelerate the pace of work at the construction site, a new road was needed. In year 1984, Rinpoche approached Mrs. Indira Gandhi, the Prime Minister of India, for assistance in building the road, and she accepted. Shortly thereafter a road was laid leading up to the Hill which made the transportation of building materials much easier. The volunteer force of people including several Japanese, worked with great enthusiasm for the construction of the stupa, which at an altitude of around 4267 metre (14000 Ft), is the highest Peace Pagoda in the world. The project was completed under the supervision of Bhikhu Nakamura. In year 1985, the 14th Dalai Lama blessed the Stupa and the temple attached to it. The Ladakh Shanti Stupa was formally opened to the public in 1991 and has become the most popular tourist attraction in Leh. Shanti Stupa is a registered society under the name "Nipponzan Myohoji Ladakh Shanti Stupa Society" of which the author is a member. It stands majestically overlooking the Leh valley with the holy relics of Lord Buddha enshrined inside it. It is a unique source of blessing for the people of Ladakh and the whole world.

Thirty-four

Meeting the 10th Panchen Lama

In Tibet, Panchen Lama is considered the highest-ranking religious leader after the Dalai Lama. Successive Panchen Lamas are considered reincarnations of the Buddha Amitabha. The title *panchen* means "great scholar", being a Tibetan contraction of the Sanskrit *pandita* (scholar) and the Tibetan *chenpo* (great). The Panchen Lamas traditionally resided at Tashilhunpo Monastery in Shigatse. Bakula Rinpoche had met the 10th Panchen Lama Lobsang Trinley Lhündrub Chökyi Gyaltsen on many occasions. Over the course of these interactions Bakula Rinpoche and the Panchen Lama had developed close mutual trust and respect. When Panchen Lama (together with the Dalai Lama) made their visit to India in 1956, Bakula Rinpoche served as their official guide and chaperone, so during that time in particular the two became very close.

It was after thirty years of separation that the two men were able to meet again. The occasion was the conference of the World Fellowship of Buddhists (WFB) which was held in Kathmandu, Nepal in 1986. Initially, Bakula Rinpoche had not intended to attend the conference in Nepal, as at that time he was already very busy with numerous engagements and duties, but when he learnt that the Panchen Lama was scheduled to attend, he immediately altered his schedule so that he too could go.

Tibet had been through a period of intense rupture and tumult during the intervening decades, so Rinpoche was very keen to meet the Panchen Lama again and re-affirm their bond as spiritual brothers. The Panchen Lama who led the Chinese delegation, was the guest of honour at the conference, the opening ceremony of which was held in an open-air stadium in Kathmandu. Huge crowds of devout Buddhists turned out to greet him. For many in the Tibetan Buddhist cultural world, even to catch a glimpse of this extremely elevated figure was considered a great blessing. I remember the event very well. The Panchen Lama was seated on a high platform. As we reached near the platform where the Panchen Lama was sitting, I remember Rinpoche greeted him from a distance. It was the first time they had seen each other in thirty years, but The Panchen Lama recognized Bakula Rinpoche immediately and without any hesitation he returned the latter's greeting by standing up from his seat. Unfortunately, the security around Panchen Lama up at the event was extremely tight, so it was impossible even for Bakula Rinpoche to get near him. The following day Raja Birendra Bir Bikram Shah Dev, King of Nepal hosted a reception in his honour at the royal palace, to which Bakula Rinpoche was also invited.

At the palace gate, the Panchen Lama was being introduced to the heads of various delegations representing different countries. Among them was Bakula Rinpoche heading the Indian delegation. Rinpoche was carrying with him a *khadag* which he offered to the Panchen Lama as they met. In return, the Panchen Lama, perhaps sensing that he would meet Bakula Rinpoche, took his own *khadag* from his pocket and presented it to Bakula Rinpoche. As I stood next to Bakula Rinpoche, I could see the simple joy on both the faces as they met again after thirty years. There was little time to talk, but the Panchen Lama immediately expressed his desire to meet Rinpoche again so that they could talk properly. While I was offering to him my own *khadag*, Panchen Lama enquired from me as to which hotel Bakula Rinpoche was staying at Kathmandu. I told him the name of the hotel and also the room number. For me personally, it was an exhilarating experience to speak directly to one of the most talked-about figures in modern Tibetan history.

That evening two invitations from the Chinese Ambassador to attend a special reception were delivered to our hotel room. Of course, Rinpoche gladly accepted the invitation. The reception was held at the Chinese embassy and it was crowded with guests. After some time, when Panchen Lama entered the hall, an awed and expected hush fell on the crowd and the famed lama was introduced to the various foreign diplomats and guests who were lined up to greet him. When his turn came, the Panchen Lama told Rinpoche very clearly that after his round of meeting the guests was complete, he would like to sit down and talk with him. Rinpoche was rather anxious about this and he was unsure how it could be arranged, given the large number of guests in the hall and the fact that they were in the premises of the Chinese embassy, which was not exactly a venue conducive to any free and frank conversation. However, after a while an official of the Chinese embassy approached Rinpoche and told us to follow him. He escorted Rinpoche out of the reception hall, and we were taken to a separate room. I could sense that Rinpoche was excited at meeting the Panchen Lama again

Rinpoche with Panchen Lama in Kathmandu, Nepal (1986)

Panchen Lama and Bakula Rinpoche in Kathmandu, Nepal.
Author standing on the left (1986)

after so many years and after so much had happened in the history of their shared culture and religion.

After a short wait, the Panchen Lama entered the room leaving behind the big gathering of distinguished people and the two lamas greeted each other in the traditional manner by touching their foreheads and exchanging gifts. I remember that Rinpoche offered Panchen Lama packets of Kashmiri saffron and apricots from Ladakh, and the Panchen Lama gave Rinpoche a *thangka* and some books. They then sat down and talked, and their conversation went on for over an hour.

I was allowed to sit there and take some photographs of this historic meeting. Initiating the conversation, Panchen Lama recalled their last meeting during his visit to India in year 1956 and also their earlier meetings in Tibet, when Bakula Rinpoche was studying at Drepung. He told Rinpoche how pleased he was to be able to meet again in "a new environment". Panchen Lama also enquired about some other Ladakhi monks from Pethub who he remembered from their time spent at Tashilhunpo in Tibet. The two then talked about the situation in Tibet, and they also broached the very sensitive subject of the Panchen Lama's relationship with His Holiness the 14th Dalai Lama. I remember Panchen Lama expressed his dismay at the attempts being made "in certain circles" to drive a wedge between him and the Dalai Lama. But, he said, any such attempts would never succeed, as he held the Dalai Lama in the highest esteem. He also asked Bakula Rinpoche to convey to the Dalai Lama his deepest respect and most profound faith.

He also spoke frankly about the severe damage that had been inflicted on Tibet's religious institutions, cultural life, and environment during the Cultural Revolution and afterwards and also about the work that was now being done to restore them. In this, he expressed confidence that they would succeed. He told Rinpoche that he was not afraid of expressing his views to the Chinese authorities. Indeed, this was evident to us, for during that very discussion we were inside the premises of the Chinese embassy, and it was more than likely that their conversation was being overheard through listening devices. But the Panchen Lama was fearless and candid in the expression of his views. To me, it was both astonishing and inspiring to see how bold he was, even after suffering so many years of manipulation, imprisonment and persecution at the hands of the Chinese authorities.

The Panchen Lama also invited Rinpoche to visit Tibet, offered his hospitality and that he would give all help so that Rinpoche is granted the necessary visa, etc. Shortly thereafter, Rinpoche received a hand-written letter from the Panchen Lama himself, again inviting him to visit Tibet. Unfortunately, the visit could not materialize during the Panchen Lama's own lifetime, which Rinpoche deeply regretted.

Back in India, Bakula Rinpoche visited Dharamshala for an audience with the Dalai Lama and gave a full account of his meeting, while also passing on the Panchen Lama personal messages of greeting and devotion. The Dalai Lama was visibly moved to hear these messages, and told Rinpoche that he too had always held the Panchen Rinpoche in high regard, despite the difficult circumstances that had separated them for so many decades.

The Panchen Lama was the single most senior and respected Tibetan spiritual leader to have remained inside China after the occupation of Tibet. Although he was criticized by many for this, the fact that he remained in Tibet actually enabled him to do a lot of valuable work in protecting the Tibetan people. He actually did as best he could during a period of intense hardship and oppression, when Tibetan culture was threatened with extinction at the hands of Chinese communism.

Initially, the Panchen Lama was in the good books of the Chinese communist leadership, and some say, with some justification, that he was used by them as a pawn. But later on, he also became an outspoken critic of Chinese policies in Tibet, and this led to some sharp divisions between him and the Chinese leadership. In year 1964, he was dismissed from all official posts, declared an "enemy of the people", and imprisoned, all at the age of only twenty-four. His situation worsened even further during the Cultural Revolution launched in 1966. It was only after Chairman Mao's death in year 1976, that his situation began to improve. In October 1977, he was released from prison, but he was still held under house arrest in Beijing for another five years, until 1982. And it was only after his release from house arrest that he was finally considered politically rehabilitated by the Chinese authorities. After that he was able, once again, to rise to important positions within the Chinese state apparatus, indicating that his spirit had by no means been crushed by these decades of adversity. He went on to serve as the Vice-Chairman of the National People's Congress, during which time he resided mainly in Beijing.

Early in 1989, the Panchen Lama returned once again to Tashilhunpo Monastery in Shigatse *(Xigaze)* which was the primary monastic seat of his lineage, and there he re-enshrined some of the bone-relics which had been recovered from the graves of previous Panchen Lamas and were desecrated in the vandalism of Tashilhunpo in the years following 1959. It was during this visit to Tibet, that Panchen Lama passed away in Shigatse on January 28, 1989, only five days after he had delivered a speech which had included an indictment of China's Tibet policies over the previous decades, and particularly during the Cultural Revolution. He had famously said that: "Since liberation, there has certainly been development, but the price paid for this development has been greater than the gains".

The death of the Panchen Lama was a great shock for many as he was still young at only 51. Officially the cause of death was said to have been from a heart attack, but many suspects there was some foul play. Many believe that his sudden death was linked to his public criticism of the government in his speech of January 28, 1989, a speech that was widely reported.

The passing away of the 10th Panchen Lama drove a further deep wedge of distrust between the Tibetan people and the Chinese government. And matters only became more contentious when it came to identifying his reincarnation. A search committee to identify his reincarnation was set up at Tashilhunpo headed by Chadrel Rinpoche, who during his search, secretly maintained communications with the 14th Dalai Lama, in keeping with traditional protocol. For several years, no incarnation was identified.

On May 14, 1995, just under six years after the death of the 10th Panchen Lama, an announcement was issued in Dharamshala, India that a child, named Gedhun Choekyi Nyima, the son of highland nomads in the Nagchu region of Kham, had been identified as the 11th Panchen Lama by Chadrel Rinpoche's search party, and that the boy had been officially recognized by the 14th Dalai Lama and given his solemn seal of approval. The reaction of the Chinese authorities was immediate and ruthless. Chadrel Rinpoche was arrested immediately and summarily sentenced to prison. The Chinese government moved swiftly to try to assert their own authority over the process, but for ordinary Tibetan people, it was already too late. News of the Dalai Lama's recognition had already spread to all Tibetan Buddhists, who almost without exception, acknowledged his authority.

It was only a few months before this, in September 1994, that 14th Dalai Lama had been visiting Mongolia, where Bakula Rinpoche was serving as the Indian Ambassador. Rinpoche was hosting a reception at the Indian Embassy in honour of the Dalai Lama. During the reception, His Holiness also paid a visit to Rinpoche's residence which was located on the first floor of the same building. It was during this private meeting that Rinpoche broached the subject of the new Panchen Lama with the Dalai Lama. He enquired whether the rumours that a boy had already been recognized were true, and also about the possibility to slip the boy past the Chinese authorities, so that he could escape to India where he would be safe. The Dalai Lama's response, unexpectedly, was one of surprise. It was true, he said, that a reincarnation had been found, but he said he was unaware of any plans to secretly bring him out to India. It seems that at that point the Dalai Lama was quite optimistic that the boy's recognition would be accepted without too much fuss by the authorities in Tibet.

Unfortunately, this was not to be. When they found out, the Chinese authorities acted fast. Not only Chagdrel Rinpoche, but also the boy (only five years old at the time) and his family were taken into custody. Chadrel Rinpoche was charged with "plotting to split the country" and imprisoned, while the boy, considered by most Tibetan Buddhists to be the true 11th Panchen Lama, simply disappeared. Gedhun Choekyi Nyima (born in Lhari County, Nagchu Prefecture, TAR on April 25, 1989) thus became the world's youngest political prisoner, and nothing has been seen or heard of him since. To this day, nearly three decades later, the whereabouts of Gedhun Choekyi Nyima remain completely unknown. This act of injustice continues to be a major source of disaffection and resentment among Tibetan Buddhists towards the Chinese state. Soon afterwards, rubbing salt in the wound, the Chinese Government made an official pronouncement rejecting the findings of the Dalai Lama as invalid, and forming their own search team to find the reincarnation of the previous Panchen Lama. It was this 'official' search party which yielded the child Gyancain Norbu, who was duly enthroned at Tashilhunpo, with Chinese state approval, as the 11th Panchen Lama on November 11, 1995.

Thirty-five

A Buddhist Leader on World Forums

Ever since his childhood, Bakula Rinpoche was well accustomed to long journeys. As a young *tulku* in Ladakh he had ventured across high passes to receive instruction and give blessings. And his epic journey to Lhasa as a young monk, covering thousands of kilometers, was an experience he would never forget. Later, his visits to Russia, Mongolia, China and several Central Asian countries helped expand his knowledge of the world and witnessed many momentous transformations taking place in various regions. Also, from close quarters, Rinpoche witnessed the destruction of life, culture and environment in different places in the garb of ideology and development.

In 1952, Bakula Rinpoche participated in the International Buddhist Conference at Sanchi, Madhya Pradesh. This marked a significant moment in his early public life. It was his first major international conference, attended by prominent figures such as: Dr. S. Radhakrishnan (Vice-President of India), Pandit Jawaharlal Nehru (Prime Minister of India), Mr. U Nu (First Prime Minister of Burma), Dr. Syama Prasad Mookerjee (President of the Maha Bodhi Society of India) and other distinguished scholars.

At this event, Bakula Rinpoche delivered a forceful speech that showcased his deep understanding of Buddhist philosophy and its relevance to the modern world. His address touched on themes of Buddhism's role in shaping moral values, fostering peace, and reviving spiritual traditions – ideas that would later define his contributions in India and abroad. This conference provided him with a platform to engage with global Buddhist leaders and set the stage for his lifelong mission of Buddhist revival, particularly in Mongolia and Russia in later years.

After Tibet, which was hardly considered a foreign land for Ladakhis, Rinpoche's next foreign trip came in 1954, when he had visited Rangoon, the capital of Burma to attend the 3rd General Conference of the World Fellowship of Buddhists (WFB). It was a historic gathering of international Buddhist leaders and representatives of Buddhist Organizations and communities with a view to revealing Buddhism to humankind and demonstrating the Buddhist way of life to the distracted and threatened world. The conference was an eye-opening experience for Rinpoche, with Buddhist leaders from so many different countries of the world in attendance. Rinpoche was accompanied on this visit by Mr. Tashi Rabgyes, a well-known scholar and a historian of Ladakh who was at that time serving as Rinpoche's secretary and interpreter. Also present was Babasaheb Dr. Bhim Rao Ambedkar, the leader of the downtrodden and one of the main architects of the Indian Constitution, who, at that time, was serving as the Law Minister of India. This was Rinpoche's second meeting with Dr. Ambedkar, since earlier, in 1950, he had helped Bakula Rinpoche retain land holdings belonging to the monasteries in Ladakh.

At this conference, Ladakh Buddhist Association (LBA) was officially registered as a regional centre of the WFB. In those days' communication was not like it is today. Many of the participants at that conference in fact, were unaware about the existence of so many different Buddhist denominations and traditions across Asia and the world. There was also clearly a lot of misunderstanding and prejudice between different groups. Rinpoche himself felt this prejudice among some of the delegates about his own Tibetan robes, and this affected him quite profoundly.

Narrating one such incident Rinpoche told me that during the conference, the delegates were brought to visit a Buddhist temple in Rangoon. The monks at the temple had perhaps never seen a monk in Tibetan robes before, which are a little different in colour and design from their own robes. This created much confusion. Besides, Rinpoche's head was not clean-shaven like the Theravada monks and at the time he had a moustache too which was not uncommon among Tibetan monks at the time (after all, the Thirteenth Dalai Lama had a moustache).

When lunch was served at the temple, the monks and lay people were seated separately. Naturally Rinpoche chose to join the monks. However, he was asked not to sit there and instead was directed to a seat alongside some lay people. Rinpoche was rather confused and taken aback but he quickly realised that the confusion was created because of his (to them) strange dress and physical appearance. It was after experiencing this, that Rinpoche's determination to build greater contact and greater understanding between the Buddhists of the world was born. He made a solemn commitment to bring different traditions closer to each other and generate better understanding and cooperation. And this was something he worked on, without wavering, throughout his long career.

Rinpoche addressed a distinguished gathering on the occasion of the First International Buddhist Conference (IBC). Seated on the dais included Mr. U. Nu, first Prime Minister of Burma, Prime Minister Nehru, Vice-President Dr. S. Radhakrishnan and Dr. Syama Prasad Mookerjee (Sanchi, Madhya Pradesh, December, 1952)

Bakula Rinpoche (centre in the first row) with delegates of World Fellowship of Buddhists (WFB) at Rangoon, Burma (1954)

In later years, Rinpoche developed close relations with a number of Buddhist leaders from variety of countries and traditions. And henceforth, to show that the various Buddhist traditions were all fundamentally aligned with one another, and to create greater understanding of this, whenever he visited a country with Theravada tradition such as Burma, Thailand, Cambodia, Laos, Sri Lanka, etc., he chose to wear Theravada robes throughout his stay.

After the conference, organizers had arranged for all foreign delegates to travel to the holy sites in the country. Rinpoche travelled to Mandalay and *Amarapura* by train. They also visited *Sagaing*, a famous centre for Vipasana meditation. They were then taken by river-steamer down the Irrawaddy river to *Pagon*, an ancient centre for spread of Theravada Buddhism in South East Asia and finally on to *Migyan*, famous for its forest meditation retreats.

While he was in Burma, Rinpoche had also established contacts with a high priest of Sri Lanka (Ceylon). After returning to Ladakh, under the auspices of the Maha Bodhi Society of India, he sent a group of young Ladakhi monks to Ceylon to study Pali and Theravada Buddhism. Six monk-students were chosen and they spent two years in Sri Lanka during which they learnt Pali and Sinhalese. After completing their studies in Sri Lanka, they returned home much enriched by their scriptural studies. In his interaction with monks from different Buddhist traditions, Rinpoche always emphasized that differences in colour and style of their dresses were superficial expressions determined partly by climate and local conditions, whereas the Buddha's holy teachings and the *Vinaya*, the core monastic discipline, was the same for all.

In December 1964, Rinpoche attended the 7th General Conference of World Fellowship of Buddhists (WFB) which was held at Sarnath, Varanasi. The WFB Conference was inaugurated by Dr. S. Radhakrishnan, Vice-President of India. Buddhist leaders from across the world attended the conference. Bakula Rinpoche represented the Ladakh Buddhist Association at the conference and addressed the gathering.

Over the years, Rinpoche travelled widely, visiting countries in Southeast Asia as well as the Soviet Union, Europe, and the United States. In every country, he interacted with the Buddhists and conveyed the message of unity and solidarity. So, in year 1969, when Rinpoche formed the ABCP in Mongolia with the Khambolamas of USSR and Mongolia (as discussed in a later section), he already had many international Buddhist contacts who associated with this organisation.

In New York City with twin towers in the background

In 1981, the United Nations hosted a special session of the General Assembly on Disarmament. People from different walks of life and from all corners of the globe were gathered there. A peace march was orchestrated which ended at New York's Central Park. Here all kinds of community leaders and activists from all walks of life, as well as native American chiefs and leaders representing all of the world's major religions gathered. They assembled to give voice to concerns regarding the deteriorating global scenario during this late phase of the Cold War, and against the nuclear arms race. Bakula Rinpoche joined Nichidatsu Fujii of Japan, Lord Philip Noel Baker from UK, Muni Sushil Kumar Jain and many others in addressing the assembled crowd. As part of a delegation comprising religious representatives, Rinpoche also met with Mr. Jan Matterson, Assistant Secretary General (Disarmament) at the United Nations Headquarters in New York.

Rinpoche Participating in a peace rally at the Central Park, New York along with Lord Philip Noel Baker, Fujii Nichidatsu Guruji of Japan and others (1981)

Bakula Rinpoche at the UN Headquarters meeting Jan Matterson, Assistant Secretary General (Disarmament) (New York, 1981)

Rinpoche addressing the International Conference on 'Saving the Sacred Gift of Life from Nuclear Catastrophe' in Moscow, USSR (1982)

Rinpoche with Prince Philip and leaders of different religious faiths at the Windsor Castle, UK (1995)

A year later in June 1982, Bakula Rinpoche visited Moscow, to attend the "World Conference of Religious Workers for Saving the Sacred Gift of Life from Nuclear Catastrophe". This was at the invitation of Patriarch Pimen of Moscow and All Russia, the Head of the Russian Orthodox Church. Participants included representatives from the World Council of Churches, All African Conference of Churches, Islamic organizations from Arab and other countries, Buddhists, Christians, Hindus, Jews, Shintos, Sikhs, and Zoroastrians. Besides many prominent religious leaders and theologians, several statesmen and scientists also participated in it. The American Evangelist Rev. Billy Graham also joined the call for a nuclear-free world. Nations were urged to resolutely renounce the policy of confrontation and hostility and to embark with renewed determination on the path of peace and cooperation for the settlement of conflicts. The conference called for an immediate halt to the arms-race and the abandonment of the aptly-named MAD (Mutual Assured Destruction) policy. It also called for an immediate freeze on the development and production of weapons of mass destruction, as a first step towards the goal of general and complete disarmament.

In 1986, leaders of the five major world religions – Buddhism, Christianity, Hinduism, Islam and Judaism – met at Assisi in Italy, the birthplace of St Francis, to discuss how their respective faiths could come together to help save the natural world. It was a unique occasion, involving some of the world's leading environmental and conservation bodies sitting down for the first time with leaders of the world's major faiths to discuss how they could combine their efforts.

Much later, as a follow-up to the Assisi meeting, a further meeting on religion and conservation was hosted by Prince Phillip, the Duke of Edinburgh (husband of Queen Elizabeth II of the United Kingdom) and co-sponsored by the World Wildlife Fund (WWF), the Pilkington Foundation and Mokichi Okada Association (MOA International). It was held in two sessions, the first of which took place in Atami, Japan, and the second in Windsor Castle, United Kingdom.

It was during the first one in Japan that Rinpoche met with Minoru Yamada, Executive Director of MOA International, an organization well-known in Japan for its museum at Atami and its model organic farm at Ohito. Mr. Yamada was passionate about the need to revive and strengthen traditional eastern values in our changing global culture. He was deeply concerned about the impact and influence of western culture on the young minds not only in Japan but in other countries too. Rinpoche was also struck by his dedicated efforts to realize the ideals of the founder of MOA, Mokichi Okada. This was Rinpoche's first introduction to the works and ideals of Mr. Okada, and he was deeply moved by Mr. Okada's vision for the future

Rinpoche with Prince Philip at the Windsor Castle, UK (1995)

At the Windsor Castle, UK with Mary Maxwell Rabbani (Baha'i) and Grand Master Xie Zongxing (Taoism) (1995)

of humanity. Apart from promoting Japanese traditional art and culture, Mr. Okada advocated organic farming at a time when the global trend was the industrialization of agriculture and the large-scale use of chemical fertilizers and insecticide to boost production. Contrary to this trend, MOA promoted organic farming and formulated clear marketing strategies which could help it succeed and gain traction in the marketplace. Rinpoche considered the MOA programmes a very good role model for dealing with the global ecological situation.

During a visit to Mongolia, Mr. Yamada accepted Rinpoche's request for training students from Mongolia and Ladakh and several young scientists from Mongolia and Ladakh visited Japan and studied organic farming under the auspices of MOA International.

In year 1995, at the First Session held in Atami, Japan, during 3-9 April 1995, it was decided to set up a new organization called Alliance of Religion and Conservation (ARC) with headquarters in the UK and Bakula Rinpoche was made one of its patrons. The main aim of this organization was to encourage interfaith dialogue on ecological conservation. Several projects have been successfully launched under its auspices and are proving to be extremely beneficial. In all these meetings, the author accompanied Rinpoche.

The second session of ARC in Windsor Castle, England, UK, from 29 April to 4 May 1995 included leaders from nine major world religions, namely Baha'i faith, Buddhism, Christianity, Hinduism, Islam, Jainism, Judaism, Sikhism and Taoism, as well as the heads of several organizations such as the World Bank, the BBC, WWF and MOA Japan. Participants included Bakula Rinpoche (Buddhism); Madame Mary Maxwell Rabbani (Baha'i); Patriarch Bartholomew (Ecumenical Patriarch of Constantinople); Dr. George Carey (Archbishop of Canterbury); Swami Chidanand Saraswati and Dr. Karan Singh (Hinduism); Prince Hasa Bin Tal and Dr. Adnan Bakhit (Islam); Dr. L.M. Singhvi (Jainism); Rabbi Arthur Hertzberg (Judaism); Jathedar Manjit Singh (Sikhism) and Grand Master Xie Zongxing (Taoism).

Martin Palmer, a Christian scholar and a good friend of Rinpoche's, coordinated all the activities. It was during this conference that Bakula Rinpoche established a strong rapport with HRH Prince Phillip, and would meet him again several times in the years to come. I remember that in the course of discussion at Windsor Castle Dr. George Carey, Archbishop of Canterbury suggested a format for a closed-door meeting. It provided that the leader of each faith would be allotted fifteen minutes to make a presentation which would be followed by a Q&A session. When his turn came, Bakula Rinpoche expressed his view which caused some flutter. He said that although western civilization had brought about major scientific progress ignited by the industrial revolution of the eighteenth century, it had led to an erosion of human values, and made people incline toward materialistic worldviews like communism and consumerism. Further, he said the main contributions of Eastern philosophy to humankind were its spiritual traditions, but unfortunately the Asian societies had also been overwhelmed by the flow of materialist ideas and lifestyles, and that this had resulted in a sharp decline in moral values as well as the rapid destruction of Nature and ecology.

I was translating Rinpoche's speech, and while making his presentation he also made some remarks which did not at all go down well with the Archbishop. For example, in his opening remarks Rinpoche had strongly disapproved of the methods and activities of some overzealous Christian missionaries, particularly in poorer countries where they exploited people's poverty and used the tactic of criticizing and undermining people's traditional faiths while offering them material incentives to convert, as he had seen in Mongolia.

These remarks clearly raised the hackles of the Archbishop of Canterbury, who intervened and asked Rinpoche what the relevance of religious intolerance and conversion was to the issue of religion and nature-conservation, which were the two subjects they had gathered here to discuss? The visibly-upset Archbishop suggested that this was not the appropriate platform to raise such issues. But in his reply Rinpoche defended his words saying that religious intolerance and coercive conversion were relevant to the issue of conservation because they have a serious adverse impact on social order, community cohesion and communal relations, all highly crucial factors for nature conservation. He cited Mongolia as an example, which prior to communism had been a Buddhist nation. He said that even after seventy years of communism, Mongolian people had never lost touch with their traditional values and were very close to nature, which according to Rinpoche, was due to their traditional faith. Elaborating his views further, he said that even today when Mongolians take a glass of vodka, even those with no overt Buddhist faith, do sprinkle drops in the four directions as an offering to nature before they drink. And when they cross a mountain pass, they do circumambulation and offering at an *Ovoo* (mountain passes). Mongolia, he said, has world's oldest protected mountains and lakes where hunting and the destruction of forests had been banned since long before modern times. These habits, customs and laws, he said, were based on ancient traditions linked with their faith in Buddhism and Shamanism. And all these values could be undermined if they converted to another faith. Rinpoche also contended that Buddhism, as a faith based on scientific inquiry and philosophy, was suited to the character of the people. As he ended his

In London with Dr. L.M. Singhvi, High Commissioner of India, Rev. Dr. George Carey, Archbishop of Canterbury and Swami Chidanand Saraswati (1995)

Rinpoche on a wheelchair at the first "Buddhist Summit" held at Kyoto, Japan with the 14th Dalai Lama, the Supreme Patriarch of Thailand Sangharaja Somdet Phra Nyanasamvara, Dr. Kyuse Enshinjoh, President, Buddhist Summit and other Buddhist leaders at Kyoto, Japan (1995)

remarks, there was thunderous applause by all the participants. Thereafter between him and the Archbishop there was no rancour.

In year 1997 Rinpoche received a letter from the Archbishop of Canterbury and the President of the World Bank. ARC had arranged a meeting at Lambeth Palace, the official residence of the Archbishop which was attended by leaders of the nine religions as well as James Wolfensohn, President of the World Bank. This time, the aim of the meeting was to explore alternative economic models consistent with religious faith, which could also help reduce poverty and environmental destruction.

The following year in 1998, Rinpoche attended the first Buddhist Summit in Japan which was a gathering of Buddhists from every tradition and every continent in which it is represented, including western and African nations. The summit was the brainchild of Dr. Kyuse Enshinjoh and was attended by the 14th Dalai Lama and Somdet Phra Nyanasamvara, the Supreme Patriarch of Thailand. It was the first joint meeting of these two supreme leaders from these two major Buddhist traditions. These events, of course, took place much later, but it was during Rinpoche's tenure as a Member of Parliament and later on the Minorities Commission, that his stature as a Buddhist leader was formed at world forums, spanning Asia and the West.

PART VI

FULFILLING DESTINY: BAKULA RINPOCHE – RUSSIA AND MONGOLIA

Thirty-six

Buddhism in Russia

The spread of Buddhism in the West during the 20th century was a major cultural phenomenon. The context which helps explain this phenomenon is that for much of the 20th century, many of the traditional heartlands of Buddhism in Asia, including Tibet came under the domination of communist ideologies which were hostile to religion, and thus crippled Buddhism in its traditional strongholds. In contrast, perhaps the single biggest factor in this 'globalisation' of Tibetan Buddhism in particular, was the exile of the 14th Dalai Lama, who arrived as a refugee in India in 1959. The oppression of Buddhism in his homeland was thus ironically the main contributing factor for its spread to every corner of the world. With the help of the Indian government, and with financial aid from well-wishers abroad, Tibetan monasteries and settlements were set up at Tibetan refugee settlements across the length and breadth of India. These monasteries have flourished and grown into major educational establishments, like the famous Nalanda and Taxila Monasteries of ancient India. They have nurtured and produced countless monk-scholars and practitioners who moved to all parts of the globe, in particular to the developed nations of the West, bringing with them the cherished teachings of Buddhism and its timeless wisdom so much needed and so relevant in today's complex world.

The spread of Theravada, Mahayana and Vajrayana in the west is well-documented and well known. What is less known is the impact that Tibetan Buddhism has continued to make quietly in the communist and former-communist countries of the former Soviet bloc. It is in this area that Bakula Rinpoche's international legacy has been most powerful, albeit little-acknowledged.

It seems that there was some kind of karmic connection which drew

Bakula Rinpoche towards the Soviet dominated world. Rinpoche was born in 1917, a year of major political and social change in the Russian Empire and the victory of the Bolsheviks and end of Russian monarchy. Secondly, Rinpoche met the pioneering Russian traveler and artist Nikolai (Nicholas) Roerich when he visited his monastery in Ladakh in year in 1925, and when Rinpoche was around nine years of age. At that time Nikolai Roerich was on his much-celebrated Altai-Himalaya expedition. Rinpoche had a black and white photograph of the famous Russian painter given to him by Roerich himself wearing a traditional Mongolian dress and a cap. Later Rinpoche would recall a faint memory of meeting a foreigner at Pethub monastery, though his recollection was that the exotic-looking foreigner was an Englishman. Nevertheless, his personality made a lasting impression. Rinpoche recalled that he had a curious-looking face above a voluminous white beard, and he was very gracefully attired. At that time Rinpoche knew nothing about Roerich. It was only several decades later when he first visited Moscow in 1968, he came to realize that Roerich was a world renowned and a very celebrated figure. In Moscow, Rinpoche was taken to an art gallery where Roerich's works were on display.

Mr. Nikolai (Nicholas) Roerich of Russia

It was then, that Rinpoche remembered a similar-looking portrait in his monastery in Ladakh. And when he saw a photograph of the painter, he recognized him at once. Rinpoche realised that the portrait he had was that of N. Roerich, (1874-1947) and that he was also the same exotic visitor he had met so long ago in Ladakh. Around this time in Ladakh Rinpoche also met Lama Anagrakia Govinda (1898-1985) and Rahul Sanskirtyan (1893-1963), who were contemporary to Nicholas Roerich and who gave a vivid description about the region.

In the decades of 1970s and 1980s, like so many other senior Tibetan lamas, Rinpoche, a Geshe Lharampa, received several requests to visit the West and talk about Buddhist teachings there. But his official duties and preoccupations in India made it difficult for him to accept these invitations. In fact, Rinpoche told me that he himself was never very interested in going to the West. His hands were already full and he put all his energy into the many duties he was carrying out in India. Rinpoche, however, always had a keen interest in and concern with helping to foster Buddhism in those eastern countries and regions of Asia, where Buddhism had flourished in the past, but in recent times had suffered rapid decline due to the suppression by communist rule. In particular, he was deeply troubled by the conditions in Mongolia and Russia.

Mongolia had long played a major role in the history of Buddhism. In the past, most Mongols had been devout followers of Tibetan Buddhism. At the same time, for many decades, Buddhism had been heavily suppressed in Mongolia under Soviet-led communist rule. During his studies at Drepung Loseling Monastery in Lhasa in the 1940s, Rinpoche had heard a lot about destruction of monasteries in Mongolia and Russia, about monks being killed or forced to give up their robes and renounce their vows and so on. This had nurtured in him a long-held desire to help the people in places like Mongolia.

Buddhism first reached Russia in the 17th century and was practiced mainly by Mongol tribes. Gradually, it gained a small presence in metropolitan cities like St. Petersburg and Moscow where many Buryat and Kalmyk Mongols had settled. By the end of the 19th century, Buddhist Studies had already reached great heights in Russia. Texts had been translated from Pali, Sanskrit, Tibetan and Mongolian into Russian and read and discussed by Russian intellectuals, who were truly impressed or influenced by Buddhist teachings. At the beginning of the 20th century, under the leadership of Lama Agvan Dorzhiev (1853–1938) many Buddhist books were printed and new monasteries and temples were built in different parts of Russia. Lama Dorzhiev was born in Buryatia, an ethnically Mongol region of Siberia where

Lama Agvan Dorzhiev (1853–1938)

Tibetan Buddhism was the main religion. He was educated at Drepung Monastery in Lhasa.

The beginning of the 20th century was "the golden age" of Buddhism in Russia. Agvan Dorzhiev was one of the most intriguing figures in twentieth-century. He maintained close contact with the Russian Tsar, while also becoming a close confidant of the 13th Dalai Lama Thubten Gyatso who later made Lama Dorzhiev his envoy to Russia and other countries. He built a magnificent new temple "Kuntsechoinei Datsan" in St. Petersburg, in a quiet quarter of the city known as 'Staraya Derevnya'. Dorzhiev arguably did more than anyone else to strengthen relations between the Russian Empire and Tibet, which at that time was an independent country. Agvan Dorzhiev's visit to the capital of Russia was aimed at furthering the goodwill between Russia and Tibet, and on the agenda of the talks with Russian Foreign Minister was the question of establishing a permanent Tibetan Mission in St. Petersburg. However, with the Bolshevik Revolution of 1917 and the subsequent communist purge of religious-minded people, Buddhism was all but destroyed throughout the USSR.

In 1929, Lama Agvan Dorzhiev was arrested and sent to a camp in Siberia. On January 29, 1938, he died in a prison hospital in Ulan Ude, the

Datsan Kuntsechoinei Temple in St. Petersburg

Buryatia capital. That same year, the last Buddhist temple in St. Petersburg was also closed. All the sacred objects were removed from the monastery and the building was converted into a scientific laboratory.

Another unique and well-known Buddhist lama of the Buryatia region, was Dashi-Dorzho Itigilov (1852–1927). He was born in the countryside of Buryatia. At the age of 15, he became a monk and joined the Aginsky Monastery. There he learned to read Tibetan and Sanskrit, so as to serve the Buddhist community. In 1911, he was appointed as the 12th Pandito Khambolama. He passed away in year 1927 and was buried in a pine box. As had been instructed by Khambolama Itigilov before his death, his close disciples exhumed the body in year 1957, and it was found in remarkably intact condition. The surprising preservation of his body has been a subject of curiosity among scientists. Under the supervision of Damba Badmaevich Ayusheev, the 24th Pandito Khambolama, the current head of Buddhist Traditional Sangha of Russia, a new temple dedicated to the Pandito Khambolama Itigilov was built in Ulan Ude, Buryatia. This temple has become a Centre of attraction and is visited by Buddhist pilgrims of the region.

Thirty-seven

Rinpoche's First Visit to Moscow and Buryatia

After his election to the Parliament (Lok Sabha) in 1967, Bakula Rinpoche was entitled to a diplomatic passport. This was a considerable privilege in the days of the Cold War, since it opened up the possibility of travelling to countries which were by-and-large closed to outsiders. As India was not fully aligned with either the United States of America or the USSR during the Cold War (if anything, it leaned more towards the latter), an Indian diplomatic passport gave Rinpoche access to many of eastern-bloc Asian countries, which were, in those days, off-limits to westerners. Being a high-profile representative of Buddhism in the land of its origin – India, Rinpoche also got the opportunity to establish contacts with a great variety of foreign dignitaries and Buddhist scholars from around the world. So, while he was an MP, and afterwards, as a member of the National Commission for Minorities, Bakula Rinpoche travelled widely, visiting many countries, not just in western Europe and the USA, but also, more importantly, the USSR, Mongolia, Korea, Japan, China, Vietnam, Laos, Cambodia, Thailand, Sri Lanka as well as several countries in eastern Europe such as Poland, Czechoslovakia, Hungary, East Germany and others.

At that time, the main government organisation responsible for overseeing the Buddhist monasteries in the USSR was known as the Central Spiritual Board of Buddhists of the USSR (known by the Russian acronym TsDUB). It was headed by a chairman with traditional Mongol-Buryatia title Pandito (Pandita) Khambolama. Its main office was in Moscow. The official residence of the Khambolama and the TsDUB, was a newly constructed temple some thirty kilometers from Ulan Ude (the capital of Buryatia, a Mongol-speaking and traditionally Buddhist region of the Soviet

Republic of Russia). A new temple was built, in an area of reclaimed swamp land, known as the Khambin Sume in 1977, after 9 years of Rinpoche's first visit in 1968. It is more commonly known as the *Ivolginsky Datsan* (Monastery). For a long time, this was the only officially-sanctioned Buddhist temple in Soviet Russia.

The first Pandito Khambolama of the Soviet era was Lobsan-Nima Darmaev who held the post from year 1956 to 1963. Later, permission was given to open a second Buddhist temple in Buryatia, this time in the Chita oblast (Prefecture), which is known as the Aginsky Datsan. Despite strict government controls over religion throughout the Soviet period, these two Datsans were together able to keep the small flickering flame of the Buddha's teaching alive during the long decades.

After Lama Darmaev's tenure, the post of Pandito Khambolama was taken by Eshi Dorzhi Sharapov and subsequently by Zhambaldorj Gomboev. About twenty monks were permitted at these two main centres. Besides these, there were about hundred former lamas still discreetly active (after their release from prison camps) in the formerly Buddhist regions. These brave individuals carried out religious ceremonies for villagers and many of them also practiced traditional medicine. A careful watch was maintained over them by the Soviet secret service. Some of the lamas informally took on disciples, outside the traditional Buddhist structures.

Despite the general suppression of religion in the Soviet Union, the authorities continued to make propaganda of the few legal institutions of Buddhism that were permitted. This served the authorities' political needs and demonstrated to the nations the "freedom of conscience" enjoyed by citizens of the Soviet Union. For this purpose, in year 1956, which also marked the 2500th Buddha Jayanti, the Central Spiritual Board of Buddhists of the USSR (TsDUB) joined the International Brotherhood (Fellowship) of Buddhists. Subsequently, a new international organization was created in 1969, known as the Asian Buddhists Conference for Peace (ABCP). It was under the auspices of this last organization, that Rinpoche was able to undertake many of his activities in the Soviet-aligned countries of Asia.

In year 1968, soon after his election to the Lok Sabha, Rinpoche was invited to Moscow for the first time by Lama Zhambaldorj Gomboev, who was at that time serving as the Pandito Khambolama, the officially recognised Supreme Head of Buddhists in the USSR. Thus, Rinpoche embarked upon his first fateful journey to the USSR accompanied by his assistant Lama Thupstan Targyes and Adv. Sonam Gyaltsan as his interpreter. The summer of year 1968 was particularly warm, and the weather was very pleasant in Moscow. Rinpoche was received at the airport by Pandito Khambolama

Zhambaldorj Gomboev and representatives of the Council of Religious Affairs of the USSR, which was the official body representing three major faiths which still formally existed in the USSR – the Russian Orthodox Church, Islam and Buddhism. As Rinpoche stepped out onto the tarmac at Moscow Airport, his long and historic association with the Soviet Union and Mongolia began.

Moscow, a city established over 800 years ago, made a very favourable impression on Rinpoche. He recalled that it was a stunningly beautiful city. It had large imposing buildings, wide roads and a general air of a prosperous and well-ordered society – quite in contrast to the hustle and bustle of the Indian capital. Rinpoche was shown around the city. He visited its landmark points such as Red-Square, Lenin Mausoleum, its world-famous underground metro system and imposing buildings such as Moscow University and Bolshoi Theater. Everyone, he said, appeared happy and there was no sign of poverty or deprivation, as was so common a sight in India and other developing countries.

Bakula Rinpoche arriving at Ivolginsky Datsan, Ulan Ude, Buryatia, USSR (1968)

Bakula Rinpoche on his maiden visit to Buryatia, USSR (1968)

Bakula Rinpoche with Pandito Khambolama Zhambaldorj Gomboev of USSR

Bakula Rinpoche at the Soviet Academy of Sciences during his first visit to Ulan Ude, Buryatia (1968)

Rinpoche with a group of disciples. This was the first-ever authorized and open teaching by Bakula Rinpoche in St. Petersburg in Soviet Union. Author is sitting to the right of Bakula Rinpoche (1988)

While there were a few scattered Buddhists and Buddhist scholars in cities like Moscow and Leningrad (now St. Petersburg), the majority of the Soviet Union's Buddhists were ethnic Mongols living in the Republics of Buryatia, Kalmykia and Tuva. Besides these traditional Buddhists, there were a considerable number of ethnic Russians who also practiced Buddhism and came to meet Rinpoche and hear him speak. According to Dr. Andrey Terentyev, a well-known Russian Buddhist scholar, besides the traditional Buddhists of Buryatia, beginning year 1970, Rinpoche was also followed closely and approached by members of the underground Buddhists group which grew in Moscow, Leningrad and some other places.

One such group was headed by Buryat Lama Bidia Dandaron. Dr. Andrey Terentyev recalls that Lama Dandaron was very much impressed with Rinpoche's intellect and would describe how when he privately requested Rinpoche for the oral transmission of Hevajra Tantra, Rinpoche averted the text provided to him and recited the whole text by heart. In 1972, Lama Dandaron was arrested for organising a "Buddhist Sect" and two years later he perished in the Soviet Gulag.[1] When meeting with these Buddhists, Rinpoche said he could observe their constant fear and sense of anxiety. This made him determined to help them as much as he could. He later also learnt that among those, who came to meet him pretending to be devout Buddhists, were undercover communist secret agents. Fortunately, there does not appear to have been any harm done.

From Moscow Rinpoche flew to Ulan Ude, capital of Buryatia. There was a lot of anticipation in Ulan Ude about Rinpoche's visit. It was summer time and for many local people, it was the first time in many decades – in living memory indeed – that a high incarnate Lama or Rinpoche of Tibetan Buddhism had visited there. Just outside the capital city, at the Ivolginsky Datsan, Rinpoche was received by Khambolama Zhambaldorj Gomboev as well as thousands of local men and women. Monks carrying traditional welcome-umbrellas, religious flags and banners lined his path, while other monks blew conch shells, long horns, and beat drums and cymbals, in the traditional welcome given to high-ranking lamas, reviving old memories of the past. In a typical Buryatia local tradition, Rinpoche was also received by people holding a large silver bowl filled with milk and others holding bread and salt. A group of senior monks jointly holding a long blue *khadag* received Rinpoche at the entrance of Ivolginsky Temple. At the time, this was the only government approved Buddhist monastery in the country. Besides this monastery, there were hundreds of empty monasteries, many lying in ruins, scattered all over the region. Inside the temple, monks made a *mandala* offering to Rinpoche while chanting prayers in Tibetan. Rinpoche stayed at

Bakula Rinpoche being received by senior monks of Ivolginsky Datsan, Ulan Ude, Buryatia, Russia

Bakula Rinpoche with Khambolama Zhambaldorj Gomboev and senior monks of Ivolginsky Monastery in Ulan Ude, Buryatia (1972)

the Ivolginsky Datsan for several days at a special guesthouse, which had been built for his visit.

Later, at the request of the lay and monastic community of the area, Rinpoche conferred a long-life empowerment, delivered a teaching and gave an oral transmission. As Rinpoche would later recollect, he was in far-away land, in a remote region of Siberia, among people whom he had never met before, yet he felt so close to them, for they shared a deep cultural affinity.

It was in Ulan Ude, that Rinpoche was first introduced to Samaageen Gombojav, the Khambolama of Mongolia who had come from Mongolia specially to meet Bakula Rinpoche. During the course of their discussion, Rinpoche learnt a great deal about the situation of Buddhism in the Soviet Union and Mongolia. Although they had to speak through a chain of interpreters, they were able to understand each other well. Rinpoche was able to share the feelings of helplessness and disgust about the piteous state of the religion in these areas.

At the same time, there was a palpable sense of sheer joy at this long-withheld opportunity to meet with co-religionists and discuss the issues at hand. Rinpoche and Khambolamas had an instant rapport and developed a close and trusting relationship. Together they resolved to give their best efforts for the cause of the Bauddha Dharma. It was the beginning of a long friendship and a historic partnership, which was to transform the fate of Buddhism in Mongolia and Russia.

The discussion between the two Khambolamas (heads of the Buddhist clergy in the USSR and Mongolia respectively) and Rinpoche was long and intense. They talked frankly about the obstacles they faced and to explore various ways and means to revive Buddhism in the regions. The sincerity and dedication of this trio – Bakula Rinpoche, Khambolama S. Gombojav and Khambolama Zhambaldorj Gomboev – was palpable and they were the pioneers and the pillars of the Buddhist revival in the region during those intensely difficult years of communist rule. More about that later.

NOTES

1. Buddhism in Russia-Tsarist and Soviet by Andrey Terentyev.

Thirty-eight

Establishment of the ABCP in Mongolia

The long and intense meeting of the three stalwarts – Bakula Rinpoche (India), Khambolama Samaageen Gombojav (Mongolia), and Khambolama Zhambaldorj Gomboev (USSR) in year 1968 in Ulan Ude, USSR had laid the foundation of an international Buddhist organization. They also discussed the obstacles they faced and to explore various ways and means to revive Buddhism in the regions. The sincerity and dedication of this trio who were the pioneers and the pillars of the Buddhist revival in those regions during those intensely difficult years of communist rule, was evident.

It was in the following year, 1969, that Samaageen Gombojav, Khambolama of Mongolia, Prof. S. Dylykov representing Zhambaldorj Gomboev, Khambolama of Soviet Union, Gunaratana Thero who represented Kushok Bakula Rinpoche, Member of Parliament and Vice-President, World Fellowship of Buddhists, Sumanitissa Thero, President, Sri Lanka Buddhist Congress, Amritananda Thero, President, Young Buddhist Council of Nepal together with some other leaders founded the international NGO called the Asian Buddhist Conference for Peace (ABCP) on 5th December 1969.

The organization had the tacit support of both the Soviet authorities in Moscow and the Mongolian Communist Government. As the first Buddhist NGO in inner Asia, ABCP facilitated mutual cooperation among the Buddhists communities struggling under communism. It also brought them into dialogue with Buddhists from other Asian countries, especially the Buddhists living in India. For Buddhists in Mongolia, it provided a platform to voice their concerns and a link to connect with the rest of the world. A significant outcome of the first General Assembly was the founding of the Zanabazar[1] Buddhist University at Gandan Tegchenling Monastery, Ulaanbaatar in 1970, which catered not only the Mongolians but also the students from neighbouring Buryatia, Kalmykia and Tuva in Russia.

The First General Assembly of ABCP was held in Ulaanbaatar from June 11-13, 1970, marking the geneses of an international voluntary coalition of Buddhists united by a shared mission to fortify global peace and safeguarding the nature and the world. This foundation also marks the inception of a voluntary movement of Buddhists of Asia who have embraced the invaluable teachings imparted by Lord Buddha as the foundational tenets of their endeavours.

The ABCP's primary function was the promotion of world peace. Although this organization, being based in a communist country, was still under a certain degree of political control, the authorities by and large allowed it to function autonomously since it served a useful propaganda function for them. It projected the communist bloc's 'soft' face and advocated for world peace, which was also a popular slogan of the Soviet regime. But these international geopolitical propaganda games were never anything more than a side-show for these three senior Buddhist monks at the helm of the ABCP. For them, the main and primary purpose of the organization was very clear. It was the restoration of Buddhism in the former Buddhist regions of Mongolia, the USSR, and all those other south Asian countries of Asia where it had suffered so many years of oppression and neglect.

The ABCP have national centres in many countries, including India, Bangladesh, Sri Lanka, Nepal, Thailand, Cambodia, Vietnam, Laos DPR, DPRK (North Korea), Republic of Korea, Japan, USSR, Mongolia, Bhutan etc. It also had a national centre, representing the Central Tibetan Administration (CTA) in Dharamshala, India. As a senior figurehead of the organization, Rinpoche travelled extensively to many parts of the world in pursuit of world peace.

In 1974, the 3rd General Conference of the ABCP was held at New Delhi's prestigious Vigyan Bhawan, with Bakula Rinpoche serving as the Chairman of the Organising Committee. It was inaugurated by Fakhruddin Ali Ahmed, President of India and attended among others by H.H. the Dalai Lama, Venerable Fujii Nichidatsu Guruji of Japan, Khambolama S. Gombojav of Mongolia, Khambolama Zhambaldorj Gomboev of Soviet Union and a galaxy of other Buddhist leaders from across Asia. Mrs. Indira Gandhi, then Prime Minister of India, hosted a reception for the delegates at her residence.

Khambolama Zh. Gomboev of Buryatia, USSR Khambolama S. Gombojav of Mongolia and Bakula Rinpoche in Mongolia (1968)

A group photo of delegates to the ABCP Executive Council Meeting in Ulaanbaatar, Mongolia (1975)

The year 1979, was a very important one for the ABCP. It was in that year, that under the auspices of ABCP, the 14th Dalai Lama visited the USSR and Mongolia for the first time from June 11–20, 1979. He also attended the 5th General Assembly of ABCP held in Ulaanbaatar. It was truly a historic and momentous occasion. Organising and preparing this visit, which, from the diplomatic viewpoint, was a very sensitive issue involving a lot of hard work and it was Bakula Rinpoche, who laid the diplomatic groundwork and played a major role in giving the visit a practical shape. The Dalai Lama's visit to the USSR and Mongolia was a very important development at the peak of the Cold War. At that time, he had not yet visited the United States of America. His maiden visit to the United States of America was a year later, from October 27–30, 1980.

The Dalai Lama arrived in Moscow on June 13, 1979. From there he travelled to Ulan Ude in Buryatia, where he spent the next two days. In the last leg of his visit, he proceeded to Ulaanbaatar, where he stayed for three nights, i.e. from June 15–18, 1979. On this visit, as on all subsequent visits to Mongolia, it was Bakula Rinpoche who was always present to receive the Dalai Lama. Bakula Rinpoche's role in re-opening the USSR and Mongolia to the Buddha Dharma was truly momentous. He was the first Tulku (incarnate lama) of the Tibetan Buddhist tradition to visit Russia and Mongolia since the Bolshevik Revolution of 1917 which incidentally was also the year he was born. Rinpoche would often talk about that period and would say how pleasantly surprised he was to see the sincere religious fervor of the people despite so many years in which the religious believers were all but suffocated. It was seeing this, he said, that made him so determined to do what he could to help bring Buddhism back into those people's lives. Nearly twenty years later, at the 8th General Conference of the ABCP held in Ulaanbaatar in September 1990, Bakula Rinpoche was elected as its President. This illustrates the long and dedicated service; Rinpoche gave to this organization.

Rinpoche welcoming Mr. Fakhruddin Ali Ahmed, President of India, New Delhi (1974)

(L to R) Bakula Rinpoche, Khambolama S. Gombojav, Mr. Fakruddin Ali Ahmed, President of India, Nichidatsu Fujii Guruji of Japan and Prof. Ch. Jugder at the inauguration of the 3rd ABCP General Conference at Vigyan Bhawan, New Delhi (1974)

Bakula Rinpoche, Khambolama S. Gombojav, H.H. the Dalai Lama, Nichidatsu Fujii Guruji and Khambolama Zh. Gomboev at the 3rd ABCP General Conference at Vigyan Bhawan, New Delhi (1974)

Delegates from various ABCP National Centres with Mrs. Indira Gandhi, Prime Minister of India at her residence in New Delhi (1974)

The Dalai Lama with Bakula Rinpoche, Khambolama S. Gombojav and Mr. Batardorj of Mongolia in Ulaanbaatar, Mongolia (1979)

(L-R) Prof. Ch. Jugder, Bakula Rinpoche, Sumanitissa Thero, HH The Dalai Lama, S. Gombojav, Fujii Guruji and Ven. Sato of Japan (1979)

Group photo of the Participants at the 5th General Assembly of ABCP held in Ulaanbaatar in 1979

Rinpoche addressing a gathering in Hanoi, Vietnam (1986)

Mapalagama Wipulasara welcoming Bakula Rinpoche in Sri Lanka

Rinpoche and members of ABCP with the Prime Minister of Vietnam (1986)

NOTES

1. Zanabazar is a Mongolian word for Gyan-Vajra.

Thirty-nine

Small Steps for Revival of Buddhism in the Soviet Union

While addressing an international conference in Leh in 2016, Dr. Andrey Terentyev, a Russian scholar spoke about the Revival of Buddhism in the USSR in the following words: "In the year of Soviet Power, the religion was totally suppressed. All 150 monasteries were destroyed and all 2000 monks and disciples repressed. Very few survived in Stalin's concentration camps. Only after the 2nd World war it was allowed to reopen small monasteries with about two dozen of monks in Buryatia Autonomous Republic of the USSR. Still both monks and believers were always under pressure and fear. Then in year 1968, as a Sun in the dark-sky, Kushok Bakula Rinpoche appeared in Russia, and all Buddhists who lived behind the iron curtain, understood that Dharma is still alive and the hope was born in their hearts. Beginning 1968, Kushok Bakula Rinpoche started to visit the USSR almost every year in connection with ABCP sessions. He conducted ceremonies, gave initiation, talked to believers, secretly met 'underground Buddhists' in Moscow and other cities. When Gorbachev came and the Soviet system started to ease, Bakula Rinpoche was the first Lama to give the authorised Buddhist Teachings for Russian Buddhists in Leningrad (St. Petersburg). Bakula Rinpoche was the first Lama to come to the Kalmykia area after more than 40 years of Communism. His role in reviving Buddhism in Russia cannot be overestimated."

It was only in year 1970, that the Soviet Union formally guaranteed religious freedom to its people, although this was largely a propaganda exercise and many restrictions still remained in place. Monks could only be enrolled after the approval of government agencies and the activities of the monasteries were closely monitored. However, even these symbolic gestures were helpful, since they re-established a crucial link with past heritage and enabled the people to keep in touch with their faith. In subsequent years, Bakula Rinpoche frequently visited Moscow and other important places in the USSR. He visited old monasteries such as Aginsky and Tsuguul Monasteries in the Chita region in Buryatia, which were in ruins. He gave advice and assistance to local Buddhists for their restoration. He also visited a small temple which was famous for its revered sandalwood statue of Buddha Shakyamuni (Zandanjowo) and Alkhanay, which is a holy-mountain park situated in the Aginsky Buryatia Autonomous District. Local authorities also arranged for his visit to the world-famous Baikal Lake.

In the summer of 1985, I got another opportunity to accompany Rinpoche on his visit to Buryatia. From Moscow, we then flew to Ulan Ude, the capital of the Buryatia Autonomous Republic and a picturesque region which includes the world-famous Lake Baikal. The flight took eight hours, with stopovers at the Siberian cities of Omsk, Irkutsk and Novosibirsk. Rinpoche was awed by the sheer geographical size of the USSR, which traversed nine different time zones. While Moscow was very much a European city, Ulan Ude which is not far from the Mongolian border, is in Asia.

At the request of local people, Bakula Rinpoche conferred Jigjed (Yamantaka) empowerments on several occasions at Ivolginsky Monastery in Ulan Ude and gave long-life initiations and teachings. A huge gathering turned up to listen to his teachings. Thousands of Rubles were collected during such occasions in the form of offerings. On each occasion Rinpoche would pass these offerings to the monastery concerned for their restoration and maintenance. All monasteries lacked facilities for religious study and rituals. The older generation of men and women looked happy to be able to visit temples. The younger generation brought up under the Soviet system visited the monasteries as curious onlookers. Despite close watch by the Soviet authorities, many people attended Rinpoche's teaching and his photographs were copied from black and white prints for their home altars. Some present-day Buryatia monks say they grew up looking at Rinpoche's picture at their home altars, consider him as one of the Buddhas and as their root Guru.

In order to protect themselves from Soviet secret agents, they would come in small groups. While some would enter Rinpoche's hotel room to receive teachings and blessings, others would stay outside to keep a watch. However, as time passed, the situation gradually eased and Rinpoche even ordained many new monks. Gradually the number of such people coming for teachings and guidance grew, and in the final years of the Soviet system, thousands of people gathered for religious congregations in Buryatia. Bakula Rinpoche said that he could feel an undercurrent of religious fervor waiting to explode.

It was during one such visit to Ulan Ude in year 1993, that Rinpoche agreed to ordain some Buddhist Nuns or Bhikkhunis. This was unprecedented as there was no such tradition in that region in the past. In an article "Bakula Rinpoche's contribution to the revival efforts and his living legacy in the Buryat Mongolian Buddhist tradition" Dr. Esuna Dugarova from Columbia University writes "Bakula Rinpoche supported establishment of "Zungon Darzhaling Women's Datsan in Ulan Ude which is the first and the only Nunnery in Russia. Rinpoche exemplifies the sophisticated transnational flow of Dharma knowledge and practice. During his pathway from the Himalaya to Lake Baikal and Mongol steppes, Rinpoche has leveraged his knowledge, experience and relations to revive Buddhism in Eurasia."

Rinpoche said that as the years passed, he came to understand the complexities of the Soviet system and its deep-rooted problems. He could feel the deep current of discontent and anger among many people, especially in the big cities such as Moscow and Leningrad (St. Petersburg). He learnt about the many aspects of hardship suffered by the people under communism. The USSR was supposed to be a classless society. That all sounded very nice, and indeed it chimed well with the Buddha's basic teachings about human equality. But this was just an appearance. Reality was quite different. Over the years, he came to realize how much impracticality and artifice there was in the Soviet Union. He learnt about the rampant corruption; both in the big cities and in the provinces as well as nepotism and abuses of power by the communist elite. He also learnt about the widespread social problems caused by a culture of excessive alcohol (Vodka) consumption. Its consequences were evident everywhere. Alcoholism and the pervasive culture of deceit, distrust and corruption created by the authoritarian system had wreaked havoc on society. Family feuds were very common, and so were divorces. It is also in human nature that the more the people are controlled and suppressed, the more they want to revolt. As science and technology developed, and especially with growing connectivity with the outside world, it was becoming increasingly difficult for the communist regime to hold down people's desire for freedom.

Reopening of 'Kuntsechoinei Datsan' in St. Petersburg

In 1985, during one of his visits to Leningrad (St. Petersburg), Bakula Rinpoche sought permission to visit the historic Buddhist Temple

'Kuntsechoinei or Gunzechoinei Datsan' which was now functioning as a laboratory. This monastery was built by Lama Agvan Dorzhiev who was a close confidant and envoy of the 13th Dalai Lama and also enjoyed patronage of the Russian Tsar. Except for the imposing building itself which still had features of traditional Tibetan architecture, there was nothing religious left about the place. Rinpoche was deeply saddened to see its ramshackle condition and could only imagine its former grandeur. In subsequent years, efforts were made in different quarters to restore it to its former status as a Buddhist Monastery. Various petitions were submitted to the city authorities by both Buryat and Russian Buddhists. In several such official meetings with the Soviet authorities, Bakula Rinpoche raised this matter with them and pleaded with them to return the temple to the Buddhist community, to whom it rightfully belonged, and who would be able to restore and maintain it properly.

In 1990, this quiet campaign bore fruit. This historic Buddhist temple was officially returned to the Buddhist community and its old name *Kuntsechoinei or Gunzechoinei Datsan* was restored. Buddhist leaders in Russia invited Bakula Rinpoche to perform the purification and consecration ceremonies for the re-opening. It was the first public Buddhist religious service in Leningrad for nearly 50 years. A large number of people attended, and Rinpoche also gave a public teaching. The delivery of this sermon was also historic. During his visits to the USSR, Bakula Rinpoche received requests for empowerments, transmissions of Buddhist sutras and teachings. But this still was the Soviet Union and Rinpoche said that he could feel the fear in the minds of the people who came to receive teachings.

Over the course of his many visits to the Soviet Union, Rinpoche met scores of people who despite hardship and severe restrictions under communism, had retained their faith and devotion towards the Dharma, and contributed a great deal to the revival of Dharma. But most of all, Rinpoche would often fondly recall; with sincere appreciation; the key role played by the Most Venerable Pandito Khambolama Zhambaldorj Gomboev (1897–1983). Others he often mentioned were Lama Jimbajamtso, Lama Gombo Tsybikov, Lama Darmadodi, Lama Munkho and Khambolama Erdeneyev. Prominent among the younger monks were Damba Ayusheev, Chimidorj, Choidorj Budaev, S. Samaev, Lama Dorjo, Lama Jamyan, Tseren Dondukbaev, etc. Damba Ayusheev later became the Pandito Khambolama of the Traditional Buddhist Sangha of Russia.

There also were other people who really made significant contributions in those years. For example, Prof. Dylikov & Dr. Algirdas Kugyavichus, (the translator of the Lamrim Chenmo and Ngagrim Chenmo into Russian)

Tom Rabdanov, Dr. Oktyabarina Volkova, Oleg Medvedev, Andrey Terentyev and his wife Margarita Kozhevnikova, Alexander Kocharov, Nikolai Karatuev, Victor Pupishev, Nick Dudka and scores of others who were truly dedicated to the Buddha Dharma. Mrs. Dulma Shagdarova, an important functionary in the Centre of Religious Board in Moscow and a functionary of Asian Buddhists Conference for Peace (ABCP), was an ethnic Buryat personality, who lived in Moscow. She was very efficient, well connected and deeply devoted and would make all the arrangements for Rinpoche's regular visits. A very kind lady, she later founded the Moscow Buddhist Society in the Russian capital Moscow.

Forty

Historic Visit to Kalmykia 1989

At the beginning of 1989, Bakula Rinpoche visited Kalmykia, a small Republic of ethnic Kalmyk Mongols in the Volga region in Eastern Europe near the Caspian Sea. It was my great privilege to accompany him on that trip and put into use the little Russian I had learnt earlier. A special Aeroflot plane was chartered to fly Rinpoche from Moscow to Elista. The Kalmyk people had endured untold sufferings and humiliation during the Soviet period. In 1931, Soviet leader Joseph Stalin ordered collectivization of farms and closed all the Buddhist monasteries. He then deported and dispersed them across Siberia, the Kalmyk language and culture suffered terribly, and possibly turned to an irreversible decline. After Stalin, his successor Nikita Khrushchev made his famous criticism of Stalin in year 1956, and the Kalmyk people were finally allowed to return to their homeland, which they began to do in year 1957. After dissolution of the USSR, Kalmykia retained the status of an autonomous republic within the newly formed Russian Federation.

Meanwhile, Rinpoche was already in close contact with many scholars including Geshe Wangyal, a Kalmyk based in the USA. When Bakula Rinpoche visited Kalmykia in 1989, he was the first Buddhist lama to do so since Agvan Dorzhiev in 1931. It was amazing to see that the Kalmyk people were still extremely warm-hearted and devout Buddhists despite having endured so much hardship. During Rinpoche's visit a small house was converted into a make-shift temple in Elista, the capital of Kalmykia Republic. There were heart wrenching scene of people crying of joy to be able to see a high lama from outside Russia. Reminiscing the day Dr. Andrey Tyrentyev from St. Petersburg (Leningrad) who had accompanied Rinpoche on this trip, told me that the Buddhist society had just been registered by the government but there was no temple or even an office of their own until the time Bakula Rinpoche arrived there. Rinpoche was interviewed by the local

Rinpoche with Geshe Wangyal from Kalmykia in New York

television where he explained the very basic Buddhists practices for the lay people and also gave teachings on the mantra *Om Mani Padme Hung*; the sacred six-syllable mantra associated with the Chenrezig *(Avalokitesvara)*, the Buddha of Compassion.

Rinpoche spent few days in Elista and during his stay Rinpoche also ordained the first group of novices. Lama Tuvandorj from Buryatia began to lead a small congregation in the makeshift temple in Elista. Rinpoche performed special prayers for absorbing the tutelary deity *Palden Lhamo*, and the accompanying rituals of propitiation and favour-seeking. He also suggested that the blessings of the protective guardian deity *Jamsring* would be particularly beneficial there. Rinpoche also gave teachings on taking refugee as well as teaching on *Tara*, and a White Tara long-life empowerment which was open to the to the public.

I remember the scorching heat outside during his teachings, but nevertheless thousands of people thronged to get a glimpse of the Bakula Rinpoche, an incarnate lama from India, and the first visitor in over seventy years. There was a festive atmosphere, and no apparent fear among the people as we had encountered in bigger cities such as Moscow. It was particularly moving to see the old people, who had been through so much in their lives, bringing their grandchildren with them and teaching them the basics of Buddhist practices as they themselves had followed in the old days, all of which was new to the younger generations.

Bakula Rinpoche on his arrival at Elista, Kalmykia.
Author is on the extreme left (1989)

Bakula Rinpoche after laying the foundation stone for a new monastery in Elista, Kalmykia (1989)

During the course of this historic visit, Rinpoche met the President of the Autonomous Republic of Kalmykia, who hosted a luncheon in his honour. The Buddhist community in Elista were keen to build a monastery in the city and they asked Rinpoche to select one of the three locations, which they had short-listed for the purpose. After prayers and divination, Rinpoche chose the site on the outskirts of capital Elista which he felt to be the most auspicious. At the site itself he also performed solemn ablution and consecration rituals for the success of the building and its future in the preservation of the Buddha's sacred dharma. Later, a new monastery was built on the site chosen by Bakula Rinpoche. It was subsequently inaugurated by the 14th Dalai Lama in 1991.

After his visit to Elista, Rinpoche returned to Moscow and from there flew to Ulan Ude. He also visited Agiinsk and Tsuugul Monasteries – where the Soviet authorities permitted small congregations of monks and lay people – Rinpoche gave a series of Empowerments. He also gave his regular teachings on the good practice of seeking refuge, on the law of karma, and on the importance of doing meritorious deeds eschewing non-meritorious actions. In this way, Rinpoche hoped to establish a sound foundation for the revival of Buddhism in a region in which it had suffered terrible decline.

In year 1989, Rinpoche was also invited to visit Kishinga in Buryatia, where he consecrated a new Stupa. During many visits to different parts of Russia, Rinpoche expressed the hope that the new generation of monks that he had ordained, who were dedicated and full of enthusiasm, would adhere to the traditional values and abide strictly by the Vinaya rules (monastic code), so that the aberrations and corruptions that had crept in during the difficult communist period, could be gradually corrected. He also expressed his deep respect for those old monks who had survived the ordeals of the past and returned to the faith. They could not be blamed, he said, for having deviated from the monastic rules and given up their sacred vows during communism. They had carried the torch of their faith alive in their hearts and could now return to the monastic fold.

In year 1991, when Bakula Rinpoche was already living in Mongolia, he again visited Buryatia on the invitation of Khambolama Damba Ayusheev and inaugurated a monastery there at Kyxta, near the Mongolian border. Thousands of people gathered to attend the ceremony. In an interview with a local Newspaper in Russia, Rinpoche said that he was very pleased with the desire and determination of the Buryats, Kalmuks and Tuvans to revive Buddhism and their culture.

When conditions relaxed and improved, he made efforts to send many young monks and lay people from Russia and Mongolia to India to study

Buddhism. Although he had no authority those days, he was able to send a few young people to India to Dharamshala, Karnataka State, South India and elsewhere. He has seen the Ivolginsky Temple coming up and many other monasteries such as Aginsky and Tsuugul Datsans reopen. He was also fascinated with the Buddhist Temple in Leningrad (St. Petersburg). The pleasure and happiness to see these changes happening is inexpressible, he quipped.

A 19th century unique Mongolian Thangka depicting the 16 Arhats with Arhat Bakula in the centre

Forty-one

Arhat Bakula's Mongolian Destiny: A Myth Comes True

In the mid-1990s, I met Prof. Dorjiin Damba, a professor of Mongolian language at the Mongolian State University in Ulaanbaatar. At the time I was working as a diplomat and taking private tuition from him in Mongolian language. On one occasion he invited me for a meal at his home in downtown Ulaanbaatar. There, in his drawing room, I saw a *thangka* depicting the Sixteen Arhats hanging on the wall. At first glance it looked like any other *thangka* of the Sixteen Arhats. But when I looked closer, I was quite taken aback. It was in fact very unusual, and I had never seen a *thangka* like this ever before. Normally, in *thangkas* of the Sixteen Arhats, Lord Buddha is seated in the centre of the composition, but this *thangka* portrayed Arhat Bakula (identifiable by his symbol, the wealth-bestowing mongoose) at the centre. Lord Buddha was depicted at the top, surrounded by the other fifteen Arhats, each carrying a Mongoose in their hands. I asked Prof. Damba about this mystery. Where did this *thangka* come from, I asked?

Prof. Damba told me that this painting had been in the possession of his family since his grandfather's time. His own father, he said, had been a monk before the revolution, who was forced to disrobe during the communist period. He then told me about a prophecy concerning Arhat Bakula that this painting referred to. I had never heard about this before. So, it came to me as a revelation. Since that time, I discovered that this legend is actually quite well-documented by scholars and that Bakula Rinpoche had an enigmatic relationship with Mongolia. So, rather than explain the significance of this *thangka* in my own words, below is the account by Prof. Vesna A. Wallace, University of California, an eminent professor of Mongolian Buddhism, in her important article on Bakula Rinpoche.[1]

"Among the earliest, eighty great disciples of the Buddha Shakyamuni and among the sixteen celebrated Arhats all venerated in Buddhist traditions for their high spiritual achievements and ethical conduct, Bakula Arhat became legendary as a contemplative hermit who endured the hardships of an ascetic life and sustained himself on plants, roots, and fruits of the forest.[2] According to the Indian, Tibetan and Mongolian sources, he never experienced illness, enjoyed an unusually long life, and healed sick monks with medicinal plants. Due to the accounts of his many extraordinary achievements such as the five extrasensory perceptions (abhijñana), knowledge of medicinal plants, and the like, he began to be worshipped as a giver of long life and as a provider of freedom from hunger, thirst, and material and spiritual poverty.

According to the popular Mongolian legend, in the 19th century, at the time of the Eighth Bogdo Gegeen, Khalka Jebtsundamba Khutagt, who was the head of Mongolian Buddhism, a Mongolian monk whose name remains unknown, predicted that Buddhism in Mongolia will be assaulted by inimical forces. He further foretold that after Buddhism among Mongols receives "a crushing blow at the hands of the red barbarians in the early twentieth century", Arhat Bakula will appear and the Mongolian Buddhist cultural heritage will be restored to its previous glory.[3] The well-known Mongolian scholar and monk, Zava Damdin (rTsa bar rTa mrgrin dka 'bcu, 1867–1937) makes reference to such a prophecy in his Golden Book (Altan Devter), but points out the Mañju´srimulatantra as the original source of the prophecy. There he appeals to Mongolians, saying: "In order to liberate [ourselves] from suffering, [we] must worship Bakula."[4] For that purpose, he composed a prayer in praise of Arhat Bakula, titled Opening the Door of the Space Treasure of a Compilation of Homage and Worship of the Elders Led by Arya Bakula ('Phags pa Ba ku las thog drangs pa'i gnas brtag phyag mchod gyi tsogs nam mkha' mdzod kyi sgo ba byed), which was read in Mongolian monasteries. According to Zava Damdin, the monks of Demchig Datsan of Sanggin Dalain Nomin aimag and the monks of Gandandarjailin of Ulaan Eregiin Nomin aimag recited that liturgical text of the offering rite to Bakula Arhat, in which he is mentioned as foremost among all the Arhats.[5]

Following the aforementioned prediction, in the Banner (khoshuu) of Agi nobleman (üizen gün) of Sain Noyen Khan aimag (province), a thangka was made for the sake of worshiping Arhat Bakula. The thangka depicts sixteen Arhats of the Buddha, with Bakula Arhat occupying a central position in the painting and holding a mongoose in his hands. He is surrounded by fifteen other Arhats and the Buddha Shakyamuni, who is attended by Sariputra and Maudgalyana, depicted above the head of Bakula Arhat. On the upper left and right corners of the paintings are depicted two Bodhisattva figures, Tara and Mañju´sri. On the bottom of the painting are the four Maharajas, the guardians of the four cardinal directions, and on the lower, right side, above the fourth Maharaja there is a representation of the seated Hashang.[6] During the years of the communist revolution, in every monastery, during daily ritual services, lamas recited the prayer 'Salutation and Worship of the Elders' (gNas brtan phag mchod), in which Bakula Arhat is mentioned as learned and holy."[7]

Discovering that it had been prophesied over a hundred years ago that Arhat Bakula would come to Mongolia to revitalize Buddhism, and that this was a part of Mongolian Buddhist belief, was to me something truly amazing. In the summer of year 2014, I was shown a collection of several such *thangka*s by Mindsaikhan Otgonbilig, Director of Bogd Khan Palace Museum in Ulaanbaatar which were preserved in that museum's archives. These were said to date back to the time of the 8th Bogd Khan or Khalka Jebtsundamba (1869– 1924) and were said to have come from his own personal collection. This recent revelation makes the story more amazing.

Later I learnt that in the 1930s, when the communist purges began and traditional Mongolian culture and their Buddhist religion faced annihilation, many ordinary devout Mongolians were actually wondering as when would Arhat Bakula come to liberate them and were praying for his manifestation. At that time, Bakula Rinpoche himself was studying at Drepung Loseling in Lhasa when he learnt about the atrocities going on in Mongolia from the numerous other Mongolian monks who were studying there. Ever since, Rinpoche had been eager to establish further contact and try to help whichever way he could. His first opportunity came in year 1956, when he met the members of the Mongolian Buddhists delegation at the 2500th Buddha Jayanti celebrations, which were being organized by the Government of India. But it was only in year1968, when Bakula was invited to visit USSR and a year later in 1969, when he visited Mongolia itself for the first time, that this long-cherished hope started to materialize. Following this visit, talk about this prophecy became more intense, especially among senior monks. And from that time onwards, due to his association with the ABCP, Rinpoche started visiting Mongolia quite often.

I recall a meeting with Geshe Ngawang-Nyima, an eminent Buryatia-Mongol monk scholar who was the abbot of Drepung Gomang Monastery in South India in the 1980s. He made some important and interesting observations. According to him, Bakula Rinpoche chose to be born in Ladakh and consequently his Indian citizenship which enabled him to travel freely to Soviet Union and Mongolia and perform many meritorious deeds. This would not have been possible had he been born in Tibet or Mongolia, he quipped. He also talked about the great personal sacrifice which Bakula

Rinpoche made in the process because had he chosen the monastic hierarchy, he would have certainly become the 'Gaden Tripa', the highest position in the Geluk tradition, a long time back and instead, chose to serve the people and liberate them from poverty, ignorance and exploitation.

Mrs. Indira Gandhi, Prime Minister of India, Mr. Yu. Tsedenbal, Prime Minister of Mongolia and Bakula Rinpoche, Member Parliament at the Rashtrapati Bhawan, New Delhi (1973)

In 1973, Bakula Rinpoche met with Yumjaagiin Tsedenbal, the longest serving communist leader of Mongolia, when he was on a state visit to India. Mr. Tsedenbal was the Chairman of the Great People's Khural (Parliament) and also Chairman of the Council of Ministers of the Mongolian People's Republic. At a reception, Mrs. Indira Gandhi, Prime Minister of India introduced Bakula Rinpoche to Mr. Tsedenbal as a senior Indian Buddhist leader and an MP. The Mongolian leader then told Mrs. Gandhi that in Mongolia, they too have monasteries and monks and that the Government of Mongolia was trying to reopen the monasteries for the public. Earlier, the communist Government had eased restrictions on religious activities and Gandan Tegchenling Monastery in Ulaanbaatar had reopened with a skeletal staff as a token of homage to traditional Mongolian culture and religion. The meeting between Bakula Rinpoche and Chairman Tsedenbal, although brief, was reported in the Mongolian press and media and this generated a great deal of interest and speculation among the people. Many years later, my Mongolian language tutor Prof. D. Damba would recall that the year of 1973 was something of a turning point. It was only after Tsedenbal's visit to India that people, especially the elders, started to feel freer to attend offering prayers and so on, and even to become monks.

But it was after 1989, when Prime Minister Mr. Rajiv Gandhi appointed Rinpoche as India's Ambassador to Mongolia, that Rinpoche's beneficial impact in the Central Asian nation really started to be felt. Mongolia had been a very close ally of Soviet Union right until its break-up. It too was a communist nation and it was closely-aligned with its neighbour. One feels the hand of destiny at work when literally within months of Rinpoche's arrival in Mongolia as India's Ambassador, the political scenario in the country suddenly changes dramatically. Following the policies of *perestroika* and *glasnost* in the USSR under President Mr. Mikhail Gorbachev, public discontent became more vocal across the Soviet Union, eventually leading to its break up in 1990. Following this, there were massive street protests in Ulaanbaatar also, as people felt emboldened to express their discontent. The winds of change swept across the Mongolian steppes and communism collapsed in year 1990, after seventy years of authoritarian rule. Working as a diplomat in Ulaanbaatar, I witnessed this wave of street demonstrations first hand as described in a later chapter. In 1921, Mongolia was the first country in Asia to follow communism, now, it was also the first to abandon it!

NOTES

1. V.A. Wallace, "Bakula Arhat's Journeys to the North: The Life and Work of the Nineteenth Kushok Bakula in Russia and Mongolia."
2. Sometimes his name is also spelled as Bakula, Vakkula, and Bakula. In Pali sources, particularly in the *Majjhima A. thakatha*, IV, the meaning of his name is derived from the word *dvi-kula* ("two families"), a derivation based on the narrative according to which, he was swallowed by a large fish when his nurse tried to bathe him in the river Yamuna – when he was five days old. A fisherman from Benares, who caught the fish found the boy alive in it, and adopted the child. Since the birth parents claimed the child to be theirs, the king decided that the child should belong to both families. According to the later Tibetan and Mongolian sources, he was named Bakula after the *Bakula* tree because he wore the clothing made of the leaves and bark of a *Bakula* tree during his life of a forest hermit.
3. *A Great Teacher of Mongolian People*, Lama G. Purevbat, 2008. In *Commemoration of the 91st Birth Anniversary of H.H. Bakula Rinpoche*. Ulaanbaatar: Pethub Buddhist Centre, p. 84. *Bakula Rinpoche: A Visionary Lama and Statesman*. New Delhi: Sonam Wangchuk Shakspo, p. 58.
4. Lhamsurengiin Khurelbaatar 1999 Bakula Rinbuchi Tuvdenchognor (Ulaanbaatar, Mongol Uls Shinjlekh Ukhaani Akademi Khel Zokhiolin khureelen, p. 85.
5. Zaya Damdi. 1, 47a, 1-3 by Lhamsurengiin Khurelbaatar 1999 Bakula Rinbuchi Tuvdenchognor (Ulaanbaatar, Mongol Uls Shinjlekh Ukhaani Akademi Khel Zokhiolin khureelen, p. 77.
6. The painting is now in the private possession of Dorjiin Damba's family in Ulaanbaatar.
7. Lhamsurengiin Khurelbaatar 1999 Bakula Rinbuchi Tuvdenchognor (Ulaanbaatar, Mongol Uls Shinjlekh Ukhaani Akademi Khel Zokhiolin khureelen, p. 77.

Forty-two

Mongolia: A Brief Introduction

Extreme cold weather, a harsh climate and boundless steppes marked by nothing but the round white tents of nomadic herders (Ger) are the main characteristics of this land. Mongolia lies in central Asia – between Siberia to the north and China to the south. Slightly larger than Alaska, it has a population of over three million and total area of 1,565,000 square kilometers, lying at an average altitude of 2000 metres (6500 Ft.) above sea level. It is a land of strong traditions, where the nomadic pastoralist way of life has not changed much in many centuries, and people live close to nature and subsist on what it can provide. The independent Republic of Mongolia does not, however, cover all the Mongol regions. Southern Mongolia (also known as Inner Mongolia) remains in the People's Republic of China, while the northern parts fall in the Buryatia Republic of the Russian Federation. Other ethnic Mongols live in regions further afield, such as Kalmykia and Tuva, both of which also fall in the Russian Federation.

It is said that the Great Wall of China was built to protect China from incursions by Mongols. The power of the historic Mongols reached its zenith during the 13th century under Chinggis Khaan and his grandson Kublai Khaan who became the emperor of China and the founder of the Yuan Dynasty. To the outside world, the little-explored land of Mongolia is known primarily as the homeland of the world-conqueror Chinggis Khaan, whose conquests extended all the way to Europe, and whose descendants extended the Mongol empire across most of Eurasia by conquering China, Korea, the Caucasus, Central Asia and substantial portion of Eastern Europe and Southwest Asia.

The word *'Khaan'* in Mongolian language means lord, king or emperor and hence the title the Great Chinggis Khaan. Before their embrace of Tibetan

Buddhism which began in the 13th century, Mongols followed diverse shamanic traditions and even today there are some who continue to follow such practices. However, recent findings of stone inscriptions written in Brahmi Script and other studies also indicate that Buddhism reached Mongolia much earlier directly from India. But in the pre-modern period (before the communist revolution) Mongolia was a predominantly Buddhist nation, mostly aligned with the Tibetan Gelug school. It was the communist revolution of 1921, which brought an end to the theocratic rule of the 8th Jebtsundamba Khutuktu, who also held the titles of Bogd Gegeen or Bogd Khan.

The Mongolian incarnations of the Jebtsundamba began in the 17th century with Zanabazar who was identified as the reincarnation of the great Tibetan scholar Taranatha. Taranatha belonged to the Jonang school of Tibetan Buddhism. Gandan Tegchenling Monastery, which today stands as the main centre of Buddhism in Mongolia, was constructed by order of the 5th Jebtsundamba in year 1838, and it included a private residence for the Khalkha Jebtsundamba. In year 1913, a temple dedicated to the 26-metre Megjid Janraisig statue was also added. In year 1904, the 13th Dalai Lama Thubten Gyatso stayed at Gandan Tegchenling Monastery.

By the time of the communist revolution, the holder of the title Jebtsundamba Khutuktu was the 8th incarnation, Agvaan Luvsan Choijinyam Danzan Vanchüg who was in fact born in Tibet in 1870. He held a position in Mongolia, very similar to that held by the Dalai Lama in Tibet. He was the most senior reincarnation and also considered the protector of the nation in worldly affairs, who after the expulsion of the Manchus and the collapse of the Qing Dynasty in China, became the country's temporal ruler. He was then deposed when Chinese troops briefly occupied the country in 1919. Soon after in 1921, Damdin Sükhbaatar seized power in Mongolia with the support of Bolshevik communist revolutionaries. He allowed the Bogd Khan to stay on the throne as a kind of limited monarchy until his death in 1924.

The 9th Jebtsundamba Khutuktu, was born as Jampal Namdol Chökyi Gyaltsen in year 1933 to Tibetan parents and recognized by the Regent of Tibet Reting Rinpoche in 1936. However, this recognition was kept secret out of concerns for his safety, given the alarming situation then prevailing in communist Mongolia. Later, like the Dalai Lama, Jampal Namdol Chökyi Gyaltsen went into exile in India, and there though he lived as a householder rather than a monk but played an important role in the modern reinvigoration of the Jonang lineage. After the end of communism in Mongolia, the 14th Dalai Lama made the recognition public in 1990. In 1992, an enthronement ceremony was held in Dharamshala – publicly recognizing and proclaiming Jampal Namdol Chökyi Gyaltsen as the 9th Jebtsundamba Khutuktu.

During visits to Dharamshala, Bakula Rinpoche who was then India's ambassador to Mongolia, regularly met the 14th Dalai Lama and apprised him about the developments in Mongolia and with regard to the restoration of the Khalka Jebtsundamba leanage in Mongolia. He also discussed the possible visit of the 9th Jebtsundamba, considered as the head of the Mongolian Buddhists to the country, to shoulder spiritual responsibility and in rebuilding Buddhism in the whole region. Meanwhile, calls for his return to Mongolia were becoming louder, especially among the monastic communities there. But some local politicians and journalists were apprehensive about such a move, as it was unclear what, if any, his political role there would be.

In July 1999 the 9th Jebtsundamba Khutuktu visited Mongolia on a tourist visa. This took everyone by surprise. Rinpoche also had no information about this visit. The visit created considerable political controversy. Much was written in the press about various theories and possible repercussions in the political process in Mongolia. Ambassador Bakula Rinpoche hosted him at the Indian embassy as well as his Pethub Monastery in Ulaanbaatar and discussed with him the situation in the country. He later returned to India.

In 2010, the 9th Bogd Khan visited Mongolia again, this time at the invitation of the Gandan Tegchenling Monastery, and with the approval of the Mongolian Government. Subsequently, he was granted Mongolian citizenship. In November 2011, he was finally enthroned as the head of all Buddhists in Mongolia at a ceremony held at Gandan Tegchenling Monastery in Ulaanbaatar. However, his health remained a matter of concern. He passed away on 1st March 2012, at Ulaanbaatar at the age of 79.

Meanwhile, the search for the next incarnation, the 10th Jebtsundamba Khutuktu continued. The Dalai Lama during his visit to Mongolia in year 1916 had indicated that the 10th Jebtsundamba has been born but made no official announcement. Subsequently, during a teaching at Dharamshala, India on 8th March 2023, for the first time, the 14th Dalai Lama declared about the presence of the 8-year-old boy A. Altannar as the 10th Bogd Khan Jebtsundamba Khutuktu. He was born in the United States of America to Mongolian parents. The news that the 10th Bogd Khan has been confirmed by the 14th Dalai Lama was a cause of celebration in Mongolia and across the Buddhist world. In September 2023, the first meeting between the 20th Bakula Rinpoche and the newly identified the 10th Bogd Khan Jebtsundamba took place at Gandan Monastery in Ulaanbaatar. I had the opportunity to witness this meeting.

For the Buddhist world, Mongolia is well-known for the erudition of its scholar-saints. Foremost among them is Zanabazar, the first Jebtsundamba, who captivated his disciples with his scholarly and artistic work and whose achievements greatly enriched Mongolia's Buddhist heritage. There have been many such Mongolian Buddhist scholars, whose works have contributed not just to the development of Buddhism in Mongolia, but also to that in Tibet, China and elsewhere.

In another significant development in the year 2021, the President of Mongolia through a decree restored the title of "Khamba Nomun Khan", which existed during the pre-communist rule in Mongolia. It is a high position next only to the Bogd Khan. Gabju Demberal Choijamts, Khambolama of Gandan Thegchenling Monastery was declared as the 29th Khamba Nomun Khan with retrospective effect to all his predecessors. He retired from this position in November 2023, and in his place Geshe Lharampa D. Javzundorj was appointed as the Khambolama of Gandan Tegchenling Monastery and the 30th Khamba Nomun Khan. He had studied at Drepung Gomang Monastery in South India and was among the early batches of monks from Mongolia sent during Rinpoche's tenure as the Ambassador of India.

Forty-three

Appointment as India's Ambassador to Mongolia

When Prime Minister Rajiv Gandhi appointed Bakula Rinpoche as India's Ambassador to Mongolia, he was already 73 years of age. He had already served as an MLA and minister in J&K, as a Member of Indian Parliament and had also and spent a decade on the National Commission for Minorities. For most ordinary people, this long career would have been enough. But Rinpoche was exceptional in the sense that he, irrespective of his age was always ready to serve and in this case, it was Mongolia, a country Rinpoche always had in his heart and had accepted Prime Minister Rajiv Gandhi's appointment in the first place.

However, Rinpoche was under no illusions that this new role would be easy. He realised that representing India in a foreign country, would be a very challenging task, especially when he had no prior experience in the diplomatic service, nor in international relations. He was concerned that he would not be able to do justice to the post and was therefore a little hesitant in accepting the offer. Ultimately it was his friends like Dr. Karan Singh, former ruler of Jammu and Kashmir and Mr. T.N. Kaul – one of India's foremost diplomats and strategic studies experts – who prevailed upon Rinpoche the importance of accepting this opportunity. They also persuaded him by saying that since Mongolia was a communist country, his work would be mostly routine diplomatic work, and that there would be other officials at the embassy to assist him. This would leave him free to pursue his duties as Buddhist monk without too much disturbance or upset. Rinpoche already knew Mongolia from his numerous previous visits, and perhaps he was also persuaded by the thought that taking this appointment would give him the opportunity to study some rare Buddhist manuscripts, which he knew were in abundance in the libraries of Ulaanbaatar and also contribute to the development of Buddhism in the country.

But even before Rinpoche could take up the assignment, he was faced with a difficult predicament. A general election had just been announced in India, and since this was a political appointment, Rinpoche naturally felt it was important for him to wait for the formation of the new government. Rinpoche's apprehensions before the election were not unreasonable. In fact, several other recent ambassadorial appointees chosen by the previous regime were later recalled by the new government in New Delhi. However, as it turned out, this assignment was anything but a comfortable posting. In fact, it proved to be not only the most challenging, but also the most tedious job he undertook in his long life of public service. Initially, his posting was for only two years. But by the time Bakula Rinpoche relinquished the office, ten momentous years had already passed.

On December 21, 1989, Rinpoche left New Delhi for Mongolia accompanied by myself, along with my family, and Rinpoche's two other support staff. Our route took us first to Hong Kong where we halted for three days, followed by an unforgettable train journey to Beijing. For Bakula Rinpoche it was his first visit to Beijing, a place he had long been eager to see. We arrived in Beijing on December 27, 1989. Elderly people and the workers still wore the Mao-style blue dress and bicycles and buses were the main modes of transport for the common people. Yet changes were already visible in the country. Under Deng Xiaoping, the Chinese Communist Party (CCP) had already embarked upon a major programme of economic liberalisation which was transforming the country. But it was also a tense time in China. The tragic events in Tiananmen Square, where so many student protestors had lost their lives when their protests were crushed mercilessly by the Red Army, which had occurred in recent past, in April 1989. The tragedy was still fresh in the minds of many in the national capital.

During our brief stay in Beijing, Rinpoche visited some historical places including the Great Wall of China, Forbidden City and the Summer Palace, throughout maintaining a low profile. His only official engagement was a meeting with Amb. C.V. Ranganathan, the Indian Ambassador to China and with Ngapho Ngawang Jigme, the highest-ranking Tibetan in Chinese political hierarchy whom Rinpoche knew from his early days in Lhasa, Tibet.

After our brief stay in Beijing, we continued our journey by the Trans-Siberian Railways to Ulaanbaatar passing through the Gobi Desert. It was mid-winter and very cold outside, but the train was well-heated and comfortable. An interesting experience of this journey was at the border town Erlian on the Chinese side. Here the train stops for a few hours and the entire wheel system of the train is changed from a wide-gauge to a narrow-gauge and vice-versa on the return journey. It was really something rather unusual. While the wheels of the train are replaced, the passengers could remain on board. This peculiar situation is a remnant of the souring of relations between the two communist giants, the Soviet Union and China in the early 1960s when the railway tracks were being laid. Such was the mutual suspicion that neither side was willing to lay any track that could potentially be used by trains of the other country. On the way to Ulaanbaatar, there was not much to see outside except for the Gobi Desert and occasional wild animals. It was just a vast barren land covered with snow. It was very cold outside. Often, we could see nothing because of billowing snow outside and the growing layer of frost on the windows.

In the year of Horse on December 31, 1989, on a cold and bright sunny day, we finally arrived at Ulaanbaatar. At the railway station there were many people awaiting Rinpoche's arrival, including some familiar faces from Gandan Tegchenling Monastery and the ABCP Headquarters. Also present were representatives of the Mongolian Foreign Ministry, the Dean of the Diplomatic Corps in Ulaanbaatar and the officials of the Indian Embassy. From the railway station we drove straight to the Indian embassy on Peace Avenue which would also serve as Rinpoche's residence for a few years, whereas the embassy was later moved to a new and grander building on the Youth Street.

In 1989, Mongolia was still under the Soviet umbrella and because of the friendly relations between India and the Soviet Union, Indo-Mongolian relations were cordial. In 1955, India was the first country outside the socialist block to establish full diplomatic relations with Mongolia and it had also strongly supported Mongolia's membership of the United Nations. And thus, Bakula Rinpoche took charge as Indian Ambassador on January 3, 1990. Just two days later, on January 5, 1990, he called on the Foreign Minister Ts. Gombosuren, and later, the same day, presented his credentials to Jambyn Batmunkh, Chairman of the Mongolian People's Revolutionary Party and Chairman of the *Great Khural* (Parliament). This was an unusual breach of protocol as the host government in normal circumstances would only accept credentials after a month or so. But in the case of Rinpoche, this norm was ignored. There was great deal of curiosity and interest in his appointment in the country. This was evident when he met the ministers and senior officials of the Government of Mongolia for the first time as ambassador. Never before in their life these officials had interacted with a senior Buddhist monk, let alone one who was a serving ambassador of a foreign country.

While some of these officials found this situation rather inappropriate or comic, for many common people in the country, Rinpoche's appointment was a matter of tremendous excitement. They were very happy to find Bakula Rinpoche living among them. Some recalled the long-forgotten prophecy made in the late 19th century, about the coming of Arhat Bakula to Mongolia.

At that time the communist party was still firmly in control and there was no apparent sense of impending crisis. As was customary, the Red Army of Mongolia presented a guard of honour for Rinpoche, as it did for all new ambassadors. As a spectator, I couldn't help but feel there was a certain irony in the scene: Here was a military show of a communist army presenting itself as a guard of honour to a Buddhist monk ambassador.

In his customary short speech following the ceremony at the presidential palace, Ambassador Kushok Bakula, as if pre-empting the momentous changes that would soon sweep the country, mentioned that: " Lord Buddha, whose teachings spread to the Mongolian steppes in the 13th century, was the first Indian envoy to Mongolia." Rinpoche spoke these words at a time when the country was still firmly under communist rule and there was no freedom of religion or speech. I wonder what went through the minds of those communist leaders when they heard those words.

Rinpoche speaking at the President House in Ulaanbaatar

Amb. Bakula Rinpoche presenting his credentials to Mr. J. Batmunkh, Chairman of the Presidium of the State Great Khural at Government House, Ulaanbaatar (1990)

Front Row: *Mr. Ts. Gotov, Secretary of Great Khural (Parliament), Amb. Bakula Rinpoche, Mr. J. Batmunkh, Chairman, Presidium of the State Great Khural and Mr. Ts. Gombosuren, Minister of Foreign Affairs.*
Second Row: *Mr. Erdenebulgan, Protocol officer, Mr. J. Choinkhor, Director of the Asia Department, Mr. Kohli, Embassy of India, Mr. B. Natsagdorj, Chief of Protocol, Mr. Sonam Wangchuk (author), Mr. Yo. Otgonbayar and Mr. Batbaatar, officers of Asia Department (1990)*

Amb. Bakula Rinpoche inspecting a Guard of Honour presented by the Mongolian Army at the Government House, Ulaanbaatar (1990)

I suspect that Mr. Batmunkh, who was then the head of the communist state was both amused and also rather pleased. He had succeeded Mr. Tsedenbal as Chairman of the Great People's Khural of Mongolia. The President of Mongolia at that time was an extremely polite and a humble man, and he warmly congratulated Rinpoche on his appointment. In Mongolian, as in Tibetan, India is known by the name 'Jagar', which in its Tibetan version means the white or pure-land, and many people in Mongolia, as in Tibet, genuinely consider India as their spiritual neighbour and teacher.

Shortly thereafter change began to sweep through the steppes. With the disintegration of the USSR and its satellites, the fall of the Berlin Wall and the economic changes going on in China; it was inevitable that Mongolia too would have to change. Within weeks, the popular reform demonstrations started in Ulaanbaatar, as ordinary and young people in particular started taking to the streets despite the sub-zero temperatures.

Perhaps the most remarkable feature of the changes that swept Mongolia in the coming years was that unlike in other socialist countries, the transformation in Mongolia was peaceful. Not a single bullet was fired nor a baton used by security forces. During the protests some Party hardliners had advocated cracking down on the protesters, but Mr. Batmunkh is said to have firmly opposed any such move, maintaining a strict policy of never using force. It was his strong and mature leadership which helped end the conflict peacefully, and bring about a smooth transition to democracy.

Rinpoche remained in close touch with Mr. Batmunkh until his death in year 1997 and always held him in high esteem.

Over the years, Bakula Rinpoche travelled the length and breadth of this vast, beautiful and empty land, often travelling for days and even weeks, often staying among the common people in their traditional *Gers* (yurts). These travels helped Rinpoche develop a genuine personal rapport with ordinary Mongolian people. He played a major role in maintaining peace and tranquility in the country during this critical and extremely difficult period of transition. While other diplomats and foreigners posted to Ulaanbaatar were often itching to get out of Mongolia, Bakula Rinpoche was entirely at ease there. Mr. Anil Trigunayat who had earlier served as the Deputy Chief in the Indian embassy in Mongolia recalls: "The British and US Ambassadors often told me that by posting Ambassador Bakula – a Buddhist Monk to Mongolia, the Government of India had done a diplomatic coup of sorts since no one could have commanded the respect and affection Rinpoche enjoyed in the host country."[1] Like a true *Bodhisattva,* he never abandoned his chosen path and was content to remain in the country, despite many hardships and its extreme weather conditions in those difficult years.

NOTES

1. 'Rinpoche Kushok Bakula Rinpoche: A Saint and an Ambassador' published in 'Kootniti', 16th April 2018.

Forty-four

The Advent of Democracy in Mongolia

By March 1990, strikes and demonstrations across Mongolia – led mainly by young students – were putting a lot of pressure on the besieged communist government. In that month, members of the first democratic alliance, called the *'Ardchilsan Kholboo'* or Democratic Union, launched a hunger strike demanding the resignation of the communist government and calling of democratic elections. Thousands joined this protest which was spearheaded by a band of young leaders. The Perestroika in the USSR and democracy movements across Eastern Europe had a profound impact in Mongolia. Prominent among them were Sanjasurengiin Zorig, Tsakhiagiin Elbegdorj, Erdeniin Bat-Uul, Baterdeniin Batbayar and Radnaasumberel Gonchigdorj. These sustained and peaceful protests finally culminated in the communist regime bowing to their demands and announcing free and fair elections to choose the future government.

Mongolia had embarked upon a new and untrodden path – the path of democracy. Since India is the world's largest parliamentary democracy, it was natural that some of the new democratic protestors looked towards India for some inspiration and support in their struggle. Having known that Rinpoche, besides a spiritual leader, he was also a prominent political figure in India, the leaders of young protestors approached him for his blessings and guidance. This led to a difficult situation for us, and especially for me personally, as Rinpoche's secretary, since we were suddenly caught in the political cross-fire at a very critical and tense juncture in Mongolia's modern history. They included S. Zorig, Ts. Elbegdorj, Dorligjav, Lama Baasan, Ninj, and others. For me, as Ambassador's Private Secretary, this was a difficult situation to handle. I explained to Ninj who had called me that for Rinpoche, as a diplomat whose job it is to deal with the government of the host nation, meeting with hunger-striking protestors would be difficult and could have serious fallout. However, these young people were adamant and they seemed sincere when they said that all they wanted were Rinpoche's blessings, and that they did not want to discuss political matters with him or raise slogans in his presence. When I conveyed the request once again to Rinpoche, he, to my surprise, agreed to meet them. So, these leaders were invited to the Indian embassy for an audience. Before the meeting, I again reminded them that political matters were not on the agenda of the meeting and that such subjects should really be avoided. This naturally was easier said than done.

As the meeting progressed, the leaders of the movement for political reforms felt comfortable and so they opened up. The young leaders broached upon their political struggle and sought Rinpoche's guidance and advice. They also knew Rinpoche's background as a politician and his close association with Pandit Jawaharlal Nehru, one of the prominent leaders of India's freedom movement. I was acting as Rinpoche's translator at the meeting, and I confess, it was a tense moment for me. But Rinpoche did not seem worried and gave them a patient hearing. He told them, among other things, that in general, genuine freedom struggles must adhere to peaceful means and shun violence at any cost. He reminded them of the tragedy that had taken place at Tiananmen Square in Beijing the previous year, which was still fresh in many people's minds. He also told them about Mongolia's Buddhist heritage and about Mahatma Gandhi's freedom struggle in India, all of which supported his main point that violence must be shunned.

The meeting ended with Rinpoche giving them his blessings and a *Zangya* (holy cords) each. As they were about to leave, one of them asked Rinpoche for a few more, which he gave. We assumed these were for their family members (as is usually the case). But there was a shock in store for us that evening. In the evening TV news bulletin, one of the protest leaders was shown distributing the holy cords among the people sitting on hunger strike at Sukhbaatar Square.

At that time there was only one national TV channel, and people were hungry for the news, so that clip must have been seen by almost everyone in the country. People in Ulaanbaatar knew exactly where these Zangya had come from, since at that time Rinpoche was the only lama who gave out such threads to the faithful. Certainly, eyebrows would have been raised at the Communist party headquarters. We were half-expecting the Government to call for an explanation and even declare Rinpoche a persona non-grata in Mongolia and asked to leave the country for interfering in the internal affairs of a sovereign country.

Mongolian youth protesting against communist rule and demanding democracy. Sukhbaatar Square, Ulaanbaatar (1990)

Author at the Freedom Square, Ulaanbaatar (1990)

When I saw this on TV, I rushed to Bakula Rinpoche who was at that time sitting at prayer. I told him what I had seen on TV. I was very impressed by the equanimity of his response. He gently told me to calm down, and to get in touch with Jalbuu Choinkhor who at that time was heading the Asia desk of the Ministry of Foreign Relations and explain to him what had happened that day. I immediately called Mr. Choinkhor. He told me that he is already aware of it and promised to get back to us if anything further was needed to be done.

The day was March 9, 1990, and the national situation took a sharp turn that very night. Intense negotiations were being held between the youth leaders and the communist regime. Fortunately, a common ground was found, and a tense and explosive situation was averted. The protestors agreed to call off their public agitation, and on their side, the communist government agreed to resign. It also decided to dissolve the ruling Politburo and hold free multi-party elections nationwide to determine the new government. There was euphoria in the air, people were really celebrating the fact that this outcome had been achieved without violence. For many people, Rinpoche's presence in Mongolia at that crucial juncture, was like a blessing and it was on this auspicious note that Mongolia entered a new era.

Unthinkable only a few months earlier, free and fair elections were held on July 29, 1990. They were closely monitored by international observers, including some from India. Ambassador Bakula Rinpoche also visited several polling booths and saw people casting their votes. This was democracy in action for the first time in Mongolia with the main contest being that between the former-communist ruling Mongolian People's Revolutionary Party (MPRP) and an assorted alliance of new democrats.

The outcome of the election was that the MPRP or the Communist Party won 85% of the seats of the 76-member parliament. Continuity was thus assured, but there was also going to be a sizable and vocal opposition in parliament. The new parliament was convened for the first time on September 3, 1990. A little more than one year later, a new constitution was formally adopted on January 13, 1992. Justice P.N. Bhagwati, a well-known constitutional expert from India also participated in the framing of the new constitution. Rinpoche was present in the parliament for this historic occasion. The new constitution not only established Mongolia as an independent, sovereign republic, it also guaranteed a number of rights and freedoms and restructured the legislative branch of the government by creating a single (or unicameral) legislature called the Great State Khural elected by universal suffrage. On June 6, 1993, the first direct presidential election took place, and this time it was won by the opposition Democratic Party candidate, Mr. Punsalmaagiin Ochirbat, who thus became the first elected President of Mongolia.

Thus, began the long and somewhat difficult process of democratization in Mongolia. Rinpoche was a witness to this entire period of dramatic transition in Mongolian history and played a distinct and significant role in ensuring that this radical transformation of the country was by and large achieved peacefully.

In later years, his formal position as Indian Ambassador came to take a back-seat to his more prominent status as a spiritual teacher and guide whose sage advice and calming presence was a boon for the country in these times of particular uncertainty and insecurity. At the time he was the highest-ranking Buddhist monk in the country and the only reincarnated lama. He offered guidance to the nascent monastic communities in the country as well as to the ordinary people of Mongolia in those crucial years. He also had the ear of many people in positions of authority, and his presence was undoubtedly a very stabilizing influence in the national capital. His contributions as Indian envoy in Mongolia during these years were also historic in so many ways. A solid foundation of Indo-Mongolian relations was laid by Bakula Rinpoche for which he is remembered in democratic Mongolia with a deep sense of gratitude.

After a peaceful transformation, a new Mongolia came into being. One of the features of the new, post-communist Mongolia was that Chinggis Khaan, who, during the Soviet period had been condemned as an imperialist, now started to be celebrated officially as a national hero. Such was the power of state propaganda in those days that a man who once symbolized Mongolia's greatest achievements, was considered anathema. But within months of the collapse of communism, such old symbols and personalities were reinstated with a great deal of nationalistic pride and fanfare. Portraits of Chinggis Khaan were printed on currency notes and the international airport in Ulaanbaatar was re-named after him. Soon Chinggis memorials of various kinds started to spring up everywhere. A new block was even added on to the front of the main Government House on Sukhbaatar Square with large statues of the Great Chinggis Khaan and his successors. And a national museum glorifying Mongolian history was opened to the public.

This new-found expression of pride in national identity was also echoed in the framing of the new constitution. At that time (early 1990s) many people wanted Buddhism to be formally inscribed as the state religion of Mongolia in its constitution, but there was opposition to this in some quarters. There was also stiff resistance from many NGOs and western missions working in Mongolia, some of which even threatened to withdraw or curtail aid and assistance if any such provision was passed by the parliament. The US in particular was very much against such a move. Rinpoche's view was neutral on the subject. He argued that as a democratic society, Mongolia should be free to draft its constitution without any outside interference or pressure. In the end, the parliament adopted a constitution in which all faiths were treated equally under law.

Needless to say, Buddhism continues to enjoy a very special place in Mongolia. Any official itinerary for a visiting head of state or other foreign dignitary will always include a visit to Gandan Tegchenling Monastery, the Centre of Mongolian Buddhists. Buddhism has regained its former pre-eminent position in Mongolian society and has become an integral part of the country's cultural identity. *Tsagaan-Sar* (the Mongolian Lunar New Year), which was banned earlier during the communist period, has now been declared a national holiday.

Although the transition to democracy in Mongolia was by and large entirely peaceful, there was one sad incident in what was otherwise a smooth transformation. On October 2, 1998, an unfortunate incident shocked the nation. Mr. Sanjasuriin Zorig, a young, 36 years old, an upcoming and popular leader of the democratic movement was murdered on the eve of him likely becoming the prime minister of Mongolia. At that time, he was serving as Minister for Infrastructure and was a sitting MP. He had earned a reputation as an upright and effective leader. The motives for his death have remained shrouded in mystery to this day. Bakula Rinpoche expressed his condolences by visiting his family and offering prayers for the departed leader. Later, his younger sister Ms. S. Oyun was elected to the parliament and set up the 'Zorig Foundation'.

In view of his seniority among the diplomatic corps in Ulaanbaatar, Rinpoche also functioned for a few years as the Dean of Diplomatic Corps in Ulaanbaatar. By the time he relinquished office, Rinpoche had already completed 10 years as the ambassador of India and set a record of sorts in the Indian diplomatic history as no other ambassador had ever done this feat before.

Amb. Bakula Rinpoche as the Dean of the Diplomatic corps in Ulaanbaatar

Forty-five

The Ambassador-Teacher (Elchin Bagsha)

The 1921 revolution, and seven decades of communism had ravaged Mongolia's Buddhist heritage, leaving it as little more than a shell. Monasteries were destroyed, their property and estates were seized and all of their former privileges were stopped. Although a few voices were still to be heard defending Buddhism in the revolutionary government as late as 1934, such voices were too few and too weak to mount any real defence against the ascendant anti-religious communist ideology. As in communist purges elsewhere, the victims of the Mongolian purges under Marshal Khorloogiin Choibalsan in years 1937–38, were mostly people from the old upper-stratum of society, such as nobles, clergy, scholars, and those who had formerly held government ranks. It is estimated that over 1000 temples and monasteries were destroyed and over 20,000 Buddhist monks executed. Additionally, though such people were the primary targets, communist purges affected the entire country. Closure and destruction of the monasteries left Mongolia's cultural landscape altered forever, and left a vacuum in the heart of its cultural life.

After decades of one-party rule, communism collapsed in Mongolia in the year 1990, and there was a dawn of freedom and democracy. The subject of the purges, which until then had been taboo, started to be talked about more openly, thus allowing the country to mourn and heal, albeit many decades had already passed. Bakula Rinpoche was taken to see remnants of Soviet purges and the mass graves. In some of them, hundreds of monks had been shot in the head and their bodies unceremoniously dumped. One could see the remains of monks' skulls riddled with bullet holes while rosaries were still clutched to their bodies. In the course of meeting with

Rinpoche, several persons who had been involved in these massacres expressed their remorse and repentance for what they had done and offered their confession before Rinpoche. They told him how they had committed crimes such as killing monks and scholars under orders from the communist hierarchy. In all such instances, I was present during this meeting and it was very poignant and moving to hear such confessions. Rinpoche also visited the "Victims of Political Persecution Museum" in Ulaanbaatar which is dedicated to the victims of the purges. The museum is housed in what was once the residence of executed prime minister Peljidiin Genden. He was the Prime Minister of Mongolia from 1932-1936. He had resisted pressure from Stalinist forces to liquidate institutional Buddhism and Soviet influence in Mongolia and is known to have confronted Stalin during their meeting in Moscow. This and the strong nationalist sentiments ultimately led to his execution in March 1937. In 1996, his daughter Mrs. Tserendulam met Rinpoche and later decided to turn her residence into a museum.

In 1991, the mass grave at Moren was officially investigated and later one at Hambiin Ovoo in Ulaanbaatar. The corpses of hundreds of executed lamas and civilians were unearthed. Later, in memory of the victims, a stupa was built at Hambiin Ovoo by Lama G. Purevbat. I remember that in year 2003, when Rinpoche was in Ulaanbaatar recuperating from pneumonia, Lama Purevbat came to inform him about the memorial stupa, which had been built at Hambiin Ovoo on the outskirts of Ulaanbaatar to commemorate the victims of the communist purges. Lama Purevbat, along with various government officials, had prepared a detailed historical and forensic report based on the excavations and had submitted these to the government. At the time Rinpoche was in extremely poor health and could barely talk. But when he heard about this, and particularly about the stupa that had been erected in memory of the victims of these horrors, he decided to go there and offer his prayers. I remember it was a very cold and windy autumn morning when together with Lama Purevbat and some monks from Pethub Monastery, Rinpoche visited the site and offered prayers at the new stupa. Unfortunately, this was to be Bakula Rinpoche's last public appearance in Mongolia. Just a few days later he had to be airlifted to Beijing for urgent medical treatment.

Lama G. Purevbat was a well-known scholar artist of Mongolia. In the early 1990s, when he was still a teenager, the young monk had once met Rinpoche at the Indian embassy. Recognizing his talent and potential, Rinpoche suggested to him that he should go to India to study thangka-painting and Buddhist art in Dharamshala, India, where there were some very accomplished teachers. He did so, and completed his studies in India. He returned to Mongolia and devoted his time and energy to the promotion

Rinpoche at the Hambiin Ovoo in Ulaanbaatar (2003)

Lama G. Purevbat (1965-2024)

of Buddhist art and teachings. He then established the Mongolian Institute of Buddhist Art (MIBA) at Gandan Thegchenling Monastery where he trained many young talents from across Mongolia in various forms of Mongolian and Buddhist art.

It may be noted that Buddhism and Mongolian cultures are in many ways inseparable. Lama Purebvat also wrote and published several books including a Mongolian version of the Lamrim. Rinpoche had seen his tremendous work of art and once described him as someone who was truly following in the footsteps of the legendary Zanabazara. Lama Purevbat's artistic skills and energy were truly inspiring. A dynamic and distinctive artist, he made substantial contributions in the making of the new statue of Mijid Chenrezig. He was best known for building the '*Aglag Buteel Monastery*' in the beautiful surrounding just about 100 kilometers from Ulaanbaatar. Some of his artifacts are prominently displayed in Mongolia's State House, which is the main seat of the national government. He was a State Merited artist of Mongolia and also received the Prince Claus Award from the Government of Netherlands. Lama Purevbat's achievements truly illustrate the great potential of Mongolian artists. Unfortunately, he passed away in April 2024, at a relatively young age of 59.

Forty-six

A Cacophony of Missionaries in New Mongolia

Besides lack of resources and qualified monks, another obstacle in the rejuvenation of Mongolia's Buddhist heritage in this period were the hundreds of Christian missionaries of various strata, mainly from the USA and South Korea, who started flooding into the country during the 1990s. Often they did not describe themselves overtly as missionaries, but came under a variety of garbs, like English teachers or volunteers, and brought with them abundant resources. The activities of such missionaries, many from very zealous protestant organizations and other cult groups, certainly made the situation more difficult for those working to revive traditional Mongolian culture. The Mormon sect was particularly active, and part of their proselytisation was to describe Buddhism as a pessimist ideology and the main cause for Mongolia's economic backwardness. They managed to impress many youngsters, who had been inundated with similar propaganda during the communist period.

Once, while travelling to the countryside, Rinpoche's car stopped at Darkhan, the second largest city in Mongolia. When a group of young people found that it was Bakula Rinpoche in the car – who was by then a well-known figure in the country – several of these youngsters ran towards our vehicle. They bowed with reverence before Rinpoche seeking his blessings. But then a man, apparently an evangelist, arrived on the scene and started yelling at them. To us, this incident demonstrated that even after indoctrination by missionaries, Mongolians often retain an instinctive reverence towards Buddhism, because of their innate faith that it is a part of their own heritage.

The arrival of such groups was completely new in Mongolia. In the pre-

Soviet era, there had only been a small Catholic mission in Inner Mongolia, a few Orthodox Russians in Ulaanbaatar and an even smaller and very short-lived community of English Evangelicals, but none of these had exerted much local influence. Then during the Soviet period, although despite a major "europeanisation" of the culture, religious missionaries were not permitted. So, the arrival of missionaries in such large numbers in the 1990s was really something new in Mongolian society. And new things always hold a certain attraction for some young people. Indeed, these missionaries would use many skillful and innovative methods to attract young people.

For example, they held popular weekend picnics combined with English language teaching, and they held out the American dream to these youngsters as something they too could attain by joining their communities. The Christian missionaries especially used their association with the rich and trendy western world to attract the poor and most vulnerable sections of society. And there were many such people in post-communist Mongolia, as people from the countryside started migrating to the city in search of work and new opportunities. Missionaries also used other less obvious channels to spread their faith, such as relief and humanitarian work carried out by NGOs. There was no vetting of foreign NGOs working in Mongolia during the liberalized period following the Soviet demise. Their methods for converting people were often very sophisticated, and of course they had abundant resources, which made them very attractive to be with, during a time of general deprivation in the country. They also used the media to spread their messages, opening private satellite TV channels and making them freely available without subscription.

Compared to the Christian missionaries, the re-emergent Buddhist monasteries had very little by way of resources and man-power. The help they received from outside was at first minimal. So, Bakula Rinpoche did what he could to raise funds from his friends in India, Japan and in the West. He also felt an urgent need of setting up a Radio and TV station in Ulaanbaatar to educate and to provide information to the Buddhist Community in Mongolia. His friends in Japan came forward for assistance in this regard. More importantly, he also helped many young boys and girls go to India for higher studies in Buddhism. He very rightly realized that only if there was a solid base of people who really knew and understood the tenets and practices of Buddhism and its associated wealth of culture, would the Buddhists have any chance of surviving amidst this onslaught of powerful and rich Christian missionaries.

Moreover, it was not just traditional Buddhists and new Christians trying to win the hearts and minds of the people in the new Mongolia. There was a kind of onslaught of all kinds of new beliefs being thrown about in this sparsely populated country of some three million inhabitants.

Forty-seven

Convening the First Assembly of Buddhist Monks

With each passing day, Rinpoche's schedule became more hectic. In addition to his diplomatic responsibilities, his role as a spiritual teacher grew rapidly. Soon, he found himself in a situation he had never imagined. Contrary to his expectation of having a restful time during his posting in Mongolia, he now found himself extremely engrossed in a great variety of quite intense and demanding situations. But, despite the mounting and hectic schedule of work he had to handle on a daily basis, Rinpoche was always very composed and quite cheerful. He often said he felt quite at home in Mongolia, which resembles Ladakh in more than one way. Its weather conditions are similar, and so are the dress, shoes and food habits and nature of the people. Even their faces are quite similar.

During these years Rinpoche gave regular radio and television interviews, and he also wrote newspaper articles. He visited many far-flung areas, often traveling on Soviet-made cargo planes, which in those days plied the routes between Ulaanbaatar and the outlying regions. These planes would sometimes land at all-but-unmanned airstrips. There was nothing like airport security or such things. Most of Mongolia is a vast steppe and, in those days, the only land vehicles capable of traversing its bumpy roads were sturdy Russian-made jeeps. These vehicles were strong, but they were far from comfortable, and to ride in them for many hours could be quite arduous. But Rinpoche never complained.

For Rinpoche it was exciting to be a witness to the dawn of religious freedom in the country after nearly seven decades of suppression. But it also was painful to see the colossal damage that had already been inflicted on Buddhist culture in Mongolia. In order to make the country's Buddhist roots take hold once again, it was imperative that there was a properly trained, ethical Sangha to whom the common people could look up to for inspiration and advice. In early 1990s, Buddhism in Mongolia was all but leaderless and in a state of disarray. Not only among lay people, but among young monks themselves there was utter ignorance about the Vinaya, the monastic code for monks and nuns. Sometimes, during a visit to a family, people would serve *Arkhi* or vodka to Rinpoche which they considered as a mark of respect, a legacy of the Soviet influence. Such was the ignorance. Gradually Rinpoche was able to spread greater awareness among the people through his many public talks and interviews.

In year 1990, during his tenure as ambassador, Rinpoche visited Harhorin (Karakorum), the ancient capital of Mongolia, where the famous Erdenezuu Monastery is located. He was accompanied by the Khambolama D. Choijamts and Gundusangpo who translated his teaching from Tibetan into Mongolian. In May of the following year, Rinpoche ordained the first batch of Gelongs (Fully ordained monk) after the fall of communism at Amarbayasgalant Monastery. He stayed there for several days. Same year, he also visited Zavkhan province. In 1992, Bakula Rinpoche visited Shankh Monastery in Ovorkhangai province in central Mongolia, 25 kms south of Harhorin city. Shankh monastery was founded by Undurgegen Zanabazar, the first Jebtsundamba Khutagt of Mongolia in year 1647.

Participants of the first assembly of Buddhist monks called by Bakula Rinpoche at Gandan Tegchenlingg Monastery, Ulaanbaatar (1990)

Bakula Rinpoche on a visit to Mongolian countryside

Rinpoche in the cockpit of a plane on his way to a Mongolian province

An Arial view of Mt. Otgontenger, the highest peak in Mongolia

At a grassland in Mongolia

Feeding water to the cattle in Gobi

Rinpoche on a visit to Gobi.

Rinpoche on a visit to Byanhongor Province

Rinpoche delivering teaching outside Shankh Monastery

Monks of Shankh Monastery displaying the robes of Undur Gegeen Zanabazar, the first Bogd Khan

In light of the challenges he faced, Rinpoche deemed it necessary to hold a gathering of monks so that he could explain such matters to them very clearly. In September 1990, he met Mr. G. Adiya, who at that time was heading the government department of Religious Affairs. Ironically, this was the same office that until the previous year, had been primarily responsible for cracking down on religious activities. But now the same department was working to promote Buddhism and to coordinate with religious organizations and public figures like Bakula Rinpoche. In a meeting that lasted more than two hours, Rinpoche and Mr. Adiya discussed many issues that were imperative to be addressed if Buddhism was to be revived. They talked about the renovation of old temples, building of new monasteries in those provincial cities and towns where the old monasteries had been destroyed. They also discussed the measures required so that people would again start joining monastic communities. These and many other aspects of Mongolia's cultural life such as celebration of Tsagaan-Sar or New Year and other religious festivals which had been banned and disrupted for so many decades, were also discussed.

In order to assess the situation and plan for future activities, Rinpoche suggested to Mr. Adiya that a conference should be convened at Gandan Tegchenling Monastery of every single monk in Mongolia. This might sound very ambitious, but at that time the number of monks in the entire country did not exceed three hundred. With everyone present, Rinpoche said, they could discuss all the issues openly and frankly and come together in rejuvenation of Buddhism in Mongolia. Fortunately, Mr. Adiya agreed to the suggestion.

The historic Assembly of Monks took place on November 15, 1990, at Gandan Tegchenling monastery and was attended by representatives from all the provinces of Mongolia. The inaugural ceremony was followed by a panel discussion which was very useful. Monks, many of them from the countryside, presented their views and sought government assistance in their efforts to revive Buddhist culture in Mongolia. Rinpoche was the key speaker at the assembly.

In his speech Bakula Rinpoche told the gathering that after seven decades of hardship and deprivation, during which hundreds of monasteries had been destroyed and thousands of monks killed, they could now enjoy freedom at last. He said that at this time it was important that the monks assessed the situation properly, reflect upon the past, and rededicate themselves virtuously to the glory and re-construction of Buddha Dharma. Crying foul and playing the blame game about past mistakes and past transgressions, he said, would not get us anywhere. Instead, he said, without wasting another moment, we should focus on the present and devote all our energies to rebuilding the religious institutions and heritage that had been lost. Though there were still many challenges before them, he said, the new political environment presented a precious opportunity to correct past wrongs. The remaining few monks in Mongolia, he said, also had a very special responsibility and duty in this respect.

Rinpoche recalled the great contributions made by Mongolians to Buddhism in the past. He spoke about the successive Khalka Jebtsundambas and many other individuals of outstanding learning and realization in Mongolia's past. Through them, Buddhism spread over the country like the illuminating rays of the sun. At its height, he estimated that there were some seven hundred active monasteries in Mongolia which were home to tens of thousands of monks. Innumerable teachers and practitioners produced volumes of invaluable teachings. Though many of these were unfortunately lost during the years of communist rule, many still remained, and the prospects of a genuine Buddhist renaissance in this traditionally Buddhist land were very real.

Rinpoche explained that the basis of the happiness of all sentient beings, including the enlightened ones, is the precious Buddha Dharma. The three duties of preserving, defending and letting such a precious resource flourish, depended on the commitment and resolve of the community of monks. Buddhist understanding, he said, is acquired in two stages: textual knowledge and comprehension. The former entails listening to, reading, and contemplating the Tripitaka or Three Baskets (*Vinaya, Sutra, and Abhidharma*). The latter entails diligently practicing the Three Trainings (moral discipline, concentration, and wisdom). In particular, it involves taking the training in moral discipline as the foundation, for it is only with bodhicitta that one can reach the higher levels of realization. Flow of the unbroken stream of the tradition depends on the moral watchfulness and virtues of the monastic communities. So, all monks should strive to be highly learned and they should adhere fully to the rules prescribed by the Vinaya (*Dulwa* in Tibetan) in their conduct.

For the benefit of the audience, many of whom had only the most basic formal training in Buddhism, Rinpoche briefly outlined the essential points of the code. It is not enough, he said, just to wear monk's robes. Society would benefit much more even from a very small number of genuinely knowledgeable and morally unimpeachable monks, than from thousands who wear the robes, but have little interest in or knowledge of what those robes really entail. So long as a person is a Buddhist monk, he said, all their activities should be in accordance with the Dulwa or Vinaya. Rinpoche also reminded the monks of Lord Buddha's teaching, "Although other creatures dare not eat the corpse of a lion, teeming worms originating from within devour it. Similarly, my teachings cannot be destroyed by others. But they will be destroyed by the ordained community's violations of ethics."

Therefore, he told them, it is very important that measures be taken immediately to prevent this from coming true. To sum up, Rinpoche told the assembled gathering that the foundation for the well-being and happiness of all sentient beings was the Buddha Dharma. All sentient beings on this earth aspire for happiness and do not desire to suffer. Since the responsibility to propagate and properly uphold the Buddhist faith rests with the monastic community, they must ensure that their external and internal conduct lives up to this responsibility. The abbots and monks of the monasteries must be role models, otherwise they would be doing more harm and no benefit to the dharma itself. The First assembly of the Mongolian Sangha was a landmark event in socio-religious history of Mongolia and paved the way for better coordinated efforts and commitments in the revival of Buddhism in the country.

Forty-eight

The Dalai Lama and Mongolia

Bakula Rinpoche had on numerous occasions met the 14th Dalai Lama and discussed the prevailing situation of Buddhism in Mongolia and Soviet Union. The Dalai Lama, given the strong historic ties between the two Buddhist nations and in particular with the lineage of the Dalai Lamas, has always taken a very keen interest in Mongolia. He often described the Mongols and Tibetans as twins and saw it as part of the duties to take care of Buddhists in Mongolia and Buryatia, Tuva & Kalmyk Republics of the Russian Federation. After freedom and democracy in Mongolia following the 1990 uprising, on many occasions, Rinpoche also discussed with the Dalai Lama about the possibility of return of the 9th Jebtsundamba or the Bogd Khan to Mongolia.

Historically, Tibetans and Mongols enjoyed an age-old and close relationship. First, it was Emperor Godan Khaan, the grandson of Chinggis Khaan who had invited Sakya Pandita Kunga Gyaltsan to visit his court and appointed him as his spiritual teacher. Subsequently, it was Emperor Altan Khaan who conferred on the third Dalai Lama Sonam Gyatso, the title of 'Dalai Lama', which literally means Ocean of Wisdom. The First Dalai Lama, Gedun Drub and the Second Dalai Lama, Gedun Gyatso were both conferred the title posthumously. The Fourth Dalai Lama, Yonten Gyatso was himself born to Mongol parents. Later, it was in the early 1640s, that Gushri Khaan, a descendent of Altan Khaan sent his forces across Tibet to unify the Tibetan regions under the Fifth Dalai Lama. He was formally declared Tibet's paramount spiritual and temporal ruler in 1642. After this, the Potala Palace at Lhasa, the symbol of Tibet's sovereignty, was built.

Incidentally, the lineage of Panchen Lamas, meaning a 'great pandita' or scholar, also had a Mongolian connection. The fourth Panchen Lama Lobsang Chökyi Gyaltsen received the title "Panchen Bogd" from the

Mongolian King Altan Khaan. "*Bogd*" in Mongolian means "holy". His three predecessors were subsequently recognized as the first to third Panchen Lamas with retrospective effect.

Therefore, among the common people of Mongolia even during communism, there was a natural and ardent desire to see the 14th Dalai Lama. Through many decades, this had remained a distant dream. A breakthrough came in 1979, when the Dalai Lama briefly visited Moscow and Ulaanbaatar. As mentioned earlier, the main architect of this historic visit was Bakula Rinpoche, who used his contacts on both the Indian and Soviet sides to find an agreement. In India, Rinpoche along with his parliamentary colleague Shashi Bhushan, held a series of meetings with Mrs. Indira Gandhi and other relevant Indian officials. At that time relations between the Soviet Union and China (which always tried to block and obstruct the exiled Dalai Lama's activities) were very poor, so it was not hard to convince the Soviet authorities. Hence, after a series of discussions, arrangements were made for the maiden visit of the Dalai Lama to USSR and Mongolia, which was planned to coincide with the Fifth General Conference of the newly-forged ABCP, which was scheduled to be held in Ulaanbaatar from June 15–18, 1979.

The visit generated keen interest in the Dalai Lama world-wide. It also was a significant development at the time of heightened tensions between the two super powers in that period. Interestingly, it was only in October 1980, that the Dalai Lama made his first visit to the USA. The visit to the Soviet Union was thus a pivotal moment in the transformation of the Dalai Lama into a world leader and messenger of peace on a truly global scale. It was no ordinary thing for the Dalai Lama to be able to visit the two super powers in the short span of few months. The Dalai Lama himself once remarked that for him this visit was, in a way, a gateway to the outside world. The visit also gave a huge amount of hope to Tibetans for Mongolia was still a communist country at that time and was geographically close to Tibet.

The Dalai Lama's visit to Moscow in June 1979 was truly historic. During that brief visit, he held meetings with the head of the Russian Orthodox Church and a number of Soviet officials. He then flew to Ulan Ude, the capital of the Buryatia Republic, where he was given a hearty welcome by thousands of devoted well-wishers. He spent two days there and gave public sermons to both the monastic community and to the local people. It was indeed a landmark visit and there was a great outpouring of emotion, especially among the formerly Buddhist ethnic Mongols of the area. Afterwards, the Dalai Lama visited Mongolia and participated in the 3rd General Assembly of ABCP from June 11-13, 1979. Incidentally this was also my first visit to Russia and Mongolia.

When the Dalai Lama returned to Ulaanbaatar on September 27, 1991, it was like a new dawn. This time he was visiting a democratic and free Mongolia, where Buddhism was not only allowed but was even starting to get official support. Of course, Bakula Rinpoche as the then Indian ambassador, who had again smoothed the way for the visit, was there at the airport to receive the Dalai Lama. The welcome accorded to His Holiness on this occasion can only be described as rapturous.

On September 28, 1991, Ambassador Bakula Rinpoche hosted a luncheon in honour of the Dalai Lama at the Indian embassy which was attended by many Mongolian dignitaries and diplomats from various countries. Outside, thousands of people had lined up on both sides of the street with their hands folded in devoted supplication as His Holiness alighted from the car and walked past waving to them. Speaking on the occasion, the Dalai Lama praised the decision of the Indian Government to appoint Bakula Rinpoche as India's Ambassador at that crucial juncture. A large crowd of people were again waiting outside to catch another glimpse of him. Peace Avenue, the city's main road, had to remain shut for a couple of hours. It was only after the motorcade carrying the Dalai Lama left, that the large crowd dispersed. As a mark of respect, we had put a yellow piece of cloth spread over the red carpet leading to the embassy gate. But as soon as the Dalai Lama's motorcade left, people got there, tore the cloth into pieces and took the pieces home as souvenirs and blessings. After all, His Holiness the Dalai Lama had put his holy feet on this piece of cloth. So deep was their faith and respect for him.

Kalachakra Initiation in Mongolia

The Dalai Lama visited Mongolia again in August 1995, this time to deliver the Kalachakra initiation at Gandan Tegchenling Monastery, Ulaanbaatar. The Kalachakra empowerment has historically been given to large crowds of people and this empowerment was particularly significant as it was the closest, the Dalai Lama had been to his homeland in eastern Tibet since his exile. Giving the Kalachakra teachings in Mongolia for the first time was also particularly poignant because this cycle has a particular connection to the lineages of Mongolian Buddhism. The great scholar Taranatha, who had founded several monasteries in Mongolia and whose reincarnations were recognized as the successive Jebtsundambas, is one of the scholar saints credited in Tibetan history for popularizing the Kalachakra teachings. So, reviving the practice in this land after so long made it truly special and memorable.

After a day's rest to recuperate from his journey, the Dalai Lama was ushered to the Gandan Tegchenling, and that same day, he began the preparatory rituals necessary for making the colored-sand mandala that accompanies the empowerment. He also gave the preliminary teachings necessary for the actual empowerment on the following day, taking the Bodhisattva vows of thousands of people. He gave a very powerful and direct teaching about realising the true nature of mind, which was the sure path to liberation from Samsara.

Next day the Dalai Lama attended a prayer assembly and gave teachings on *Tendrel Toepa* (a text which translates as in Praise of Dependent Origination) (*Pratityasamutpada*). The assembled monks offered him an elaborate Guru-yoga Puja, a long-life-prayer and a mandala. Expressing his happiness and gratitude, His Holiness said that the precious Buddhist message, and in particular the untainted teachings of the Great Lama Je Tsongkhapa, had flourished in Mongolia for hundreds of years. The dawn of religious freedom after so many decades of suppression, he said, was a precious opportunity for the public at large. He advised young people to respect their ancient culture and traditions and cautioned them against falling prey to a materialistic lifestyle. He asked them to stay away from the menace of alcohol and instead drink Airag, fermented mare's milk which is a traditional Mongolian drink and considered very healthy. Many elderly people shed tears of faith and gratitude, while others were visibly deeply moved. His Holiness then gave a blessing to help them be on course for attaining a better rebirth (*Ngontho*) and a blessing for the dawning of the wisdom of selflessness, known as the blessing of "definite goodness" (*Ngeleg*). While to the faithful, he dispensed Mani pills and protection cords. He ended the session with a prayer for the flourishing of the Buddhist faith.

During this very visit he also conferred the long-life empowerment on thousands of people at the *Tov Tsengeldekh Khureelen* or the National Sports Stadium. On that occasion, monks from Namgyal Monastery in Dharamshala performed ablution ceremonies for sacred religious objects and for the land. Several Buddhist scholars from abroad as well as celebrities such as Richard Gere also attended the teaching. Later, when giving a profound teaching on Lamrim, in its condensed version, to tens of thousands of devotees, unperturbed by heavy rain, people reported seeing His Holiness in his true Buddha-manifestation, surrounded by an aura of light. The fortunate ones who were present were put on the road to liberation from the samara. These visits and the profound teachings had a tremendous and enduring influence across Mongolia and throughout the ethnically Mongol regions of Buryatia, Tuva, Kalmykia and even Inner Mongolia (now a northern province of China).

There was another incident in 1995, which captures Bakula Rinpoche's character. During his visit the Dalai Lama was scheduled to address a gathering of people representing different faith organizations, since the promotion of harmony between different faiths was one of Dalai Lama's

The Dalai Lama arriving at Chinggis Khaan International Airport in Ulaanbaatar (1991)

Bakula Rinpoche in conversation with H.H. The Dalai Lama inside Ih-Ger at the Gandan Monastery, Ulaanbaatar (1991)

The 14th Dalai Lama Tenzin Gyatso outside the Indian Embassy, Ulaanbaatar (1991)

core commitments. In the meeting, the Dalai Lama recalled his close friendship with the Pope John Paul-II and also gave a lavish praise to the Christian missionary activities, especially, among the poor. Bakula Rinpoche, unlike The Dalai Lama, was well aware of the charged atmosphere of intense missionary activity going on in Mongolia at that time.

Later that evening Bakula Rinpoche went to meet the Dalai Lama at Ih-Tenger, the state guesthouse in Ulaanbaatar and told him of his misgivings. He explained very candidly about the ground reality in Mongolia – the unhindered influx of missionaries and their attempts to convert Mongolian youth in every conceivable way. Rinpoche said that every word spoken by His Holiness would have a deep impact on young minds in the country. So, he requested the Dalai Lama to speak more at length about Buddhism and its importance and relevance with their past and for the future.

The next day at the teaching His Holiness then gave a detailed and profound explanation of Buddhism, and it's extremely rich heritage based on logic and science, which called upon people to examine by themselves the deep question of life. It was then that he spoke at length about Buddhism and its relevance to the modern world. Addressing the people, he said that while Christianity is more bearing to the western culture, Buddhism is to the east. After the teachings were over, His Holiness jokingly asked Bakula Rinpoche if he was satisfied with his teaching that day. I remember seeing Bakula Rinpoche bowing down his head in agreement.

Forty-nine

Resuscitating Mongolia's Buddhist Heritage

Over the years, Rinpoche helped reintroduce many religious and cultural events, which had until then been forgotten in the country. For example, an important day in the Buddhist calendar – the Buddha Purnima, which is celebrated all over the world as *Vesak* (and even at the United Nations), to commemorate the birth, enlightenment and the maha-parinirvana of the Gautama Buddha, was banned in Mongolia.

In March 1992, Rinpoche invited several prominent people to his residence in Ulaanbaatar and discussed with them the significance of the Vesak Purnima or the "thrice-blessed day". He explained to them how in India, as well as in many other Asian countries, this day is celebrated on a grand scale. L. Enebish, Governor/Mayor of Ulaanbaatar, N. Enkhbayar, Minister of Culture, Choijamts, Khambolama of Gandan Tegchenling Monastery, Ch. Dambajav, Khambolama of Dashchoiling Monastery, heads of other monasteries, as well as O. Dashbalbar, a popular poet, Luvsanvandan, a scholar and President of the Mongolia-India Friendship Society and some other prominent citizens, were among those present in that meeting. The result of this gathering of influential figures was that the government agreed to Rinpoche's suggestion and constituted an organizing committee headed by L. Enebish, Governor of Ulaanbaatar who would be responsible for organizing the event for the first time in 70 years.

Buddha Purnima in Ulaanbaatar

It was two months later, on May 18, 1992, that the Buddha Jayanti was celebrated with great fanfare in Mongolia. The main event took place in

Ulaanbaatar's sports stadium and was attended by a large gathering. On a huge open platform in the sports ground, an ancient sacred thangka scrolls depicting the Buddha radiating a thousand rays, was unfurled and put on display. The President of Mongolia, P. Ochirbat, was in attendance, and this was the first time ever that the President of Mongolia, ministers and officials had joined in a religious celebration without any fear and apprehension. In his address, President Ochirbat spoke of this new environment in the country. Condemning the atrocities committed during the decades of communist rule, he vowed that Mongolia would never allow such brutalities again. He also called for a new beginning in restoring national culture and Buddhism across the country.

The festival began with the recitation of the prayer '*Gewa Yenlag Dunpa*' by monks. Scholars spoke about the significance of the day and also about the life and teachings of Buddha Sakyamuni. Rinpoche addressed the gathering in Tibetan, with Mongolian translation by Khambolama D. Choijamts. He reminded the crowd of the long and illustrious history of Buddhism in Mongolia, the subsequent decades of degeneration, and the consequences this had for society. To help repair society, he called upon people to make efforts to regenerate the lost Buddhist culture of the country. He also repeated his call for non-violence and unity within Mongolia, so that the transition from communism to democracy would not become an excuse for a descent and petty feuding. He spoke specifically about the harm done by alcohol. He said that irrespective of religious belief and for enjoying good health, people should avoid all intoxicants, which includes *arkhi* (vodka) and all other types of alcohol. He called for a popular campaign against alcohol to be launched. As a start, he said that people should abstain from drinking alcohol and consumption of meat on important days, such as the full moon day of every lunar month. He also spoke about the merits of avoiding meat, especially on religiously significant days.

As was typical in his style of public address, Rinpoche combined comments such as these on social issues, with religious teachings on how to take refuge. On this occasion, he talked about the *Migtsema* (prayer to the three Bodhisattva Protectors and to Lama Tsongkhapa). He also explained the significance of the teacher, the vajra guru, in Tibetan Buddhism, and explained the six-syllable mantra, *Om Mani Padme Hung*, which is dedicated to the Bodhisattva of Compassion. This was followed by a mass recitation of a rosary-round of *Om Mani Padme Hung* by the gathering and a mini-Naadam.

Rinpoche addressing the Vesak celebration in Ulaanbaatar (1992)

Rinpoche at the first celebration of Vesak Purnima in Mongolia after 70 years of communism. Mr. P. Ochirbat, President of Mongolia is seated third from the left (1992)

It is to be noted that in Mongolia wrestling is the most important of what in traditional Mongolian culture are known as the "three manly skills", other two are horsemanship and archery. This concluded the first historic observance of Buddha Jayanti in modern Mongolia. The event was a resounding success. Since this revival in 1992, the day is now enthusiastically celebrated every year in Mongolia. In his address Bakula Rinpoche also emphasised that Vesak-Day is the most important occasion for Buddhists world-over and therefore, urged the Government of Mongolia to consider declaring it as a public holiday in the country. Years later in 2019, in a significant move, the Government of Mongolia declared Vesak or Buddha Purnima as an official Public Holiday.

Land for Mongolian Monastery in Bodhgaya

Uppermost in Rinpoche's mind, of course, was always the effort to promote and revive the Nalanda tradition and ancient spiritual ties between India and Mongolia. In this regard, Rinpoche was closely involved in the initiative to build a Mongolian Buddhist Temple at Bodh Gaya. This initiative began when Mrs. A. Oyunbileg, the first lady of Mongolia, was invited to India on an official visit. Before her departure, she met Rinpoche at the embassy to seek his advice. It was then that Rinpoche suggested she put a request to the Indian government for the allotment of a piece of land at Bodh Gaya for building a Mongolian temple. There were temples from many Buddhist countries and traditions, but nothing to represent Mongolia. Later during her meeting with the Indian officials, the first lady Oyunbileg duly raised this request, and with this, a beginning had been made. Lama J. Gonchigsuren, a monk, who accompanied the first lady, confirmed this to me. Rinpoche then followed this up vigorously at the highest level in New Delhi. There was a lot of communication from both sides and finally, the request was accepted and a piece of land was granted by the Government of India to Gandan Tegchenling Monastery, free of cost. A beautiful Mongolian-style monastery has now been built at the site, adding another attraction to the vibrant Bodh Gaya, and providing a home for Mongolian Buddhists pilgrims at this holiest of sites in the Buddhist world.

Buddhist Teachings in Mongolian Language

Ordinary people in Mongolia did not understand the few Buddhist texts available at that time, since for the most part these were either in Tibetan, or in the old Mongolian script, which had been abandoned and replaced with an adapted Cyrillic alphabet under communist rule. At that time, since some seventy percent of the Mongolian population were below thirty-five years of age, the need for new books on Buddhism written in simple language using the modern Mongolian script was keenly felt. So, this was an issue and Rinpoche organized translation of basic Buddhist teachings into Mongolian language. During a visit to Japan, he also raised this matter with Buddhist organizations dedicated to educational projects. Rinpoche requested the *Bukkyo Dendo Kyokai*, a Japanese organization which publishes Buddha's teachings in different languages, to produce a Mongolian-language version of their core publication called *The Teaching of Buddha*. This is a collection of the Buddha Shakyamuni's teachings. Nambar Enkhbayar, Minister for Culture, took up the task of translating the book himself from English into Mongolian. Many copies of the Mongolian-language version were then printed in Japan and shipped to Mongolia where they were distributed nationwide free of cost. This was the first such publication of religious books in the country.

Mr. N. Enkhbayar, Prime Minister of Mongolia greeting Bakula Rinpoche (2002)

Mr. Nambar Enkhbayar, who is an important figure in modern Mongolia, had been well-acquainted with Bakula Rinpoche ever since the latter's early days in Ulaanbaatar. They first met in 1990, at the Association of Mongolian Writer's Union, where Rinpoche had been invited to deliver a lecture. Later Mr. Enkhbayar became Minister of Culture and worked closely with Rinpoche in organizing cultural events and in the production of various books mentioned above. He later became General Secretary of the MPRP,

Speaker of Parliament, Prime Minister and finally the President of Mongolia. He also led the government committee which oversaw the installation of a 26 metre-tall statue of Chenrezig, (*Avalokitesvara*), which is considered a masterpiece of contemporary Mongolian art. Like several other prominent public figures at that time, Mr. Enkhbayar is a disciple of Bakula Rinpoche. And despite the very important positions he held, he always remained a humble person. He always stayed in touch with Rinpoche, who considered his contributions to the development of the country worthy of praise. To me personally too, he has been a very dear friend and we have maintained close contacts over the years.

Reviving the Buddhist Traditions

Every year on the occasion of *Tsagaan-Sar* (Mongolian New Year), which literally means "white moon", Bakula Rinpoche would visit Gandan Tegchenling Monastery to attend the night-long prayer vigil, a tradition which had been banned during communist regime. But with the changes that were sweeping the Mongolian steppe, Tsagaan-Sar once again became the most important annual national holiday. Every year people throng the temple dressed in traditional attire, many carrying snuff bottles which they exchange while greeting one another. People visit the monasteries on this auspicious day to seek blessings and attend the prayer rituals which continue throughout the night. The day before Tsagaan-Sar is known as '*Bituun*', when people thoroughly clean their homes and the nearby surroundings. Herders (the traditional occupation of most Mongolians) also clean any livestock barns or shelters they have. Then they seek blessings. Typically, the Bituun ceremony at the home also involves lighting butter lamps to their protector or deity, who is believed to visit every household on this day. In this way, people greet the New Year afresh. Each year, on the morning of the first day of the New Year, Rinpoche would also address a large gathering in the courtyard of Gandan Tegchenling and convey his greetings to the nation on this festive occasion.

On the first day of the New Year, a typical Mongol family will gather at the home of the eldest member of the extended family. Dressed in national sheepskin-lined costumes called 'Del' which is similar to Ladakhi dress (*Goncha*) people greet their elders by performing what is known as the *Zolgokh*, grasping them by the elbows to show their respect and support. Traditionally, the eldest receives greetings from each member of the family. During the greeting ceremony, family members drink tea and hold *Khadag*. They also exchange ornate snuff bottles made of precious stone and decorated with gold and silver. After the ceremony, the extended family and guests eat mutton, dairy products, and 'Buuz', the Mongolian name for

Monks participating in the Vesak (Buddha Jayanti celebration) in Ulaanbaatar.

Rinpoche addressing the people on the occasion of Tsagaan-Sar (Mongolian New Year). Khambolama Choijamts is also seen in the picture

Momos, and drink *'Airag'* (fermented mare's milk) and Mongolian milk tea. Guests are also given gifts.

In March 1991, as part of Tsagaan-Sar, Rinpoche gave a teaching to a large gathering on the Lamrim Chenmo (the Great Stages on the Path to Enlightenment) at the newly opened Zuun Huree Monastery. The teachings of the Buddha have manifested in many forms and traditions within Tibetan Buddhism, but the most prominent and popular traditional explanations of his teachings, in both Tibet and Mongolia, are the Lamrim ("Stages of the Path"), as composed by Je Tsongkhapa, the founder of the Gelug tradition. Lama Tsongkhapa's concise yet profound teachings made Buddhism accessible to all by clearly explaining the interconnection of the different paths and stages, showing that there are teachings suitable for any practitioner. As the title suggests, it leads practitioners through stages towards the attainment of Buddhahood. Rinpoche started by giving its preliminary teachings, then established a Lamrim lineage and then, on April 20, 1991, he gave the full blessings, ending with a long-life ritual through Guru Puja (Lama Choepa). On that day, he also gave a teaching on the Eleven-Faced Chenrezig and explained the practice of reciting the Mani mantra a hundred thousand times (Mani Dhungdrub), as had been requested by Khambolama Dambajav of Zuun Huree Monastery on several occasions. This was practiced by a large gathering over several days. Rinpoche was also requested by Khambolama Dambajav to give a new name to the Zuun Huree monastery, which is located in the centre of Ulaanbaatar. At his request Rinpoche gave it a new name 'Tashi Choeling Monastery' which is how the monastery is known today.

Opening Tugsbaisagalan Nunnery

In November 1990, several women who had earlier received layperson's ordination (Genyenma in Tibetan) from Rinpoche, invited him to their makeshift ger temple near Gandan Tegchenling in Ulaanbaatar. At their request, Rinpoche conferred the transmissions of the Preparatory Practice of Kelsang Dringyen, Neljorma Self-Generation (both elaborate and brief versions), Guru Puja and Tara. Later, he also ordained a few nuns. This, at that time, was a rare phenomenon in Mongolia. Even during pre-communist Mongolia, the ordination of nuns as found in Tibet, was not common in Mongolia. So, when the news spread that some women had been ordained by Bakula Rinpoche in Ulaanbaatar, there was some muted opposition to the move. When people questioned Rinpoche about it, he explained to them in detail about the tradition, and in this way put their doubts to rest.

Another important phase in these developments was the opening of

'Tugsbaisagalan' Centre. In subsequent years, other nunneries also came up. With the help of Lama Zopa Rinpoche and the Sakyadhita International Association of Buddhist Women, Rinpoche sent several Mongolian nuns from this and other centres to study Buddhism at nunneries in India and Nepal. Many of them have since returned to Mongolia and continue their spiritual pursuit. Rinpoche was particularly impressed by the deep devotion to Buddha Dharma he saw among the women of Mongolia. Women also shoulder many responsibilities; not only of raising children but also, in many cases, contributing to the family finances by earning through sheer hard work.

Resumption of Monastic Studies in India

Despite the horrors that had been inflicted on Buddhism in Mongolia, it had somehow survived in the hearts of the people and Rinpoche had a strong belief that no external forces could ever completely sever Mongolians from their faith in the Buddha Dharma. Even so, Rinpoche's path as a leader in the Buddhist revival was far from an easy one as Buddhist culture had suffered serious erosion in the country. Monastic discipline or Vinaya, considered to be the core of Buddhist monastic tradition, was almost non-existent. And most people, especially those under thirty, had very little understanding of Buddhism. Some even had very distorted views about the past and about the nature of monasticism, due to what they had been taught at school during communism. So, to rebuild the religion on a proper foundation was a very daunting prospect. Every aspect of Buddhist culture had to be carefully planned. Apart from logistical tasks associated with re-building Buddhist institutions, people also needed spiritual and emotional help to overcome their spiritual and emotional loss. These were enormous challenges, since there were only a handful of well-educated monk teachers in the entire country.

Although open Buddhist practice was impossible during communist rule, the rituals, practices, prayers, and chants had never been completely destroyed, as many practitioners and families pursued their spiritual practices discreetly. So, despite decades of communist rule and persecution, and in the absence of qualified teachers, many people had maintained quiet reverence for Buddhism throughout that period. Gandan Tegchenling Monastery was established in 1838 by the 5th Jebtsundamba Khutuktu. However, in year 1938 it was closed down and reopened in 1944. It had been the only officially authorised functioning Buddhist monastery in the country during the communist period. It was natural for it to take a central role in the Buddhist revival of the decade of 1990s and beyond. Its elderly monks were already well-versed in prayer services, chanting and in performing rituals. Its younger monks were also enthusiastic and diligent in performing prayers, chants and in memorizing religious texts. The main rituals and practices that had been carried on by the successive Khalka Jebtsundamba had largely survived.

To rebuild Buddhism in the country, a new generation of monks had to be prepared and sent to the monasteries in India. To ensure their uninterrupted study, Rinpoche took-up with the Indian Government and arranged for long term Student's visas for hundreds of Buddhist monks to study at Drepung Gomang, Sera, Gyume and other major monastic institutions. This facility remains in force even today. A few monks were also sent to Monasteries in Dharamshala and Sakya Monastery in Dehradun. Rinpoche also coordinated with the Central Tibetan Administration and arranged stipend for these monks and also sent them to institutions such as the Buddhist School of Dialectics in Dharamshala, Central Institute of Higher Tibetan Studies, Varanasi for financial support for the monks to enable them to undertake these courses of study.

In 1992 Rinpoche sent the first batch of five young Mongolian monks to study in India at Drepung Gomang Monastery which is located in the southern Indian state of Karnataka. Before the Chinese occupation of Tibet, monks from Mongolia used to go to Drepung Gomang and to other monasteries in Lhasa for higher studies. People were happy that the re-connection with Buddhism which so many had wished for, was taking concrete shape after decades of suppression. When Rinpoche began the process, several hundred boys turned up for the interview. Such was the enthusiasm and interest among the common people. This gave Rinpoche and Jhado Rinpoche whom Bakula Rinpoche had invited to Mongolia, and all of us associated with the school, tremendous joy. There was high appreciation amongst the public for what was being initiated. Over the years, their number grew to hundreds and in the 2019-20, there were over 600 Mongolian monks studying in various monasteries in India. In order to enable these and future Mongolian monks, Ambassador Bakula Rinpoche ensured that monks as well as nuns received long-term student visas.

Mongolian Buddhist Cultural Centre

In order to facilitate the Buddhist regeneration and its social impact as well as to further contacts with Buddhists outside Mongolia and coordinate their activities, Bakula Rinpoche suggested the formation of a social organization in Ulaanbaatar. This was to be on the same lines as the Ladakh Buddhist Association that had been so effective in his native Ladakh. Rinpoche made

The first batch of young monks sent to India for Buddhist/monastic studies after the fall of communist regime (1992)

this suggestion to Mr. Enkhbayar, who was then serving as the Minister of Culture. But rather than constituting it as a voluntary social organization (as in Ladakh), it became an official state-sanctioned body. On November 12, 1992, Buddhist Culture Centre was inaugurated by Bakula Rinpoche in the presence of many dignitaries. The event was held at a heritage building near Natsagdorj Library in Ulaanbaatar, which henceforth was to be its headquarters.

O. Dashbalbar, a devout Buddhist and a popular poet, was appointed the first director of the centre. Unfortunately, this was not a very long-lived venture. Due to financial constraints and the untimely death of Dashbalbar, who was a great inspiration for many people, it later had to be closed down. Dashbalbar was a dynamic young man who took deep pride in traditional Mongolian culture. He was also a Member of Parliament and played a significant role in promoting traditional values when there were sweeping changes disrupting Mongolian society. He passed away at a young age. Had he lived longer; he would have undoubtedly left a deep mark on Mongolian society. Rinpoche was deeply saddened by his death.

Reconstruction of the Mijid Chenrezig Statue

As the situation stabilized in the country and trained and qualified monks started to return from monasteries in India, various temples which were completely destroyed during the communist purges and were closed down, began to reopen and function again one by one. Opening of the new temples such as Dungkor Dratsang, Idga Choiling Dratsang, Jud (Gyud) Dratsang, Manba Dratsang, Gunga Dratsang etc. further consolidated the religious structure in the country and helped restore the lost glory of Gandan Tegchenling Monastery, the Centre of Mongolian Buddhists. Rinpoche was very pleased with these initiatives and provided his assistance and guidance in every possible way.

October 26, 1996, was a typical cold autumn day in Ulaanbaatar. The occasion was the unveiling of the newly completed giant statue of Avalokitesvara (Mijid Chenrezig) at Gandan Tegchenling. After Mongolia had freed itself from Manchu rule, a large statue of Chenrezig was erected at Gandan in year 1911-14. But in the late 1930s or early 40s – during the darkest days of the communist purges – the gold-gilded copper statue had disappeared. Nobody seemed to know what had happened to it. Popular belief is that it was dismantled and melted down to make ammunition for the Soviet forces. When religious freedom was restored in the 1990s, an investigation was launched by various governmental agencies and non-governmental organizations to ascertain what had happened. Unfortunately, they made little headway.

Among the people, this holy statue had come to be seen as a symbol of Mongolia's independence. So, under the new order in post-communist Mongolia, the government decided that a new statue of Chenrezig should be erected in place of the missing one. A special committee was set up headed by the Minister for Culture Mr. Enkhbayar. Prominent on this committee was Mr. Mend Oyo, a well-known Mongolian scholar who was put in overall charge of the project which was funded by the state. He would consult Rinpoche regularly and the project began in earnest. Rinpoche would often visit the site where the statue was being made and was impressed by the artistic skill of many young Mongolians working on the project. For Mongolian artists this was a great opportunity to exhibit their skills. The height of the new gold-plated copper statue was to be over twenty-six metres.

After more than eighty years, the Mijid Chenrezig Temple gate was declared open to the public once again. The statue of Chenrezig was restored to its original site. Holy relics received from the 14th Dalai Lama were placed in this new statue. A ceremony dedicating this new statue to the nation was held on October 26, 1996, in which President Mr. P. Ochirbat was the chief guest.

In addition, there was a huge turnout of high-ranking government officials, diplomats, as well as a sizable public gathering. In his address,

Mijid Chenrezig statue

Rinpoche expressed his happiness at the reopening of the historic Mijid Chenrezig Temple and congratulated the Government of Mongolia and the people on the completion of this magnificent project.

Bringing Lord Buddha's Holy Relics to Mongolia

Mr. N. Enkhbayar, Minister for Culture, would often visit the Indian embassy and discuss various issues with Rinpoche related to bilateral cooperation and the restoration of Buddhism in Mongolia. During one such meeting, Rinpoche mentioned the holy Buddha relics kept at the National Museum in New Delhi. Rinpoche narrated the history of the relics to him, and conveyed to Enkhbayar that the pieces were undoubtedly the holy remains of Lord Buddha, as had been authenticated by the archeologists. His interest and reverence were very much aroused, so he started discussing with Rinpoche ways in which the holy relics might be possible to bring to Mongolia for public exposition in due course of time.

A few days later Enkhbayar came to Rinpoche with an official letter of request from the Government of Mongolia to the Government of India. He asked Rinpoche, if he might forward the request to the relevant departments in New Delhi in the hope that the holy relics would be brought to bless the Buddhist land of Mongolia. Rinpoche said he would try his best in this regard. However, he also cautioned that it would not be an easy task, since the relics were considered a national treasure and had never before been taken out of the country. Nonetheless, Rinpoche promised to try, since he felt this was a very apt request. Later, it was decided that the request would be formally carried to New Delhi by Jalbuu Choinhor, Mongolia's Deputy Foreign Minister.

However, things did not move as smoothly as was wished by everyone. The officials were not prepared to take any risk and there was a long delay. When other measures failed to convince the authorities in New Delhi to release the relics, Rinpoche as the last resort, wrote to Prime Minister P.V. Narasimha Rao. He wrote about the hardship Buddhists in Mongolia had faced over many decades under communism and said that such a gesture from India would not only help to lift the morale of the people going through a difficult period, but would also generate a great deal of goodwill for India. So, he requested the Prime Minister to make personal intervention to get the bureaucracy unstuck. To the great joy of the people of Mongolia, Prime Minister Narasimha Rao gave his approval.

As a result, the holy relics of the Buddha Sakyamuni arrived in Mongolia on September 1, 1993. The delegation accompanying the holy relics was led by Kumari Selja, Union Minister of State for Education and Culture, Government of India. The delegation included Dharmapala Maha Thero, a senior Buddhist monk and former President of the All India Bhikkhu Sangha, and several officials from the National Museums of New Delhi and Calcutta. A grand ceremonial reception was held at the airport to welcome the holy relics, and a Mongolian military band played the national anthems of India and Mongolia. Thousands of people came out to line either side of the airport road as the holy relics were carried to the city.

Bakula Rinpoche with Mr. N. Enkhbayar, Minister for Culture and Mr. J. Choinkhor, Ministry of Foreign Relations holding the Holy relics of Lord Buddha

(L to R) Mr. N. Enkhbayar, Minister for Culture, Government of Mongolia, Kumari Selja, Minister of State for Culture, Government of India, Mr. P. Ochirbat, President of Mongolia and Amb. Bakula Rinpoche (1993)

Rinpoche blessing faithful in Mongolia

Dharampala Bhikshu, President All India Bikkhu Sangha carrying the holy relics of Lord Buddha with the author by his side, Ulaanbaatar (1993)

On the first day, the relics were visited, amidst a lot of media coverage, by the country's top leadership including the president, the prime minister, and the speaker of the parliament. A large crowd of people had gathered outside the Cultural Palace on Sukhbaatar Square. President Ochirbat, speaking at the inaugural function, thanked the Indian government for its gesture and hoped that this gesture would help further strengthen the ancient ties between the two countries. President Ochirbat also opened an exhibition entitled "Path of Buddha" displaying Buddhist art objects drawn from different museums in India. The holy relics were kept at a specially made enclosure at Ulaanbaatar's Cultural Palace to enable as many people as possible to pay their respects.

As Attaché (Culture) at the embassy of India, I was responsible for the security and upkeep of the holy relics for which special arrangements had been made by the Government of Mongolia. The response of the public was massive. For a whole month, long queues were seen outside the Cultural Palace. People from every segment of Mongolian society and from all across the country came to offer their devotions.

On October 1, 1993, on the final day of the public exhibition, a closing ceremony was held after which the holy relics were carried through the main streets of the capital on an open-back and beautifully decorated truck with monks praying and carrying a religious umbrella. Thousands of people again lined the streets as the motorcade moved slowly towards the airport. At the airport Mr. Enkhbayar handed the relics over to Bakula Rinpoche. Rinpoche himself carried the holy relics for the return journey to India accompanied by the author. This was a historic trip because instead of going back to India directly, we flew via Beijing where we spent three days. Although there was no official programme for the holy objects in Beijing, Rinpoche felt that their mere presence on the Chinese soil was deeply significant and would help pave the way for further beneficial developments in China. Only a few people, including a handful of Tibetans and Rinpoche's Chinese disciples knew about Rinpoche's arrival in Beijing. The relics remained with Rinpoche throughout our journey, and he offered prayers before them constantly. From Beijing we then flew to Bangkok and from there to Calcutta, where the holy relics were handed over to the director of the National Museum. For Rinpoche, this had been a very precious time. As for myself, I really do not have words that can express my feelings of joy and peace at having accompanied Bakula Rinpoche in the presence of such sacred objects during this historic journey.

The 41st Sakya Trizin Visits Mongolia

The Sakya lineage masters, such as Sakya Pandita Kunga Gyaltsan and his nephew Pagpa Lama had played a pivotal role in spreading Buddhism among the Mongol tribes in the 13th century. In 1253, Mongolian Emperor Godan Khaan, grandson of Chinggis Khaan, had invited Sakya Pandita to his court and accepted him as his spiritual teacher and established a "patron-priest" relationship between the two. Sakya Pandita is the author of "*Subhashita*" one of the most popular Buddhist books among Mongolians, even today. Pagpa Lama was Sakya Pandita's nephew and travelled with him to the emperor's court. Later he became the spiritual teacher of Qubilai Khan who established the Yuan Dynasty which ruled China for a century. Pagpa Lama is also credited with having invented the first Mongolian script, known as the Pagpa script, or the square alphabet, which was based on Tibetan and was on official Yuan Dynasty seals. Given these long-standing connections between the Sakya tradition of Tibetan Buddhism and the Mongols, which were still remembered and felt keenly among the people, Bakula Rinpoche felt they needed to be restored.

Bakula Rinpoche had known the 41st Sakya Trizin Rinpoche, the Sakya Dagchen of the Dolma Phodrang and head of the Sakya school of Tibetan Buddhism. They first met in 1955, when as young tulkus, they, together, attended teachings at the Potala Palace in Lhasa. After escaping to India in 1959, Sakya Trizin visited Ladakh several times. He had also visited the Ladakh Bauddh Vihar in Delhi, founded by Bakula Rinpoce and stayed there for several weeks.

Rinpoche had been mulling to invite Sakya Trizin to Mongolia for some time. So, during a routine visit to India, Rinpoche called on him at his residence at Rajpur, Dehradun, to extend an invitation in person. Sakya Trizin was naturally very pleased at the suggestion, since he too was well aware of the long-standing historic links with Mongolia and the continued faith of many people there in the Sakya tradition. He accepted the invitation and promised to visit soon.

On June 9, 1995, he arrived in Ulaanbaatar on a nine-day visit to Mongolia. Upon his arrival at Chinggis Khaan International Airport, he was accorded a warm and ceremonial reception by Bakula Rinpoche along with the abbots of various monasteries. Bakula Rinpoche also hosted a luncheon in his honour at the Indian embassy. His schedule in Mongolia included meeting with Mongolian leaders, visits to various institutions, as well as visits to various monasteries, where he gave suitable empowerments to the faithful. The visit was very successful and Bakula Rinpoche was happy that the historic links between the Mongol and the Sakya tradition seemed to be

41st Sakya Trizin Rinpoche on his arrival at Ulaanbaatar (1995)

Bakula Rinpoche talking to 41st Sakya Trizin (Ulaanbaatar, Mongolia 1995)

Author speaking at the dinner hosted in honour of the 41st Sakya Trizin. Ulaanbaatar, July 2010

The 41st Sakya Trizin, Mr. N. Enkhbayar, Former President of Mongolia and the Author watching a mini-Nadaam (Ulaanbaatar, July 2010)

on the path of restoration. Rinpoche also facilitated many Mongolian monks, particularly those from Erdenezuu Monastery, the opportunity to study at Sakya Monasteries in India. Among them was Venerable Otgonbaatar Shastri who studied at the Sakya Monastery at Rajpur near Dehradun.

In early 2010, I got an audience with Sakya Trizin at his residence in Rajpur. At that meeting, on behalf of the Ulaanbaatar Pethub Monastery, I requested him to visit Mongolia and also conveyed to him the wish of the late Bakula Rinpoche to have him visit Mongolia again. Although his schedule was already filled up for the year, he told me that he would very much like to visit Mongolia again and would adjust his schedule, accordingly.

The 41st Sakya Trizin arrived in Ulaanbaatar on July 20, 2010. This second visit of Sakya Trizin lasted for ten days, during which he gave teachings to thousands of devotees at Ulaanbaatar's Wrestling Palace and also laid the foundation-stone for a new Sakya Monastery in Ulaanbaatar. He also visited Darkhan, the second largest city in Mongolia, Sakya Rinpoche also held a meeting with Mongolian scholars and academicians. He was also received warmly by many Mongolian dignitaries including Tsakhiagiin Elbegdorj, the newly elected President of Mongolia. A mini-Naadam (festival) was also arranged for him by the former president N. Enkhbayar, so that Sakya Trizin could witness something of traditional Mongolian culture, with displays of the three Mongolian national sports – archery, horse racing and wrestling.

Fifty

Bakula Rinpoche and his Association with Korea

In 1945, when Japan surrendered to the Allies, the Korean peninsula was split into two zones of occupation – the U.S. controlled South Korea and the Soviet-controlled North Korea. In 1948, two separate governments were established in Pyongyang and Seoul. The painful suffering resulting from the country's division and separation of people and families is a familiar story and is well documented. People's pain and agony are too deep to be described in words. The Korean war of 1950s had ended in 1953, in an armistice and since then the people in Korea, unfortunately, were living in a hostile and dangerous environment.

Korean Peninsula has also been a stronghold of Buddhism which was introduced to it from China in the fourth century CE. Statues and paintings of 16-Arhats are a common yet distinctive feature in all the major Buddhist monasteries and temples. As we all know, Buddhism is practiced and adapted in different countries to their distinctive local conditions. North Korea, unlike Mongolia, was alien to Rinpoche. However, it changed in the early 1970s when after the establishment of ABCP, contacts could be established with the Buddhists there. Chang Tae Song of the Korean Buddhist Federation in Japan, an affiliate of the North Koreans, and with Pak Tae Ho of the Buddhists in the Democratic People's Republic of Korea (DPRK, North Korea) became active members of ABCP.

Like every contemporary communist country, in North Korea too, any contact with foreign organizations was closely monitored and regulated by the communist regime. However, Bakula Rinpoche, having worked in Mongolia and USSR, was able to deal with the situation smoothly. He was also a staunch supporter of the re-unification of the Korean peninsula and had also raised this issue at the ABCP conferences and other international forums.

Over the years, Rinpoche's association with the North Koreans became closer. He invited a North Koreans delegation to visit India. They also attended ABCP conferences and were a part of the ABCP delegation received by Mrs. Indira Gandhi, Prime Minister of India. In 1985, Bakula Rinpoche visited North Korea as part of the Indian Buddhist delegation. In North Korea, the delegation visited some ancient temples in the most serene and enchanting mountain surroundings.

Coming to the conditions in North Korea, the regime actively discourages the practice of religion, including Buddhism. Places of worship and activities of Buddhist monks were monitored closely. However, it is also reported that several ancient monasteries and historical relics including the famous Pohyonsa Temple, survived complete annihilation and were protected by the regime. In contrast, Bakula Rinpoche's first visit to the capital of South Korea, Seoul happened much later in 1993. This was on the invitation of A. San Jung Woo, the head of Gu Ryong Sa temple of *Jogye order*, who enjoyed a close connection with the Buddhists in the Himalayan regions of India, including Ladakh.

In Seoul with Prime Minister Narasimha Rao

I remember another notable anecdote from the years, when a regional conference of Indian ambassadors in the East Asian region (China, North and South Korea, Japan, Hong Kong and Mongolia) was held at Seoul in South Korea in 1993, by the Ministry of External Affairs. The meeting was to be chaired by Prime Minister Narasimha Rao, who was there for an official visit to South Korea. We had received instructions that each head of mission shall make a presentation on India's relations with East Asia, in the presence of the prime minister and the minister for external affairs.

The prime minister was staying at the Hotel Shilla in Seoul, so Rinpoche and all other ambassadors were also put up there. The meeting was convened in the hotel. All the other ambassadors, who were career diplomats, had come prepared with a written text for presentation. It was a very formal and rather intimidating occasion. On one side of the table sat the Prime Minister, the Minister for External Affairs, National Security Advisor, Foreign Secretary and other officials and on the other side were all the ambassadors. Rinpoche was seated right opposite the prime minister. When the meeting started, the prime minister asked 'Bakula ji' to begin with his presentation. Rinpoche began by saying that he had not prepared a formal

Bakula Rinpoche with Buddhists representatives from the DPRK, North Korea

Rinpoche with A San Jung Woo, Gu Ryong Sa, Korea Buddhist Chogye Order, Tongdo-Sa Temple in Seoul, Korea

presentation and would speak his thoughts extempore. He also said that since his knowledge of the wider region was limited, he would focus his comments only on Mongolia, China and Tibet. He then began his presentation in Ladakhi, which I translated. The prime minister was pleased with his ideas and several of the suggestions that he had made. He asked the Foreign Secretary to follow up on those important points on an urgent basis. Then it was the turn of the next ambassador to make his presentation. As he took out his paper, PM Narasimha Rao interrupted and said that everyone should follow the example set by Bakula ji. No paper would be read, and instead they should speak their thoughts. All the ambassadors, thus, had to follow suit and instead of being a staid formality, the meeting ended with a very lively discussion.

Later that evening, there was a reception in honour of Prime Minister Narasimha Rao Several hundred guests were invited. When the prime minister entered the hall, there was a mad rush of people trying to get near him and take a picture with him. Seeing the crowd, Rinpoche moved away and stood in a corner. Prime Minister Narasimha Rao saw Rinpoche from a distance. He walked straight through the crowd to meet him and chatted with him. This story is typical of Rinpoche. His effectiveness was in his humility as a simple Buddhist monk. Prime Minister requested Rinpoche to join him to visit a Buddhist temple in Seoul where Rinpoche was introduced to the members of the South Korean Buddhist clergy and other guests.

Fifty-one

Meeting with Mikhail Gorbachev

Rinpoche with the leader of Soviet Union (1985-91)
Mr. Mikhail Gorbachev (1996)

In 1995, Rinpoche received a personal invitation (**Annexure 27**) from Mr. Mikhail Gorbachev, the former Soviet leader. He had ended the Cold War and initiated the reforms of glasnost (openness) and perestroika (reconstruction or reformation) which unleashed such powerful forces of change, that the entire Union was dissolved in 1991. His invitation to Rinpoche was in connection with the State of the World Forum to be held that year in San Francisco. The forum had been set up by Gorbachev with the purpose of connecting partners worldwide to search for solutions to critical challenges facing the world. As such, he sought out a cross-section of individuals which included senior statesmen and women, current political leaders including, scientists, spiritual leaders, intellectuals, artists and youth leaders. He invited a number of global figures to join him in San Francisco to discuss the state of the world and formulate new directions for the future of the nation-state. For me it was a privilege to accompany Rinpoche on this trip.

During the conference, Rinpoche met with Mr. Mikhail Gorbachev and his wife, Mrs. Raisa Gorbacheva, on several occasions. The former Soviet leader was very popular in the West but was viewed very differently in his homeland of Russia and in other parts of the former Soviet Union. Many people felt that the collapse of the USSR had been a terrible calamity and he was to be blamed for their economic hardships. Rinpoche, as always, was impervious to such controversy, and met Mr. Gorbachev simply as a good human being, as he did with everyone. The encounter was very pleasant, and Rinpoche said he was struck by Gorbachev's warmth and his friendly nature.

The event lasted four days in total and a vast array of subjects were covered. In his address, Rinpoche spoke about the problems of a divided world, and emphasized the point that extreme ideologies would never be able to solve global problems. In a world polarized by competing political ideologies, he said, the 2500-year-old teachings of Lord Buddha were as relevant as ever and that understanding of the principles of interdependence and impermanence were like a beacon of hope for humanity. In the Himalayas, he said, people had lived in some of the world's harshest environments, and yet, he contended, they had created one of the most peaceful places on earth. Today, he said, excessive human activity is causing climate change and melting of the Himalayan glaciers poses grave risks to the entire region. As the world's population continued to grow and urbanize, the impact of human activity on the earth's ecology was only getting worse. Rinpoche thus appealed to the assembled audience and the international community at large to realize the gravity of the situation and take immediate measures in order to safeguard future generations.

After the conference, Rinpoche took the opportunity to visit several cities in the USA and call on some of his many acquaintances there. Mr. Jalbuu Choinhor, the Mongolian Ambassador to the United States and his wife Mrs. Maijargal, had invited Rinpoche to Washington DC where he spent a couple of days in their home, and also gave a public talk for the Mongolian community in the city. He also visited the home of Khwaja Haq, an old friend from Ladakh who had settled down in the USA. In Michigan, Rinpoche was the guest of Gelek Rinpoche, who had established a centre called 'Jewel Heart' and gave a lecture at the centre which was attended by a large gathering. He also visited New York before returning to his duties in Mongolia.

Fifty-two

Strengthening Indo-Mongolian Relations

India established formal diplomatic relations with Mongolian People's Republic on December 24, 1955 and thus became the first country outside the Soviet bloc to do so. Since then, there has been lively diplomatic interaction between the two countries. In 1961, it was India that sponsored Mongolia's candidature for membership of the United Nations despite the opposition by both Taiwan and China (at that time Taiwan held China's seat at the UN). Even at the height of the cold war, Mongolia and India had each other's backs. As Mr. K.P. Nayar wrote in The Telegraph, (Calcutta) on May 18, 2015, "Few people now remember that when India fought a difficult diplomatic battle with its back to the wall for the creation of Bangladesh four decades ago, it had one unwavering ally: Mongolia. In 1972, when Indira Gandhi, Prime Minister of India instructed India's permanent mission in New York to move a resolution in the UN General Assembly for recognizing the new nation that had seceded from Pakistan and drum up support. But it could persuade no more than two countries to co-sponsor that resolution. One of those two co-sponsors was Mongolia, the other was Bhutan. As soon as Mongolia signaled the president of the General Assembly that it was co-sponsoring the Indian resolution, Pakistan broke off diplomatic relations with Mongolia. But in Ulaanbaatar, the leadership did not waver. Instead, it conveyed greater support to Indira's efforts to position Dhaka securely on the global diplomatic stage.

An immensely pleased Indira immediately invited Mr. Yamjaagiin Tsedenbal, the then Prime Minister of Mongolia, to visit India. He accepted the invitation forthwith because he had earlier enjoyed her father's gracious hospitality when Jawaharlal Nehru hosted him in 1959 as the first high-level visitor from Mongolia after India's independence."

Rinpoche had met Mr. Tsedenbal for the first time in New Delhi. It was during this visit of Yumjaagiin Tsedenbal to India, in February 1973, that a path-breaking Indo-Mongolian joint declaration was signed. This was then further consolidated by a Treaty of Friendly Relations and Cooperation signed in February 1994, during the Mongolian president Punsalmaagiin Ochirbat's state visit to New Delhi in which Rinpoche had played a pivotal role.

Though good relations had long been a feature of Indo-Mongolian relations, Bakula Rinpoche's tenure as ambassador coincided with an era of tremendous insecurity and change in Mongolia, which could have taken matters in many different possible directions. During the early period of structural reform and the introduction of a free-market economy, Mongolia, like many of the former republics of the Soviet Union, faced enormous challenges. The steady flow of financial aid and assistance, which used to come from the USSR and other relatively advanced East European socialist countries, dried up almost overnight. The sudden withdrawal or radical reduction of state funding from the social sectors of health, education, farming, industry and so on, made life very difficult for the common people.

Many people made their way to the capital city in search of opportunities, but there they found little respite from their difficulties, and in addition had to adapt to the relative rootlessness of urban existence. Soon there were acute shortages of food and other essential goods. Imports disappeared from shelves, as the government faced an acute crunch on its foreign paying. Services such as free education, subsidized food, healthcare and job security, all guaranteed under the old regime started to fall apart, with many services abruptly terminated for want of funds. Long queues of people waiting to buy even the most basic food provisions became a common sight in the city.

Of course, those of us in the embassies were the fortunate ones. There were exclusive shops for diplomats and foreigners trading only in foreign currency, but living conditions in the far-flung rural areas were getting hard. The abrupt dismantling of the co-operative system and the sudden creation of a free market economy was a rude shock for ordinary people. As the privatization process picked up momentum, free social services began to be withdrawn leaving people to fend for themselves. Unemployment was unknown before, but very quickly it became almost the norm. Highly-trained skilled workers such as doctors and engineers suddenly found themselves jobless and having to take up menial tasks just to make ends meet. The Mongolian government was forced to look to UN agencies and elsewhere for assistance. To add to their woes, the country was hit by some extreme weather events, such as an unusually heavy snowfall in 1990, and a windstorm in 1993, which wreaked havoc in some regions.

Dr. Shankar Dayal Sharma, President of India, welcoming President of Mongolia at the courtyard of Rashtrapati Bhawan, New Delhi (1994)

Mr. P. Thungon, Union Minister, President of Mongolia Mr. P. Ochirbat, Mrs. Tsevelmaa, spouse of the President, Amb. Bakula Rinpoche, Mr. Tsogt, Trade Minister at Agra (1994)

Fortunately, Mongolians are known for their resilience, perseverance and camaraderie. These qualities of theirs became invaluable assets during these difficult years. Despite extreme hardships, people remained stoical. There were very few public protests unlike in other countries that were also undergoing structural reform at the time. Some say that the ability to deal with hardship while staying calm is a legacy of the people's Buddhist and nomadic heritage. There may be some truth in it.

As India's ambassador, Bakula Rinpoche focused his attention on helping Mongolia in areas related to what in developmental terms is called human resources. His expertise lay in the realm of nurturing the good qualities of the human spirit, and this is what he did, providing sage counsel and voice of calm and kindness in difficult times. Of course, work at the Indian embassy had many dimensions. Indian experts and advisors in various fields, including those for drafting the Mongolian constitution and conducting elections were made available. Bakula Rinpoche strongly advocated with the Indian government to increase the number of scholarships available for Mongolian students to study in India under the CEP (Cultural Exchange Program). As a result, the number was increased to over one hundred from the mere handful of slots available to Mongolians when he had assumed office. A lot of arrangements were also made to ensure that Mongolian students and professionals could access Indian government scholarships for higher education and specialized training at various universities and institutions in India under ITEC scheme (Indian Technical and Economic Cooperation), under which all expenses are borne by the Indian government. Thanks to Bakula Rinpoche's own contacts, special arrangements were also made to send Mongolian students to the Central Institute of Tibetan Higher Studies at Sarnath, where they would study Buddhist philosophy and Tibetan language. Further through some private channels, as already described earlier, arrangements were made to send young Mongolian monks to study at various Tibetan monasteries in South India and Dharamshala.

In year 1999, Mongolia was hit by one of its infamous Zud spells. This happens when a summer drought is followed by cold blizzards resulting in the loss of thousands of livestock and thus leading to severe food shortages. In such times Rinpoche's actions were always decisive. He argued forcefully with the Government of India to provide emergency assistance in the form of aid as well as a soft credit line and other material supplies. India also extended modest developmental assistance during these years in areas such as education, training (especially in IT), agriculture, defence and in the field of culture. Rinpoche helped build an all-party Mongolian-Indian Parliamentary Group to complement the activities of the Mongol-India Friendship Society, which had branches in all the Mongolian provinces. Rinpoche was ever ready to assist the people in any way possible.

Here I remember an interesting anecdote. It was in 1994 when the Mongolian President Mr. Ochirbat was on a State Visit to India. At the President's House Rashtrapati Bhawan in New Delhi there the leaders including Prime Minister Narasimha Rao and President Ochirbat were sitting together informally and discussing various bilateral issues. During the conversation, referring to Rinpoche's role as an ambassador, Mr. Dinesh Singh, India's External Affairs Minister in a lighter note said "Rinpoche is so focused on Mongolia that sometime I get confused whether he is our ambassador or Mongolian ambassador" and everyone present there had a hearty laugh.

The Government of India also approved grants for a vocational training centre to be opened in Ulaanbaatar which was named after the late prime minister of India, Rajiv Gandhi. Under the terms of agreement for the establishment of this centre, the Mongolian government agreed to house the school, and pay for its upkeep, while the Indian government was to meet the costs of machinery, faculty, transportation and the training of personnel. This school provides vocational training in computers, leatherwork, radio/TV repairs, plumbing, polishing of precious stones and motor vehicle repair work. Thus, it has helped many unemployed youths find jobs. In 1995, when Mrs. Sonia Gandhi, president of the Indian National Congress Party, visited Mongolia, she visited this vocational training school and presented it with a portrait of her deceased husband Mr. Rajiv Gandhi.

Inside Rashtrapati Bhawan with Prime minister Mr. Narasimha Rao, President Mr. P. Ochirbat, Mr. Dinesh Singh, Minister for External Affairs, Dr. Sachidanand Murty and Dr. Lokesh Chandra (1994)

At Rashtrapati Bhawan with Prime Minister Narasimha Rao, Mr. A.B.A. Gani Khan Choudhury, Member of Parliament, Lok Sabha and Mr. Dinesh Singh, Minister of External Affairs (1994)

Official talk during the visit of Dr. Shankar Dayal Sharma with the Mongolian Government headed by Mr. D. Byambasuren

She was also the guest of honour at that year's Naadam National Day celebration. A joint venture for a cement plant was also set up in Khovd Province with funds drawn from India and discussions had begun to set up an Indian school in Ulaanbaatar.

There was also a need to boost the production of fruits and vegetables in Mongolia. At that time cabbage, potatoes and carrots were, by and large, the only vegetables available in the market. The staple diet of Mongolians has long been meat – mutton in particular – which is considered essential due to Mongolia's harsh climate. In his interaction with the people and officials, Rinpoche often brought up this issue of promoting the cultivation of vegetables as a supplement to meat and dairy products. In 1996, in cooperation with the Mongolian Ministry of Agriculture, an Indo-Mongolian Friendship Farm was established at Darkhan, the second largest city in Mongolia, which Rinpoche inaugurated jointly with the Mongolian Minister of Agriculture. Different varieties of seeds were brought from India and were successfully tested and grown in Mongolia.

Another important development was the establishment of an Indian Cultural Centre in Ulaanbaatar, aimed at reviving and strengthening old cultural ties between the two countries. In March 1992, a MoU was signed which provided for the establishment of such a centre in Ulaanbaatar. The provisions of the memorandum were similar to the ones for the establishment of the vocational training school. The Government of Mongolia would provide a rent-free space to house the centre and staff to run it, while the Government of India would set up a library, provide all the training materials, teaching staff, equipment and so on. On January 20, 1993, the Indian Cultural Centre was opened with an inaugural ceremony attended by Mr. R. Gonchigdorj, Vice-President of Mongolia, Mr. N. Enkhbayar, Minister for Culture, and many other dignitaries. This centre has since become a symbol of the close relationship between the two countries, providing facilities for teaching Hindi, English, Indian classical dance and music, yoga and other things. A remarkable feature of this centre is that it is successfully run jointly by the two countries.

Several important high-level visits from both sides took place during the ten years of Rinpoche's tenure as India's ambassador in Mongolia, and bilateral relations undoubtedly strengthened between the two countries over these years.

An Uneasy Protocol Duty

I recall one incident in Mongolia which indicates the extent of Bakula Rinpoche's popularity in the country. Rinpoche had been in Mongolia for about 3 years by the time Dr. Shankar Dayal Sharma, Vice-President of India paid a visit to the country in 1992. A warm reception was extended when the IAF plane carrying the Vice-President of India landed at the Chinggis Khaan International airport in Ulaanbaatar. It was a landmark visit and an agreement for cooperation between the parliaments of the two countries was also signed.

After the bilateral meetings were over, the Vice-President Dr. Shankar Dayal Sharma's itinerary provided a visit to Erdenezuu Monastery at Harhorin, the ancient capital of Mongolia. The Vice-President and the delegation were to go there by helicopter. As the visit came nearer, Rinpoche told me that he would like to excuse himself from that trip and that I should check with Lakhan Mehrotra, Secretary, Ministry of External Affairs (who was accompanying the Vice-President) if he could do so. Mr. Mehrotra, however, told me that he would check with the Vice-President and get back to us. Later he told me that the Vice-President was not very pleased with the idea and therefore requested Rinpoche to go with the delegation.

So, Rinpoche agreed to go. However, he told me to contact the protocol officer in the Mongolian Foreign ministry, who was handling the visit to say that while Rinpoche would be accompanying the delegation, he desired that his name should not be included in the list. As we landed at Erdenezuu in Harhorin, there was only the local Governor and some officials present at the airport to welcome the delegation. But soon the news spread that Rinpoche had also landed with the delegation. People started to gather there just for a glimpse of Rinpoche. The last phase of the visit to Erdenezuu, was a visit to the main temple. As the delegation was coming out of the temple, a very large crowd waiting to see Rinpoche and seek his blessing, started jostling without caring for the VVIP visitor. It was then that the Vice-President understood why Rinpoche was hesitant to come with the delegation. Dr. S.D. Sharma had seen Rinpoche's popularity in Mongolia firsthand. He later narrated this incident in his speech in the Rajya Sabha (Upper House) of Indian Parliament.

Mr. R. Gonchigdorj, Vice-President of Mongolia, Dr. S.D. Sharma, Vice-President of India and Amb. Bakula Rinpoche, Ulaanbaatar (1992)

Amb. Bakula Rinpoche and Mr. K.R. Narayanan, Vice-President of India at the Embassy of India, Ulaanbaatar (1996)

Rinpoche meeting Dr. Shankar Dayal Sharma at his residence in New Delhi

Rinpoche with Mr. P. Ochirbat, President of Mongolia and Mr. P. Jasrai, Prime Minister of Mongolia

Bakula Rinpoche receiving the 'Polar Star' State Award from Mr. N. Bagabandi, President of Mongolia (2001)

In Ulaanbaatar, the Indian embassy was functioning in a dilapidated old building on rent. Once the Polish ambassador, a good friend of Rinpoche made a farewell call on Rinpoche. He told Rinpoche that not only was he leaving but that the Polish embassy, a property of the Mongolian Government, will stop functioning in Mongolia altogether. He wondered if Rinpoche would be interested in moving into the Polish embassy building. The Polish embassy was an imposing large building and was situated in an open spot. Americans had just opened their mission in Mongolia and wanted the building for themselves. However, thanks to Rinpoche's presence, the Mongolian Foreign Ministry intervened, and the building was allotted to the Indian embassy in 1996. Subsequently it was purchased by the Government of India.

After a decade in Mongolia, Rinpoche returned to India in February 2000. On May 6, 2000, having formally relinquished his office, Rinpoche called on the Prime Minister Mr. Atal Bihari Vajpayee in New Delhi and subsequently met with the Minister for External Affairs Mr. Jaswant Singh, to submit his final appraisals. He told them that despite several initiatives, Indo-Mongolian cooperation has not yet reached its full potential. Being far away from one another and not sharing a land border has meant that the volume of trade between the two countries has remained rather small. He also emphasized that with Mongolia's vast underutilized natural resources

Bakula Rinpoche meeting Prime Minister Atal Bihari Vajpayee in New Delhi. Author is also seen in the picture

and India's technological advancement, skilled manpower and vibrant economy, there are many opportunities for both sides to explore further avenues of cooperation in future. The prime minister recognized and praised all the work done by Rinpoche in strengthening ties between the two countries and in rebuilding Buddhism in Mongolia. Although geographically far apart, India and Mongolia are two ancient civilizations with a common heritage of Buddhism. It is therefore entirely fitting that in the modern period the two countries enjoy close and friendly relations.

Acknowledging Rinpoche's immense contributions to bilateral cooperation and in the revival of Buddhism in the country, Mr. P. Ochirbat, the first democratically elected President of Mongolia (1992–97) praised the work of Bakula Rinpoche in the following words: "Amb. Bakula Rinpoche was a statesman, a diplomat and a Buddhist clergy who carved out his own niche in the history of Mongolia. He recognized the historic necessity to develop Mongolia's national culture to restore the glory of Buddhism, an inseparable part of its cultural heritage. He was a divine messenger at the time of peaceful transformation from communism to democracy and a source of inspiration to our people. In 1994, I paid a State Visit to India during which the two countries signed the historic "Treaty of Cooperation and Friendship". It was an unprecedented and a landmark agreement in the history of bilateral relations and here I would like to emphasize on the personal efforts made by Bakula Rinpoche in the accomplishment of this feat."

Describing the enormous role played by Bakula Rinpoche in rebuilding Buddhist culture and democracy in Mongolia, Mr. N. Enkhbayar, Prime Minister of Mongolia stated: "Unlike in other socialist countries, transition in Mongolia from communism was peaceful. Rinpoche was an integral part of this great transformation and he played an active role in these changes through his advice, assistance and participation. Who, if not Bakula Rinpoche, could have guided the people through these changes? Rinpoche had been my guide and teacher. I remember Rinpoche's advice to me to have a vision for my country, to share the same with the rest of the people and to work hard to make the vision come true. I will be expressing the sentiments of all Mongolians when I say that we shall always remain grateful to Rinpoche for what he had done and accomplished for Mongolia."

Rinpoche maintained a close contact with Foreign Minister, Mr. Ts. Gombosuren who was considered a liberal and who ably assisted Chairman Mr. J. Batmunkh in those critical days. In an article Mr. Gombosuren wrote: "When Bakula Rinpoche finally came to Mongolia as India's ambassador, we were keen that he presented his credentials as soon as possible. In our first meeting, we exchanged views on the internal situation of our countries, development of bilateral relations and other issues. Rinpoche expressed his views on policy matters and the purposes underlying them. He could sense a major transformation taking place in Mongolia. These were the words of a genuine and a far-sighted statesman who wanted to inspire and encourage us. There was no mention of 'religion' but behind the words 'history and culture' he obviously meant that Buddhism must be restored. Seven month later, the first ever democratic and free elections were held in Mongolia. Thus, in a way, Ambassador Bakula Rinpoche had predicted the future of our country. Unfortunately, some people felt that the Ambassador was interfering in the internal affairs of our country. Some 'conscious' men even suggested to 'send back' the Indian ambassador. But His Holiness enjoyed tremendous respect and support among people who felt proud of their national history and culture. In more recent times some important steps were taken to promote bilateral relations between our two countries and one could clearly see the role and tremendous contributions made in this regard by Amb. Bakula Rinpoche. This is a common assessment of many individuals which I fully endorse."[1] Rinpoche's legacy was acknowledged even long after his departure from office. Even today he is a household name in Mongolia, and for many he symbolizes the unbreakable bond between the two countries, united by the common culture.

NOTES

1. Bakula Rinpoche. Published by Pethub Buddhist Centre, Ulaanbaatar, 2008.

Fifty-three

Establishment of Pethub Monastery in Ulaanbaatar

Rinpoche's many visits to the Mongolian countryside over the years, and meeting people from across the length and breadth of the country brought home to him the confusion and ignorance about Buddhist practice in Mongolian society. He also realized that this was the result of seventy years of communism in the country. Not only did people have very little clarity about the teachings and practices of Buddhism, but they had also been fed with inaccurate and derogatory information about Buddhism and its role in the past as well. Something needed to be done. The re-opening of several old monasteries was a positive step, but these monasteries were poorly equipped. There were educated teachers, but their number was not sufficient. As a result, the quality of the monks' education was low and their numbers were few. In order to help rebuild the Sangha, or the community of monks, Rinpoche decided to build a new monastery in Ulaanbaatar, Mongolia. This was Rinpoche's personal initiative and which he thought would serve as a model for others.

With this idea in mind, Rinpoche requested the Government of Mongolia to release land for building a branch of Pethub, his monastery in Ladakh. He met Mr. L. Enebish, the then Governor and Mayor of Ulaanbaatar, as well as a prominent young leader. Rinpoche discussed with him the proposed monastery and its objectives. Mr. Enebish, whole-heartedly supported the proposal and assured his full cooperation. Rinpoche was thus given a free hand in choosing the appropriate land for the purpose. He chose a piece of land in Ulaanbaatar's Chingilte District which was allotted to him in 1991, through a government order.

The 14th Dalai Lama blessed the construction site for the Pethub Monastery in Ulaanbaatar (1991)

Karan Singh inaugurating the Pethub School in Ulaanbaatar, established by Bakula Rinpoche on 9th September 1992

On September 28, 1991, the Dalai Lama blessed the site. With this auspicious beginning, Rinpoche entrusted the construction work to the Mongolian Army Construction company. He felt that the involvement of this company, which was an outgrowth of the Soviet military institutions built up during communist rule, would be meaningful and symbolic. However, although work started quickly, the building work soon had to be suspended due to sky-rocketing inflation, which was making it difficult to keep pace with the cost of construction. Rinpoche was putting all the personal resources available with him into the project, but the economic situation in Mongolia in those days was too volatile to continue. When construction was resumed, it was put in the hands of a private company.

Meanwhile, Rinpoche had rented a portion of the Natsagdorj City Library in Ulaanbaatar where he had started a school for monks in preparation for the proposed monastery. On September 9, 1992, Dr. Karan Singh, former Maharaja of J&K, a renowned scholar and an old friend of Rinpoche, whom he had known since the early days in post-independence Kashmir, inaugurated the school.

Jhado Rinpoche and Bakula Rinpoche in Ulaanbaatar (1993)

Bakula Rinpoche also enlisted Jhado Rinpoche, a young and erudite scholar, to help with the establishment of the school and the monastery. Later H.H. the 14th Dalai Lama appointed Jhado Rinpoche as abbot of Namgyal Monastery in Dharamshala. Subsequently, he also served as abbot of Gyuto Monastery in Dharamshala. Jhado Rinpoche subsequently returned to Mongolia. Over the years, Jhado Rinpoche gave extensive teachings across Mongolia and in neighbouring Buryatia. In year 2020 he gave Kalachakra teaching at Ulan-Ude, Buriat, Russia and in year 2024 in Ulaanbaatar, Mongolia. He also learnt Mongolian language and could freely communicate with the people. His simplicity and humble nature won the hearts of people in Mongolia and elsewhere. At the school, Geshe Thubten Tashi and Stanba Tsewang from Ladakh taught Tibetan and Buddhism while Rinchen Wangmo, my wife, took English classes for the young monks. Bakula Rinpoche would spend 2-3 hours every day teaching the student-monks and his emphasis was always on the Vinaya.

In doing so, Rinpoche was inspired by the following words of Je Lama Tsongkhapa:

Where the great Buddha Dharma had either not spread,
Or having spread, had undergone a decline, in that direction,
Through the gracious intercession of Chenrezig,
May this treasure-mine of happiness and well-being illuminate all!

Meanwhile, the construction work at the site had resumed and Rinpoche was very pleased with the idea that the building would be ready before his scheduled return to India. Lama G. Purevbat, an eminent artist and a close disciple of Bakula Rinpoche, made the thangkas and supervised the interior decoration of the monastery.

Finally, with just a few months before his return to India, the inauguration ceremony for the Ulaanbaatar Pethub Monastery, which he named Pethub Stangey Choskorling, was held on August 26, 1999. Mr. Krishan Kant, Vice-President of India was the chief-guest. Also present were Mr. C. Saikhanbeleg, Minister for Education, as well as members of the diplomatic corps in Ulaanbaatar, and various other guests including Mr. T. Kawai, President of MOA International, Japan, whose organization had also supported Rinpoche wholeheartedly in his endeavor. Messages of congratulations were also received from the 14th Dalai Lama and the presidents of the neighbouring Buryatia and Kalmyk Republics of the Russian Federation.

The inaugural ceremony was followed by a traditional Mongolian cultural programme. Mongolian wrestling tournaments are quite ritualized.

The wrestlers pair off so there can be as many as forty wrestling matches happening in the arena at the same time. The competitor brought to his knees first is the loser. When they finish, they do this slow movement, somewhat like a dance, with their arms outstretched like eagles. The winner goes and carries a pose like an eagle to show he is the victor. Even in a hundred bouts, no one gets upset, because the ritual keeps it together and maintains the dignity of the occasion. When a wrestler wins a contest, he takes on the winner of another contest and so on until only two champions are left.

Bakula Rinpoche with Avarga B. Baterdene

I remember that on this occasion the crowd was getting very excited because one of the final two contestants Mr. B. Bat-Erdene was the national champion of ten years standing. He was something of a national hero. Himself a devout Buddhist, he would often visit the embassy to take Rinpoche's blessing, and despite his celebrity status, he always struck me as an honest and straightforward man. To this day, he is regarded as one of Mongolia's most successful, long lasting and celebrated wrestlers. Now retired from the sport, he has served as an elected member of parliament and was the Defence Minister and Sports Development.

Also present on the occasion was Gelek Rinpoche, a nephew of the 13th Dalai Lama Thubten Gyatso, whom Bakula Rinpoche had known since his days in Drepung Monastery in Lhasa in the 1930s. Like Bakula Rinpoche, Gelek Rinpoche was among the last generation of lamas educated in Tibet before the Chinese communist invasion. A Geshe Lharampa degree holder,

Rinpoche meeting herdsmen in the countryside

Mr. Krishna Kant, Vice-President of India in conversation with Amb. Bakula Rinpoche (Ulaanbaatar, 1999)

he was also a well-known Buddhist scholar and taught many western students. He also founded Jewel Heart, a Tibetan Buddhist centre in Michigan, United States. Lama Zopa Rinpoche, spiritual head of the Foundation for the Preservation of the Mahayana Tradition (FPMT) and Gosok Rinpoche, old Dharma friends of Rinpoche also came to attend the ceremony, as did many of Rinpoche's students from Beijing. During his meeting with Lama Zopa Rinpoche, Bakula Rinpoche suggested to him that a branch of his organization – the FPMT be established in Mongolia. Lama Zopa accepted the proposal and today the FPMT Centre, through its various activities, is making great contributions to the development of Buddhism in Mongolia.

To mark the solemnity of the occasion and with the generous help of Indian Council for Cultural Relations (ICCR), a group of 15 monks from Pethub Monastery in Ladakh also attended the inaugural ceremony. Besides performing an elaborate consecration ceremony along with monks from Mongolia, it was they who performed the ritualistic mask dance (Cham in Tibetan). This was the first such performance by Buddhist monks in the Mongolian capital after seventy years and was attended by thousands of devotees.

Mongolia had long shared Tibet's advanced traditional Buddhist medicine system, but this too, needless to say, had all but collapsed during communism. It needed to be revived too. So, Rinpoche decided to start a traditional medicine clinic within the premises of the new Pethub Monastery. The Tibet Foundation, an organization based in the UK, headed by Mr. Phuntsog Wangyal, came forward with financial support. As a result, a separate block was constructed and the Naidan Clinic was inaugurated on June 24, 2002 by Mr. N. Enkhbayar, Prime Minister of Mongolia. Ms. Sue Byrne, coordinator for the Tibet Foundation's project "Buddhism in Mongolia" also attended the opening ceremony.

Over the years many dignitaries, especially those on official visits to Mongolia from India have visited the monastery and appreciated the tremendous hard work and goodwill created by Bakula Rinpoche. One such visit occasion was the visit of Mrs. Prathibha Devisingh Patil, President of India, who visited Pethub Monastery on 23rd July 2011. She paid her floral tribute to Bakula Rinpoche and gifted a bus which I received on behalf of the monastery.

Complimenting the work done by Bakula Rinpoche Prime Minister Narendra Modi, in his address to the Mongolian Parliament in 2015, described Pethub Monastery as an "enduring symbol" of links between India and Mongolia.

Rinpoche with young monks of Pethub monastery in Ulaanbaatar

Pethub Monastery, Ulaanbaatar, Mongolia

For me personally, it has been a great honour and privilege to be closely associated with this project from the very beginning and work as its Executive Director for over 25 years. Today, the monastery is an important landmark in Ulaanbaatar and has come to symbolize Indo-Mongolian cultural links. It was Rinpoche's hope that the two Pethub Monasteries – one in Ladakh and the other in Mongolia – would forge a close bond and support each other's dharma activities in future. 'Pethub' means a model or an example. Rinpoche also wanted to see his monastery living up to its name.

PART VII

In Pursuit of Peace in China and Tibet

Fifty-four

Teaching Dharma to Chinese Disciples in Beijing

During the ten years he served as India's ambassador in Ulaanbaatar, Bakula Rinpoche visited Beijing regularly, as much as once every three months. Typically, on each visit, he would spend the weekends in the capital. He would also meet his Chinese acquaintances and disciples and visit holy places in and around the city.

In the early 1990s, China was still a very closed society. The economic reforms had just begun and religious practices were still a taboo and forbidden. As word got out about the presence of Bakula Rinpoche in town, people approached him for teachings and expressed their wish to become his disciples. Like those in other communist countries, the devotion of these Chinese students to the Buddha Dharma was truly moving. The keenness with which they listened to the teachings, and their sincerity in practicing touched Rinpoche deeply. However, being in the Tibetan tradition and a foreigner, Bakula's position in China was a sensitive one. He was a diplomat serving the Government of India and had close contacts with the 14th Dalai Lama, further complicated the matters. The situation became increasingly complex and difficult following the intensified crackdown on practitioners of Falun Gong during the 1990s, Shugden controversy in India and the Chinese government ruthless suppression of student protest in Beijing. The Chinese authorities viewed all religious teachers with deep suspicion. I always accompanied Rinpoche during these trips. So, Rinpoche had to maintain a difficult balance between the two roles – one as serving diplomat and the other, as a Buddhist monk and a well-respected senior lama.

Following the crackdown on the Tiananmen protests in 1989, the government was making widespread arrests, cracking down on all forms of protest and dissent around China. The foreign press, critical of the government, was expelled from the country. The strictly controlled coverage of events in the Chinese press became the only source of information. Members of the communist party who were deemed to have any sympathy for the pro-democracy protesters and Falun Gong were prosecuted. Several high-ranking members were placed under house arrest. Although there was widespread international condemnation of the crackdown, the communist regime simply ignored or condemned them as attempts to interfere in its domestic affairs. As time passed, the leadership reasserted its firm grip on society, and then only did they resume and even accelerate the pace of economic reform.

Considering the tense situation, on several occasions, I had to intervene with Rinpoche, reminding him of the fragility of the situation in China and requesting him to refrain from giving religious discourses too openly as this was officially prohibited by law in China. But Rinpoche was fearless and always had the same answer. "As a Buddhist monk, how can I refuse people who come asking for teaching?" For him, to do so would be a betrayal of his solemn vows as a monk. But, at the same time, Rinpoche always insisted that his interactions with Buddhist disciples was entirely ethical and spiritual in nature and had nothing to do with politics.

Initially the groups coming to see Rinpoche in Beijing were few in number. It was just a few individuals, both Chinese and Tibetans coming to meet him in his hotel room. I am sure, there were secret agents of the government among them, listening closely to whatever was said. The meetings still always took place discreetly. Many would have found such clandestine meetings awkward or intimidating, but Rinpoche had prior experience of such situations in the Soviet Union. He knew exactly how to handle them. As the number of attendees at these informal gatherings began to grow, he also started receiving requests for more detailed teachings and specific transmissions. It is a small miracle that given the political situation in China and Bakula Rinpoche's position as a senior diplomat and someone who was in close contact with the 14th Dalai Lama, no untoward incident occurred during his many visits to Beijing, which spanned over a decade.

At the request of his disciples, Rinpoche passed on several sacred transmissions in Beijing. Initially, such teachings were performed at the residences of expatriate disciples from Taiwan, Hong Kong or western countries, since foreigners were at greater liberty than the domestic Chinese themselves. But later Rinpoche also started giving teachings at the residences of local people. Later still, when the situation became more relaxed, he gave public teachings in halls. Such gatherings for religious discourses are technically forbidden in China even today, but in practice the authorities increasingly turned a blind eye. However, that situation could easily change overnight as there was no legal protection for religious freedom in China.

In Beijing Rinpoche also started meeting many academics and high-level officials. There was a strong sense that Buddhism was gradually being restored and re-legitimized in China, but without any official or explicit government declaration to that effect. Meanwhile, the strong wave of free-market economics, which had been unleashed by Deng Xiaoping (paramount ruler from the late 1970s until his retirement in 1989) was transforming China rapidly. The emerging Chinese consumerist society was blatantly capitalist, in stark contrast to the Chinese communist ideology. "Socialism with Chinese characteristics" was the slogan. In reality it was free-market economics, combined with a one-party state and strict political control over things like press freedom. One could observe a growing gap emerging between the rich and poor. It was also seen in the context of differences between the old-guard generation, who had lived under the austerities of communism, and the new generation of urban youth, or "little emperors." They were known as little emperors because of the overprotective up-bringing given over-indulgently during China's one child policy. These social changes were creating new challenges for the leadership. The rapid economic reform process also coincided with a growing number of young people experiencing a spiritual void. China's ancient traditions of Confucianism and Buddhism had suffered deep erosion, especially during the Cultural Revolution. As a result, materialistic consumerism devoid of moral or spiritual values, was becoming rampant. In his interactions with the people in China, both then and in subsequent visits, Rinpoche often called for the resuscitation and rejuvenation of Chinese traditional culture, in which Taoism and Buddhism were firmly rooted.

However, the Chinese government's contradictory attitude towards Buddhism was notable. In some respects, religious persecution against Tibetan Buddhism continued unabated, but on the other hand, the government interfered in areas of religion, such as identification of new re-incarnations and patronized large-scale Buddhist projects including building the largest Buddha statue in the world at Lushan County, Henan in year 2002. Government also started funding for international conferences on Buddhist studies.

One of the most momentous experiences which Rinpoche particularly cherished, during our many visits to China, was meeting Mr. Yang Deneng and his wife Madam Hu Jiou. At the time of our first meeting in 1990, they were already in their seventies. Meeting them was both moving and exhilarating. They were both sincere Buddhist practitioners. Mr. Yang was the president of Beijing Layman's Association, which was an officially-recognized organization of lay Buddhist practitioners, which he was able to set up despite various obstacles. Rinpoche maintained close contact with them which continued until the death of Yang's wife in year 2000. Mr. Yang Deneng himself passed away a year later. Both of them had been students of Kyabje Trijang Rinpoche, the junior tutor of the 14th Dalai Lama and received teachings from him in Lhasa. Both, Mr. and Mrs. Yang could speak Tibetan fluently. As years passed, with their help, Rinpoche started giving teachings to large gatherings of students in Beijing. Several Tibetan masters, including Alag Shardong Rinpoche, would help in the translation of more difficult teachings into Chinese. This old couple always held their faith with tremendous sincerity and they had a small number of students whom they had been training over many years. Besides them, there were scores of other young people, from all walks of life, such as artists, businessmen, doctors, students, farmers, professionals and even policemen. Some were even children of important Chinese dignitaries. All were sincerely interested in learning Buddhism and many became Rinpoche's devoted disciples.

Rinpoche also used these visits as an opportunity to visit Buddhist holy sites and other historical monuments not just around Beijing, but further afield in provinces across the Chinese mainland. In Beijing itself there are many holy sites. The so-called Lama Temple, which is known as *Yonghegong* in Chinese, is built in a mixture of Chinese and Tibetan architecture. Most of its resident monks are from Inner Mongolia, an ethnically Mongolian but now a Chinese province. There are also several stupas in and around Beijing.

On September 25, 1993, Rinpoche set off on a pilgrimage to *Riwo-Tse-Nga*, the "Five-Peaked Mountain" or Wutaishan in Chinese. This is the abode of the Bodhisattva Manjushri and is considered amongst the most sacred places of pilgrimage for Buddhists. Accompanied by a group of students, Rinpoche paid obeisance to the mountain, covering all its peaks. The serenity and tranquility of the surrounding mountains in the early morning was both soothing and exhilarating. It is a highly suitable place for contemplation. Rinpoche spent several days at this mountain location. There was a great sense of satisfaction for Rinpoche in making this pilgrimage. He had a deep desire to go there. So, with this visit, his lifelong wish was fulfilled.

Rinpoche offered prostrations and prayers. He also visited the cave in which, it is said, the 6th Dalai Lama Tsangyang Gyatso, sat in meditation for six months. The cave has an extraordinary ritual spring. This trip to Wutaishan was the first leg of Rinpoche's historic visit to the north-eastern Tibetan province of Amdo and on to Lhasa, a trip which is described in greater detail in a later chapter.

Rinpoche with Mrs. Hu Jiou and Mr. Yang Deneng in Beijing (1993)

Rinpoche with Chinese disciples in Beijing, China (1994)

Rinpoche's spiritual activities in mainland China continued for over a decade. An important occasion came in 2002, when he received an invitation to visit Shandong province and consecrate the famous Prince Pagoda in Wenshang County, which is said to contain the tooth of the Lord Buddha. According to local officials, the holy relic was found in a silver casket within a stone box. The box had an inscription in Chinese script, which mentioned the history of this relic which had come from India. It is also decided that the casket containing the holy relic should be placed facing the direction of India, the birthplace of Lord Buddha. While renovating the ancient pagoda, the local government had to remove the relic for its safe keeping. After the renovation was complete, they organized a ceremony to re-enshrine the holy relic back in its original place. So, on May 19, 2002, on the invitation of local authorities Rinpoche visited the temple to perform the auspicious task. Hundreds of people including senior provincial officials, attended the ceremony. The day coincided with Lord Buddha's birthday (in accordance with the Chinese calendar) which incidentally also happened to be Rinpoche's birthday, so the occasion was considered very auspicious on many counts and his students threw a grand reception at a hotel.

Rinpoche with author and his family at the Great Wall of China

As mentioned earlier in detail, Bakula Rinpoche had already had a long involvement with protecting Lord Buddha's holy relics in India – advocating for their proper housing, display and bringing them to various places. In year 1951, he had arranged for the holy relics of Lord Buddha and of his two principal disciples, Sariputta and Maudgalyayan, to Ladakh. In 1993, he facilitated bringing the holy relics to Mongolia. Now, in the later years of his life, he had this further auspicious opportunity to pay his respects to holy relics in China.

Fifty-five

Engaging with Tibetan Politics in China

Rinpoche's interactions with students and disciples in China was purely spiritual and never political in nature. However, the Tibetan issue, naturally, continued to be something that preoccupied Rinpoche, and he kept trying to do what he could, to help find a resolution to the ongoing suffering of the Tibetan people. By the 1990s, the political landscape around the Tibet issue had shifted considerably since his days as a Member of Parliament. The Dalai Lama had made the public declaration that it was not about seeking independence from China, but only demanding genuine autonomy for Tibet. He had formulated the so-called Middle-Way policy, in the hope that this would peacefully resolve the issue of Tibet and ensure the peaceful co-existence of the Tibetans and Chinese in the future, based on equality and mutual co-operation. For many Tibetans, the early 1990s was a period of considerable hope and optimism that a resolution to the Tibet issue might soon be found.

When Bakula Rinpoche had visited Lhasa in 1955, as an official representative of the Government of India, he had become acquainted with the Ngapho Ngawang Jigme, a prominent member of the Tibetan Government at that time. He was the main figure in the old Tibetan Government, who was working with the new Chinese communist authorities. Ngapho had been the Tibetan official in charge of the Tibetan army, when it surrendered at Chamdo to the invading Chinese communist forces in the winter of year 1950–51. He had also been one of the Tibetan government's signatories to the Seventeen Point Agreement between the Tibetan and Chinese governments in 1951, which in theory guaranteed Tibet's autonomy within China. Since the Chinese forces were already on the doorstep of Tibet at Chamdo in Kham region when this agreement was signed, many believed that it was signed under duress and therefore invalid. Anyway, after the Dalai Lama's escape to India in 1959, Ngapho Ngawang Jigme stayed in Tibet as the highest-ranking Tibetan functionary in Chinese-occupied Tibet and remained in senior Chinese governmental positions for many decades.

In December of 1989, before Bakula Rinpoche travelled to Beijing for his two-day stop-over on the way to taking up his post as India's ambassador in Mongolia, he requested the Indian Embassy in Beijing to try and set up a meeting for him with Ngapho Ngawang Jigme. The latter was then a resident in Beijing where he held the position of Vice-Chairman of the Standing Committee of the National People's Congress (NPC) as well as Chairman of the Standing Committee of the People's Congress of the Tibet Autonomous Region (TAR). He also held a senior position on the NPC Ethnic Affairs Committee and was Honorary President of the Buddhist Association of China.

Rinpoche in conversation with Ngapho Ngawang Jigme in Beijing, China (1992)

Rinpoche met with Ngapho at the latter's residence in the centre of Beijing not far from Tiananmen Square. I, with another official from the Indian embassy accompanied Rinpoche. It was a well-guarded house with a large iron gate manned by police and security officials. Ngapho lived there with his wife and children. It was a courtesy call and the meeting itself was uneventful, but it certainly was a significant step towards building trust between Rinpoche and the Chinese authorities. The two men had met after over four decades and both expressed their pleasure at meeting again after so many years.

As I recall, Ngapho Ngawang Jigme looked quite healthy despite being in his late eighties. In subsequent years, Rinpoche and Ngapho would meet frequently in Beijing. It was during one such meeting that Rinpoche touched upon the situation in Tibet and the potential will to find a solution to it. Rinpoche expressed the view that the issue of Tibet was getting more and more complex and there was no sign of any resolution in sight. Ngapho had an important role in the historic events that shaped the Tibetan situation and he had been in senior positions in the Chinese government. For these reasons, Rinpoche wondered if Ngapho might be able to intervene in order to accelerate the effort to find a resolution which would be acceptable to both sides. Rinpoche said that the Dalai Lama had already clarified that the Tibetan issue is no longer a struggle for political independence. He had agreed to be part of China provided his demand for a genuine autonomy for Tibet was accepted by the Chinese Government. Couldn't this help in finding a solution?

Ngapho Jigme replied that he shared Rinpoche's concerns, and confided to Rinpoche that he had already made several attempts in the past to bring the two sides closer. In particular, he said that after the passing away of the 10th Panchen Lama in 1989, he had advised the Chinese leadership that the Dalai Lama should be invited to Tibet to participate in the traditional and customary religious rites for deceased Panchen Lama. He said that this was a golden opportunity for both sides to meet without any pre-conditions. According to Ngapho, the Chinese had actually accepted his suggestion, and were prepared to allow the Dalai Lama to participate in the last religious rites. Later, the Chinese also sent feelers to the Tibetan administration in Dharamshala. According to Ngapho, he was completely taken aback to learn that the Tibetan Government-in-Exile in Dharamshala had turned down the proposal. Apparently, the CTA officials in Dharamshala were distrustful of Chinese intentions. It was feared that if he went back to Tibet, they would not allow him to return again to India. This suspicion, according to Ngapho, was uncalled for. That this visit did not materialize, he said, was a source of great regret and disappointment for him. Later, Rinpoche made enquiries about these claims. Tenzin Namgyal Tethong, who had served as a senior member of the Central Tibetan Administration in Dharamshala and had met Rinpoche in Leh and told him that such a proposal had indeed come from China, but that it was turned down by the CTA out of fears for His Holiness security.

Ngawang Jigme Ngapho was the face of Tibetan people at the senior levels of the Chinese government. He passed away in Beijing in 2009 at the ripe old age of ninety-nine years.

Fifty-six

Rinpoche's Visit to Tibet 1992–93

From Mongolia, Tibet was near yet very far away in some special sense. After he settled down in the Indian embassy in Mongolia, Bakula Rinpoche set about trying to get a visa to visit to Tibet, but each time we applied, the visa was refused on one or the other pretext. It was only after Ngapho spoke to the Chinese Foreign Minister in Beijing and gave his personal guarantee, that the Chinese government issued the visa. This information came from Ngapho himself, who confidentially requested Rinpoche not to make any political statements during his visit to Tibet. As a result of Ngapho's intervention, not only was a visa granted, but also Rinpoche's visit to Tibet was hosted by the Tibet Development Fund (TDF), which is an NGO founded by the 10th Panchen Lama. Being hosted by TDF was very significant, since it enabled Rinpoche to meet all the important political leaders in the Tibet Autonomous Region (TAR) as well as with religious figures. It also gave him access to many holy places, from which he would otherwise have been barred from visiting.

Rinpoche was on a pilgrimage, but even then, Rinpoche became one among the first few Indian diplomats and a high dignitary to visit Lhasa since 1962 Sino-Indian war. I had the good fortune to accompany Rinpoche on this tour. We left Ulaanbaatar on August 1, 1992, by air for Beijing where we stayed for a few days. In Beijing, Kunga Tsering, representative of Tibet Development Fund (TDF), whom Ngapho Ngawang Jigme had deputed to manage the trip, also joined us. Before our departure for Lhasa, Rinpoche met Salman Haidar, Indian Ambassador to China and also an old friend of Rinpoche. Interestingly, his grandfather Hashmatullah was the Wazir-Wazarat of Ladakh or the administrator under the Dogra regime.

From Beijing we flew to Chengdu, the capital of Sichuan province and stayed there for two days visiting the city. From Chengdu, we flew on to Lhasa. The landscape below was breathtaking. For us, it was the same very familiar scene – ranges of high snow-clad mountains and long stretches of barren land with small patches of cultivated land. All of this reminded us of Ladakh. On arrival at Lhasa, we were received at Gongkar airport by a team of TDF, which included Jigme Yontan (Jigyonla), the Deputy Director of the TDF, and the youngest son of Ngapho Ngawang Jigme and Jigme Taring.

Rinpoche's pilgrimage in Lhasa began on July 4, 1992, with a visit to the Jokhang temple and Barkhor street in Lhasa. Before 1959, there used to be many Indian and Nepalese traders in Barkhor street. For all Tibetan Buddhists, irrespective of school or sect, the Jokhang Temple is considered highly sacred. It was established during the reign of King Songsten Gampo, the first Tibetan Emperor to introduce Buddhism in the Land of Snow in the 7th century CE. According to tradition, the two brides of the king, Princess Wencheng of the Chinese Tang Dynasty and Princess Bhrikuti of Nepal, are said to have brought with them important Buddhist statues from their respective homelands, which were enshrined here. Many Newari Nepalese artists worked on the construction of the temple, which is also known simply as the Tsuglag-khang, the house of wisdom. This is so because the Tibetan term "Tsuglag" refers to all forms of traditional knowledge. Today, it is more commonly known as the Jokhang, meaning the "House of the Buddha", since it contains the famous Jowo statue. The Jokhang has been at the centre of Tibetan Buddhism since its very beginning. The famous Indian Buddhist Master, Atisa Dipankara Srijanana, upon whose teachings the Lamrim were later developed, taught here in the 11th century. For many, it is the most important temple and sacred site, not only in Lhasa, but in the entire Tibetan cultural sphere. The same, to the horror of all devout Buddhists, during the Cultural Revolution in July 1966, was ransacked and desecrated by Red Guards. Buddhist scriptures kept there were looted and burnt to ashes.

Rinpoche went around the temple with great interest and reverence. He was also shown the room of the Dalai Lama, upstairs, where some of his personal belongings were preserved there. For Rinpoche, it was very moving to be back in the inner courtyard of the Jokhang after so many decades, for, this is the Sanctum Sanctorum of Buddhism in Tibet. It was right here in this same courtyard, that over half a century ago Rinpoche had taken part in a debate during the course of his Geshe examination in 1940.

The place was thronged with pilgrims as well as a considerable number of foreign tourists (as this was a period during which Tibet was relatively open). There were large numbers of Chinese soldiers in uniform as well as plain-clothes operatives. Some of them were posted on the roof tops. The

Bakula Rinpoche paying homage to the Jowo Rinpoche at Jokhang, Lhasa, Tibet (1992)

Rinpoche at the Potala Palace in Lhasa (1992)

circular street, which surrounds the temple, known as the Barkhor, was full of devotees, tourists, traders and lay people. We also saw that some renovation work was going on in one corner of the temple. On our arrival, a young monk, Nyima Tsering, who was the senior priest at the Jokhang, received Rinpoche and guided us around. He gave us detailed descriptions and information about the temple and the changes that had taken place over the years.

In the coming days, we also visited the Norbulingka and the Potala, the summer and winter palaces of the Dalai Lamas respectively. Rinpoche was very happy to be back in Tibet, but at the same time he was deeply saddened and anguished over the massive destruction of old monuments that had taken place over the years, especially during the Cultural Revolution and much of which was still visible.

During his time in Lhasa, Rinpoche also visited his alma mater, Drepung Monastery which in earlier times housed around 7700 monks. Drepung (literally meaning "rice heap" because of its appearance from afar) lies at the foot of Mount Gephel, about 5 kms west of Lhasa. It is the largest of Lhasa's "three great monasteries". It was founded by Jamyang Choje Tashi Palden, one of Tsongkhapa's main disciples, in the year 1416. Since then, it has been the primary monastic institution of the Gelugpa school. Before the construction of the Potala palace by the Great Fifth Dalai Lama in the 17th Century CE, the Ganden Phodrang, or "Ganden Palace" in Drepung was in fact the traditional residence of the Dalai Lamas. Drepung was renowned across the Tibetan Buddhist world for the high standards of its academic study, especially the rigour of its training in Buddhist philosophy. And of course, it was here that Bakula Rinpoche himself had spent fourteen years between 1927 and 1940, studying Buddhist philosophy as a young monk. When Rinpoche paid homage at the main temple over half a century later, and after such a momentous and traumatic period in Tibet's history, Drepung's entire congregation of monks assembled to conduct a special prayer. To sit again, with the monks at prayer, in the great assembly hall of Drepung, for Rinpoche was a moving and joyous experience.

The next stop, naturally, was Drepung's Loseling Dratsang (college), within Drepung where he had studied. The monks at Loseling had been informed about Rinpoche's visit. There was a palpable feeling of anticipation, as a large number of monks waited for Rinpoche's arrival. A good number of them were actually Rinpoche's contemporaries and had studied with him decades ago. He was given a ceremonial welcome by the monks. There was a great sense of jubilation at being reunited after more than five decades. As Rinpoche entered the precincts of Loseling, he saw his old acquaintances and classmates waiting for him with khadag in their hand. After the initial joy of the greeting, they settled down in a room specially prepared for Rinpoche's visit. Rinpoche and the monks started to reminisce about their good old days. Gradually, the discussion became more somber as the monks recounted with great sadness the tragedy that followed. Even Rinpoche could not help himself from becoming overwhelmed with grief as they shared their experiences, and I could see tears rolling down his cheeks. It was a deeply moving scene.

The visit to Pethub Khangtsen – Rinpoche's residence in Lhasa which in the old days had also served as the main hostel at Drepung for monks from Ladakh – was also a moving and nostalgic experience for Rinpoche. Traditionally, this elegant complex had belonged to Pethub Monastery in Ladakh, since it had been established by the previous Bakula. In the 1950s, during Rinpoche's last visit, a major renovation and improvement had been carried out there. But now, as we drew closer, we could see how dilapidated the buildings had become. Parts of the roof had caved in and many doors and windows were missing. There used to be a platform outside the gate for Rinpoche to mount his horse, which was still there, though rather rickety. The portion of the building containing Rinpoche's own quarters, however, was more or less intact. The room was locked and the monk who was occupying it had gone away to Nepal. However, the monks managed to open the door and Rinpoche was able to go inside. The altar in his prayer room, which had been made of high-quality sandalwood, was missing. Rinpoche spent some time in the room, and then went around the premises once again, lost in his thoughts. He also discussed with local authorities about the possibilities of renovating Pethub Khangtsen and reclaiming its ownership. But there was no headway in this regard.

Sera Monastery was our next destination. Sera Monastery is also one of the "great three" monasteries, located about two kilometers north of Lhasa. It is said that the origin of the name 'Sera' is in the fact that before the monastery was built, the area was surrounded by wild roses (se ra in Tibetan). During the 1959 revolt in Lhasa, Sera Monastery suffered severe damage from artillery shelling. Its colleges were destroyed and many monks were killed. Rinpoche went around the monastery complex and paid his obeisance in the main temple, where there was a large gathering of monks performing prayer rituals. At Sera, Rinpoche also met Geshe Singye, a native Mongolian who was at that time the monastery's abbot. Rinpoche had already met him earlier in India. Now he was in his eighties, and Rinpoche received an oral transmission from him. Rinpoche also told Geshe Singye about the changes that had taken place in Mongolia and how the communists were no longer in power there. He asked Geshe Singye if he would like to return to his native place in Mongolia. But the horror of communist atrocities

Rinpoche reminiscing old times in his room at Pethub Khangtsen, Drepung Losaling Monastery, Lhasa (1992)

With Geshe Singye (Mongolian), Abbot, Sera Monastery, Lhasa, Tibet (1992)

was so deep in Geshe Singye's mind that he felt insecure and declined the offer.

On July 5, 1992, we left Lhasa to visit Ganden monastery, the third of "great three" monasteries of Tibet. It was founded by Je Tsongkhapa himself in 1409. Traditionally, the Ganden Tripa or "throne-holder of Ganden" is considered the head of the entire Gelugpa School. Ganden consisted of two principal colleges, Jangtse and Shartse, meaning North Peak and East Peak respectively.

After a journey by jeep, we caught a glimpse of this historic monastery from a distance. However, our joy and excitement were short-lived. As we drew closer to the structure, we could clearly see the enormous destruction this ancient monastery had suffered. While recalling its past grandeur, Rinpoche felt very sad, and was lost in thought for some time. At that point, Rinpoche explained to me the doctrine of impermanence as being the nature of life. Clearly his understanding of Buddhism was what helped him cope with the enormous sense of loss he felt on seeing the scale of this destruction. The majority of the complex, which housed an estimated 5,000 monks, was in ruins and rubble. It had been completely emptied of monks after the uprising in 1959, and then in 1966, during the Cultural Revolution. Its buildings had been shelled by Red Guards. The closer we drew to the monastery, the more he felt hurt and saddened.

We spent a full day there touring the monastery. The three main sites there are the Serdung, which contains the holy relics of Tsongkhapa, the Tsokchen or main Assembly Hall, and the Ngamcho Khang which is the chapel where Tsongkhapa traditionally taught. The monastery also houses artifacts which belonged to Tsongkhapa. In a rare gesture of respect, the monks displayed and showed Rinpoche these objects and holy items. The monks there also gave Rinpoche a full account of the events leading to its present condition. Deeply saddened, Rinpoche made a long kora or circumambulation of the monastery, which took nearly three hours. One old monk, who was well-known within the monastery for his extensive knowledge about the holy spots around the monastery, was specially deputed by monastery administration to escort Rinpoche. He gave a detailed narration of the holy sites on the way.

On July 7, 1992, we left for Shigatse. After seeing the city's neighborhood, Rinpoche visited Tashilhunpo monastery, which he had first visited as a boy in the 1920s. The attendants of the late Panchen Rinpoche received Rinpoche at the monastery gate. Tashilhunpo (whose name means something like "heap of glory") was founded by Gedun Drub, the nephew and disciple of Je Tsongkhapa who was later retrospectively considered the First Dalai

Rinpoche at the ruins of Ganden Monastery, Tibet (1992)

Holy-relics shown to Rinpoche at Tashi Lhunpo monastery

Lama. It is a historic and culturally important monastery occupying an imposing location on a hill dominating Shigatse, which is the second-largest city in Tibet. Pilgrims circumambulate the monastery on the Lingkor (sacred path) outside its walls. Although many of the buildings there had been destroyed during the Cultural Revolution, these were mainly the residences of the four thousand or so monks who used to live there. However, the monastery itself was not as extensively damaged due to the favour that the Panchen Lama enjoyed with the Chinese authorities in the early years of their occupation.

Even at Tashilhunpo, during the height of the Cultural Revolution in 1966-68, Red Guards had led the crowds to break statues, burn scriptures and open the stupas containing the relics of the 5th to 9th Panchen Lamas and other holy objects. Only a few holy relics were saved and preserved. In 1985, the 10th Panchen Lama began reconstruction of a new stupa to house these and honour his predecessors. This new stupa was finally consecrated on January 22, 1989, just six days before the Panchen Lama died here at Tashilhunpo at the young age of fifty-one. Paying homage to his old friend and spiritual brother was again a moving experience for Rinpoche. He recalled with regret how the Panchen Lama had invited him to Tibet after their meeting in Kathmandu in 1986. Rinpoche offered prayers before the stupa which enshrined Panchen Lama's holy relics.

Later, the monks of the monastery and of Ngagpa Dratsang in particular held a reception in honour of Rinpoche. Here many monks shared their agonizing recollections of the past. Nevertheless, they were confident about the future and were determined to fully rebuild the monastery. At that time, the Chinese Government was also investing in rebuilding the monasteries in Tibet, with the idea that they could become major tourist attractions.

But this was also a strange paradox. This was the same Chinese Communist Party rebuilding the very monasteries, which it had earlier plundered, burnt and destroyed. There was something hollow and unwholesome in this newfound state support for the monasteries. Monks were still fleeing to India in large numbers to receive authentic Buddhist teachings at the Tibetan monasteries, which had been re-established there. Again, and again, this came up in our conversations with the monks in Tibet that as long H.H. the Dalai Lama, who was the most important symbol of their faith, and all the other revered Buddhist masters remained in far-off India, a genuine renaissance of the religion in Tibet itself was impossible. Without the Dalai Lama and all the other great masters, they could restore the grand buildings, but could not secure the purpose they were built for. It was like having a body without a living heart!

Heavy rains then prevented us from going on to Sakya Monastery, and instead Rinpoche visited Zhalu Monastery. On July 10, 1992, we reached Gyangtse, the town, which in Rinpoche's youth had been a major trading point with India, as an official Indian Trade agent was based there. We visited all the monasteries and temples in and around. From there we left for Samye, the first monastery ever built in Tibet. It was built during the reign of the Tibetan Emperor Trisong Detsen in the 8th century CE. Its construction was overseen by the trio of Shantarakshita (a former abbot of Nalanda Monastery in India), Padmasambhava and Trisong Detsen. At the time of our visit, Samye was undergoing a major renovation.

On July 12, 1992, we left for Tsethang, where we visited the Yumbu Lhakhang, said to be the oldest building in Tibet, and the Tradrug Lhakhang the oldest Buddhist temple in Tibet. We also visited the Songtsen Gampo Medicine School and the exhibition hall at Cheonggye County, where the tombs of the old Tibetan kings are located.

Back in Lhasa, Rinpoche again visited Drepung where he made mang-ja, tea offering for the Drepung Loseling monks. He also visited Ngagpa Dratsang and Gya Khangtsen. There he met Choezey-la and Geshe Lamrimpa Chenpo, two of the few remaining masters of the old tradition. Geshe Lamrimpa Chenpo, a renowned master of the Lamrim (Stages of the Path) was a very popular teacher among local Tibetans as well as having followers across China. Geshe Lamrimpa also presented to Rinpoche a set of Lamrim (Brief, Intermediate, and Elaborate versions), and on the trio of Sangwadueba (Guhyasamaja), Demchog (Cakrasamvara) and Jigjey (Yamantaka).

Next day we visited Nechung Monastery and spent some time meeting old monks there. On July 15, 1992, we visited the Ramoche Tsuglag-khang, and the Men-tsee Khang, the centre for traditional Tibetan medicine where Rinpoche was received by well-known scholar Dr. Jampa Yontan who gave Rinpoche an introduction to the Mentsi Khang's activities. Later that day Lobsang Gelek, Governor of Lhasa hosted a dinner in honour of Bakula Rinpoche which was attended by several senior dignitaries.

During his stay in Lhasa, Mr. Ragdi, Chairman, Regional People's Political Consultative Conference, who held the position in the political hierarchy next only to the Party Secretary of the Tibetan Autonomous Region. He hosted a lunch in honour of Bakula Rinpoche. It was attended by several CCP leaders in Tibet as well as some officially-recognised religious leaders. In his speech, Mr. Ragdi informed Rinpoche about the major development projects which had been undertaken by the CCP in Tibet. He also reiterated the official government position regarding the preservation of Tibetan language and culture. He expressed a hope that border trade

Amb. Bakula Rinpoche at a banquet hosted in his honour by Mr. Lobsang Gelek, Governor of Lhasa, Tibet Autonomous Region (1992)

between India and Tibet would be resumed in the future which, he said, would be to the mutual benefit of both sides.

In his speech, Bakula Rinpoche thanked the local government for the warm hospitality extended to him, and the precious opportunity to visit Tibet once again. Always frank and honest, Rinpoche then said that he had mixed feelings about the visit. On one hand he had greatly enjoyed being in the holy land once again and was impressed by the infrastructural development in Tibet. On the other hand, he said, he was also deeply saddened by the destruction that had taken place in Tibet, particularly of the monasteries which are the repositories of traditional knowledge. He expressed the hope that the Chinese government would do everything possible to help the monasteries regain their former glory and that the monks and nuns of Tibet would, in future, enjoy uninterrupted freedom of religious practice. He expressed his optimism about the early return of the 14th Dalai Lama to his homeland Tibet. He also hoped that Tibet's distinct cultural and ethnic identity would be preserved.

Rinpoche then reiterated and fully endorsed the comments of Mr. Ragdi with regard to the prospect of reopening border trade, and informed him about the efforts he himself had been making in this regard from the Indian side. He also reiterated a long-standing call from the people of India, particularly the people of Ladakh, for the opening of a travel route via Demchok in Ladakh. This could facilitate a much shorter and smoother journey for pilgrims to Mount Kailash and Lake Mansarovar and would also boost the economy in these border regions on both sides. He also informed his audience about the major infrastructural developments in

Ladakh, such as, road and airport connectivity and expressed his hope that the Chinese government would look upon Indian proposals in this regard favorably. The lunch was then followed by a colorful cultural programme of Tibetan dance and music.

During the discussion, Mr. Ragdi informed Rinpoche of the recent announcement about the recognition of the 17th Gyalwang Karmapa Urgyen Trinley Dorje Rinpoche, head of Karma Kagyu school of Tibetan Buddhism. He told Rinpoche that a reception was also being hosted in honour of the newly-recognised Tulku, and invited Bakula Rinpoche to attend. The previous incarnation, the 16th Karmapa Rangjung Rigpe Dorje, is considered to be one of the great meditation masters of the 20th century. He was highly respected across the Himalayas and in many parts of the world. Bakula Rinpoche had known the 16th Karmapa well. The 16th Karmapa had passed away in 1981.

The boy recognized as the 17th Karmapa, named Urgyen Trinley Dorje, was born on June 26, 1985, in a nomad community in Bakor, in the eastern Tibetan province of Kham. The 14th Dalai Lama gave his confirmation of the recognition in June 1992, and on July 17, of the same year he was given his formal name in a traditional ceremony which took place in front of the sacred Jowo statue of the Buddha in the inner sanctum of the Jokhang.

At this reception Bakula Rinpoche was seated with the young Karmapa along with several other high dignitaries including Mr. Ragdi, head of the Communist Party in Lhasa. The parents of the 17th Karmapa were also present and incidentally, I happened to share a table with them, so we could talk. They were simple highland nomads or drogpa, who lived at high altitude in the traditional black tent of Tibetan nomads with their herds of Yak, Dri and Dzo. I found the parents to be tremendously humble, honest and generous people. During our conversation, the mother told me that this was the first time they had ever been to Lhasa. Coming from a remote Tibetan nomadic area, I could see how uncomfortable they felt sitting at a formal dinner which they had never experienced in their life. I remember seeing the mother of Gyalwa Karmapa covering her mouth with her sleeves as she could not stand the smell of Chinese food.

Meeting Stagtsang Raspa Rinpoche in Lhasa

In Lhasa, Bakula Rinpoche was also reunited with His Eminence Stagtsang Raspa Rinpoche, the head lama of Hemis Monastery, which is the largest Monastery in Ladakh. Stsagtsang Rinpoche was born in a Tibetan family, but after his recognition as the reincarnation of his predecessor, he was brought to Ladakh, where he spent several years of his childhood. Bakula

Bakula Rinpoche meeting Kyabje Stagtsang Raspa Rinpoche in Lhasa, Tibet (1992)

Rinpoche had known him since his childhood. He had then returned to Lhasa to pursue higher studies. But unfortunately, in year 1959, while he was studying there, the Tibetan uprising occurred, after which the Chinese authorities, who were aware of his credentials, prevented him from leaving Tibet. He then had to renounce his monastic vows and take employment as an ordinary worker. He had endured extreme hardship under Chinese communist rule. However, during the 1990s the situation had eased considerably and by the time of our visit he had been appointed a member of Tibet's Buddhist Association.

Stagtsang Rinpoche came to the hotel in Lhasa to meet Bakula Rinpoche. In fact, he and his wife visited, most of the days we were there, bringing Tibetan tea for Rinpoche. The two Rinpoches were extremely happy to see each other again after so many years. Stagtsang Rinpoche was in good health. Earlier some years ago he had visited Ladakh, but eventually decided to return to Lhasa much to the disappointment of the monks of Hemis and the people of Ladakh. In the course of their conversation, Bakula Rinpoche broached the subject of Stagtsang Rinpoche visiting Ladakh again. Conveying the sentiments of all Ladakhis, Bakula Rinpoche urged him to return to Hemis. Bakula Rinpoche promised that he would help secure the necessary Indian visa and so on. Stagtsang Rinpoche, while appreciating the offer of help, confided to Rinpoche that for the moment, he was not contemplating a return. He gave no specific reasons for this, but said that he would return to Ladakh at an appropriate time. Let us hope that Stagtsang Raspa Rinpoche returns to Ladakh soon and thus ends the long separation with his followers there.

Thus, after completing this long cherished and historic visit to Tibet, and being reunited with many friends and acquaintances there, Rinpoche departed again for Beijing and later returned to Ulaanbaatar.

A Visit to Amdo (Qinghai Province)

A year later, Rinpoche visited the Amdo region of Tibet, most of which today falls within Qinghai province. From Ulaanbaatar we flew to Beijing, and on July 29, 1993, we flew onward to Xining, the capital of Qinghai Province. For this visit, no special permissions were required. In Qinghai we realized that in the main cities, Tibetans were a minority, being outnumbered by ethnic Han Chinese and Muslim Hui. But in most of the countryside the Tibetans were still the predominant ethnic group.

Rinpoche's visit covered all major towns of Qinghai. In particular, we made the pilgrimage to the monastery of Kumbum, founded in year 1583, by the 3rd Dalai Lama near the place where Je Tsongkhapa had been born in year 1357. Kumbum, which is affiliated with Drepung in Lhasa, is situated in a narrow valley close to the village of Lusar in a Tibetan cultural region of Amdo. Kumbum is regarded as second in importance only to the "great three" monasteries of Lhasa. On a nearby site where Tsongkhapa was born, it is said that there was a sandalwood tree and a small stupa built by Je Tsongkhapa's mother. The leaves and the bark of this tree were reputed to bear impressions of the Buddha's face and various mystic syllables, and its blossoms were said to give off a uniquely pleasing scent. This tree became known as the "Tree of Great Merit". Later, when Kumbum Monastery was established at the site, a four-storied temple with a golden roof was built around this tree. This, it is said, is how the monastery got its name, Kumbum meaning the "hundred thousand enlightened bodies" of Buddha.

At Kumbum, Bakula Rinpoche was received by the 8th Arjia Rinpoche Lobsang Thubten Jigme Gyatso, the head of the monastery. In 1993, Arjia Rinpoche was relatively young. He was actually born into a Mongolian family. During the Cultural Revolution, he had been forced to leave his monastery and attend a Chinese school. Yet, he told Bakula Rinpoche, he had been able to secretly continue his Buddhist practice and study with his tutors. But his sufferings were deep. He was sent to a labour camp, where he was forced to work for sixteen years. After the Cultural Revolution, Arjia Rinpoche returned to Kumbum, where he served as its Abbot, and oversaw major renovations and the re-establishment of monastic studies. In 1998, Arjia Rinpoche escaped and finally settled down in the United States of America. His life is committed to the preservation of Buddhist teachings, art and culture within and outside of Tibet and Mongolia.

Next day, Bakula Rinpoche met Venerable Gungthang Rinpoche in Labrang's Tashi Kyil Monastery. Gungthang Rinpoche was a highly learned and influential lama and a very popular scholar in Amdo. He too had endured a great deal of suffering under the Chinese Red Army. Along with many other monks and lamas he had been imprisoned in 1958, during the period of the communist "Democratic Reforms" which had sparked a widespread uprising in Amdo. After his release in 1979, he became very active as a spiritual leader and a scholar, whose fame spread across Eastern Tibet. He also undertook a major reconstruction of his home monastery.

During our visit, we also had the rare opportunity to visit Takser, a small village on high grounds near the famous Blue Lake (known as Tso-ngon or Kokonor). It is the birthplace of the 14th Dalai Lama. Rinpoche met and tried to converse with local Tibetan villagers. However, it was quite hard to communicate with them as most people in the village spoke only Chinese. Rinpoche prayed at the site where H.H. the 14th Dalai Lama was born.

After this, Rinpoche visited Shaqun (Shachung) Monastery located in the south of Siling (Xining) city. This is considered to be one of the four great monasteries of northern Tibet, where Je Tsongkhapa had himself received the novice's precepts and begun his monastic life, receiving teachings and transmissions from many different Buddhist lineages. Rinpoche was welcomed by Shardong Rinpoche, the head of Shardong Monastery. Like many other Tibetan masters, Shardong Rinpoche had also suffered humiliation and hardship during the Cultural Revolution and had to work as a laborer. He had also been publicly denounced by the communist government for his alleged anti-party activities and paraded around town in an act of ritualized humiliation with written slogans hanging from his neck. Bakula Rinpoche and Shardong Rinpoche kept in close contact and used to meet occasionally in Beijing. Since Shardong Rinpoche knew Chinese well, he was often able to assist Rinpoche when he gave teachings to Chinese disciples in Beijing.

Like in TAR, it was distressing to see the discontent and unrest among the Tibetans in the Amdo region. We could see that the Chinese controlled every sphere of life. To make matters worse, there were simmering ethnic tensions in the region between the Tibetans and the Chinese Muslim settlers whose number, according to the local Tibetans, was growing with each passing year.

Fifty-seven

Advocating Indian Mediation on the Tibet Issue

By the mid-1990s, negotiations between the Tibetans and Chinese government had unfortunately come to a grinding halt. This too could not make Bakula Rinpoche resign himself to situations of impasse. According to him, what was required was a further diplomatic push. The stakes were high, since a peaceful resolution of the long-standing Tibet issue would be an immeasurable benefit to the people of both China and Tibet.

In a letter from Ulaanbaatar, dated May 4, 1998, addressed to Prime Minister Atal Bihari Vajpayee, Bakula Rinpoche put forward a proposal that India should play the role of an impartial mediator in the conflict, keeping in mind the interests of all concerned parties **(Annexure 28)**. He wrote that the question of Tibet and its future dispensation had been hanging unresolved for more than forty years. The periodic demonstrations and disruptions by Tibetans in India were a direct consequence of this lingering problem. Such conflicts carried serious potential for further escalation if nothing was done to resolve it. He also wrote about the recent demonstrations in Delhi, which had culminated in the tragic self-immolation of a Tibetan youth protesting against the official visit of a senior Chinese leader to India. He said it was wrong to treat such events as isolated or minor incidents, since they were connected directly to an ongoing political problem and would only get worse if the problem was not seriously addressed.

The Dalai Lama had already declared his willingness to negotiate with the Chinese government if only they would accept the principle of genuine autonomy for Tibet. The Chinese, for their part, had also periodically expressed their willingness to open talks with the Dalai Lama, on the condition that he refrained from calling for Tibetan independence. So, in his letter Rinpoche wrote that his own well thought out opinion was that it would be in the best interest of both China and Tibet to find a solution to the Tibetan question while the present Dalai Lama's Middle Way (Madhyamika Marg) policy still held sway among the Tibetan populace. He also expressed his dismay that although the official Chinese position and the Dalai Lama's own views could hardly converge any further, there was no positive development towards a high-level and substantial meeting. Therefore, Rinpoche urged the Government of India to take a more active role than just a mediator between the two.

In response to this letter, Bakula Rinpoche received a letter dated June 12, 1998, from Mr. K. Raghunath, Foreign Secretary, Ministry of External Affairs, Government of India. The Foreign Secretary agreed with Rinpoche's opinion that the issue was not one of "playing the Tibet card". However, he felt that since the Chinese had never accepted India's neutrality on this issue, and often accused India of collusion with the Dalai Lama and anti-Chinese elements, they would be unlikely to accept Indian mediation. He, therefore, felt that further discussions on the matter were required and that India would have to wait for an opportune time to raise this issue with the Chinese. The letter gave some grounds for the hope that India might soon step up and address this issue, but unfortunately, there was no further movement on the proposal.

PART VIII

The Final Years

Fifty-eight

Atal Bihari Vajpayee: An Old Friend

As mentioned above, while remaining loyal to Congress Party ideology, Rinpoche had always maintained a very cordial relationship with leaders of other political parties. Atal Bihari Vajpayee was from the opposition BJP. But they held each other in great esteem. They were together in the Lok Sabha and over the years developed a very close relationship. Going back, there were also other senior leaders in the Saffron party such as Balraj Madhok, Dr. Syama Prasad Mookerjee and Prem Nath Dogra who worked for total integration of J&K with India and fought against the policies of National Conference led by Sheikh Abdullah.

In 1969, it was on Bakula Rinpoche's call that A.B. Vajpayee, then a member of parliament of Jana Sangh Party and an opposition leader in Parliament, visited Leh to support the ongoing Buddhist agitation in Ladakh. According to Tsering Samphel, a close associate of Bakula Rinpoche, the immediate results of this agitation were that the State Government agreed to settle Tibetan refugees on the Igoo-Phey canal command areas in Leh, introduction of Bhoti or Bodyig language in school curriculum and for creation of the posts for Bodhi teachers.

After the state of emergency declared by Prime Minister Indira Gandhi in 1977, the Jana Sangh merged with several other parties to form the Janata Party which defeated the Congress Party in year 1977 General elections. But three years in power, the Janata Party was dissolved in year 1980, and the members of the erstwhile Jana Sangh re-assemble to form the Bharatiya Janata Party (BJP) and made a humble beginning.

In year 2000, after a decade in Mongolia as India's ambassador, Rinpoche returned to India. On May 6, 2000, he called on Prime Minister Vajpayee at his residence in New Delhi. Prime Minister heaped praise for his outstanding achievements as a diplomat and recognized all the work done by Rinpoche in strengthening ties between the two countries and in re-building Buddhism in Mongolia after seven decades of communism. He described Rinpoche a role model for other diplomats to emulate.

There was another incident which demonstrated the close bond these two veteran leaders shared. In year 2003 Rinpoche had a relapse of Pneumonia in Mongolia and he had to be rushed to Beijing for treatment. There was no improvement in his condition and the doctors in Beijing feared for his life. At this critical juncture it was Rinpoche's old friend Prime Minister Vajpayee, who came to his rescue as explained in a later chapter.

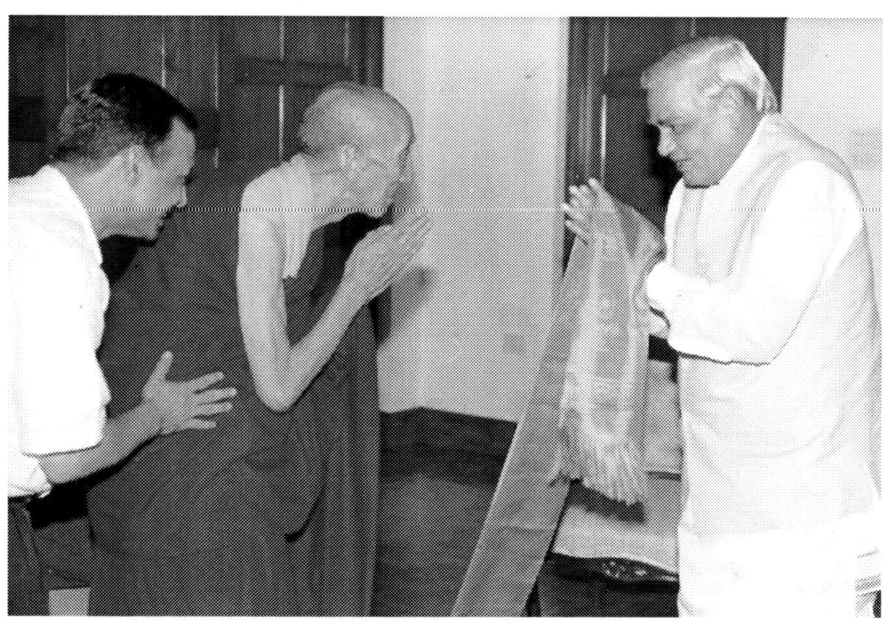

Rinpoche meeting Mr. Atal Bihari Vajpayee, Prime Minister of India in New Delhi (2000). Author is on the left

Fifty-nine

At the Buckingham Palace with Queen Elizabeth-II

As mentioned in an earlier chapter, for several years, Rinpoche had been in close contact with Prince Philip, husband of Her Majesty Queen Elizabeth-II of the United Kingdom. In 1993, the British Ambassador to Mongolia called Rinpoche to inform him of an official visit by Princess Anne (the Queen's daughter) to Mongolia. This was to be the first official visit by a member of the British royal family to the country. The British ambassador had been asked by Buckingham Palace to arrange a meeting with the Venerable Kushok Bakula Rinpoche, Ambassador of India. Later, when Rinpoche met Princess Anne at the British embassy, she passed on Prince Philip's warm greetings and said that she had heard a lot from her father about the great work Rinpoche was doing in Mongolia and elsewhere. Later in 1995, during the conference of the ARC (Alliance of Religions and Conservation), Rinpoche was put up for several days at the famous Windsor Castle.

In year 2002, Rinpoche received another formal invitation from Buckingham Palace. I accompanied Rinpoche on this journey too. Before the meeting, there was a lot of correspondence and instructions regarding Do's and Don'ts at the palace, the dress code for each occasion and other issues of social etiquette. But of course, such dress code issues were irrelevant to Rinpoche, since as a monk he would of course wear his usual robes and would not eat dinner. I myself had to don a black Band-gala suit, which is the official formal dress for Indian diplomats.

Buckingham Palace is the official residence of the Queen and has seven hundred and seventy-five rooms, including no less than nineteen staterooms for receiving visitors. It was on October 12, 2002, when Her Majesty Queen Elizabeth-II hosted a celebration dinner at Buckingham Palace, that Rinpoche met her for the first time. For me, it was a particularly special moment as I had never imagined myself going to Buckingham Palace, let alone having dinner there. We drove right up to the palace porch where Rinpoche was received by officials, and we were ushered inside. The exterior of the building was imposing, with big granite pillars, and the palace guards standing like statues in their unique uniforms. But inside, it was warmly lit and beautifully decorated. The long corridors, adorned with grand paintings and other works of art were mesmerizing. The beautiful thick carpets all around gave it a very quiet and tranquil atmosphere. The grand staircase with its painted ceilings was a thrill to see as was the courtyard as one enters the building. So many echoes of the Empire and times past.

The guests, which included religious leaders from different faiths, were received in the palace lounge by Her Majesty and her husband Prince Philip. Welcoming Rinpoche to the palace, she said that she had heard a great deal about Rinpoche from Prince Philip and was very happy to have met him at last. After a brief chat, we were escorted to the adjoining dining room. There was a large dining table with chairs on both sides. At the dinner table, Rinpoche was seated next to Her Majesty, on her right side. I was seated on a chair a little behind the two to do the translation. During the dinner, which lasted an hour and a half, Rinpoche and the Queen conversed throughout. Her Majesty apologized to Rinpoche for not being able to offer him dinner. Rinpoche said that was quite alright. He did not eat dinner because of his monk's vows. While others enjoyed the dinner, he only had a cup of Darjeeling tea.

At the beginning of the dinner, I was rather nervous, but as the conversation progressed, I felt quite at ease and was able do my duty as an interpreter without any hiccups. Her Majesty was interested to learn about the Buddhist perspective on the environment and also about current conditions in the Himalayas. She was also very curious about the peaceful transformation of Mongolia, as well as a host of other issues including Kashmir, Ladakh, Tibet and the state of Buddhism in China. During our conversation she also expressed her desire to meet the Dalai Lama, whom she held in very high esteem and regretted that she had not yet had the opportunity to meet him. Throughout the entire dinner, the Queen had spoken to no one but Rinpoche. After dinner, she apologized to the other dignitaries whom she had not been able to talk to, since she had been so engrossed in her conversation with Rinpoche.

Bakula Rinpoche, Prince Philip and other religious leaders at the Buckingham Palace, London (2002)

A few months later, Martin Palmer, who was the secretary-general of the Alliance of Religions and Conservation, informed Rinpoche that Her Majesty had expressed a desire to meet Rinpoche again, and another formal invitation was received by Rinpoche. However, this visit could not materialize due to Rinpoche's deteriorating health and instead her message of condolence was received after his passing away. This clearly is a testimony to the great admiration the Queen had for Rinpoche. **(Annexure 29)**

Sixty

Return to the Homeland

After a momentous decade in Mongolia, it was time for Rinpoche to return home in February of year 2000. He was 83 at that time. Far from being a retirement posting, his tenure as ambassador in Ulaanbaatar had been the most hectic and perhaps the most productive period of his long life. What made it so was his role in rebuilding Buddhism in Mongolia and Russia and in laying a solid foundation for India-Mongolia relations. After making his farewell calls to the Mongolian leadership and the diplomatic corps, Rinpoche left Mongolia. Being the longest serving ambassador, Rinpoche was also the head of the diplomatic corps in Ulaanbaatar. At the railway station in Ulaanbaatar a large number of people had gathered to bid farewell to him. Next day, we arrived in Beijing, where we stayed for two days. All of Rinpoche's disciples were eagerly awaiting his arrival. Then from Beijing, we flew to Hong Kong and onward to New Delhi.

Later that summer, Rinpoche visited Leh. The road from Leh airport to Leh town was lined on either side with thousands of people carrying *khadag* who had come out to welcome him home. Large number of people from all communities – Buddhists, Muslims and Christians also came to meet him at his residence at Samkar Monastery in Leh, where he spent a couple of months. Rinpoche was overwhelmed with emotion at being back in his native Ladakh after so long.

The IALS Conference in Leh

For many years, Bakula Rinpoche had been a patron of the International Association of Ladakh Studies (IALS), which had originally been created under the initiative of an Englishman named Henry Osmaston to bring together academic research related to the culture, history, language, literature, ecology and society of Ladakh and its neighbouring areas. In July 2003, the 11th colloquium of the IALS was co-hosted in Leh by the J&K Academy of Art, Culture and Languages headed by Nawang Tsering Shakspo. Rinpoche was invited to the inauguration of the conference at the government auditorium at the landmark Polo Ground in Leh. Mufti Mohammed Sayeed, Chief Minister of J&K, was the chief guest, and there were scholars from many different countries and different parts of India too. In a brief speech at the inauguration, Rinpoche recounted the transformation of Ladakh that he had witnessed over the course of his long and eventful life and emphasized an urgent need for greater efforts to be made in the future to save Ladakh's fragile culture and ecology. Taking advantage of the presence of the chief minister, Rinpoche asked him to sanction a new convention hall for Leh with proper equipment and facilities to replace the old Leh auditorium, which had been built in the 1970s and was now in a dilapidated condition. Chief Minister Mufti Sayeed was magnanimous in his response, and gave his approval for a new convention hall.

Rinpoche meeting with local elders of Muslim community at Samkar Monastery, Leh after his return from Mongolia (2000)

Prior to the conference, the Chief Minister had visited Rinpoche's residence at Samkar Gonpa to enquire about his health. He was accompanied, among others, by Nawang Rigzin Jora, the newly elected MLA-Leh, who has been inducted as a cabinet minister and other local leaders. Rinpoche already knew the Chief Minister Mufti Mohammed Sayeed well, as he had been a senior Congress Party leader and a former Union Home Minister, before he founded his own breakaway party called the People's Democratic Party (PDP).

After the usual exchange of pleasantries, Rinpoche thanked the chief minister for inducting Rigzin Jora, a young and dynamic youth leader as a minister at the cabinet rank. But never one to lose an opportunity, he, at the same time, requested Mufti Sahib to change Rigzin Jora's cabinet portfolio from Science and Technology to some other department where he could contribute more to the development of Ladakh region. This had been a spontaneous request from Rinpoche which took Rigzin Jora by surprise. Since I was translating for Rinpoche (as he was speaking mostly in Ladakhi), Rigzin Jora intervened to ask me not to translate that portion (the spontaneous request) of what Rinpoche had said relating to him. I was in a dilemma and did not know what to do. Mufti Sahib could see my dilemma. This piqued his curiosity and asked me what had happened. So, I told him Rinpoche's wish, while making clear that the request came only from Rinpoche. Mufti Sahib was amused and reassured Rinpoche that he would look into the matter. Rigzin Jora has held ministerial positions in successive J&K governments and contributed to the development of the region.

Rinpoche also pleaded with the Chief Minister to pay attention to the plight of the people of Zanskar; to allocate more seats for them in the proposed LAHDC, Kargil and reiterated the demand of the people of Zanskar to declare Zanskar a separate district.

Meeting with the Home Minister

Despite his advanced age, he never ceased to work for the benefit of others, and in that sense, Rinpoche never retired. For example, in the summer of 2002, when India's Home Minister Mr. L.K. Advani visited Leh, Rinpoche was not in good health. But all the same he went to meet the Union Minister at the ITBP guest at Choglamsar. Incidentally it was Mr. Advani who, during one of his earlier visits to Leh, had discovered that the river overlooking the guest house at Choglamsar, was actually the upper reaches of the Indus river. Being a Sindhi himself, he was emotionally attached to this river and subsequently initiated a festival called the "Sindhu Darshan" which is now held in Leh every year.

In a wide-ranging discussion, Rinpoche pleaded with Mr. Advani to engage in a serious dialogue with the leadership in Ladakh over their long-standing demand for Union Territory (UT) status. Rinpoche conveyed to him his bitter disappointment at the lackluster attitude of successive central governments in this regard. He told the Home Minister that he had been effectively coerced by the Indian leadership not to press on this demand, on the grounds that it would weaken India's position in J&K, since such a move would no doubt be vigorously and vociferously opposed by the various factions in J&K. On the other hand, as Rinpoche argued that UT status for Ladakh would actually strengthen the Centre's hand, not weaken it. After all, he reminded the Home Minister that Pakistan had brought the territories of Pakistan occupied Kashmir (POK) under its control, while the Indian government continued to hesitate about doing the same in Ladakh – despite the overwhelming support of the people there for such a status.

Rinpoche impressed upon Advani that the time had now come for the Government of India to put this issue back on the table. The Home Minister trotted out a well-worn response about needing to build consensus on the matter. For Rinpoche, it was a constant source of wonder that – in India, even while supporting, the people at the highest positions of government would still find reasons not to do it.

President APJ Abdul Kalam visits Pethub Monastery

Dr. APJ Abdul Kalam, popularly known as the 'People's President', visited Leh on June 27, 2003. Keeping his tryst with the frontier region of Ladakh, the President also visited Pethub Monastery to meet Bakula Rinpoche. Both the leaders had a passionate conversation and expressed their views on varied subjects including spirituality, peace and development. I was present in the meeting translating for Rinpoche. After pleasantries and exchange of

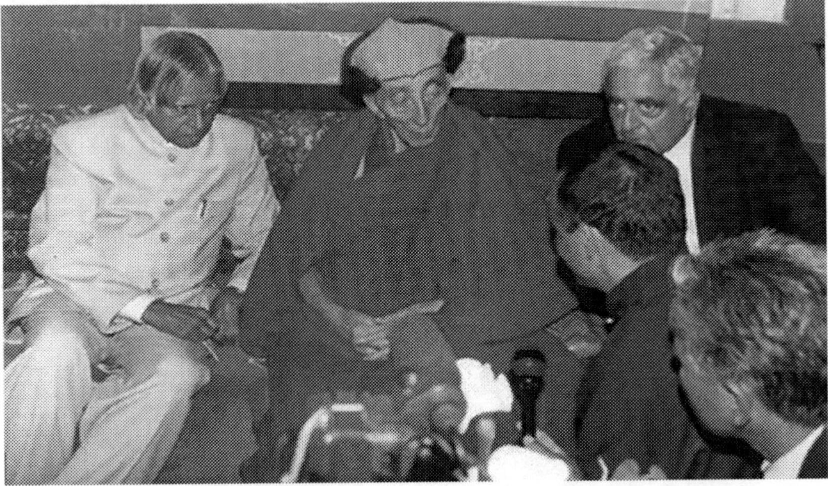

Dr. A.P.J. Abdul Kalam, President of India, Bakula Rinpoche and Mufti Mohammed Sayeed, Chief Minister of J&K, Leh. Author is seen translating the conversation. (2003)

gifts, Dr. Kalam applauded Rinpoche's role in building a new Ladakh and also recalled his contributions to nation building and friendship with other countries. He also appreciated his role as ambassador of India to Mongolia. After the meeting, the President participated in the prayer ceremony in the main assembly hall of Pethub monastery and paid his homage to the statue of Lord Buddha. The President was accompanied by the state Governor, Mr. S.K. Sinha, and Chief Minister Mufti Mohammed Sayeed and other dignitaries.

The Dalai Lama Pays a Visit to ailing Rinpoche

In the summer of year 2002, construction of the new residence for Bakula Rinpoche at Samkar Monastery, was completed. The old residence was by then had become over one hundred years old and had a very steep staircase which made it impossible for Rinpoche to climb. So, Gelong Thupstan Targyas, Rinpoche's *Chagzot* (Manager) and his longtime assistant, decided to construct a new residence. Rinpoche moved into the new residence and stayed there convalescing, as by now his health was very fragile.

On August 13, 2003, while Rinpoche was recuperating there, the 14th Dalai Lama paid a holy visit at this new residence at Samkar. He spent about two hours with Rinpoche. For Rinpoche it was an unbounded joy to have His Holiness by his side. A few days later, Rinpoche had another audience with the Dalai Lama at Zhive-tsal, his residence at Choglamsar. This was to be their last meeting. The Dalai Lama perhaps having a premonition about the inevitability of the Samsaric cycle and Rinpoche's imminent end, gave his old friend and spiritual brother a special *Khadag* as a token of his respect and appreciation for everything that Bakula Rinpoche had done over a long period of six decades.

The Last Meeting with the Dalai Lama at Leh.
The author is standing behind Rinpoche (2003)

Sixty-one

Recounting the Final Days

Bakula Rinpoche's motive had always been crystal clear, and it was this clarity that enabled him time and again to rise to the challenges that presented themselves before him, without ever losing heart. This was evident in the way events unfolded during the final months and days of his life. It was as if he had planned everything beforehand.

August of year 2003 was a very difficult month. Rinpoche had again come down with pneumonia in Leh. When his condition did not improve, even after sustained medication, he was airlifted to New Delhi. He was admitted at the Sitaram Bhartia Institute under the care of the eminent physician Dr. J.S. Guleria. There, his condition improved gradually and later he was discharged from the hospital. At that time, it was hot and humid in New Delhi. Travelling back to Leh in his condition was not an option because of the high altitude and the lack of high-caliber medical facilities there. Rinpoche loved Mongolia and had a strong urge to go there and spend some time at his monastery. However, he couldn't go as his health was not robust enough to undertake such a long journey. Yet, he kept on persisting and insisting on going there leaving me in a quandary as to what I should do. It was at this juncture that I consulted Rizong Sras Rinpoche for his advice. He instructed me to follow Bakula Rinpoche's own wish. And so, we did. As we had done so many times together before, we flew via Hong Kong and Beijing, to Ulaanbaatar. The weather in Mongolia at that time was fine, and Rinpoche's condition seemed to start improving day by day.

Unfortunately, after two months or so in Ulaanbaatar, he had a relapse of pulmonary pneumonia. When his condition did not improve after treatment, he was flown to Beijing where arrangements were made for him at Capital Hospital, reputed to be one of the best in the city. When we flew into Beijing, many of Rinpoche's students as well as Col. Prasad, Military Attaché from the Indian embassy in Beijing was at the airport to receive us and take him directly to the hospital. For three weeks Rinpoche was under intensive care, but his condition remained unchanged. Finally, the doctors expressed their helplessness, and advised us to take Rinpoche back to New Delhi immediately. Rinchen Wangmo, my wife was also with us throughout this difficult period.

By now, Rinpoche had become extremely weak, and it was impossible for him to take a regular commercial flight. Time was running out and we were in a desperate situation. It was then, that we learnt about the air ambulance service. I went to the Indian Embassy in Beijing to apprise Ambassador about the situation. But I refrained from seeking any financial help from him. Moreover, Rinpoche had already relinquished his ambassadorial post and held no official position at the time, so he would not be entitled to reimbursement from the government exchequer.

The ambassador immediately called the Prime Minister's office in New Delhi to apprise them of the situation. He had been put through to Prime Minister Atal Bihari Vajpayee himself, who directed him to provide whatever assistance was needed for Rinpoche's treatment and travel, including the air ambulance. He also told me that a special room had been set aside for Rinpoche at the All India Institute of Medical Sciences (AIIMS) in New Delhi.

October 10, 2003, was a gloomy day in Beijing. There was a heavy downpour. When we reached Beijing airport, rain falling from the sky seemed to echo the tears pouring from eyes of Rinpoche's many disciples, who had come to the airport to bid what we all feared was a final farewell to their master. Accompanied by a Bolivian doctor, an Australian nurse and Ms. Jiang QiQi, a disciple of Rinpoche, we left Beijing in an executive aircraft which had been converted into an air ambulance. The flight made a single stop at Kunming, China to refuel and then the journey continued. Throughout the flight, Rinpoche's condition remained stable, and he was actually quite cheerful, though very weak. By the time we landed in New Delhi, it was late in the night. An ambulance was waiting at the airport which took us directly to AIIMS. With Rinpoche safely back in India I was able to heave a sigh of relief, a sentiment that was shared by others. After a brief stay at AIIMS, Rinpoche was then shifted to the Sitaram Bhartia Institute, where he had previously been successfully treated by Dr. J.S. Guleria.

In the hospital, Rinpoche remained calm throughout, spending most of his time in prayer. He never complained of any pain or discomfort. In order to help him rest, I would sometimes remove the *mala* (rosary) from his hand, but even then, in immobile state, he continued to murmur prayers with his fingers holding the oxygen pipe, in the same position as he had been holding the rosary.

Meanwhile, Rizong Rinpoche and several other monks from Pethub Monastery had come to New Delhi. There was some sudden improvement too in his condition. Doctors at the hospital were baffled by this unexpected recovery. A couple of days later, Rinpoche was feeling much better and requested the doctors to allow him to return to his residence, to which they agreed. Rinpoche was delighted to be back at his residence in New Delhi.

On the fateful evening of November 4, 2003, Rinpoche developed a breathing problem and was administered oxygen. Till late that night, Rizong Rinpoche stayed with Bakula Rinpoche in his room, leaving only at around 1 a.m., when Bakula Rinpoche was peacefully resting. I continued to stay by Rinpoche's side. On all other nights, Rinpoche would have woken me up for any help he needed. But that night there was no call at all.

I woke up around 4 a.m. and when I looked at Rinpoche, I saw something unusual about his condition. I rushed towards him, asking if he was all right. As before, he was in an upright sitting posture with rosary still in his hands, and his face calm. I called out to him, asking him if he is all right, and to my great relief he opened his eyes, looked at me and nodded. Then he closed his eyes again. Wondering what to do, I rushed to Rizong Rinpoche who was in the next room. He came immediately, checked his breath and asked all of us to leave the room. He sat down and opened his holy scriptures. After some time Rizong Rinpoche announced that his master was now in *samadhi* and that no one should disturb him for the next 48 hours.

It was early on Tuesday, November 4, 2003, when I had to perform the most painful task of my life to announce the Parinirvana of Bakula Rinpoche at the age of eighty-six. First of all, I called the Private Office of H.H. the Dalai Lama in Dharamshala. I then informed the authorities in New Delhi and in Leh. I also made a call to Mr. N. Enkhbayar, by now the Prime Minister of Mongolia. The news was flashed on TV and was reported also in newspapers of both India and Mongolia. Ladakh plunged into darkness of grief.

A few hours later, I received a call from the Prime Minister's Office that Mr. Atal Bihari Vajpayee had expressed his desire to visit Rinpoche's residence at Saket, New Delhi to pay a floral tribute. Police personnel were by now already camped outside Rinpoche's residence. I informed Rizong Rinpoche about the Prime Minister's intention. Rizong Rinpoche however, asked me to request the Prime Minister's Office to postpone the visit and instead come to the Kashmir House, New Delhi which I duly conveyed to the Prime Minister office.

For the next two days Rinpoche's mortal remains, or the *Kudung* as it is known honourifically, stayed untouched and undisturbed at his residence. Rizong Rinpoche asked me to check on his condition as now the mortal remains was to be taken to Kashmir House, New Delhi to enable people to pay their last respects. I, along with Lobzang Lundup, a monk of Pethub monastery, entered the room. We found that Rinpoche's body was unchanged and his face still had a kind of radiance. In fact, we sensed some pleasant smell emanating from it.

On November 6, 2003, after all the necessary religious rituals had been performed, Rinpoche's mortal remains was moved to J&K House, Prithviraj Road, New Delhi where a steady stream of highest dignitaries came to pay their last respect. These included Prime Minister Atal Bihari Vajpayee, Mrs. Sonia Gandhi, President of Indian National Congress, Lt. Gen. Sinha, Governor of J&K, Chief Minister Mufti Mohammed Sayeed, Vinod Khanna, Minister of State for External Affairs, as well as ambassadors from several countries and scores of other dignitaries and religious leaders of different faiths. A large number of Ladakhi and Tibetan residents in New Delhi also came. In the state of J&K, a day of mourning was declared. Floral wreaths were also laid on behalf of the President of India, the Prime Minister of Mongolia and other dignitaries.

Mr. Atal Bihari Vajpayee, Prime Minister of India paying floral tribute to the mortal remains of Bakula Rinpoche, New Delhi (2003)

On November 7, 2003, Rinpoche's mortal remains were carried from Palam Airport, New Delhi in a special Indian Air Force plane to Leh piloted by Wg. Cdr. Stanzin Thinles, a young Ladakhi air force officer and coordinated on the ground by Flt. Lt. Thsering Namgyal Shakspo. It traversed the Himalayas and landed at Leh, where a sea of grieving people was waiting. The entire ten kilometre route from the airport to Leh town was thronged with people, including hundreds of *jawans* of the Ladakh Scouts, all mourning the loss of their long-standing and inspirational leader who had shaped Ladakh's destiny for over half a century. It was a poignant sight. Even Buddhist monks, for whom life and death are too well-understood to mourn, were seen crying. The holy body was first taken to the Jokhang at Leh and from there to Pethub Monastery.

A special plane of Indian Air Force lands at Leh airport with the mortal remains of Bakula Rinpoche

The final journey

The mortal remains of Bakula Rinpoche in Leh City to enable the general public to pay their last respects

An emotional moment. Women and children holding their tears

The people of Ladakh lined-up to mourn the passing away of their beloved leader

At the Leh airport, Jawans of Ladakh Scouts lined up with Khadags in hand to pay their last respects to the mortal remains of Bakula Rinpoche

Mufti Mohammed Sayeed, Chief Minister of Jammu & Kashmir, arriving at Pethub Monastery to pay his respects

Mr. Ghulam Nabi Azad, Congress Party leader and former Chief Minister of Jammu and Kashmir, paying floral tributes

Rinpoches and high-ranking monks assembled for the last rites

Hiroshi Fujikura, Secretary General of Buddhist Summit, Japan reading out the Message from Dr. Kyuse Enshinjoh, President, Buddhist Summit, Japan

Sonam Wangchuk (author) reading out the condolence messages received from world leaders on the demise of Bakula Rinpoche

On November 16, 2003, the mortal remains of Bakula Rinpoche were consigned to flames on the hills above Pethub monastery with full state honours. The funeral service was led by Rizong Sras Rinpoche with over a thousand monks in attendance, representing all the monasteries of Ladakh. Rinpoches as well as Mr. Sanghpriya Gautam, Minister for Agro and Rural Industries, representing the Union Government, Mufti Mohammed Sayeed, Chief Minister of J&K and the special Envoy of the Dalai Lama were among those present. Columns of police personnel presented a guard of honour, and shots were fired in the air as a mark of respect, as the mortal remains of the 19th Bakula Rinpoche were consigned to flames amidst the chanting of prayers by monks and thick clouds fragrant of juniper smoke. Bakula Rinpoche, the savior of poor Ladakhis and a spiritual teacher of the faithful in so many countries had departed for his heavenly abode. It was the end of an era.

Expressing his deep sadness on the passing away of Bakula Rinpoche, H.H. the 14th Dalai Lama wrote in his condolence message: "...After having received the teachings of Sutra and Tantra from many renowned teachers, and putting them into practice in his daily life, he worked for the people of Ladakh and Mongolia to help grow a firm seed of enlightenment in their mind. He also worked for the preservation, dissemination and restoration of precious teachings of Buddha Shakyamuni. Rinpoche held highly respectable posts during which he offered many services that received appreciation from the Government and people of India. The assistance rendered to Tibetans by him during the difficult times is to be remembered with gratitude. The passing away of Bakula Rinpoche is a great loss to all. May the reincarnation appear soon, by the power of his own prayers and the faith of devotees, to take over the responsibilities of Dharma activities for the sake of all sentient beings."[1]

Atal Bihari Vajpayee, Prime Minister of India, while offering his condolence wrote: "...In the passing away of the Most Venerable Kushok Bakula, an eminent Buddhist scholar, a saint, a guide and a source of inspiration for all, is lost. It is difficult to imagine Ladakh without Kushok Bakula ji."[2]

Recalling her close relations with Bakula Rinpoche, President of Congress Party Mrs. Sonia Gandhi, wrote: "...The entire country has been saddened by the death of Kushok Bakula ji. There has been grief in many other countries as well at his passing away. He had a very close association with my family, starting with India's first Prime Minister Jawaharlal Nehru himself. Indira Gandhi and Rajiv Gandhi had profound respect and regard for him. His death was, therefore, a personal loss for me. But much more than that, Kushok Bakula ji was a great scholar acknowledged for his erudition, deep learning and for his wonderful sense of compassion. Throughout his long and distinguished career at the state, national and international levels, Bakula Rinpoche epitomized and upheld the glorious traditions of India's religious diversity and secular heritage. May we all continue to be inspired by his thoughts, by his teachings and indeed by his life."[3]

Mr. N. Enkhbayar, Prime Minister of Mongolia sent a special emissary to attend the last rites of Bakula Rinpoche. He also sent his condolence which said: "...We recall his most active and dynamic work in Mongolia. For me personally, it was a privilege to be his disciple and have the opportunity to work with him. Elchin Bagsh (Ambassador Teacher) Bakula Rinpoche will always remain in our hearts as a great friend of Mongolia."

In her condolence message Her Majesty Queen Elizabeth II wrote: "...I am very sad to learn about the passing away of Sri Kushok Bakula and to say how fondly I recall our most interesting discussions at London in 2002. I know also how significant a part Sri Kushok Bakula played in the Alliance of Religions and Conservation's (ARC) work and his wisdom and counsel will be sorely missed."[4]

In 2004, a memorial stupa dedicated to Rinpoche was completed and enshrined at Pethub Monastery, Ladakh. A grand consecration ceremony was attended by hundreds of monks from across Ladakh and guests from many countries. On June 10, 2004, Dr. Manmohan Singh, Prime Minister of India visited Leh to rename Leh airport as "Kushok Bakula Rinpoche

Dr. Manmohan Singh, Prime Minister of India renaming Leh Airport after Kushok Bakula Rinpoche. Leh (2004)

Airport". Speaking on the occasion he said: "In doing so [dedicating this airport], we pay tribute to the memory of the Most Venerable Kushok Bakula Rinpoche, the architect of modern Ladakh. Venerable Kushok Bakula was a noble saint, a teacher, a patriot, a beloved leader, a true Buddhist and, above all, a great Indian. It is only appropriate that we name this airport, the link between the high Himalayas and the world below, after this son of Ladakh and this man of God... Bakula Rinpoche, as he was widely known, was a unique Lama of great talent and exceptional gifts. He was revered for his erudition, his dedication to the education of a new generation, his gentle humility and his wisdom and compassion."

In the Mongolian capital Ulaanbaatar, the municipal authorities renamed the road leading to Pethub Monastery as "Bakula Rinpoche Road" in 2008. A grand silver stupa weighing 160 kgs., donated by the people of Mongolia and made by Lama Purevbat, was installed at Pethub Monastery.

On June 30, 2014, Nobel Laureate the 14th Dalai Lama today unveiled the statue of 19th Kushok Bakula Rinpoche at the newly created 19th Bakula Memorial Park near Leh Airport. This statue was later moved to Pethub (Spituk) village community Hall.

On October 21, 2014 Mr. Raman Bhalla, Minister for Housing and Mr. Nawang Rigzin Jora, Minister for Urban Development, Government of J&K renamed the main road leading to Jammu City Railway Station after the 19th Bakula Rinpoche.

Narendra Modi, Prime Minister of India addressing the Mongolian Parliament

HH The 14th Dalai Lama unveiling the statue of Bakula Rinpoche in Leh (2014)

Mr. Raman Bhalla, Minister for Housing and Mr. Nawang Rigzin Jora, Minister for Urban Development, Government of J&K after naming a Road in Jammu City after Bakula Rinpoce (2014)

Addressing the Mongolian Parliament on May 17, 2015, Prime Minister Narendra Modi stated "...Today India and Mongolia are telling the world that the bonds of hearts and minds have the strength to overcome the barrier of distance. It lives through the work of Kushok Bakula Rinpoche, India's Ambassador here from 1990–2000. The Pethub Monastery that he established here will be an enduring symbol of our links."

In Ladakh, Bakula Rinpoche had remained a father-figure to all, for his tireless work in both the political and religious spheres. Followers of different Buddhist traditions as well as other communities were united in their recognition of his unshakable integrity and dedication. Even those few people, who were his political opponents, they would vouch for his integrity. Thanks to his leadership, post-independence Ladakh, could maintain a united front throughout its long and arduous struggle to achieve the recognition it deserves. It was Rinpoche's wish that the people of Ladakh remain united in the political landscape as well as in the society in general, so that they are able to overcome the obstacles and in preserving and safeguarding their cultural identity.

NOTES

1. Bakula Rinpoche – A Tribute (2004).
2. Ibid.
3. Bakula Rinpoche – A Tribute (2004).
4. Ibid.

EPILOGUE

Sixty-two

Appearance of the Mongoose (Neola)

On the 4th day following the last rites, Rizong Sras Rinpoche, along with many monks and a large gathering of devoted laypeople, gathered to take part in a ceremony to collect Bakula Rinpoche's ashes. There were elaborate prayer rituals amidst thick and fragrant juniper smoke. A close watch was being maintained to observe any signs, which might help finding Bakula Arhat's next reincarnation. Rizong Sras Rinpoche and Jampa Rinpoche from Drepung Losaling oversaw the ceremony. Earlier we had seen them placing an enclosed metal-cover over sand inside the funeral pyre. Then sometime later, the pagoda-shaped pyre was carefully opened to see if any special signs had appeared, as is customary after the passing away of high incarnate lamas. Inside, under the metal cover, was a clearly visible impression of footprints. The direction of these impressions was interpreted as indicating the direction in which the next incarnation would be found.

Until then, it had been a clear sunny day, but suddenly a small cloud appeared in the sky and just as Rizong Rinpoche and other monks were collecting the holy ashes from the pyre, snow started to fall. This was extra-ordinary. For everyone present there, this was no ordinary snowfall, but rather a blessing from the heavens. Thick petals of snow covered the area. Strangely, this snowfall was confined only to the area where the ceremony was taking place, while nearby it remained dry, and the sky was clear.

Many more surprises were in store. Rizong Rinpoche and the monks had just left the courtyard of Pethub Monastery bearing the vase containing the holy ashes. Suddenly one monk clearly saw a *neola* (mongoose) appear under the platform where Bakula Rinpoche normally sat during the monastery's annual Gustor festival. This sighting of a *neola* was for us truly miraculous and joyous, since the mongoose is the particular symbol of Arhat

Bakula, as seen in all the *thangkas* and statues depicting him. Never before had anyone seen a *neola* in the area. It was a very strange phenomenon and filled everyone with awe. The *neola* appeared calm and was not afraid of the people looking at it with intense curiosity. Immediately, Rizong Rinpoche, who had gone upstairs, was informed. He came down and he too saw the *neola*. This was no ordinary phenomenon and Rizong Rinpoche in a lighthearted way commented that Arhat Bakula, who is normally depicted holding the mongoose, has now released it.

There were more surprises to come. The next day, Tharchin Malik, the monk in charge of Bakula Rinpoche's personal rooms at Pethub Monastery, was amazed to see the *Neola* leisurely walking around in Rinpoche's rooms. The animal was roaming around everywhere and also onto Rinpoche's bed, where it rummaged around in Rinpoche's Ku-dam (a gown-like dress for monks). It accepted food offered by Lama Tharchin Malik and seemed completely unafraid of the curious people around. The news spread fast and people from all over the area started to come to witness this unusual phenomenon. The *Neola* was there in the monastery for over a month. In the meantime, a statue of Bakula Rinpoche was installed in the monastery. But on a day when the consecration prayer for the holy statue was performed, the *Neola* mysteriously disappeared and was never to be seen again.

Mysterious appearance of a Neola (symbol of Arhat Bakula) at Pethub Monastery, Ladakh (2003)

In December 2003, we had an audience with HH the Dalai Lama at his residence in Dharamshala and made a fervent appeal to His Holiness to pray for the swift return of Bakula Rinpoche's reincarnation and also requested him to compose a special prayer. His Holiness accepted the request and later composed a prayer which was regularly read in various Monasteries in Ladakh and Mongolia. During the course of this meeting, the Dalai Lama praised the notable accomplishments of Bakula Rinpoche in his life and recalled his personal association with him. He praised Rinpoche's humility and simplicity in life and dedication to the service of Dharma. The Dalai Lama said that among Rinpoche's many facets, he considered the rôle he played in the development of Ladakh and rebuilding Buddhism in Mongolia and his ability to reach people under communism in the Soviet Union and Communist China, most notable. He felt that the legacy of Bakula Rinpoche and his work should be carried forward.

Sixty-three

Celebrating the Birth Centenary of Bakula Rinpoche

The test of a truly great man is his humility, and Bakula Rinpoche embodied this virtue. However, as his birth centenary approached, there was a growing sense that more should be done to honour the contributions of a person who had redefined the art of building a harmonious society. In response, an Organising Committee was formed to celebrate Bakula Rinpoche's birth centenary.

On December 24, 2017, I had the privilege of meeting Shri Narendra Modi, the Hon'ble Prime Minister of India, at Parliament House in New Delhi. On behalf of the Birth Centenary Celebration Committee, I invited him to grace the concluding celebration of Rinpoche's birth centenary, scheduled for May 19, 2018, in Leh. The Prime Minister graciously accepted the invitation and attended the ceremony.

As a prelude to the year-long celebrations, an International Conference titled "Bakula Rinpoche: A Saint and Statesman" was held in Leh from October 1-3, 2016. It was organised by the Indian Council of Cultural Relations (ICCR), the conference featured delegates from 15 countries who presented papers on the life and works of Bakula Rinpoche. The conference was inaugurated by Mr. Salman Haider, former Foreign Secretary of India.

The main event of the Birth Centenary celebrations was organised by the Ladakh Autonomous Hill Development Council (LAHDC) and commenced on May 19, 2017, at the historic Polo Ground in Leh. The celebration included a vibrant cultural programme, where school children presented tableaus depicting Rinpoche's life. Zagd-Ochir Sumiyabazar, a Mongolian singer captivated the audience with traditional long songs, an important aspect of Mongolia's musical heritage.

The Dalai Lama releasing the author's book on Bakula Rinpoche at Dharamshala (2018)

After the centenary celebrations, different events were also organised to celebrate the life and work of Bakula Rinpoche:

1) On March 31, 2018, His Holiness the Dalai Lama released first edition of my book, "Kushok Bakula Rinpoche: The Architect of Modern Ladakh," in Dharamshala. The book has been translated into several languages. The Embassy of India, Moscow published the book in Russian, and it was officially released during a ceremony held in Moscow in 2021. Similarly, in 2022, a ceremony took place at the Ministry of Foreign Relations, Government of Mongolia, in Ulaanbaatar to mark the release of the Mongolian edition of the book. A commemorative stamp issued by Mongol Post was also released on that day.
2) In Mongolia, where Bakula Rinpoche spent 10 crucial years and is revered as 'Elchin Bagsh' (Ambassador-Teacher), commemorative events were organised. On April 25, 2018, a ceremony was organised by the Ministry of Foreign Relations in Ulaanbaatar, attended among others by Mrs. Sushma Swaraj, India's Minister for External Affairs, and Mr. D. Tsogtbaatar, Mongolia's Minister for Foreign Affairs.
3) In New Delhi, a commemorative function took place in November 2018 at Mavalankar Hall, with Smt. Sumitra Mahajan, Speaker of Lok Sabha, serving as the Chief Guest. Special events were also organised in over 40 universities across India.

4) On August 5, 2021, a Hindi version of the book, "**एक युग प्रवर्तक भिक्षु - कुशक बकुला रिन्पोछे - एक जीवनी**," translated by Mr. Nitin Vaidya and published by the National Book Trust, New Delhi, was released at the Assembly Hall of the LAHDC, Leh, by Adv. Tashi Gyalson, Chairman and CEC of the Ladakh Autonomous Hill Development Council, Leh.
5) A bronze bust of Bakula Rinpoche was installed at the LAHDC Secretariat in Leh on August 5, 2021, coinciding with the anniversary of Bakula Rinpoche laying the foundation stone of the building.
6) On May 19, 2025, a 12-foot bronze statue of Bakula Rinpoche, sculpted by the renowned artist Ram Sutar, was unveiled at the 'Bakula Rinpoche Memorial Park' Leh, Ladakh. Sh. Kiren Rjijiju, Union Minister for Parliamentary Affairs and Minority Affairs was the Chief Guest. Dr. (Brig) B.D. Mishra, Lt. Governor of Ladakh, Sh. Tashi Gyalson, Chairman & CEC, LAHDC, Leh, H.E. Mr. Dambajav Ganbold, Ambassador of Mongolia to India, Kyabje Drukpa Thuksey Rinpoche and a large number of monks and people from across Ladakh, were also present on this joyous occasion.

   Incidentally, on the same day, another statue of Bakula Rinpoche was installed at the Chenrezig Temple in the Gandan Thegchenling Monastery, Ulaanbaatar, the Centre of Mongolian Buddhists.

His Legacy and Inspiration

The centenary celebrations culminated on May 19, 2018, in Leh, where Prime Minister Narendra Modi paid a heartfelt tribute to Bakula Rinpoche for his service to the nation. The Prime Minister's address highlighted Rinpoche's contributions to Ladakh, India, and the world.

Bakula Rinpoche is also deeply respected by Russian Buddhists for his pivotal role in revitalising Buddhism in the Soviet Union and later in Russia. In 2021, at the request of Russian Buddhists from Moscow, St. Petersburg, Kalmykia, Tuva, Irkutsk, and Buryatia, the Government of India gifted ten bronze statues of Bakula Rinpoche to various Russian republics.

The legendary Bakula Rinpoche, with his compassion, courage, and fortitude, continues to inspire people worldwide. Like the Arhat Bakula, who is associated with granting the requisites for understanding the Buddha's teachings, the 19th Bakula Rinpoche, Lobzang Thupstan Chognor, manifested qualities of love, wisdom, and compassion that brought joy and enlightenment to countless lives.

May his life and teachings continue to inspire generations to come.

Birth Centenary celebrations organized by the Ladakh Autonomous Hill Development Council (LAHDC), Leh. May 19, 2017

Birth Centenary celebrations organized by the Ladakh Autonomous Hill Development Council (LAHDC), Leh. May 19, 2017

Mrs. Sushma Swaraj, Minister of External Affairs at the Birth centenary celebration organized by the Ministry of Foreign Relations of Mongolia, Ulaanbaatar (2018)

Shri Narendra Modi, Prime Minister of India offering tribute to Bakula Rinpoche on his birth centenary, Leh (2018)

Shri Om Birla, Speaker, Lok Sabha offering floral tribute to Rinpoche's bust at LAHDC, Leh (2021)

Release of the Book in Russian language oraganised by the Embassy of India, Moscow. Also seen in picture: Alikber K. Alikberov, Suresh Soni, Amb. Venkatesh Verma, Dr. Sachidanand Joshi, Shakti Sinha, Sonam Wangchuk and Aashish Bhave (2021)

Release of Book in Mongolian language in Ulaanbaatar. Also seen: Amb. MP Singh, State Secretary, MFR, Bakula Rinpoche, Kiren Rijiju, N. Enkhbayar, Ts. Gombosuren, D. Choijamts, Director, Mongol Post and Sonam Wangchuk (2022)

Author with the Director, Mongol Post at the ceremony to release the commemorative stamp (2022)

Mr. N. Enkhbayar, former President of Mongolia, Amb. M.P. Singh, Mr. Kiren Rijiju, Union Law Minister, Secretary of State, Ministry of Foreign Relations, Khambolama D. Choujams, Director, Mongol Post at the ceremony marking the release of Postal stamp (2022)

Book in Hindi released by Adv. Tashi Gyalson, CEC, LAHDC and Togdan Rinpoche at Leh at Leh (2021)

A group photo after the unveiling of Bakula Rinpoche's Statue at the LAHDC, Leh and the release of the book in Hindi

12 ft. Bronze statue at the Kushok Bakula Rinpoche Memorial Park at Leh, Ladakh.

(R to L) Release of the book ***"Kushok Bakula Rinpoche: The Architect of Modern Ladakh – Life and Times"*** *published by* ***Pentagon Press LLP, New Delhi.*** *(L to R) Sh. Sonam Wangchuk Shakspo (author), Sh. Tashi Gyalson, Chairman & CEC, LAHDC, Leh, Amb. Dambajav Ganbold, Ambassador of Mongolia to India, Dr. (Brig.) B.D. Mishra, Lt. Governor of UT Ladakh, Sh. Kiren Rijiju, Union Minister for Parliamentary Affairs & Minority Affairs, Kyabje Drukpa Thuksey Rinpoche, Kyabje Urgyan Rinpoche and Geshe Lobzang Wangchuk, Chogzhi-lama, Pethub Monastery.*

ANNEXURES

Annexure 1

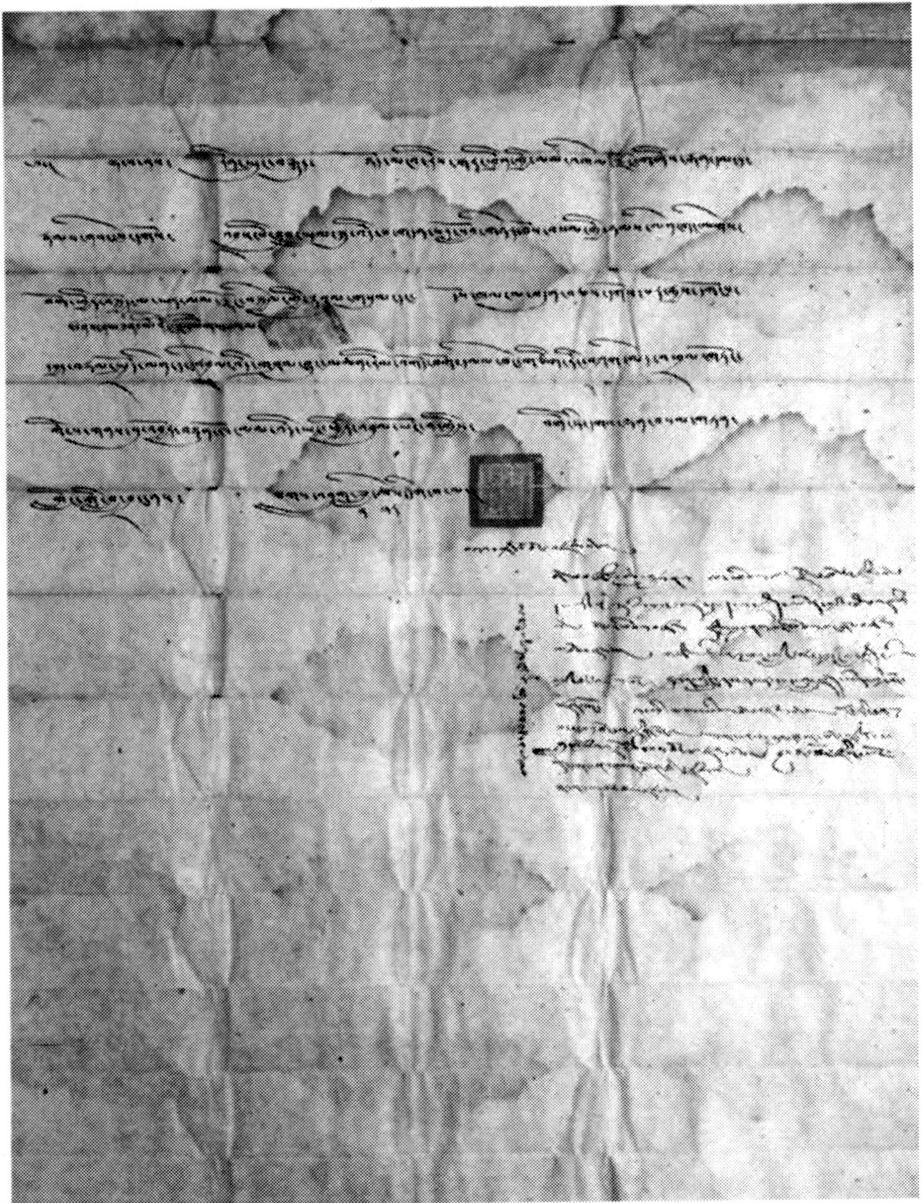

Annexure 2

(Translation of Bodhi Letter)

To,

The Hon'ble Pt. Jawahar Lal Nehru

It is a matter of great pleasure that you are quite hale and hearty. Due to the splendid achievements and adventures of Indian military officers like Col. Hari Chand, etc. the enemy has been defeated and made to flee. The ryots have become fearless and happy and the state is in full bloom. We were very glad to know that you would come to this desert next year and we will thus get the opportunity of having your 'darshan'. We, therefore, request you to be kind enough to come to this deserted state without fail and see all the renowned and holy places. May God provide us this auspicious opportunity in very near future and may peace be established soon.

Yours truly,

Sd/

(Gyalsras Bakula)
Head Lama Spituk Ganpa Tehsil Leh, Ladakh

Annexure 3

प्रधानमंत्री

ता. 29–03–1949

प्रिय मित्र,

आपका पत्र मेजर हरिचंद द्वारा मिला। बड़ी प्रसन्नता हुई। हिंद सेना की जो आपने प्रशंसा की है उसके लिए हार्दिक धन्यवाद।

आपके सुंदर और पवित्र देश जाने की मेरी बड़ी इच्छा है और आशा है कि अवकाश मिलने पर यह इच्छा पूरी हो सकेगी।

आपका शुभचिंतक

(जवाहर लाल नेहरू)

प्रधान लामा ग्यास शास बकुला,
पेतुप-गोनपा,
तहसील लेह, लद्दाख

Unofficial Translation

Prime Minister

29-03-1949

Dear friend,

Received your letter sent through Major Hari Chand. It was heartening to read your letter. I sincerely thank you for the words of praise for the Indian Army.

I have a strong desire to visit your beautiful and holy country and I do hope that I shall have the opportunity and be able to fulfill this wish.

Yours Sincerely,
(Jawaharlal Nehru)

Head Lama Gyalsras Bakula,
Pethub Gonpa, Tehsil, Leh, Ladakh.

Annexure 4

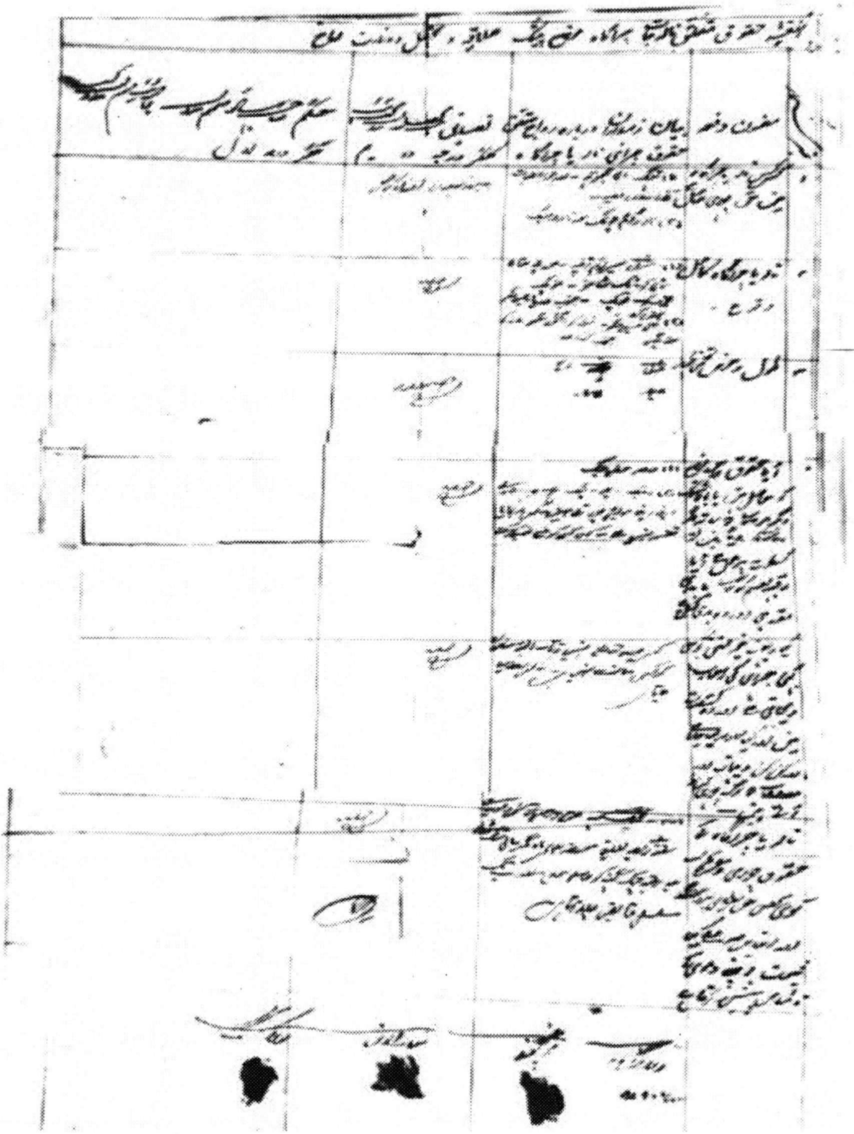

Revenue records about the airport land belonging to Pethub Monastery.

Annexure 5

Text of speech made in the State Assembly on May 12, 1952. Mr. Speaker and Hon'ble members.

The Budget Estimates, presented by the Finance Minister evoked varied reactions among the members of this House. My own reaction, I must say clearly, can hardly be called pleasant. The budget estimates, if I describe them lucidly, are extremely disappointing for us, the unfortunate people of Ladakh who are professedly the most backward and woefully poor in the whole State. If the estimate is read from one end to the other, no mention of Ladakh is found anywhere in it. What to speak of the economic and other requirements of Ladakh, which being so urgent and necessary; merit prompt attention for their fulfillment? No mention is found with regard to education facilities in Ladakh. Similar is the case with the expansion of elementary education in the area, which depicts the beckoning and crying picture of the District. The Frontier Scholarships granted to the students of elementary, secondary and college in the district by the erstwhile government have been withdrawn with a stroke of a pen by the present government. The old government had sanctioned grants in aid to three primary schools run by Shias, Sunnis and Buddhists communities, which the present government withdrew. The Bodhi language is being taught in high schools. But no books have been published for the same and the subject is being taught to the students of middle and high schools without any books. No budget has been provided for preparation and publication of such books. In the schools, Urdu, which is a foreign language for our children, is still the medium of instruction. This unnatural medium of instruction proves to be a great stumbling block in the educational development of our children. But no provision for the development of Bodhi in our area has been made in the Education budget. These essential requirements have been totally ignored even though it is crystal clear to all that so far, our area has not been able to produce not more than one dozen matriculates or half a dozen graduates. Technical education, which is making great strides in J&K, does not exist even nominally in our area.

No arrangement for the rehabilitation of the Zanskar refugees has been shown in the budget in spite of the fact that these helpless people have been wandering like beggars in the Kullu Valley. Dozens of these wandering refugees have succumbed to death. Nor is there any mention in the budget about the repairs of the religious places (Gonpas), which have suffered tremendous damage at the hands of the Pakistani tribal raiders. Apathy does not end here. The economic development of our area has not come to the thought of budget makers because there is no mention of it even by mistake in the budget. We were confident that the Cooperative, Panchayati and Rural Development programmes would include our neglected area as well in their sphere of activities. But alas, all these aspirations turned to ashes as usual. No mention of this either was found in the budget. In this respect, our disappointment is much more woeful for those at the helms of affairs, had, on many occasions, assured us of establishing such developmental departments in our area as well. Here I recall that historic event when the Prime Minister of the State of J&K and Mr. Jawaharlal Nehru, Prime Minister of India, had visited us and promised that the Chief Engineer and other engineers would be deputed to our area to see the possibilities of digging canals where the water supply is meagre, making the land cultivable, thereby resolving the troubles of the area. But I regret that this promise remains merely a promise and is yet to be fulfilled. The matter does not end here. The erstwhile, condemned government had undertaken in Kargil a survey of the Khurbathang canal. But so far, our own government did not take any effective step towards the digging of the canal. I need not emphasize how profoundly bound with our life, is the construction of irrigation canals. In view of this principle, in J&K where there already exist many canals, a provision of Rs. 25 lacs have been made in the budget for construction of new canals. But no mention is made of constructing even small canals for thousands of acres of dry land in Ladakh.

I want to draw your attention to one more urgent, significant matter, which has a connection with the progress of our area. Our area is remote and cut off from other areas of the state and its parts are remote from one another. There being a tremendous paucity of roads in our region, construction of roads is essential for linking this area with other areas and the possibilities of trade may open up. But no impetus is given to the development of our means of communication and transport. Not even a hint is made in the estimates. In this connection, I cannot remain without mentioning the gratitude, we owe to the Indian Army for they have constructed a jeep-able road up to Kargil. No step is being taken by the state to carry forward this feat.

There are two posts and telegraph offices in our area at Leh and Kargil towns. In Zanskar, the people get post and telegraph facility only after going to Kargil. But can you estimate as to how far Padum, Zanskar is from Kargil? 150 miles of hilly journey across two high mountain Passes, which are more than 4400 metres high in altitude? Now, under such circumstances, can you imagine how impatient we are that adequate provision is earmarked for the development of the means of communication in our area and a scheme is formulated which could create the conditions for our development a possibility within a few years? But I am concerned that in this Budget of the Hon'ble Finance Minister, I do not find even half a word about Ladakh. From the Budget it seems that in the mind of the Budget makers, there is no locational existence of Ladakh, nor has this area been considered any part of the state.

Perhaps some people might argue that from our 'Illaqa' (area) the government gets a meager income of rupees two lacs and the government has to bear the burden of expenditure of about Rupees nine lacs. But I cannot help submitting that this pretty heavy amount of Rupees nine lacs is not spent on the development of our area. This is spent solely on the salaries of the government employees and other such type of expenditure. In this connection, our area cannot be grateful to the Government. Perhaps the very burden of the expenditures of the salaries of the Government employees is a reason for no steps being taken for the development of our area. Does it not substantially indicate that for very long our area has been left backward and that for lifting it out of poverty and squalor nothing has been done?

Yes, one ordinary type of work has been implemented. A Special Forest Officer, whose status in the Department is no more than that of a Ranger, has been appointed for promoting plantations. But here too, I would like to draw the attention of the Hon'ble members to the fact that the major portion of the fund provided for it is spent only on the salaries and just a meagre sum is spent on the development of plantations. This useless scheme of development is the exception, which proves the rule that our area has been left to remain backward. We had profound expectations that a board of experts would be set up to survey the natural resources of our area, to explore the possibilities of taking advantage of these, and to formulate schemes which, when implemented properly and permanently, could put an end to the economic backwardness of our area. But in the Estimates, this point has not even been touched. And it seems that our area has been regarded as an occupied territory.

The allegation of the government ministers that others put the demands of the Ladakhis into their mouths has come to be heard more than once. On this occasion I strongly contradict this point, which is an accusation or an insult or whatever you may deem fit to call it. This allegation is not based on truth. When we are oppressed by starvation, you may kindly tell whether we need someone else to convince us that rats are running into our stomachs. When a supply of cloth is sent to us from Srinagar and out of the same not a piece is available to us and we roam about naked, at that time, do we need a sermon from someone from outside that we are shivering from cold and burning from heat? From Srinagar, a stock of kerosene oil is dispatched for us. But it is not known where the stock is spent, whether this goes to the black market or how it is used. But the fact, which appears, is that even at this time we are required to buy every bottle of kerosene oil at an exorbitant price. Even in such circumstances, to understand as to what price we have to pay for any article, would we need lessons from outsiders? From us land revenues are realized at rates that have not been heard of even in the worst of extortionist times. And we are crushed under the burden of this rate. Then, at times, our cries of agony are echoed in the air. Is this voice, this cry, also that of outsiders? Is this the expression of other people's sentiments? Responsible officers loot our people. For the first time in the history, police called from outside is posted in our area. Such things we had not even imagined. But they appear at the present time on behalf of the new people's government. From all these policies, we suffered damage, humiliation and insult. Are these causes of indignity, insult or damage for others that they involve us in their net? Besides this, we have borne other hardships also patiently and we have been crying under those hardships. Were those cries and lamentations of ours in those moments of suffering and embarrassment the voice of others? Undoubtedly, we are simple people. Will this mean that we do not have those feelings, those sentiments, and those aspirations, which are in other people? Although we had not expressed our difficulties so far, that does not mean that we will remain dumb forever. Like little children we were unfamiliar with the big world; we kept playing the role of the dumb. But as and when in this connection we grow into adulthood, our thoughts and sentiments cannot remain unexpressed in writing and speech. Even a worm crawls in anguish if it is trampled upon. Our problems got aggravated day by day and it is not unusual to express these aspirations and sentiments in our writings and speeches. When a few years ago under the leadership of Jenab Sheikh Abdullah, Kashmiris launched their freedom movement, did not those at the helms of the Government say that they were being instigated by foreigners and their voice was not their own voice, but that of others? So far, the people of Ladakh have remained suppressed under the burden of restrictions and they kept repressed their sorrow and feelings. But at this present critical juncture of the world when the movements for freedom and self-determination are echoing in the skies and have got assimilated among people everywhere, and when 'New Kashmir' and 'New China' in particular are found taking new turns, it will be unfair to expect that the people of Ladakh would remain unconcerned with these movements, and on the lines of the past would remain dumb in the expression of their feelings and sentiments. The world has completely awakened and is fully giving expression to its individuality. Then why is it being hoped that the people of Ladakh will go on sleeping and be dumb? When, for other people, self-expression and aspiration for progress are considered virtues, why then, is the awakening of Ladakh looked upon with eye of suspicion? Why is this being said that the people of Ladakh do not take in their own welfare such interest, as other people take? At the end, my request is that this accusation, this allegation that we are talking the talk of others like a gramophone is a hallucination, is a deception and we do not have the patience for the repetition thereof for the second time.

I am grateful to the honourable members for giving patient hearing to my speech and I hope that the members of the government and hon'ble members would give the attention which my words deserve.

Thank you.

Annexure 6

Note from HRD Minister on VKV. Dy No 4716/P/C/HRD/2002 Office of Human Resource Minister

Enclosed is a letter (in original) from Shri Kushok Bakula Rinpoche, Ex MP addressed to HRM regarding restoration of the status of Vishesh Kendriya Vidyalaya (VKV) Ghaziabad. HRM has desired that the case may be examined in detail and till a final decision is taken, the previous status of VKV vis a vis admission of the students from border states be maintained.

Sd/ (Alok Tandon)
PS to HRM

29.7.2002

Commissioner, K V S

Copy for kind information to Padma Bhushan Shri Kushok Bakula Rinpoche, Ex MP with reference to his letter dated July 8, 2002.

Annexure 7
Prime Minister

New Delhi November 5, 1997

Dear Bakula Jee,

I have your letter No ULA/103/4/97 dated October 3, 1997 regarding firing by the Pakistani Army on civilian areas of Kargil.

I share your feelings at the loss and distress undergone by the people on account of the unprovoked and totally senseless shelling by Pakistan. Our security forces responded swiftly and sent the message that any such act of misadventure would be met with a similarly appropriate response. We have made it clear that we seek friendship with all our neighbours but let there be no doubt that we will take all measures, necessary to safeguard our borders and protect our people.

I have sanctioned Rs. one crore from the Prime Minister's National Relief Fund for the provision of immediate relief to the families of those killed or those injured in these firings and for reconstruction of damaged houses and properties.

With best wishes,

Yours sincerely,

sd/-

(I.K. Gujral)

Ven. Kushok Bakula,

Ambassador of India,

Ulaanbaatar, Mongolia

Annexure 8
Chief of Army Staff

General VP Malik,
PVSM, AVSM, ADC

New Delhi-10011
Army Headquarters

A/00043/1/COAS 19 Aug 99

Excellency,

Thank you for your letter of July 20, 99 and your appreciation on the performance of our men in OP VIJAY. The victory has been achieved due to the grit and determination of our troops and the sterling leadership displayed by your officers.

I can understand your special word of praise of the officers and men of the Ladakh Scouts. They have performed in an exemplary manner, displaying extraordinary courage and determination. We are increasing their number in the Amy.

I am sending a copy of your letter to the Colonel of the Ladakh Scouts with a request to convey your condolences to the bereaved families of soldiers in Ladakh.

With warm regards,

Yours sincerely,
Sd/- (V.P. Malik)

Shri Kushok Bakula
Ambassador
Embassy of India
CPO BOX 691, Ulaanbaatar, Mongolia.

Annexure 9

Speech made by Kushok Bakula, M.P. in the Lok Sabha on March 29, 1968 (Unofficial translation from Hindi)

Hon'ble Deputy Speaker, I support the demands raised by the Defence Minister and I heartily congratulate him. Ladakhi soldiers took part in the war of 1947 and 1962 to repel the invaders. In view of the courageous feats of Ladakhi Jawans in 1947, 'Ladakh Scouts' was formed incorporated into the Indian army and for which I want to congratulate Defence Minister. I also want to congratulate Defence Minister for making arrangements for allowing civilians to fly by military planes during those six months when Leh-Srinagar road is closed due to heavy snowfall and no road communication is possible. In 1947, 1962 and 1965 wars many young Ladakhis sacrifices their lives. In 1962 on the Daulatbeg Olvi and Demchok fronts, our Ladakhi youths exhibited their tremendous spirit of patriotism and bravery, which is well known. They were awarded medals for their supreme sacrifices and chivalrous deed, but unfortunately, neither their families have been given any job nor their sons have been given any scholarships or allotted any land by the State Government. Troops from Punjab and Rajasthan have been given many facilities, their families have been allotted land and their children have been provided scholarships. I have to say with a deep sense of regret that in spite of repeated demands, the State Government has not provided such facilities to our Ladakhi soldiers. Dependents of those persons who sacrificed their lives in the defence of our country, were given bare 300 to 400 by the State Government of J&K whereas the local people, through their small contributions have provided more assistance to the families than what the State Government has given to them. We should not forget how bravely these soldiers faced difficult situations and by doing so they brought good name and fame to Ladakh, J&K. So, it is imperative for the Government to provide them more financial assistance. I request Defence Minister to give due attention to this aspect.

I want to say that the facility of using Indian Air Force aircrafts by civilians should be continued for some time more. Ladakh, Jammu & Kashmir are the three regions of the State but if one looks at the reality, one can easily say that Ladakh has no place in the scheme of things in the State Government. I have every hope that Dr. Karan Singh who is present in the House will surely make some arrangements and that the Defence Minister will look into our requests definitely in the near future.

Leh town to aerodrome, which is barely 8 kms, gets blocked during winter and people have to wait for days together in the extremely cold days of the winter months. Due to inclement weather, flights do not operate regularly causing much hardship to the people. Some arrangement must be made for the passengers to stay at the airport. There is no such arrangement these days. The Defence Minister has been kind enough to allow the civilians to travel by military aircrafts; we would request him to also make some arrangement for civilian passengers to stay at the airport during their long wait for catching the flights.

It is essential to construct Leh-Manali road. Late Pt. Nehru visited Ladakh in 1949 and I had put forward this request to him at that time. Thereafter when Dr. Karan Singh visited Leh as the 'Sadar e Riyasat', I had also laid stress on the construction of Leh-Manali road but unfortunately at that time it was not considered necessary. Whenever I met Pt. Nehru, I emphasized the need for the construction of this road. Today, I want to reiterate this demand in the House and to say that the construction of Leh-Manali road is absolutely necessary, both in terms of providing an alternate road link to Ladakh and to take into account defence need for the country. Traders who come to Ladakh from Delhi and Amritsar have to take a longer route via Kashmir. If Leh-Manali road is constructed, the distance will become short and it will also benefit the traders.

This road is also extremely important from national security angle. The construction has now started but I would like to say that the work must be given priority. There should be no complacency in this work. We had said in 1954 that Chinese who have come to Tibet are also aiming at India but because we are insignificant people, nobody listened to our voice. When in 1959 the Dalai Lama had to flee his homeland and take political asylum in India along with Tibetan refugees, then only the Government of India awakened to the realities of the situation and realised the gravity of situation. We have been saying this since 1954–55 that the Government of India should pay attention to the defence of our country as the Chinese were preparing to invade India. History bears witness that our apprehensions were correct and China did attack India. So, I want to repeat again that the construction of Leh-Manali road is essential and it must be constructed at the earliest.

Pakistan in collaboration with China wants to endanger our independence. Pakistan army is still sitting at the top of high hills of Kargil. During Indo-Pak war of 1965, our Indian army had twice cleared the hills from Pakistani invaders and captured these hills but later on due to Tashkent Agreement and also with a view to have friendship with Pakistan, our army had to leave those strategic hills. I am not criticizing Tashkent Agreement but I would definitely like to say that we will suffer tremendously due to our decision to leave those hills. Pakistan in collaboration with China can destroy our airport in minutes. Why the government leaves these places of strategic importance to the defence of our country unattended? Are you doing so under the impression that it would help strengthen bond friendship between India and Pakistan? Do you think Pakistan will keep quiet on Kashmir issue? If this can happen, then your action to leave the strategic hills unattended is justified. But it is not so.

Similarly, to foster friendship with Pakistan, India handed about 350 to 500 kms. of Indian territory in the Rann of Kutch to Pakistan. If this could foster friendship with Pakistan, I will have no regrets for giving these areas to Pakistan. But it appears difficult to have Indo-Pak friendship at least during the reign of Ayub Sahib. Today we see that China and Pakistan are bent upon attacking India and they are also inciting internal disturbances. So, it is necessary that there should be no complacency on the defence front and we should provide for adequate funds to meet our full requirements.

Earlier one Hon'ble member said that defence budget is too high and that it should be reduced. But in my view, this provision should be actually enhanced even more. Do we not know that China and Pakistan are bent upon creating trouble on the border and also instability within the country? Therefore, it is extremely important that there is no crunch of funds for defence needs of the nation and instead we should allocate as much funds required for this.

I am a new person in this House and I came here with high hopes that I will learn good lessons from here but I have to say with anguish that I am disappointed. Members sitting on the opposition benches only believe in criticizing the government all the time. I do not say that they should not raise valid and necessary objections against the government and criticize only for the sake of criticism. Instead, they should play a constructive role in the interest of the country. Today I see that there is lot of agitation in the country on the question of language and other problems. These problems have been created to disrupt the unity of our country. The opposition should desist from raising issues which endanger the unity of our people. In the present context, I feel, it is essential to strengthen our forces. We must defend the unity of our country and make its border impregnable.

I want to bring to the notice of Defence Minister that when our soldiers cross Sonamarg, they get an altitude allowance of '30 only. This allowance is very meagre for such a high altitude. This allowance should be increased to give our soldiers required facilities. When our civil officials visit those areas, they get special allowances. Considering the difficult conditions our soldiers live, their allowance is too meagre. They have to go to the height of 20,000 feet and stay at the height of 15, 16 or even 17,000 feet. Ladakh experiences severe cold and cannot live without heating the rooms but our soldiers stay there day and night at a higher altitude. Therefore, the altitude allowance for soldiers should be increased from at least '30 to 60 or even more.

Similarly, I would like to mention about the police force. Generally speaking, we do not require any police forces in Ladakh. But our State Government, for whatever reasons, sends substantial police forces. It is all right. Let them send. But I would like to say that we do not need many officers, just send ordinary personnel.

There are 12 companies of Ladakh Scouts, of which two companies are stationed in Nubra and one in Demchok. These places are extremely cold, even in the months of June and July. While posted in these places, Government Employees go home but our soldiers have to remain there for long period even at that height. It is therefore, necessary that more allowances be given to these soldiers. I say this because if ever there is a threat to Ladakh, it affects the security of not only Ladakh but of India as well. Whatever I am saying today is not only for the wellbeing of Ladakhis. They are not so many in numbers, around 90,000. They can even take shelter elsewhere. But the land of Ladakh is extremely crucial for India.

I want to say that if Ladakh is threatened, it will severely harm our national interest and security and territorial integrity of the country. If Ladakh slips out of our hands then take it from me that nothing is safe. It is, therefore, not good to lose Ladakh because you have seen what happened to Tibet which has harmed our country.

It is regrettable that we do not care for Tibet and have done nothing to save Tibet from Chinese occupation. When questions were asked, Mr. Chagla, the Defence Minister had replied that they will do something for Tibet. What steps you have taken during the last five years? Will you take step only when Tibet is completely ruined? In fact, Tibet is already lost. The magnificent monasteries, great learned scholars, have all been destroyed. Buddhists live in Tibet. The way things happened in Vietnam; the Chinese want to do the same there. Chinese have even betrayed Pandit Nehru and they will do so the same again in future. This time they have deceived India and next time it will be Pakistan. I appeal to the Government of India to take measures to protect Tibet's culture and identity, which is a common heritage for Buddhists all over.

Therefore, I appeal to the government to enhance the allowances of all defence personnel stationed in Ladakh and provide them with all necessary facilities. Unlike other areas, Ladakh has no place for entertainment and means of comfort. So, what can anyone do? You step out and it is only barren mountains.

I congratulate the Government for establishing hospital at Leh for the army personnel where civilians too can get medical treatment. I am indeed grateful to the Central Government for it. These services should have been provided by the State Government but this they are not doing adequately. The Central Government is, on the other hand, providing us with all such facilities.

I do not want to take much time of this House. I once again thank the Defence Minister.

Annexure 10

Speech made by Kushok Bakula, M.P. in the Lok Sabha on March 26, 1969. (Unofficial translation from Hindi)

Thank you for allowing me to speak on the demands of the Home Ministry. I am indeed grateful to you for giving me this opportunity. I support these demands. It is necessary to strengthen police set up in the present circumstances in order to curb those activities which are based on violence and destruction. Enemies of the country are bent upon harming our secular and democratic traditions and incite tensions in the country. It is also necessary to strengthen police force because of internal and external dangers that we often face.

I did not want to speak on the demands of Home Ministry but circumstances have compelled me to speak. Two days ago, I had given a Call attention notice on the incidents that had taken place in Ladakh. I was told by the Hon'ble Speaker that the Home Ministry demands will be discussed in the House and I could speak on that occasion.

How vast is the area of Ladakh can be easily ascertained from the fact that Ladakh constitutes 37,753 miles in the total 53,664 miles area of the entire State of J&K. It is such a vast area and its border extends to Pakistan, China and Afghanistan. But I regret to say that in spite of this, no attention has been paid to Ladakh. I know that Central Government provides 90% grant to Ladakh through that State Government but I regret to say that these funds are not utilized fully or fruitfully for development of Ladakh. I do not want to say anything in detail about it. I will convey the same to the Home Minister when I meet him.

Secondly, I have repeatedly said in this House that the people of Ladakh should be given Scheduled Tribe status. I was told that there are some laws, which cannot be imposed in J&K. I do not want to go into this question whether those laws can be imposed or not in the State of J&K but I want this provision should be made applicable to Ladakh. Our region is backward in so far as education is concerned. They are very poor. Unless our people are included in the category of Scheduled Tribe, no development of this region is possible.

As you know Ladakh is predominantly Buddhist area of our country. But lately the Buddhists have been facing threat to their very existence. I have never said anything like this in the past but today I have received a telegram which I would like to read out.

"Recently some people have desecrated Buddhist prayer flags and thrown them down in Sabu village. Buddhists of Ladakh have been deeply offended by this act. Local administration has not taken any action against the culprit which prompted many people including Kushok Togdan, Kushok Thiksay, Kushok Stakna, head of Phyang, Thiksay and Stakna monasteries and President Ladakh Buddhist Association to protest. They have demanded strict action against those indulging in hurting the sentiments of Buddhists. For two days people have been observing Bundh in Leh. Situation is deteriorating. Age old tradition of communal harmony is being threatened. Local people will be satisfied only when the guilty are brought to book. Buddhists of Ladakh feel threatened in secular India. Situation may go out of hand if no action is taken, for which local administration and State Government will be held responsible. – President, Ladakh Buddhist Association."

The above telegram is dated March 25, 1969. I am forwarding a copy to the Hon'ble Home Minister. Such incidents are happening there regularly but I fail to understand why no action is being taken by the police and local administration. Hon'ble Speaker, there have been many such incidents in the past. Kashmiri conspiracy is at work again and the Buddhists of Ladakh are being threatened, suppressed and discriminated against and many incidents of high-handedness are taking place in close connivance with the State Government. The Buddhists of Ladakh wanted to build a temple and a Dharamshala in Kargil on their own land, but they were not allowed to do so neither there is any place for a funeral for Buddhists in Kargil. The Muslims of Ladakh have been living in harmony with Buddhists since ages. It is a new trend unknown to Ladakh.

The situation is deteriorating. At the time, when I was in the Council of Minister, I tried to put an end to this tense situation and made both the communities to realize the implications of such a conflict. I told them that both Buddhism and Islam have to co-exist and both religions should get protection. India is a secular country where there are many religions; all religions are protected then why Buddhist religion in Ladakh should be treated differently. It is a serious problem.

On another occasion, some miscreants said that Buddhism will be liquidated and that Pakistani flags will be hoisted. There was stiff opposition at that time also and processions were to be taken out. I was present at that time but I did not allow the processions to be taken out. The State Government assured that action will be taken and that a Committee will be constituted comprising representatives of Ladakh Muslim Association and Ladakh Buddhist Association and this Committee will stop re-occurrence of such incidents but I have to say with regret that no action was taken.

Now this is the third incident. I would request the Home Minister to talk to the Chief Minister of J&K on phone immediately. Miscreants must be punished otherwise Buddhism will be endangered in Ladakh. You are aware that after Tibet, we consider Ladakh as second Tibet and a great Centre of learning. It is considered to be the centre of Buddhism. Buddhists in Ladakh are a micro minority in the State and therefore, it is the responsibility of the Central Government to protect our interests. Failing to do so, Central Government will be held equally responsible. Earlier, Ladakh only faced external threat from China and Pakistan. There was no internal threat which unfortunately is now developing. Therefore, swift punitive action must be taken against those found indulging in such acts.

Hon'ble Speaker, there is no Minister representing Ladakh in the J&K Council of Ministers. I was a member of the Council of Minister in J&K Government for 10–12 years but ever since I have been elected M.P., there is no Minister from Ladakh region in the State Government which is causing great turmoil in the region. We are trying our best to stop such incidents from getting out of hand but how long can you suppress the sentiments of the people?

I had submitted a memorandum last year on August 24, 1968 wherein it was urged that NEFA type administration be established in Ladakh. At that time there was allegation that I was attempting to separate Ladakh from the State of J&K. It was not my intention. Ladakh could remain a part of the State of J&K but the Central Government should control this region in the way it is being done in NEFA. We had discussions with the Prime Minister and the Home Minister. They told us that the time was not ripe for it and that we should drop this idea. After looking at these incidents, I feel that time has come. I had told Pt. Jawaharlal Nehru in 1949 that Ladakh should be taken under the direct control of the Centre.

J&K is a Muslim majority State in the country but we never said that because of large population of Muslims, Ladakh should not be a part of it. The intention behind our demand is that since Ladakh is backward and it has not progressed, by putting it under the Central control, its progress will be possible. We were told at that time that there were some legal hurdles and as such it was not possible. Our intention was that Ladakh should become strong which in turn will make India also strong. The danger has come to the fore because we did not take a firm stand in favour of Tibet. There are no communists in Ladakh and there are no pro-Chinese feelings in Ladakh but if we ignore the development of Ladakh, the situation can change. I want that the Central Government should tell the State Government that such incidents can create adverse circumstances and as such we should take immediate steps.

Ladakh has no power. There were only two diesel engines of 90 KW in Ladakh, out of which one is out of order. Only one engine is not sufficient to meet electricity requirements of entire Ladakh.

Kargil has a large Muslim population equally backward and lagging behind. They also need education and development of the area. It is not difficult to generate electricity in Kargil because there is sufficient water and there are many rivers. But it is regretted that no efforts have been made so far to produce electricity in Kargil. No representation has been included in the State Council of Ministers from Ladakh. I don't want to say much on this issue now because Chief Minister Mr. G.M. Sadiq has said that he will include one representative in the State Cabinet after the Budget session. If it is done, it would be welcomed and if it is not done, the trouble would start again and the Government of India will be held responsible for it, because the State Government would do what you ask it to do.

Last year Union Deputy Minister of Information and Broadcasting had visited Ladakh and she had assured that an AIR Kendra (radio station) will be set up in that area but nothing has been done so far in this direction. When Mrs. Indira Gandhi was in the Cabinet, she too had assured but nothing happened. The main requirement in that area is power and Ladakh is in complete darkness.

Many MPs have seen with their own eyes during their visit to Ladakh that many resources are locally available for power generation. You have said that vegetation has grown in that area but that alone is not sufficient.

We had placed our demands before Gajendragadkar Commission. The Commission sent its repot to the State Government. It is specifically mentioned in the Report that Ladakh got less funds and no development has taken place. The Commission has also suggested that there should be a full-fledged Minister from Ladakh, a degree college be set up and a powerful Development Council be established. It has made many other recommendations, which should be fully implemented without any further delay. I thank the Hon'ble Speaker for giving me this opportunity to speak.

Thank you.

Annexure 11

No. 9687

Lok Sabha

Ministry of Information and Broadcasting Unstarred Question

(To be answered on 14.5.1970)

Sub: EXPANSION OF A.I.R. STATION, LADAKH

Shri Kushok Bakula

Will the Minister of INFORMATION AND BROADCASTING AND COMMUNICATIONS be pleased to state?

a) The details of the programme broadcast regularly by the A.I.R. Ladakh Unit to counteract the false propaganda broadcast by the Peking Radio through the medium of the language used in Ladakh and its adjoining areas;

b) Whether Government proposes to expand the said Unit so as to make it more effective in the Kashmir State itself instead of preparing relay records for that Unit in Delhi; and

c) If so, the details thereof?

ANSWER

Minister of State in the Ministry of Information and Broadcasting, Department of Communication (Shri I.K. Gujral)

a) Radio Kashmir, Srinagar, broadcast daily a programme of 1 hour and 25 minutes duration in Bodhi for listeners in Ladakh and the adjoining areas. The programme consists of news commentaries, talks, music, documentaries and newsreels. The programme is produced by a unit in Delhi and it air-freights it daily to Srinagar.

b) Work in connection with the setting up of a radio station at Leh is already in progress and when the station starts functioning the programmes for listeners in Ladakh and its neighbourhood will be increased considerably.

Annexure 12

Minister of External Affairs

No. 319M(S)79

February 27, 1979

My Dear Bakula ji,

Thank you for your letter No. F3-1/79 dated February 10, 1979, where you were kind enough to wish me success in my mission to Peking.

During my conversation with the Chinese leaders when the question of the Dalai Lama and Tibetans was referred to, I informed them that we had made it clear that it was in deference to the Dalai Lama's spiritual position and in recognition to the needs of the Tibetan refugees, who voluntarily came to India, that asylum and resettlement facilities were extended by India. If the Dalai Lama and the Tibetans consider that the conditions are suitable for their return to the places of their origin, we, from our side, would not stand in their way in doing so.

I had earlier met his Holiness in Delhi on January 22, 1979, when we had a very useful conversation.

Yours sincerely,

Sd/-

(A.B. Vajpayee)

Ven. Kushok G. Bakula, Member,
Minorities Commission Government of India, New Delhi.

Annexure 13

Minister of Defence Government of India

No. 117/DM/68

New Delhi, April 17, 1968

My dear Shri Kushok Bakula,

During discussion on the Demand for Grants of the Ministry of Defence for the year 1968–69, you had suggested that the construction of Leh-Manali road should be expedited.

Leh-Manali road is being constructed as a project of Border Roads Development Board. The funds required for this and other roads included in the programme of the Board are provided out of Transport Ministry's budget. I had not sufficient time to deal with all important points raised by the Honourable Members in course of my reply on the floor of the House. I, therefore, thought I should let you know the position in regard to this road, which is within my area of responsibility as Deputy Chairman of Border Road Development Board.

The work on Leh-Manali road was started in 1964. In order to achieve maximum speed, its construction was taken up from both ends. About 65% of the formation cutting work has been completed. Our engineers expect that a fair-weather road should be available for use by vehicles by the end of the next year. Considering the limited construction season and formidable problems of logistics, the tempo of work has been satisfactory. A close watch, however, is being kept on the progress of work because, like you, we are conscious of the importance of this road both from Defence and development angles.

Yours sincerely,

(Sd/- (Swaran Singh)

Shri Kushok Bakula, M.P. 26 Janpath, New Delhi

Annexure 14

Kushok G. Bakula

Member, Minorities Commission

No. F1-2/79

C-1/9, Tilak Marg,
New Delhi
February 26, 1979

Esteemed Sir,

I am sorry to bother you with this letter regarding the Leh-Manali highway. This road, as I understand, was constructed primarily to provide an alternative to the traditional Leh-Srinagar road from the defence point of view. Though the road has been completed, it has not been thrown open to civil and military traffic. In fact, a big stretch of this 449 metres road remains to be metalled.

The importance of the Leh-Manali road from the defence point of view need not be over emphasized. The commissioning of this road would considerably cut down expenses on transportation of defence equipment and provisions etc. for defence personnel in that sensitive area. Among other things, the road is not vulnerable at all and hence its importance from the security point of view also.

The road would have its own civil utility. The traditional Leh-Srinagar-Pathankot road being longer and more difficult takes considerable time for transportation of essential items of human consumption for the people of Ladakh. As a result of this, the poor people of the area have not only to pay higher prices for essential commodities, but also have to put up with their non-availability at times. I personally feel the position would considerably case with the opening of the Leh-Manali road which is shorter and easier than the other road. Incidentally, the new road would also be more convenient to the intending tourist to Ladakh.

In view of the above facts, I would request you Sir, kindly to consider the matter favourably and early as it is vitally connected with the defence of the country and the economy of Ladakh.

With regards,

Yours sincerely,
(Sd/-)
(Kushok G. Bakula)

Shri Morarji Desai, Prime Minister of India New Delhi

Annexure 15
Prime Minister of India

No. 748-PMO/79

New Delhi
March 8, 1979

Dear Kushok Bakula,

Please refer to your letter of February 26, 1979 regarding Leh-Manali road. I have had enquiries made. It appears that at one time the Army authorities had projected this need but now in view of the development in the situation and other facilities that are available they are not interested in this road. The possibility of civilian traffic on this road is also very thin particularly since there are many physical difficulties to be experienced on the way to Leh. There are 4 mountain passes of Rohtang, Baralacha, Lechalang and Tangla which are 12,000 to 17,500 feet high. While it is true that this provides a shorter route to Leh than via Srinagar, you will appreciate that most of the traffic must naturally be via Srinagar. Even the tourist traffic is more likely to be combined with a visit to the Kashmir Valley rather than with a visit to Manali, particularly in view of the difficult road journey of Leh to Srinagar which is 135 kilometers. As against Manali to Leh which is 477 kms. Though the total journey from Pathankot to Leh via Manali is shorter than via Srinagar by nearly 200 kms. It has also been estimated that the Keylong to Upshi portion of the Leh-Manali road which covers about 307 kms. would cost about Rs. 14 crores as capital expenditure and the maintenance cost would be very high. Taking all these factors into consideration I do not think it would be possible for Government to improve the road so that it can be used by civilian traffic, nor would it be easy to use this road as an alternative to the Srinagar-Leh road when that road is blocked for the simple reason that at that time even this road is likely to present numerous difficulties.

With kind regards,

Yours sincerely,
(Sd/-)
(Morarji Desai)

Shri Kushok G. Bakula, C-1/9, Tilak Marg, New Delhi

Annexure 16
Prime Minister of India

No. 389-PMO/79

New Delhi

October 11, 1979

Dear Shri Kushok Bakula,

Kindly refer to your D.O. letter No. F.1-1/79 dated September 26, 1979 regarding the completion of the Leh-Manali Road.

I have had the matter examined again. The assessment is that further improvement of the road is not an operational requirement. As such, utilization of BRDs funds for this work would lack justification. As regards the development of the road of non-military purposes, the investment will be substantial; and is not likely to be cost-effective. The considerations against it have been explained to you in Shri Morarji Desai's letter No. 748-PMO/79 dated March 8, 1979. These remain unchanged.

With regards,

Yours sincerely

(Sd/-)

(Charan Singh)

Shri Kushok G. Bakula Member,

Minorities Commission, C1/9,

Tilak Marg, New Delhi

Annexure 17
Press Statement

The people of Ladakh have been eagerly awaiting the implementation of the assurances given to the Ladakh Action Committee sometime back by the State Cabinet Sub-Committee with regard to their genuine demands for which the Ladakhis had launched an agitation. Despite its commitments regarding declaring the entire area of Ladakh as a Scheduled Tribe and conceding regional autonomy to the region within the framework of the State etc., the State Government has not apparently taken any step in this regard. The indifferent attitude of the State Government is causing deep anxiety among the people of Ladakh who are pressing the Action Committee to act decisively.

The apathy of the State Government regarding implementation of its commitments made to the Ladakh Action Committee is clear and understandable in the context of the existing deteriorating state of affairs in the entire State which are its own creation and for which it blames the Central Government. The top echelons of the State Government and the leaders of the Party in power there are engaged in diverting the attention of the people from pressing domestic problems towards imaginary issues of their creation. This explains the indifferent attitude of the State Government towards the problems and demands of the people of Ladakh.

I would like to make it clear that in the event of the failure of early implementation of the assurances given to the Ladakh Action Committee by the State Cabinet Sub-Committee, the people of Ladakh would be driven to resume the agitation on an intensified scale for which the responsibilities would rest entirely on the State Government. Ours is a peace-loving area and we would not ordinarily like to resort to actions which are not in keeping with our tradition. But if we are driven to desperation for our survival we will not hesitate to strike. I hope the State Government would soon realize the gravity of the situation and meet the agreed demands of the people of Ladakh to avert unpleasant repercussions.

Kushok Bakula

Chairman Ladakh Action Committee,
New Delhi, May 14, 1981

Annexure 18
Press Statement

1. The persistent denial of legitimate demands of the people of Ladakh particularly those relating to the declaration of the people of Ladakh as Schedule Tribe, granting Regional Autonomy to Ladakh within the State framework and allocation and distribution of plan funds etc. on the rational basis drove the peace-loving Ladakhis into passive yet effective peaceful demonstration of their anguish towards the known apathy of the State Government regarding their just demands.

2. It is regrettable that the State Government should have backed out from its commitments given to the Ladakh Action Committee regarding acceptance of its demands, over a year ago, as a consequence of the discussions between the two sides. Such an attitude on the part of the State Government could not be held for long and ultimately drove the Ladakhis to rise again in defence of their legitimate rights and demands. To start with, Shri Sonam Wangyal, Ex-Minister in the State, Tsering Stobdan and Nasir Ali Khan, all prominent locals initiated an indefinite hunger strike before the Deputy Commissioner's Office under –20°C temperature in open. They were followed by scores of volunteers of Ladakh Action Committee who staged relay hunger strike with them. The hunger strike, it may be mentioned, was resorted to after two weeks' notice for conceding the demands.

3. On January 24, 1982 when the demonstrators were proceeding peacefully towards the venue where three volunteers of Ladakh Action Committee were observing indefinite hunger strike to express their solidarity with the demands of the Action Committee, the police resorted to unprovoked lathi charge and tear gas shelling. This provoked the peaceful crowd to retaliate in self defence. Subsequent unwarned police firing resulted in the death of a senior monk and a young man and injury to many others. This police high-handedness added fuel to the fire resulting in worsening of the situation.

4. As a situation like this which was charged with tension, the local administration aggravated the situation further by requisitioning several truckloads of army personnel fully armed. This created a scare resulting in dispersal of the crowd and their seeking shelter wherever possible. In this process the police exploited the situation by chasing the fleeing crowd to wherever they went for protection. They did not stop at that, but rushed into residential houses where they indulged in

indiscriminate lathi charge on men, women and children besides looting their valuables. As the police chased, the crowd took to its heels and sought shelter in the nearby Buddhist monastery. The police did not hesitate even to chase them there and indulged in lathi charge and tear-gas shelling within the premises of the monastery. Apart from the fact that this action of the police was condemnable in violating the sanctity of the holy premises, it was unlawful, unwarranted and far from the protective role which the police is supposed to play. The total toll of the police high-handedness was two dead and injuries to about hundred civilians and minor bruises to only three police personnel. The entire area was put under police rule till the next day-the January 25, 1982 when curfew was imposed for continuous four days in Ladakh for the first time in its history. Innocent people were beaten, arrested and kept under unlawful police custody for a number of days. To project its innocence, the administration made a false statement over the AIR that no detentions were made. The hardships experienced by the people during the curfew are too deep for expression.

5. The question of the cremation of those who were killed in police firing was planned for January 28, 1982 and for this purpose negotiations were entered into with the local administration which was adamant not to hand over the dead bodies to the Ladakh Action Committee. But the Ladakh Action Committee insisted on getting possession of the bodies of the martyrs in order to give them a befitting funeral. The District Administration was still reluctant in handing over the bodies. However, on the express assurances by Ven. Kushok Bakula, Mr. P. Namgyal, M.P. and other prominent citizens and members of Ladakh Action Committee, the District Administration conceded the demand of handing over the bodies and also promises to withdraw the curfew that day from 7.00 a.m. to 5.00 p.m. It was made clear to the District authorities by Ladakh Action Committee that there should be no trace of the police personnel throughout the curfew relaxation period. It is no exaggeration that for the first time in the history of Leh town a record gathering of about 10,000 mourners of all communities witnessed the last rites of the martyrs without any untoward incident. After expiry of the curfew relaxation period, the authorities re-imposed curfew which continues till 7.00 a.m. of January 29, 1982. This, however, was followed by imposition of Section 144 in the area. The volunteers of Ladakh Action Committee, however, defied this prohibitory order and courted arrest daily in groups. It is interesting to note that the police were not registering cases against defaulters under section 144 but

instead under section 107/151 of the Ranbir Panel Code so as to leave room open for their future harassment.

6. Shri P. Namgyal, M.P, was man-handled twice by the police, first, on January 24, 1982 when he was trying to pacify the crowd and putting off fire to a Government vehicle and secondly, on January 24, 1982 when he was returning to his residence even though he was holding a curfew pass issued by the District Magistrate. This particular incident is indicative of the unwarranted police high-handedness which is reprehensible. The incident aroused the passions of the people but they were somehow pacified by the Action Committee leaders and thus further deterioration of the situation was averted.

7. The recent happenings have brought home to the people of Ladakh and to the outside world that the Ladakhis could not expect a fair and honourable deal at the hands of the State Administration which obviously is determined to crush them, divide them on communal basis and what to speak of conceding their legitimate demands. The situation could have assumed greater dimensions but for the intervention of the members of Ladakh Action Committee which persuaded the hunger strikers to give up fast and pacified the masses with assurances that their demands would be taken care of and sorted out. In order to curb future police high-handedness, it was urged that a Central Judicial probe be ordered into the police firings resulting in loss of human lives and injury to about 100 peaceful demonstrators it comprising men, women and children. It is painful to note that the State Authorities did not at this moment utter a single word of sympathy to the bereaved families, what to speak of their granting any financial relief to them and to the injured and much less about conceding the demands which led to this unpleasant and tragic situation. We appeal to the Government of India to take appropriate action with regard to the police firings and indiscriminate lathi charge and the demands of the Ladakhis whose endurance has reached the saturation point. The Ladakhis will not rest content unless their demands are implemented in the right spirit and until they find a place of honour in the State set-up.

Kushok Bakula
Member, Minorities Commission
P. Namgyal M.P.

New Delhi, February 3, 1982

Annexure 19

Kushok Bakula
Member, Minorities Commission

Lok Nayak Bhawan
New Delhi
September 22, 1989

Esteemed Shri Gandhi,

Kindly refer to my letter dated September 18, 1989 forwarding therewith a detailed report about the unfortunate recent developments in Ladakh. Normally I should have awaited action on the letter but I am constrained to write to you again as there is hardly any day when I do not receive distressing calls from Leh. The brutal manner in which the State Government is coming down on the Buddhists of Ladakh is too deep for words. Three innocent people have already lost their lives and many injured as a result of unprovoked police firing on peaceful demonstrators on August 27, 1989—three days after my arrival at Leh. It was a calculated attempt by the State Government to malign me and to achieve their malicious ends. Indiscriminate desecration of religious places, intrusion into the Buddhist houses under the cover of curfew, beating people mercilessly and looting their cash and valuables has been the style of functioning of the State's custodians of law and order.

It appears that the Government of India is oblivious of the gravity of the situation or is not taking it seriously. The separatist forces of the State which have made a mockery of the State Government by openly indulging in anti-national activities in the Valley are now raising their ugly heads in the sensitive Ladakh region also. If these anti-national activities are not checked in time, these would not only erase the identity of the Buddhists in their own land but prove disastrous so far as national security is concerned. I hope you are aware that the secessionist forces of the Valley have sneaked into the peaceful Ladakh region with a view to propagating secessionist ideologies and fanaticism beyond the Zojila Pass. These subversive elements, with the connivance of the State Government, are indulging in activities which are aimed at eroding the identity of the Buddhists which would ultimately result in compromising, the security of the region.

The denial of legitimate rights to the people of Ladakh by the successive State Government is an open secret. While the two constituents of the State viz. Jammu and the Valley of Kashmir enjoy the satisfaction of having the seat of Government at their door steps in turns in a year despite the enormous expenses and all that follows, the third constituent of the State namely Ladakh does not even enjoy the small satisfaction of having a divisional Commissioner at Leh. The people of Ladakh have been thus left to their fate and the outcome of their neglect and discrimination is apparent today.

As you are aware, Pt. Jawaharlal Nehru entertained inexpressible concern for the well-being of the people of Ladakh for their peaceful and cheerful disposition. The Ladakhis, in return, left no stone unturned in defending the borders of the country in successive wars against China and Pakistan through supreme sacrifices. In the hour of distress of these helpless people, even a simple word of sympathy would have been a matter of solace.

As a representative of the Buddhists in the Minorities Commission, I have been apprising the Government of India, of the problems faced by the Buddhists minority. Even with regard to the disturbances in Leh, I lost no time in apprising you of the developments there from time to time in the hope that govt. would take some action to protect this vital region and its rich cultural heritage. But unfortunately, things did not move that way. The feeble voice of Ladakh is unable to make any impact on the Government whose compulsions in the Valley seems to outweigh the vital interest of the strategically important Ladakh region. I am afraid, making the Ladakhi Buddhists a scape-goat may not be in the overall national interest in the long run.

As my sincere efforts in safeguarding the interests of the microscopic Buddhist minority of the J&K State are not bearing the desired fruit, it is becoming extremely difficult for me to justify my association with the Minorities Commission and safeguard my cherished credibility. It is surprising that even conferment of the Scheduled Tribe status on the people is eluding them because of the pressures of the State Government. I would, therefore, request you to kindly intervene into the matter as inaction on the part of the Government has given a big jolt to the people. Your personal intervention in the matter would also go a long way in re-infusing a sense of confidence among the Ladakhis. The following steps would help attain that objective and improve the situation:

Declaration of the people of Ladakh on Scheduled Tribe as recommended by the Registrar General of India; Visit to the trouble torn Leh town by a senior Central Minister and holding of a Tripartite Talk comprising the representatives of the Central Government, the State Government of J&K and the representatives of the agitating Buddhists of Ladakh to discuss the demands of the Ladakh Buddhist Association.

The Srinagar Leh highway will close down for winter months in less than a month's time. Should stock of essential commodities be not rushed to Leh expeditiously, we may have to witness starvation deaths.

Equally important is the calling off of the strike by the Buddhist employees, as the Governmental machinery including essential services has come to a dead halt.

With best regards,

Yours sincerely,
(Sd/-)
(Kushok Bakula)

Shri Rajiv Gandhi, Prime Minister of India,
New Delhi

Annexure 20

Jagmohan
Minister for Tourism and Culture

DO No 826/M (T&C)/2002

Transport Bhawan
New Delh-110001
December 18, 2002

Dear Shri Kushok Bakula Rinpoche ji,

I acknowledge with thanks your letter dated December 2/13, 2002 regarding enshrining the holy Buddha relics.

Your suggestion is important and deserves most earnest consideration. I am discussing the matter with the authorities concerned and will do whatever I can in the matter.

With kind regards,

Yours sincerely,
(Sd/-)
(Jagmohan)

Shri Kushok Bakula Rinpoche
Ex-Member of Parliament
J-177, Saket
New Delhi-110017

Annexure 21

Tour Report of Ven. Kushok Bakula, Member, Minorities Commission, on his Visit to Leh from August 24–31, 1989

On my return from tour of the Soviet Union recently, I learnt with deep anguish about the traumatic happenings in Ladakh which, not only rocked the proverbially peaceful region, but also smeared its fair face with almost indelible stains. An account of the cataclysmic incidents and the trail of bitterness they left behind is given below. To my mind, it seems to be a calculated affair to serve some ulterior purpose – most probably it being political in nature.

Causes of the Turmoil

1. Kashmiri Muslims, based at Leh, had been instigating the local Muslims against the Buddhists for quite some time past, resulting in occasional minor clashes. A Buddhist youth leader, who was going for shopping on July 7, 1989 in the main market of Leh was, without any provocation, given a rough beating by four Muslim youths, which resulted in his sustaining some injuries. It is significant that the day happened to be a Friday and the victim was a Buddhist youth leader. While Muslim boys were arrested by the police, their victim was removed to the Civil Hospital for treatment.
2. Never before in the history of Ladakh has there been a Buddhist Muslim problem, more so of such aggressive nature. However, if there was any, it was with the handful of Muslims from Kashmir and some locals.
3. On hearing about the detention of four youths, Muslims went to the Police Station to see them and, perhaps, to try for their release. By this time, the situation had already got tense. Tension, however, aggravated when at the Police Station, someone wrongly reported that stones had been pelted at the local mosque and, surprisingly enough, his identity is still shrouded in mystery. Muslims, however, rescued the detained youths from the Police Station, but by that time tension had mounted very high.
4. Meanwhile, Buddhist youths had gone around the town calling shopkeepers to close their shops as mark of protest for beating the Buddhist youth and the Police inaction towards the culprits. On the other hand, some people from the Muslim crowd left the Police Station and during their march towards the market, pelted stones on a building

of the famous Hemis Monastery property in Leh resulting in damage to its glass-panes etc. While marching, this crowd shouted anti-India and Pro-Pakistani slogans. Anti-Buddhist slogans were also heard in Leh for the first time – a sad reflection on the age-old communal harmony of the region. As the slogan shouting mob was advancing towards the main market, a clash ensured between it and the Buddhists advancing from the opposite direction. The District Magistrate imposed an indefinite curfew in the area, thus bringing the situation under control.

5. The Buddhist leadership had announced 'Ladakh Bandh' on August 7, 1989 – the day disturbances completed one month. Unruly Buddhist mob set on fire some Government buildings which prompted the Police to fire about 30 rounds on the demonstrators who had gathered around a hillock near Leh. Fortunately, there was no casualty. Besides imposition of Section 144, the town was under round the clock curfew from July 7, 1989 itself, which was later relaxed in a phased manner.

6. The sequence of events convinced the Ladakh Buddhist Association that it was a pre-planned attack on the Buddhists and demanded appointment of a Commission of Inquiry to go into the matter. This demand was made by the Ladakh Buddhist Association on July 10, 1989 to the Divisional Commissioner and the D.I.G. of Police, who had flown into Leh, in the presence of Shri P. Namgyal, Union Minister of State for Chemicals, Petro Chemicals and Parliamentary Affairs. It was re-iterated by Shri Namgyal when he subsequently met the Chief Minister at Srinagar. The demand of the Ladakh Buddhist Association, it may be mentioned, was in the nature of an ultimatum, failing which the Association would embark upon an indefinite agitation demanding Union Territory Status for Ladakh.

7. As the State Government did not appoint the Commission of Inquiry, the Ladakh Buddhist Association announced launching of an agitation to ventilate their grievances and to expose the apathetic attitude of the State Government towards Ladakh. The theme of the agitation centred around demand for a Union Territory status for their homeland. It would be recalled that it is an old demand of the Ladakhis which is being pressed again to protect their vital interests and identity which, they are convinced, are not possible under the present dispensation. They feel, and perhaps, rightly so, that Ladakh's salvation does not lie with the State of J&K.

8. If the State Government had conceded the demand of Ladakh Buddhist Association for appointment of a Commission of Inquiry, the course of

events would have shaped differently and peace would have prevailed in the sensitive region. Above all, those responsible for fomenting trouble would have been exposed and brought to book. As the State Government did not concede the demand for appointment of a Commission of Inquiry, the Buddhists, in keeping with their ultimatum, took unfortunately to a violent agitation.

9. Some Kashmiri Muslims who are allegedly associates of the outlawed Kashmir Liberation Front and are stationed at Leh as traders have been instigating the local Argons and Sunni Muslims against the Buddhists. This instigation was simmering for a long time resulting in minor clashes between the two communities. Such instigation with the connivance of the State Government authorities has infused a sense of insecurity among the Buddhists, despite their being in a majority in the district. It is unfortunate that communal clashes took place for the first time in the sensitive region resulting in damage to some Muslim properties.

10. The allegations and counter allegations by the two communities helped perpetuate the trouble and misgivings they nursed against each other. However, the situation could have improved and normalcy been restored if the State Government authorities had willed so. I am sorry to record that the State Government did not feel interested in resolving the tangle. Certain quarters, whom I would not like to mention, are blaming the Buddhists for the unfortunate happenings in the region. While both the communities are to be blamed for all that happened, it is totally unfounded to blame the Buddhists exclusively for the violent turn which the developments took. If my memory serves me well and if we cast a glance over the history of the region, our amicable relation between the Buddhists and the Muslims would be more than testified. It has, unfortunately, been an unseen third hand which has wrought havoc in the proverbially fraternal and peaceful region.

11. As stated above, I was in the Soviet Union when the trouble started on July 7, 1989. On my return to India and on learning about the disturbances, I flew to Leh on August 24, 1989 where I immediately held discussions with District Officials, representatives of Ladakh Buddhist Association, Ladakh Muslim Association, the Merchant's Association etc. As a result of the discussions and my personal appeal for harmony to the two communities, peace seemed to be around the corner. But, unfortunately, the local police (JKP) and CRP were withdrawn from Bazar patrolling duty and instead Armed Police from Kashmir (JKAP) were deployed for such sensitive duty with some obvious ulterior motive.

12. It is unfortunate that when, on my intervention, peace was gradually returning to the area, the JKAP was unnecessarily inducted into the area to create trouble and disturb peace. Though the two communities professed to renounce violence against each other, the Buddhists peacefully continued to violate Section 144 to court arrests. But on August 27, 1989 the district authorities appeared to have decided to come down on the Buddhists with lathis and bullets and silence them by force. This is testified by the fact that the market area outside the Jokhang from where the Buddhists procession was coming out and was about to leave the temple for courting arrests by defying Section 144, was cleared. As soon as the people started coming out of Jokhang, the police lathi charged them without any provocation in order to provoke the Buddhists for retaliation. The people started pelting stones on the police and later set one bus on fire. The police opened fire without the usual warning, instantly killing three innocent persons and injuring many.

13. When I asked the Superintendent of Police about the gravity of the provocation which promoted opening of fire on peaceful demonstration, he told me that bombs were hurled from the temple on the police. When I further asked him as to what the impact of such alleged bombs was, he had no answer. The JKAP did not even spare the sacred temple with their bullets but fortunately there was no damage or loss of life. The same day viz. August 27, 1989 the police entered the precincts of the Jokhang Temple and arrested hundreds of people who had gathered there for a routine Puja, those who had taken shelter after the Police opened indiscriminate fire on the people in the street outside the Temple, and also those who had assembled to court arrest in violation of Section 144. The arrests included, among others, the President of the Ladakh Buddhist Association. The District Magistrate imposed indefinite curfew in the town and the rural areas were handed over to the Army. An unprecedented happening took place during curfew hours. The JKAF intruded into Buddhists houses, beat their inmates indiscriminately, desecrated the objects of worship and made good their escape with whatever fell into their hands.

14. The next morning, i.e. August 28, 1989 the President, Ladakh Buddhist Association and some others were taken to Srinagar for detention in the Central Jail there. For two reasons, I tried to impress upon the District Magistrate the desirability of detaining the leaders of Leh itself. First, because no negotiations could ever take place in the absence of the President, and secondly, such a move could be counter-productive

as people would not relish their leader to be detained in distant Srinagar. He did not agree to my suggestion and, as expected, unpleasant reactions followed at Leh.

15. I continued to appeal for peace and amity through statements and A.I.R. Leh. While this had an impact on the people, the police atrocities continued unabated as the JKAP whose numbers had by now swelled up, were anxious to justify their presence in the region. It is unfortunate that the peaceful town of Leh had turned into a virtual Police camp.

16. In support of the agitation and to protest against the arrests of the President, Ladakh Buddhist Association and others and indiscriminate Police atrocities, all Buddhist State Government employees went on an indefinite strike from September 2, 1989 paralyzing even the essential services. The strike has since been called off on the appeal of Ladakh Buddhist Association in the larger interest of the people.

The long-standing demands of the Buddhists:

(i) There has been a systematic endeavour of various elements to reduce the Buddhists into a minority in their own land through their conversions to other communities, namely, Islam and Christianity.

(ii) There is no denying that the Buddhists are being discriminated against in every sphere of life and developmental programmes.

(iii) District Leh is discriminated against in Plan funds, Services, provision of educational facilities (no College in the entire district), Power generation, Land distribution etc., etc.

(iv) Agriculture, which is the main source of sustenance of Buddhists, is gravely neglected.

(v) Rampant corruption in Government Offices, particularly in PWD, and a sense of general apathy on the part of higher echelons of administration.

(vi) False and unfounded allegations against Buddhist monks and the Jawans of the renowned Ladakh Scouts of the Indian Army and motives attributed to malign them have caused great resentment amongst the Buddhists.

(vii) The misuse of the State legislatures against the Buddhists, and irresponsible and baseless remarks against the Buddhists by Muslim MLA's and MLC's have gravely hurt the sentiments of Buddhists of Ladakh.

(viii) The Ladakh Affairs Department in the State Cabinet, which was set up through the good offices of Pandit Nehru to save the interests of Buddhists of Ladakh and to play a meaningful role for the benefit of Ladakhis, has been reduced to a mere farce.

(ix) Even in the all-time largest J&K Council of Ministers comprising 30 Ministers, Ladakh has no representative therein. What could be more discriminating than this?

(x) Out of four seats for the Ladakh region in the State Legislature, the Buddhists share is just one.

Points for Action

(i) The Ladakh Buddhist Association's demand for a tripartite talk comprising of representatives of the Government of India, the State Government and the Ladakh Buddhist Association has not so far been conceded by the State Government as it apprehends that is might become a precedent for future. But, in view of Ladakhi Buddhists' past experience in talks with the State Government, the Ladakh Buddhist Association is not prepared to hold talks unless Government of India is also represented therein.

(ii) Creation of congenial atmosphere for a dialogue for which unconditional release of the President, Ladakh Buddhist Association and others is essential.

(iii) A Commission of Inquiry be appointed to go into the violent incidents in Leh.

(iv) Leh being under indefinite curfew and winter being around the corner, the essential stocks be rushed to the region before the Zojila Pass closes in November to save people from starvation.

(v) Despite the tragedy which befell Leh, it is unfortunate that no State Minister or Central Minister has visited the area to boost the sagging morale of the people. As such our attitude of neglect and alienation could prove detrimental to national interests. It is high time that at least a Central Minister visited the area.

It is, however, gratifying that the long-standing and just demand of the people of Ladakh for conferment of Scheduled Tribe status on them has just been finally conceded. People are now looking forward to its speedy implementation.

Annexure 22
Agreement

The initiatives taken by the Hon'ble Prime Minister Shri Rajiv Gandhi and the Hon'ble Minister of J&K Dr. Farooq Abdullah, to restore peace and normalcy in the Ladakh region was greatly welcomed by the Ladakh Buddhist Association. The visit of the Union Home Minister Sardar Buta Singh, Shri Mohd. Shafi, Agriculture Minister of J&K and Shri Mangat Ram Sharma, Transport Minister of J&K to Leh on the 29 October 1969 was also welcomed and greatly appreciated. It was further agreed that a meeting would be held very soon after the General Elections in the second week of December 1989.

(i) To find a satisfactory and mutually acceptable solution to the problems of the people of Ladakh region. In this context the memorandum of the Ladakh Buddhist Association, which includes the demands of the Autonomous District Hill Council, was received for detailed consideration.

(ii) To discuss the developmental needs of the people of the region so that an integrated tribal sub-plan could be formulated to be implemented within a specific time-frame.

In all these matters the Central Government would lend its good offices to the State Govt. at all stages.

The Ladakh Buddhist Association agreed to withdraw their agitation and the demand for Union Territory Status.

As a matter of good-will, the State Govt. agreed to withdraw all cases in connection with the agitation, except those involving serious offences. Prohibitory orders would also be withdrawn immediately. Efforts would be made to create an atmosphere of harmony and brotherhood and a sense of security among the people and measures will be taken to rehabilitate all those who have been affected during the agitation in which Ladakh Buddhist Association will render all possible assistance.

Leh, October 29, 1989

Sd/	Sd/	Sd/
(Thupstan Chhewang) President, Ladakh Buddhist Association	(Ashok Jaitley) Addl. Chief Secy. Govt. of J&K	(P.P. Shrivastav) Addl. Secy to the Govt. of India, Ministry of Home Affairs

Annexure 23

Kushok Bakula
Ambassador

Embassy of India
Ulaanbaatar,
Mongolia

No. ULA/103/1/90

March 5, 1990

Esteemed Shri Singh,

I am sorry to bother you with this letter when you are pre-occupied with important national and international matters. I am writing these few lines regarding Ladakh which, for the past some-time, has been undergoing a very strained and difficult period of its history. The Buddhists of Ladakh have been for decades subjected to discrimination and neglect at the hands of successive State Governments in Kashmir. While, I would not like to go into the causes of the problem in detail as they are well known to you, it certainly needs to be mentioned that the present problem is a direct outcome of the involvement of the secessionist and fundamentalist forces of Kashmir and, therefore, needs to be viewed accordingly. I had apprised the previous Government as well as Home Minister, Mufti Mohd. Sayeed that the simmering discontent among the Buddhist minority in Ladakh exploded when the local agents, trying to carry out the nefarious activities of the secessionist elements of the Valley, for the first time in the peaceful history of Ladakh, these elements traded anti-India and pro-Pakistani slogans in the heart of the Leh town. This was preceded by beating up of a Buddhist youth leader and damage to property of a local Buddhist Monastery by Muslim youth. The Buddhists and Muslims of Ladakh, it may be noted, have been, for centuries, living in peace and harmony. The partial role played by the District Administration in those unpleasant incidents added fuel to the fire resulting in total loss of confidence among the people of Ladakh in the State Administration. This was clearly seen as a provocative move of the Muslim fundamentalists who perhaps were over-confident of their strength in the Valley and who wanted to extend their activities to the Ladakh region. The Buddhists sensing the danger lying ahead demanded strong action against the culprits and an inquiry into the whole incident. But unfortunately, this did not happen and as a result, the Buddhists had to launch a peaceful agitation demanding the Union Territory status for Ladakh. In view of their past experience with the State Administration, the agitating Buddhists would not agree to participate in any discussion for a settlement without a representative of the Government of India also present in the talks. Accordingly, an agreement was signed in November last in Leh in the presence of the then Union Home Minister and two Cabinet Ministers of the State. The Additional Secretary, Ministry of Home Affairs, the Additional Chief Secretary, J&K State and President, Ladakh Buddhist Association (LBA) were signatories to the agreement. It promised solution to the problem facing the Buddhist minority and an early consideration of the demand of the LBA. It may be mentioned here that by this time, the LBA in the overall national interest, had dropped the demand for UT status for Ladakh and would be satisfied if a Darjeeling-type District Council is given to them. I am also a witness to the agreement. The President, LBA had agreed to sign the agreement only when he was assured by all the parties concerned that the demand of Hill Council would be favourably considered in due course.

In the meanwhile, the Elections to the Lok Sabha took place resulting in the formation of a new Government at the Centre under your dynamic leadership. The elections and the formation of the new Government at the Centre, however, delayed the process of any early settlement of the problem. While I have still not lost hope, it appears that a solution to the problem will elude the people of Ladakh for some more time. Ever since my joining as Ambassador here, I have been watching the developments in Ladakh with great concern. It appears that the feeble voice of Ladakh is unable to make any impact on the Government whose compulsions in the Valley seem to out-weigh the vital interests of Ladakh. I may, however, emphasise that making Ladakhi interest a scapegoat on this account may not be in the overall national interest. In order, therefore, for an early amicable solution to the Ladakh problem, I request that the demand of LBA for District Council as agreed upon be kindly conceded early. Such a step, I am sure, can alone bring peace in the region. I shall be grateful if you kindly intervene in the matter and help in finding an early solution to this important matter.

With best regards, Yours sincerely,

(Sd/-) Kushok Bakula

Hon'ble Shri V.P. Singh,
Prime Minister of India,
New Delhi-110 011

Annexure 24
Prime Minster

New Delhi
December 29, 1992

Dear Shri Bakula,

This has reference to your letter of November 30, 1992 regarding establishment of Autonomous Hill Council for Leh District in Ladakh. I understand that you have already met the Union Minister who has discussed this with you.

Efforts are continuing for developing a framework for appropriate institutional safeguards, which could meet the aspirations of the people and the development needs of the region. I am sure that with the co-operation of all concerned, we would be able to work out suitable arrangements in this regard expeditiously.

With regards,

Yours sincerely,

Sd/- (P.V. Narasimha Rao)

Kushok Bakula
Ambassador Embassy of India Ulaanbaatar

Annexure 25

Secretary

Ministry of External Affairs

New Delhi

No. E.VIII/55/2/94-MG

May 18, 1994

Dear Ambassador,

Please refer to your letter No. ULA/AMB/KB/1/94 dated May 9, 1994 addressed to the Prime Minister seeking the restoration of Ladakh's traditional trade routes with Tibet and the opening of Demchok for pilgrimage to Mount Kailash and Lake Manasarovar.

We have proposed to the Chinese side last year that Demchok be opened for border trade. We are still awaiting their consent and continue to remind them whenever a suitable opportunity presents itself.

As far the proposal to open Demchok for pilgrimage to Kailash and Manasarovar, we hope to process this as soon as details of the necessary facilities and services and available from the local authorities in Ladakh.

With regards,

Yours sincerely,

Sd/-

(Shivshankar Menon)

Ven. Kushok Bakula Ambassador
Embassy of India, Ulaanbaatar (Mongolia)

Copy to:

Ms. Sujata Mehta

DS(M), PMO, New Delhi TCA Rangachari

Joint Secretary (EA) Ministry of External Affairs New Delhi

Annexure 26

Arun Kumar, IAS

Secretary to Government Ladakh Affairs Department,
Civil Secretariat, Camp-Leh.

No. Camp Leh/93/1 August 21, 1993

Dear Sir,

This is with reference to the meeting that we had on August 5, 1993 in your office chambers in Delhi regarding Kailash-Manasarovar Yatra through Ladakh.

As desired, I have now made extensive local enquiries (including ones from veterans who have travelled on this route to Lhasa) and would like to reconfirm that indeed it is possible to cover the 633 kms. route to Tarchen/ Parakha the case camp for Kailash-Manasarovar from Leh two days. The road is free from rains, a snow or avalanches (it is a high-altitude desert after all) and therefore can be used round the year. This in fact is such a good route, that it should be made use of even by the 350 or so pilgrims going by the conventional route via U.P. for their return journey as well as for emergencies, medical or otherwise.

Leh airport is connected by Indian Airlines flight to Delhi thrice a week. In additional there is a flight each, every week, to Chandigarh to Srinagar and Jammu as well as Army flights to Chandigarh. The State Government has a standing arrangement with the Indian Air Force for helicopter services which the Government of China permitting can be used to rescue people even from Manasarovar within 3 hours or so of such requisitions. The hospitals at Leh have every facility to tackle high altitude health problems, including a pressurized chamber (with the Army) to enable patients to get treatment at sea level atmospheric pressures. Nyoma, 441 kms. away from Mansarovar, has a Government Public Health Centre, while Koyul 33 kms. from Manasarovar, and ITBP medical facilities. On the Chinese side, Tashigang and Garzong 35 and 115 kms away from the Indian border are supposed to be small townships, where additional facilities for tourists can be created in a reasonable short time. For reasons of acclimatization, however, I would recommend that pilgrims be advised to reach Manasarovar after five-night halts from Leh. The first two nights' halt should be made at Leh which will help pilgrims to acclimatization at 12000 ft. as well as enable them to have at least day's sightseeing at Leh. The third night halt is proposed at Nyoma 182 kms. away from Leh. The 4th at Demchok 134 Kms away from Nyoma where formalities for crossing into China will have to be completed. The 5th night halt can be made at Garzong in China 115 kms. away from Demchok and the can be at Tarchen/Farakha 117/192 kms. away from Gorzon. After this, the pilgrims can do the two Parikramas. The details are available at PP 11/12 of the Ministry's on this Yatra. The proposed route-map is enclosed at the Annexure-I.

The return journey can be performed the same way a little faster by climating a night halt or two at Nyoma of Garzong. We can thus have a 17–20 days yatra in reasonable comfort through this route.

The arrangement in Ladakh as well as from Delhi to Leh (via Manali or Jammu – **Annexure-3**) shall be made by the J&K Tourism Development Corporation (J&K TDC). This shall include journeys in luxury buses halts with full board and lodging, electricity through portable gen-sets, wherever required etc. Detailed pricing exercises shall be conducted after we receive the green signal from the MEA. The rates on the Indian side from Delhi to Demchok and back are, however, likely to be within the limit of '5,000 which the KMVN is charging for the U.P. route. No additional charges for porters or ponies would, therefore, be leviable on the Ladakh route.

The recommended season is May 1 to September 30. The route capacity is proposed to between 20 to 40 pilgrims a day for about 100 days during this period. July-August would be the most comfortable months to undertake this Yatra, as in Delhi, May-June pilgrims would be able to reach Leh only by air because of the closure of the Zojila and Rohtang passes.

Border Trade

In case MEA (and the Government of China) be very kindly favourable to the idea of opening this alternate route in the interest of Indian pilgrims, I would also recommend considering opening the Demchok border for border trade on a permanent basis. The population on both sides of the border have had age old ethnic, religious and commercial ties and they get very emotional at the prospect of restoring such ties. Traditionally, wool, silk, velvet, salt and meat in both sides used to give locally produced barley, sattu, wheat, butter, fruits, carpets, animal skins, Indian textiles etc. This trade at a smaller scale, goes on even now and, if legitimized by establishing a regular customer office at Demchok, can have the potential of growing to the extent of ₹ 10.50 lacs a day. The banking facilities can be provided by opening an extensive counter of the J&K Bank at Demchok.

In case, any more details are required please contact me immediately (at the address given on page 1) or Shri S.S. Mathur, IAS, Resident Commissioner, J&K Government, 5, Prithviraj Road, New Delhi.

With regards,

Yours Sd/-

(Arun Kumar)

Shri S.S. Menon,
Joint Secretary (China)
Ministry of External Affairs
Room No. 174,
South Block
New Delhi-110001

Annexure 27

March 14, 1995

His Excellency Kushok Bakula, Embassy of India,
P.O. Box 691
Ulaanbaatar, Mongolia.

Your Excellency,

It is my personal honor to invite you to participate in an historic and timely endeavor, the State of the World Forum, to be held in San Francisco September 27-October 1, 1995.

As we leave the Cold War behind, we face many complex problems whose solution will require not only physical and financial resources but also political and moral will. We need a critical reassessment of all our assumptions and a new combination of players to envision the next phase of human development.

We are inviting to the Forum those individuals whose expertise and concern enable them to critically analyze and constructively shape the issue pertinent to the future of our planet. They include senior states people, current political leaders, business executives, scientists, spiritual leaders, intellectuals, artists and youth. Each has an important and complementary part to play as we enter the next century and a new millennium.

I have invited as Co-Chairs for the Forum several friends and colleagues who are particularly interested in these issues: President Askar Akaev, President Oscar Arias, Prime Minister Tansu Ciller, President Vaclav Havel, Prime Minister Ruud Lubbers, Nobel Laureate Rigoberta Menchu, Prime Minister Yasuhiro Nakasone, President Julius Nyerere, Secretary George Shulz, Mr. Ted Turner and Archbishop Desmond Tutu.

It is my hope that those of us who gather for the Forum will consider how we might collaborate in the future.

Please allow me to present as a gift the enclosed selection of my personal reflections on humanity's future, which I hope will prove useful as you review the materials and consider your personal participation.

I believe you would make an important and valuable contribution to this international endeavor and I look forward to meeting and working with you at the opening of this initiative in San Francisco.

Sincerely
Sd/-
(Mikhail S. Gorbachev)

MSG/jb Enclosure

Annexure 28

Kushok Bakula Ambassador

No.ULA/103/98

Embassy of India,
Ulaanbaatar, Mongolia.
May 4, 1998

Esteemed PrimeMinister,

As you are aware, the question of Tibet and its future has exercised the world for the last 40 years. We, in India, are directly connected to the problem considering the presence of H.H. the Dalai Lama and a large number of Tibetan refugees on our soil.

Periodic demonstrations by the Tibetans in India are also a direct fall-out of the lingering problem which, no doubt, also carries the potential of escalating further if nothing is done to resolve the issue. We have recently seen such demonstrations in New Delhi, this time culminating in a tragic self-immolation. While they are invariably tied to the official visits of senior Chinese leaders to India, perhaps it is no longer sufficient to treat them as a minor aberration or irritant.

You are, no doubt, aware that the Dalai Lama has been saying for quite some time now that he does not aim for secession from China. His objective is an autonomous Tibet within the PRC where the Tibetan religion and unique way of they could be preserved. The Chinese too have periodically stated that they would be willing to open talks with the Dalai Lama if he were to refrain from a call for independence. Only last week, the Chinese Foreign Ministry spokesman re-affirmed this at a press conference after the visit of US Secretary of State Madeline Albright.

It is my considered opinion that it would be best for China to attempt a resolution of the Tibetan question with the Dalai Lama while he still bolds centre-stage. This is on account of his publicly stated position that Tibetan independence is not his objective. After him, I fear that the Tibetan movement would pass into the hands of younger and more radical elements who may well espouse the cause of Tibetan independence.

While the official Chinese position and the Dalai Lama's views could hardly coverage any further, it is dismaying to see that there is no positive movement towards actually sitting down across the table. I feel that this is an opportunity that is begging for us to play the role of an honest broker. We must desist from any temptation to consider Tibet as a 'card' that we hold against the Chinese, a view held by several of our foreign policy and military pundits. Any dispassionate and objective analysis will show that this card has no meaning especially considering that it is our well-considered aim to improve relations with our northern neighbor and that any antagonism would only work against us.

An honest mediation between the Chinese and the Tibetans, on the other hand, would certainly work in our favour and genuinely clear the misgivings that China still holds vis-à-vis our policy towards Tibet. We must, therefore, take immediate steps to convince both sides to commence discussions. This should be attempted, in the first stage, through sustained covert diplomacy essentially because one can anticipate Chinese objections to 'meddling in internal affairs' as also hard-liners among the Dalai Lama's advisers) aimed at setting an acceptable agenda and venue for talks. If and when discussion can start, we can then decide how active a role we need to play.

I would also like to mention that the contents of this letter are my personal opinion and that I have neither discussed these with the Dalai Lama nor with any Chinese authority. However, it is no secret that the Dalai Lama would like India to play a more active role in the settlement of the Tibetan issue.

Equally important is the fact that while countries like the United States and the EU have been taking up the issue with the Chinese, although more n the human rights context, India which has close historical and cultural links with Tibet, has not made any serious attempt to initiate a dialogue between the two sides. While our silence in the past was understandable, there is a marked change in the scenario now. The unequivocal statement of the Dalai Lama on Tibet's relations with china and the Chinese conditions on the dialogue with His Holiness has brought substantive change in the situation. I do not think that an initiative on our part at this stage could cause any harm in our relations with China. On the other hand, any successful conclusion at any time in future would benefit our interests tremendously.

With profound regards, Yours sincerely,

(Sd/-)

(Kushok Bakula)

Shri Atal Bihari Vajpayee,
Hon'ble Prime Minister of India,
New Delhi

Annexure 29
Buckingham Palace

January 30, 2004

Christopher Geidt

Asstt. Pvt. Secretary to the Queen

Message

Thank you for your letter of 15th January which I have shown to the Queen. Her Majesty was very sad to learn that Sri Kushok Bakula died last month and has asked me to say how fondly she recalls her most interesting discussions with him in London in 2002.

I know also how significant a part Sri Kushok Bakula played in the Alliance of Religions and Conservation's work and that his wisdom and counsel will be sorely missed. It was kind of you to ensure that The Queen was notified of this most unwelcome news.

Yours ever,

Sd/-

(Christopher Geidt)

Martin Palmer, Esq.